Miriam F. Stimpson teaches courses in modern architecture and furnishings at Brigham Young University in Utah.

A Field Guide
of Modern
in the

Prentice-Hall, Inc., Englewood Cliffs, New Jersey 07632

MIRIAM F. STIMPSON

to Landmarks Architecture United States

Library of Congress Cataloging in Publication Data

Stimpson, Miriam.
  A field guide to landmarks of modern architecture
in the United States.

  "A Spectrum Book"—T.p. verso.
  Bibliography: p. 427
  Includes index.
  1. Architecture—United States—Guide books.
2. Architecture, Modern—20th century—United States—
Guide-books.   I. Title.
NA712.S75   1985   917.3'04927   84-24774
ISBN 0-13-316571-X
ISBN 0-13-316563-9 (pbk.)

*A Field Guide to Landmarks of Modern Architecture
in the United States. Miriam F. Stimpson*
© 1985 by Prentice-Hall, Inc., Englewood Cliffs, New Jersey 07632

A Spectrum Book.

Printed in the United States of America

10   9   8   7   6   5   4   3   2   1

Production coordination: Fred Dahl
Manufacturing buyer: Frank Grieco
Interior design: Maria Carella
Cover design: Hal Siegel

This book is available at a special discount when ordered
in bulk quantities. Contact Prentice-Hall, Inc., General
Publishing Division, Special Sales, Englewood Cliffs, N. J. 07632.

ISBN 0-13-316571-X

ISBN 0-13-316563-9 {PBK.}

Prentice-Hall International (U.K.) Limited, Inc., *London*
Prentice-Hall of Australia Pty. Limited, *Sydney*
Prentice-Hall Canada Inc., *Toronto*
Prentice-Hall of India Private Limited, *New Delhi*
Prentice-Hall of Japan, Inc., *Tokyo*
Prentice-Hall of Southeast Asia Pte. Ltd., *Singapore*
Whitehall Books Limited, *Wellington, New Zealand*
Editora Prentice-Hall do Brasil Ltda., *Rio de Janeiro*
Prentice-Hall Hispanoamericana, S.A., *Mexico*

Contents

Preface

Never in the artistic history of mankind has there been a more innovative and technically advanced period of architecture. During the past 100 years, modern structures have delighted the world—engineering masterpieces reflecting the current attitudes and aspirations of a modern society. The majority of these significant structures are located in the United States—a leading world force in the field of architecture.

This guide directs travelers to the finest building wonders of the modern era. Illustrations, brief descriptions, and maps make it easy to locate the most famous modern structures in America. Buildings are presented in alphabetical order, by state and city. Additional modern buildings of interest are listed at the end of the illustrated sections.

Over 10,000 buildings were examined for this compilation. An honest effort has been made to present the best-known modern structures in America—those that are considered landmarks. These buildings have received national and international acclaim. I have taken the prerogative to include important structures found in less populated areas so that all states could be represented. Some states, such as New York, Texas, California, Illinois, and other significant architectural centers, boast hundreds of modern structures that could fill volumes. In those instances, only the most famous buildings have been included. The majority of

buildings presented are public and commercial buildings, many open to the public, with an emphasis on those designed since 1965.

Dates for buildings have been as accurately recorded as possible, but they may vary as a function of whether they indicate the date of commission, date of ground breaking, or date of completion. Additionally, dates vary somewhat in research materials available.

This illustrated guide book was compiled for all those interested in the hallmarks of modern architecture. The reader should find it convenient, engaging, and understandable. The author welcomes correspondence with readers and professionals in the architectural field suggesting changes, additions, or other significant alterations.

ACKNOWLEDGMENTS

Gratitude is expressed to The American Institute of Architects, individual architectural firms, Chambers of Commerce, and owners of modern buildings across the nation whose help was invaluable in compiling this guide book.

Special thanks are also given to Tina M. Jackson, Sally Sharp, Kineteder & Smart, architects, Caryn Pulsipher, and Suzy Stratford whose talents as illustrators have contributed to the overall effectiveness of the material.

Introduction

"Make no little plans; they have no magic
to stir men's blood."

DANIEL BURNHAM

Modern architecture in the United States, as
in Europe, did not spring full-blown from a
select group of great minds. As in other
notable periods of architectural development,
what can be seen as a total departure from
the past is actually part of an historical
process with many threads that relate the
apparently novel to the notion of architecture
as a continuum, an ongoing concretization of
human creative thought. "When modern
architecture departs from the past," writes
Lewis Mumford, "it does so with good
reasons, either because the conditions of life
generally have changed, or because fresh
technological facilities offer fresh incentives
for their imaginative use, or because new
feelings and values demand a fresh form of
expression, or for all these reasons together."
Certainly modern architecture in the United
States, while part of a world-wide movement,
reflects a particular political climate, combination of myths and traditions, regional
characteristics, technological developments
and capabilities, and interests of clients, that
together form a unique set of conditions for
architectural expression.

Miriam Stimpson's *A Field Guide to Landmarks of Modern Architecture in the United
States* offers a comprehensive field guide to
hundreds of notable public, corporate, and
domestic buildings of the last one hundred
years. With this guide, the visitor is given the
necessary information to find and experience
these buildings; fortunately, since most of the
buildings are open to the public, one's visit
need not be limited to merely viewing the
building's exterior facade. The guide's regional
organization offers the opportunity to compare
buildings within a particular locale, to explore
the issue of regional or contextual influence,
and to examine the question of whether these
factors in architectural design have been
absorbed into a homogeneous national voice.
By including domestic as well as corporate
buildings and public institutions, Miriam
Stimpson enables the visitor not only to
compare different building types by the same
architect, but also to explore the effect of
varying constraints—including attitude of the
client, or a shift in the architect's concern, or a
particular technological development—that are
integral to the final form of any building.

A major voice in the growth of modern
architecture in the United States is seen in the
work of H. H. Richardson (1838–86). Firmly
rooted through education and training in the
European historical tradition, Richardson is
generally seen as the first original American
architect. Both Glessner House (Chicago,
1885–87) and Allegheny County Jail and Court
House (Pittsburgh, 1884–88), although disparate
in function, reveal through the building form
and use of materials an attitude of stability and
strength that is particularly American; both

reflect the muscular energies of the age, creating a new type of monumental architecture.

Richardson's work influenced the seminal architect of the period, Louis Sullivan (1856–1924). With his partner, Dankman Adler (1844–1900), Sullivan created one of the outstanding public buildings in Chicago—the recently restored Auditorium (1886–90). Sullivan's overall design—including interior ornament with flowing lines derived from natural forms—reveals his belief in organic forces as a vital source of energy, both in life and architecture. His steel frame skyscrapers, notably the Wainwright Building (St. Louis, 1890), and the Guaranty Building (Buffalo, 1894) are humanist expressions of what was then a totally new building type.

The skyscraper, this particularly American form, had developed from the use of an iron frame, with its height limitations, to a steel frame in the 1880s. Encouraged by the business community in Chicago, many early examples of this building type are seen there. The Reliance Building (Burnham and Root, 1890); the Monadnock Block (Burnham and Root, 1889–92) and Holabird and Roche's Tacoma and Marquette Buildings of 1886 and 1894 are outstanding illustrations of the early skyscraper: not only is the steel frame utilized, enabling the buildings to be taller and lighter, but the frame itself is used as an architectural expression. Until the First World War, the tallest building in the world (792 feet) was Cass Gilbert's Woolworth Building (New York City, 1913). This "Temple of Commerce" is a skyscraper in the guise of a Gothic cathedral.

The greatest American architect, Frank Lloyd Wright (1869–1959) received his early training in the office of Adler and Sullivan. The Prairie Style, developed after he opened his own office, focused changing architectural concerns on domestic architecture, creating a point of departure from the then current Victorian styles. Many examples of the Prairie Style, with long horizontal lines that follow

the ground plane, overhanging roof, flow of interior spaces that extend to outdoor terraces and gardens, and interplay of planes and volumes, are found in the Oak Park and River Forest suburbs of Chicago, where Wright also built his own house and studio. The Robie House (Chicago, 1908–10) is the major residential statement of the Prairie Style. The Larkin Building (Buffalo, 1904) incorporates Prairie Style features in an office building; Unity Temple (Oak Park, 1905–06) is a further development of these themes. Wright's career covered sixty years and several distinct periods. The 1936 house, Falling Water (Bear Run, Pennsylvania) reflects the influence of the International Style, but with Wright's particular sensibility, use of materials, and attitude toward the house as home—as well as the dramatic form and siting. Completed at the end of his career, the Guggenheim Museum of Art (New York, 1956–59) illustrates his continued concern with shaping enclosed space, creating flow of movement, and the use of architectural form as a means to this end. The Morris Shop (San Francisco, 1948–49) is an earlier exploration of these design concerns.

In contrast to Wright's distinctively American architectural voice, several major figures in European modern architecture brought their various backgrounds to the United States and continued careers here, influencing both students and practicing architects. Walter Gropius, Mies van der Rohe, Eero Saarinen, Alvar Aalto, Le Corbusier—all are represented in American modern architecture. Mies van der Rohe's elegant Lake Shore Drive Apartments (Chicago, 1948–51) hold a dramatic position at the edge of city and lake. Mies' work at Illinois Institute of Technology (Chicago) included the design of Crown Hall (1955–56) and other campus buildings. These buildings express his interest in the creation of the clear span, unitary volume, as well as in careful and articulated detailing. The Seagram Building (New York City, 1954–58), with Philip Johnson, is the most admired of his buildings. The choice of materials, the precise detailing, the siting which, in its setback from the street, creates a plaza acknowledging the 1917 Racquet Club (McKim, Mead, and White) across Park Avenue—all contribute to this grand urban gesture.

In the years after the Second World War, expressive and sculptural designs in modern architecture are seen. For example, Eero Saarinen's TWA Terminal (JFK International Airport, NY, 1958) is a bold formal statement that uses concrete in a particularly fluid manner. Baker House (Cambridge, Massachusetts, 1949) by Alvar Aalto is an undulating brick building, with enclosed staircases seemingly hung on the exterior wall.

Among American architects of the post-war period, the work and theory of Louis Kahn (1901–1974) is significant. As artist and architect, with images gleaned from wide travels, Kahn in his buildings (as with his students) addressed basic questions of architecture: the derivation of form, use of light, nature of materials, and relationship and articulation of spaces and volumes. The Richards Laboratories (Philadelphia, 1957–61) and the Salk Institute (La Jolla, California, 1959–65) express Kahn's focus on the *architectural* solution to pragmatic requirements, while respecting each site's particular demands and character.

Kahn's poetic and reverent approach to architectural theory and design shares the roots of Robert Venturi's (1925) work; but the latter assumes a very different set of concerns and images. Using popular contemporary culture as a reference, Venturi and his partners Rauch and Scott-Brown—as seen in the Guild House (Philadelphia, 1960–63), Allen Memorial Art Museum (Oberlin, Ohio, 1973–77), and Gordon Wu Hall (Princeton, NJ, 1981–83)—attempt to communicate directly with the viewer, utilizing highly readable "signs."

Perhaps the most inclusive movement in modern architecture is the evolving Post-Modernism. Philip Johnson's AT&T Building (New York City, 1978–82) has been called by Paul Goldberger the first "major monument of Post-Modernism." With its traditional skyscraper form and applied decoration at the top, clearly visible in the Manhattan Skyline, the building is a distinct development from Johnson's earlier International School affiliation. But perhaps Post-Modernism is best represented in the work of Michael Graves, whose Portland Building (Portland, Oregon, 1980–82) is a monumental civic building that expresses the architect's interest in myth and allegory as a means of enriching the user's understanding of the building. Color, ornament, and formal references are utilized to articulate these concerns.

Certainly American architecture, seen as an expression of a particular spirit, also recognizes a relationship to a world-wide architectural community. Faith in the historical development of architectural expression, in the nature of growth and the sharing of ideas within this community, offer an optimistic attitude for the future of American architecture. But unless we, as users, clients, and citizens, are consistently discriminating and demanding in what we expect from architecture—both in a particular building and in its contribution to the built environment—we will live with what we deserve.

S. M. DAVIS

To the students at B.Y.U.,
fellow colleagues, friends,
and family for their
encouragement and support.

• Huntsville

Anniston •

Birmingham •

Auburn •

Tuskegee •

• Daphne

Robertsdale

Alabama

BIRMINGHAM

Birmingham-Jefferson Civic Center (1969–76)

ARCHITECTS: Geddes Brecher Qualls Cunningham
LOCATION: 9th-11th Avenues N between 19th and 21st Sts.
OPEN: During business hours and special events

This functional and flexible Civic Center was inspired by the powerfully expressive architecture of German designer, Hans Scharoun, architect of the famous Berlin Philharmonic Hall. Massive, thick walls and strong forms provide a barrier from the noise of air and land traffic. Comprised of four attached units, the large multi-purpose complex houses an exhibition hall, a concert hall, a theater, and a coliseum.

BIRMINGHAM

The Theater of Birmingham-Southern College (1967–68)

ARCHITECTS: Warren, Knight, & Davis
LOCATION: 8th Avenue (US 78) at 8th Street
OPEN: During school hours and performances

An exquisite small theater plan, the Theater of Birmingham-Southern College employs all the latest technical advancements in theater production. The interior treatment has been brilliantly designed responding to aesthetics as well as function. Lighting, acoustics, the stage and other facilities are superbly executed. Additional spaces for workshops and classrooms are located in the basement.

LOACHAPOKA (EAST CENTRAL ALABAMA)

United Methodist Church
(1980)

ARCHITECT: Nicholas Davis
LOCATION: Take Auburn exit from I-85
from Auburn, Take Hwy #14 W. to
Loachapoka
OPEN: Sunday services at 10:00 A.M.
Contact Parsonage next door for
information

An innovative and sensitively designed structure, the United Methodist Church is situated in a small farming community. The architect, a professor at Auburn University, wanted to create a church that reflected the spirit and surroundings of the natural, homey farm-town setting. The unpretentious church is primarily constructed of wood and glass. Forms employed throughout the building are suggestive of a barn or chicken coop.

TUSKEGEE

The Tuskegee Chapel, Tuskegee Institute (1968–69)

ARCHITECTS: Paul Rudolph, with Fry & Welch

LOCATION: West of Tuskegee on ALA 126
OPEN: Mon.–Fri. 8–4:30, Sun., 7:30 A.M.-12 noon. Closed Sat.

An inventive structure, the Tuskegee Chapel breaks dramatically with traditional approaches to ecclesiastical design. The combination of brick, wood, and glass bring a spectacular textural effect throughout the complex. This effect is further enhanced by streams of light from the ceiling that wash the walls with light. The positioning of various functions is played up through the dynamic use of form and space.

ADDITIONAL MODERN STRUCTURES OF INTEREST

ANNISTON

Anniston High School (1970–71)
ARCHITECTS: Caudill, Rowlett, & Scott
LOCATION: The Educational Park.
Woodstock Avenue at 12th St. (3 blocks E
of Quintard Avenue (US 431)

BIRMINGHAM

South Central Bell Telephone Company
(1980s)
ARCHITECTS: Giattina & Partners
LOCATION: Off Hwy. 280 (100 ft. below
hwy level)

This precast concrete structure is interestingly
arranged in bold horizontal bands that span a
pond in a densely wooded area.

DAPHNE

Marion Corporation (1982)
ARCHITECTS: Loftis Bell Downing and
Partners
LOCATION: One Marion Avenue

Unusual slopes and angles are employed for
this wood and glass headquarters for an oil
refining, distribution, and drilling corporation.

HUNTSVILLE

Vonbraun Civic Center (1970s)
ARCHITECTS: Smith, Kranert & Tomblin &
Associates with Dickson and Davis
LOCATION: 700 Monroe Street, S.W.
Huntsville

An admirably planned complex functional for
many community facilities.

ROBERTSDALE

St. Patrick's Catholic Church (1972–73)
ARCHITECTS: J. Buchanan Blitch, Bill Argus
Jr., and Eduardo Camacho
LOCATION: Highway 59, North

A religious structure of dignity and simplicity
nicely sited in a grove of pine trees.

Fairbanks •

Anchorage

Sitka

Alaska

ANCHORAGE

William A. Egan Convention and Civic Center (1984)

ARCHITECTS: Hellmuth Obata Kassabaum with C.C. of Alaska
LOCATION: Between F and E Street, on W. 5th Avenue
OPEN: During business and shopping hours, special events

At the present time, Anchorage is undertaking an ambitious downtown development program consisting of plans for expansion, additions, preservation, and beautification. The impressive new three-level Convention Center with 98,318 square feet, is one of the first completed projects. Conveniently located by hotels and shopping, the rectangular complex features a dazzling rounded glass extension enclosing an atrium lobby.

ANCHORAGE

Historical and Fine Arts Museum (1968–1974/1984)

ARCHITECTS: Schultz/Maynard (1968); Kenneth Maynard (1974) Mitchell/Giurgola (1984)
LOCATION: 121 West 7th Ave.
OPEN: Tues.–Sat. 9–6, Sun. 1–5; (except holidays); summer, Mon. 9–6, Tues. and Thurs. 9–9

Recently expanded to three times its original size, the Historical and Fine Arts Museum is devoted to Alaskan art and cultural displays. Exterior walls are uniquely topped with a decorative frieze by Anchorage artist Alex Duff Combs, depicting the flora and fauna of the Cook Inlet region. Other features include traveling shows, special lecture and film series, and art programs.

FAIRBANKS

Rasmuson Library and Fine Arts Center (1969)

ARCHITECT: Francis R. Mayer
LOCATION: College Road (AK 3)
OPEN: Mon.-Fri, 8-5, Sat. 1–6, Sun 11–6

This fresh and clear complex of reinforced concrete is clad with pebble concrete wall panels and copper tinted windows. The large library is the focal point on the campus with additional facilities for the Fine Arts Center adjoining.

SITKA

Centennial Building (1966–67)

ARCHITECT: Allen McDonald
LOCATION: Harbor Drive
OPEN: June–Sept., daily 9–9, Oct.-May, 9–5

Commanding a sweeping view of the ocean, mountains, and nearby islands, the Centennial Building is located on a steep hillside by the beach. The simple stone and wood structure functions as a museum for the area and a place for community activities. An interesting Tlingit Indian canoe is effectively placed in an outside plaza near the entry creating a focal point for the complex.

ADDITIONAL MODERN STRUCTURES OF INTEREST

ANCHORAGE

Anchorage Natural Gas Building (1969)
ARCHITECTS: Crittenden, Cassetta, Wirum & Cannon
LOCATION: Spenard Road at 31st Street

Well articulated with bands of anodized aluminum panels and tinted glass, this small office building is neatly and attractively planned.

Arco Building (1983)
ARCHITECTS: Wirum & Cash
LOCATION: 700 "G" Street

The Arco Building, sheathed with metal and copper reflective glass, is Anchorage's largest complex to date.

Cook Inlet Building (late 1970s)
ARCHITECTS: Maynard and Partch
LOCATION: 2525 C Street

One of the city's most dazzling architectural projects, the Cook Inlet Building creates a strong silhouette on the skyline.

Federal Building/Courthouse (1979–82)
ARCHITECTS: John Graham Co. & Associates
LOCATION: 701 "C" Street

A well-designed building that sets an admirable architectural standard.

George M. Sullivan Arena (1983)
ARCHITECTS: Wirum & Associates
LOCATION: 1600 Gambell

A boldly designed multi-use sports arena named in honor of a past mayor of Anchorage.

Holy Family Cathedral (1951)
ARCHITECT: A.A. Porreca
LOCATION: Corner of 5th and H Street

An interesting cast concrete monolithic structure.

Performing Arts Center (to be completed in 1987)
ARCHITECTS: Hardy Holzman Pfeiffer

LOCATION: Block of 5th & 6th-G & F

This beautifully designed center is now under construction and will cover one square block.

Sohio Building (1970s)
ARCHITECTS: Hellmuth, Obata & Kassabaum
LOCATION: 3111 "C" Street

This impressive tower is constructed of metal and glass. The new *Sohio Building,* located on the corner of Benson & Northern Lights, is also designed by Hellmuth, Obata, & Kassabaum, featuring a cluster of low- and high-rise structures.

FAIRBANKS

Commons-University of Alaska (1969)
ARCHITECTS: Crittenden, Cassetta, Wirum & Cannon
LOCATION: On College Road (AK 3)

This important structure plays an introductory role to the growing university. Traffic plans have been planned effectively to channel traffic throughout the complex. Glass and wood have been extensively employed.

- Second Mesa

- Sedona

Cordes Junction •

Glendale •
Phoenix • • Scottsdale
Tempe • • Mesa

• Tucson • Willcox
• Kitt Peak

Arizona

CORDES JUNCTION

Arcosanti (1970-)

ARCHITECT: Paolo Soleri
LOCATION: 2.5 miles NE of Cordes Junction. Exit off IS 17 (70 miles N of Phoenix)
OPEN: Daily tours at 9, 11, 2, and 4

Soleri is one of the most extraordinary and individualistic architects of our times. Migrating to the United States from Italy to work with Frank Lloyd Wright at Taliesin, Soleri later began working on his "cities in the desert." Arcosanti, a prototype of "archology," Soleri's term of ecology and architecture, is a city of raw concrete expressed in amazing forms. A tour through the city, still being built, is an exhilerating experience.

KITT PEAK

Robert R. McMath Solar Telescope (1966)

ARCHITECTS: Skidmore, Owings, and Merrill
LOCATION: 39 miles W of Tucson on AZ 86, then 13 miles on AZ 386
OPEN: Daily 10–4

A forceful, yet simple structure of white painted copper, this Solar Telescope makes a dynamic impression against its desert setting. The form and total design concept of the structure expresses many of the new challenging architectural functions of our cybernetic age. The Kitt Peak Solar telescope, with dimensions measuring the largest in the world, allows observation of the sun. Architectural forms, technology, and materials support this fascinating function.

PHOENIX

Arizona Biltmore Hotel (1929)

ARCHITECT: Frank Lloyd Wright
LOCATION: 24 Street & Missouri
OPEN: Always

A fabled and glamorous hotel on thirty-five acres of desert terrain, the Arizona Biltmore has attracted some of the world's most famous people. During the 1920s Wright became fascinated with the Aztec Indian culture after visiting Mexico. Motifs throughout the hotel complex are modern designs inspired by ancient Aztec Indian temples. Interior spaces and furnishings were also executed by the great master of modern architecture. The landmark hotel was restored after a fire in 1973 by Taliesin Associated Architects, founded by Wright.

SCOTTSDALE

Civic Center (1968–75)

ARCHITECTS: Bennie Gonzales Associates
LOCATION: George Avenue between 1st and 2nd Streets
OPEN: During office hours and for performances

This large public facility consists of a library, City Hall, and Center for the Arts. The Civic Center's design employs thick walls and small windows recalling a unique Arizona vernacular—modified in a contemporary approach. Always concerned with the human element, the architect designed unit facilities surrounded by a lovely park providing space for many public activities.

SCOTTSDALE

Taliesin West (1938–59)

ARCHITECT: Frank Lloyd Wright
LOCATION: Maricopa Mesa, N on
Scottsdale Road, E on Shea Boulevard, 4.8
miles to the gate
OPEN: Tours daily 10–4, on the half hour

Situated on 800 acres of desert terrain,
Taliesin West was planned as a winter
quarters for Wright's students. (Taliesin East is
located in Spring Green, Wisconsin.) Chal-
lenged with the materials and spirit of the
desert, Wright used purplish-red desert stone
blocks set in concrete supporting his
"organic" philosophy that "a house must grow
out of the land."

SECOND MESA

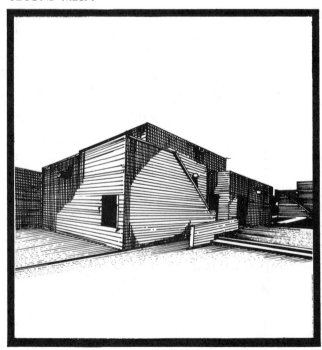

Hopi Cultural Center (1970–71)

ARCHITECT: Bennie Gonzales Associates
LOCATION: AZ 264, 5.3 miles W of
intersection with AZ 87
OPEN: Daily

Echoing the Southwest Adobe architecture of
the early Indian culture, the Hopi Cultural
Center is appropriately located in a desert
setting on the Hopi Reservation. Situated on a
Mesa rising 6,450 feet, the Cultural Center is a
simple museum, restaurant, motel, and shop.
The Center is an enticing place to begin a
tour of the reservation, the oldest continually
inhabited area in the United States, and
experience the Indian culture.

SEDONA

Chapel of The Holy Cross
(1965)

ARCHITECTS: Anshen & Allen
LOCATION: off AZ 179, 3.8 miles S of
intersection with US Alt 89
OPEN: Daily 9–5

A small but monumental structure, the Chapel
of the Holy Cross is nestled within the
majestic red sandstone cliffs of Arizona. The
chapel of poured-in-place-concrete conforms
to a soaring 90 feet high cross that dominates
the exterior and interior space. Access to the
chapel is only possible by means of a winding
foot path that adds to the drama of approach-
ing this remarkable building. It is one of the
first modern religious structures in Arizona.

TEMPE

Grady Gammage Memorial
Auditorium (1959–66)

ARCHITECT: Frank Lloyd Wright
LOCATION: Arizona State University
campus
OPEN: School hours and for performances

Completed after the great modern architect's
death, the Grady Gammage Auditorium is a
fascinating building on the University's campus. The design concept of the structure
reflects Wright's preoccupation with spirals
and circular forms toward the end of his life.
Classical forms and motifs blend with a
contemporary interpretation in a unique
manner.

ADDITIONAL MODERN STRUCTURES OF INTEREST

GLENDALE

Schubach Jewelry Shop
ARCHITECTS: Frank Lloyd Wright Foundation
LOCATION: Valley West Mall

MESA

Desert Samaritan Hospital (1974)
ARCHITECT: Cardell R. Scott
LOCATION: 1400 South Dobson Road

An excellent building example designed for optimum patient care and comfort.

Mesa Community Center
ARCHITECTS: Frank Lloyd Wright Foundation
LOCATION: Center St. & 2nd Street (201 N. Center St.)

PARADISE VALLEY

Ascension Lutheran Church
ARCHITECTS: Frank Lloyd Wright Foundation
LOCATION: Mockingbird Lane

PHOENIX

First Christian Church and Bell Tower (1957–)
ARCHITECT: Frank Lloyd Wright
LOCATION: 6500 North 7th Avenue

This church was completed after the master architect's death by the Frank Lloyd Wright Foundation according to the original design. The free-standing bell tower is the focal point.

Office of Lewis & Roca
ARCHITECTS: Frank Lloyd Wright Foundation
LOCATION: 100 W. Washington

Lath House at Heritage Square (1980)
ARCHITECT: Robert R. Frankeberger
LOCATION: Heritage Square

This delightful open-air pavilion, and the latest addition to Heritage Square has been praised across the country. Used for special exhibits and events the structure is constructed of hundreds of Douglas fir poles.

Mountain View Estates
ARCHITECTS: Frank Lloyd Wright Foundation
LOCATION: Tatum & Shea Blvd.

Phoenix Civic Plaza (1972)
ARCHITECTS: Charles Luckman Associates
LOCATION: 225 East Adams

Covering a six-block area, the Phoenix Civic Plaza features the bold multi-purpose CONVENTION CENTER with its striking recessed triangles, and the SYMPHONY HALL. The angled striated concrete Symphony Hall is connected to the Convention Center by a plaza.

Security Mortgage Corporation Building
ARCHITECT: Tom Hite
LOCATION: 3507 North Central Avenue

An unusual inverted tiered pyramid has been employed giving this structure a unique dimension.

Valley National Bank (early 1970s)
ARCHITECTS: Welton Becket & Associates
LOCATION: Valley Center

This soaring tower is sheathed with energy efficient reflective glass and features a panoramic view from a restaurant at the top.

SCOTTSDALE

Cosanti Foundation Workshop (1962-)
ARCHITECT: Paolo Soleri
LOCATION: 6433 Doubletree Road, 1 mile W of No. Scottdale Rd.

Open daily from 9–5, Cosanti is equally as fascinating as Arcosanti. Cosanti functions as a workshop of meandering spaces constructed of roughly formed concrete shapes and also as a dwelling quarters and small museum. Visiting Cosanti is a memorable architectural experience.

Har-Zion Synagogue (early 1960s)
ARCHITECTS: Bennie M. Gonzales Associates
LOCATION: 5929 East Lincoln Drive

Expressing a part of its natural surroundings, the Synagogue has swirling forms suggesting sand dunes. The building has been called "an oasis of faith."

Hopi Post Office
ARCHITECTS: Frank Lloyd Wright Foundation
LOCATION: Pima Road

Mountain View East
ARCHITECTS: Frank Lloyd Wright Foundation
LOCATION: Hayden Road & Timbre

TEMPE

ASU Music Building
ARCHITECTS: Frank Lloyd Wright Foundation
LOCATION: Arizona State University Campus

TUCSON

Great Western Bank Building (1975)
ARCHITECTS: Mascarella
LOCATION: 5151 E. Broadway

Pima County Junior College (1970-)
ARCHITECTS: Caudill Rowlett Scott with Wm. Wilde & Associates
LOCATION: Anklam Road, 2.3 miles W of IS 10

Tucson City, County, and Federal Building
ARCHITECTS: Various architects: Federal Building by Friedman, Keim, and McFerron.
LOCATION: 250 W. Alameda (City of Tucson)
131 W. Congress (Pima Library)
301 W. Congress (Federal Building)

An admirable and striking group of civic buildings located in downtown Tucson. Also noteworthy is the *MUSIC HALL AT TUCSON CONVENTION CENTER* by CNWL which Friedman, Keim, and McFerron designed in 1971.

WILLCOX

Cochise Visitor Center (1971)

ARCHITECTS: Dinsmore, Kulseth, & Riggs/ Architecture One, Ltd.
LOCATION: near Willcox, on Interstate 10, Far SE part of state

This bold, simple structure of white stucco is planned around a 40-foot-square courtyard and functions as an introduction to the exciting history of the area.

Mesa Temple, Church of Jesus Christ of Latter-Day-Saints (1928)
ARCHITECTS: Don C. Young and Ramm Hansen
LOCATION: 121 South Le Sueur

Constructed of reinforced concrete and faced with terracotta glaze, this Temple was inspired by pre-Columbian temples. Styles from the past were popular during the modern Art Deco period.

- Eureka Springs

Blytheville •

- Conway

- Little Rock

- Hot Springs

Arkansas

CONWAY

Bailey Library at Hendrix College (1967)

ARCHITECTS: Philip Johnson with Wittenberg, Delong & Davidson
LOCATION: Washington Ave. and Independence Street off US 64 & 65B
OPEN: During school hours

Flanked by an inviting open air plaza, the long low Bailey Library is a popular meeting place on campus. Built partially underground, the design enhances the surrounding landscape and provides a spacious visual concept much appreciated on the crowded campus grounds. Various levels and forms contribute to the overall design effect.

EUREKA SPRINGS

Thorncrown Wayfarers Chapel (1981)

ARCHITECT: Fay Jones
LOCATION: A few miles NW of town on US 62W (follow signs)
OPEN: Sun.–9, 11, & 6. Open daily at various times during year

Located on a hilltop in the Ozark Mountains, this light and airy chapel commands a panoramic view of the area. Glass and wood members are secured by X-shaped connectors that give structural interest to the design. The chapel was built on the property of James Reed who wanted a place where travelers could rest and enjoy the view. Jones, a follower of Frank Lloyd Wright's philosophies, met the challenge of preserving the natural beauty. He feels that "good architecture has the potential to nourish."

HOT SPRINGS

Mid-America Center (1982)

ARCHITECTS: Stuck Frier Lane Scott Beisner, Inc. with E. Verner Johnson & Associates
LOCATION: 400 Mid America Blvd. (Take Highway 270 West) c. 6 mi. from downtown.

Nestled in a wooded area and straddling a stream, the new Mid-America Center was commissioned by the Arkansas State Department of Parks and Tourism of Little Rock. Constructed of steel, glass and wood, this inviting building houses a "see, touch and do" museum. The architects have created a spacious interior environment where children and adults can "experiment," build mountains, pump up a balloon, see diamonds in a mine, and view many other marvelous exhibits.

LITTLE ROCK

Metrocentre Mall

(completed 1978)

ARCHITECTS: Cromwell Neyland Truemper Levy & Gatchell, Inc. with Blass/Riddick/Chilcote
LOCATION: Between Fourth St. and Seventh St.

Conveniently situated in a downtown location in Little Rock, the well-planned Metrocentre Mall is a welcome addition to the area. The efficient arrangement of shops, restaurants, office space, and other public facilities are designed to harmonize and complement the surrounding landscaped spaces. The project won a prestigious design award from the American Institute of Architects. A large abstract sculpture by Henry Moore is the Mall's focal point.

ADDITIONAL MODERN STRUCTURES OF INTEREST

BLYTHEVILLE

Mississippi County Community College
(1980)
ARCHITECTS: Cromwell, Neyland, Levy, &
Gatchell, Inc.
LOCATION: Mississippi County College
campus

Constructed primarily of steel, aluminum,
polystyrene sandwich panels, and fiberglass
built-up roofing, this College employs an
advanced system of passive and active solar
techniques.

LITTLE ROCK

Worthen Bank (1970)
ARCHITECTS: Erhart Eichenbaum Rauch and
Blass
LOCATION: 200 West Capitol

The Worthen Bank is one of the first high-rise
concrete towers of its kind in the state of
Arkansas.

Terra Linda •
San Rafael •

Mill Valley •

San Francisco

• Berkeley
• Oakland   • Lafayette

• San Lorenzo

Pacifica •

San Mateo •

Palo Alto •
Santa Clara •

Los Altos
Santa Teresa •

Los Gatos •

• Santa Cruz

• Redding

• Sea Ranch

Santa Rosa

San Francisco Area

Squaw Valley
Lake Tahoe

• Sacramento
• Stockton

Seaside

Monterey
Carmel

Carmel
Valley

• Fresno

• San Luis Obispo

• Ojai
Santa Barbara

• San Bernardino
• Redlands

• Palm Springs
• La Jolla

Malibu

Santa Monica

Burbank •

Beverly Hills •

San Diego
Pasadena
Los Angeles

• El Segundo

San
Pedro   • Long Beach

Palos Verdes

• Garden Grove
• Santa Ana

• Newport Beach

California

BERKELEY

First Church of Christ, Scientist (1910–12)

ARCHITECT: Bernard Maybeck
LOCATION: 2619 Dwight Way at Bowditch Street
OPEN: Tours Sun. 12:15; or telephone church office for an appointment: (415) 845–7199

Considered Maybeck's finest work, the Christian Science Church is an excellent early example of incorporating modern techniques with traditional aspects—an approach the architect was known for. Maybeck, who started the School of Architecture at U.C. in his own home, was particularly fond of employing Gothic, Classical, Oriental, Spanish, Tudor, and Swiss elements with his modern interpretations.

BERKELEY

University Art Museum University of California (1968)

ARCHITECTS: Mario J. Ciampi & Associates
LOCATION: Bancroft Way between College Ave. and Bowditch St.
OPEN: Wed.–Sun. 11–6

This simple, massive concrete structure is enlivened with a delightful Alexander Calder sculpture near the entry. As one enters the museum, a fascinating environment of unusual form and space invites the visitor to explore the display areas. The complex series of platforms seems to provoke comparisons to Frank Lloyd Wright's Guggenheim Museum in New York City, but with realization that this museum is more flexible and offers extensive visual freedom.

BURBANK

Warner Brothers Office Building (1981)

ARCHITECTS: Luckman Partnership
LOCATION: 3903 West Olive Avenue
OPEN: During business hours

A slick, high-tech structure, the Warner Brothers Office Building makes a dazzling impression. No mullions protrude from the thin-skinned building. Staggered curved forms add to the drama with no window frames employed—the glass has been glued in place. Natural greenery placed on the first levels creates strong contrast against a gleaming background. The interior space, featuring soaring atriums, carries out the design image.

GARDEN GROVE

Community Church (1959–61)
Crystal Cathedral (1979–)

ARCHITECTS: Richard Neutra (Community Church) Philip Johnson/Burgee (Crystal Cathedral)
LOCATION: 12141 Lewis Street, N of CA 22 and W of IS 5
OPEN: Usually open daily and for Sun. services, Tours

An innovative design concept incorporating a drive-in amphitheater facing a pulpit, the Community Church is constructed of concrete and natural stone. A "Tower of Hope" was added in 1967. Nearby is Johnson's spectacular Crystal Cathedral. The striking "monument to imagination" features 10,661 glass panes suspended beyond a stark white frame. The four-pointed star design has been compared to the "prow of a vast glass liner."

LA JOLLA

The Salk Institute (1964–66)

ARCHITECT: Louis Kahn
LOCATION: Genessee exit off IS 5, W on
Genessee St. to 10010 N. Torrey Pines Rd.
OPEN: Tours, Mon.–Fri. 11, 12, 1, and 2,
except holidays.

One of Kahn's finest works, the sprawling
symmetrical Salk Institute is boldly situated
on a hilly wooded site overlooking the Pacific
Ocean. All functions and details connected
with this efficient research facility have been
meticulously planned by the architect. Strong
form and use of material effectively convey
the spirit and solidity of the building's
function. The two major buildings are separated by a sunwashed travertine plaza with a
narrow waterway down the center.

LOS ALTOS HILLS

Foothill College (1959–61)

ARCHITECTS: Ernest J. Kump and Masten &
Hurd
LOCATION: 12345 El Monte Ave., just W of
IS 280
OPEN: Daily

The architects were more concerned with the
total environment of the campus than with
individual buildings. The complex, consisting
of thirty-nine units, radiates around walkways,
patios, and courtyards with facilities for
parking. Building materials are of rough sawn
redwood with huge projecting exposed
wooden beams that serve as outside
corridors.

LOS ANGELES

Bonaventure Hotel (1975–77)

ARCHITECTS: John Portman & Associates
LOCATION: 5th at Figueroa
OPEN: Always open

A magnificent cluster of five glass cylinders, the Bonaventure Hotel makes a striking impression on the Los Angeles skyline. Portman's dramatic hotels around the nation have become exciting landmarks of architecture often featuring vast central open spaces. Surrounding these atriums are shops, restaurants, lounging areas, and other convenient facilities.

LOS ANGELES

Bradbury Building (1893)

ARCHITECT: George H. Wyman
LOCATION: 304 South Broadway
OPEN: Mon.–Sat. 10–4, except holidays

Restored to its original condition in 1969, this building may seem an odd selection for a guide to modern design, but its significance lies in the extensive and delightful use of iron and glass construction - a quite modern treatment during that time. A number of commercial structures around the nation during this period exploited iron in this manner-frankly exposed and decoratively wrought.

LOS ANGELES

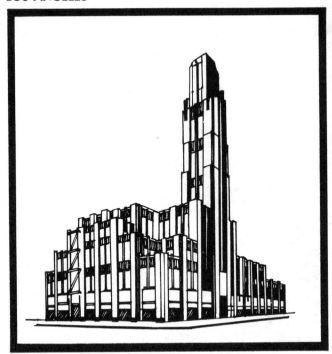

Bullocks Wilshire (1929)

ARCHITECTS: John and Donald Parkinson
LOCATION: 3050 Wilshire Boulevard
OPEN: During shopping hours

An elegant and supreme example of Art Deco design, Bullocks Wilshire is one of California's architectural treasures of the Art Deco period. During the twenties and thirties designers were inspired by many influences and styles of the past that were resurrected in the name of modernism. The design of Bullocks takes advantages of this design direction to capture various Art Deco themes in each department of the store. The detailing throughout the building is exquisite.

LOS ANGELES

Hollyhock House at Barnsdall Park (1920–21)

ARCHITECT: Frank Lloyd Wright
LOCATION: 4800 Hollywood Boulevard just W of Vermont Ave.
OPEN: Tours Tues., Thurs., first Sat. in month at 10, 11, 12, and 1, except holidays.

Reflected in the Hollyhock house is Wright's involvement with the Oriental and Aztec Indian cultures. Motifs with this influence are repeated in many details but especially in the continuous exterior frieze. Wright employed a textile block system of concrete units he felt had "organic" harmony. THE ARTS AND CRAFTS CENTER by Rudolf M. Schindler, who worked under Wright for a short time, is also an interesting early modern building, on the grounds and open to the public.

LOS ANGELES

Pacific Design Center (1975)

ARCHITECTS: Cesar Pelli and Gruen Associates
LOCATION: Melrose Avenue at San Vicente Boulevard
OPEN: First floor Mon.–Fri. 9–5

This well-known Argentine-born American architect's work exemplifies the high tech approach to design primarily through the use of hard reflective and colorful materials. The Pacific Design Center, a showroom for furnishing manufacturers, is surrounded by smaller-scaled buildings. The mammoth ultramarine structure has been nick-named "The Blue Whale."

LOS ANGELES

Simon Rodia Towers/Watts Towers (1921–54)

DESIGNER: Simon Rodia
LOCATION: 1765 E 107th St., E off Harbor Freeway (CA 11) on Century Boulevard, S on Central Ave., E on 108th St.
OPEN: Open daily

Rodia was a logger, miner, construction worker, and tilesetter—an immigrant from Italy. For over 30 years, he lovingly built this eccentric masterpiece consisting of pipe, broken bottles, seashells, bed frames, tile, and all manner of odds and ends to achieve his fantasy creation. Rodia departed after the towers were completed. Today they are maintained by the city and appreciated by art lovers around the world.

LOS GATOS

Civic Center (1964–65)

ARCHITECTS: Charles D. Stickney and
William R. Hull
LOCATION: 110 East Main Street at Fiesta
Way

OPEN: During office hours

Situated in a charming wooded park setting,
this unpretentious brick and concrete Center
was efficiently planned to accommodate various public functions. Plazas, a fountain,
seating, and plantings provide a welcoming
introduction to the complex that includes a
library, administration offices, police, and
public facilities. The much admired Civic
Center has become a prototype for similar
government buildings across the the nation.

OAKLAND

Oakland-Alameda County Coliseum and Stadium

(1966–68)

ARCHITECTS: Skidmore, Owings, and
Merrill
LOCATION: 5 miles S of downtown
Oakland off CA 17 at 66th Avenue
OPEN: For various events

A dynamic circular structure of steel, glass,
and concrete, the Coliseum and Stadium was
designed to house a vast audience and
playing field. SOM's San Francisco office
planned a series of large X-shaped exterior
concrete supports that are independent of an
inner glass wall. The effect is both striking
and functional. The structure is especially
brilliant at night when lit.

OAKLAND

Oakland Museum (1967–69)

ARCHITECTS: Kevin Roche/John Dinkeloo & Associates
LOCATION: 1000 Oak Street between 10th and 12th
OPEN: Tues.–Sat. 10–5, Sun. 12–7

An inviting composition of tiers, plazas, and gardens are arranged around various exhibition spaces and welcome the visitor to the Oakland Museum. One of the most inventive, effective, and appealing structures of its type in the nation, the interior spaces were planned for displays that include California art, history, and natural science.

OAKLAND

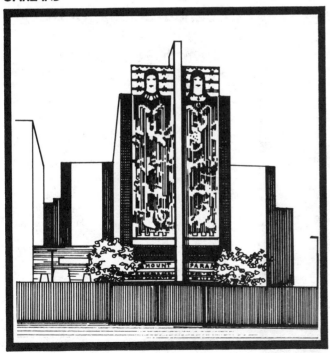

Paramount Theatre (1931)

(Restored in 1973)

ARCHITECTS: Miller & Pflueger
LOCATION: 2025 Broadway
OPEN: For performances. Tours by appointment

The glamour of the cinema played an important role during the Art Deco period of the roaring 1920s and 30s. Movie houses around the nation were built laden with popular motifs such as palm trees, Egyptian and Aztec themes, geometrics, and other decorative designs. The dramatic exterior mosaic work soars the full height of the facade creating a colorful addition to downtown Oakland. This mosaic is matched only by the vast interior lobby space that has been beautifully restored. The facilities throughout the complex feature dazzling surfaces and design treatments.

PALOS VERDES

Wayfarers' Chapel (1949–51)

ARCHITECT: Lloyd Wright
LOCATION: Palos Verdes Dr. South, 1 mile E of Marineland
OPEN: Daily 11–4

Wright, son of the famed architect Frank Lloyd Wright, designed this building to fulfill a dream of "a chapel on a hillside above the ocean where wayfarers could stop to rest, meditate, and give thanks to God for the beauty and wonder of creation." This small but breathtaking glass church is supported by a memorial to the theologian Eamnuel Swedenborg, founder of the Church of the New Jerusalem.

PASADENA

Art Center College of Design
(1974–75)

ARCHITECTS: Craig Ellwood Associates
LOCATION: 1700 Lida St., W off Linda Vista Ave., 1 mile W on Lida
OPEN: Tours Mon. and Wed. at 2 PM, Fri. at 10:30 AM

Spanning 192 feet over a deep irregular ravine, the frankly exposed black-painted structure with bronze tinted glass windows makes a spectacular impression on the sprawling hillside. This single building provides facilities for 1,000 students, including a library, cafeteria, art studios, darkrooms, and other spaces for art projects. The structure is a true offspring of Miesian architecture.

PASADENA

David B. Gamble House

(1907–08)

ARCHITECTS: Greene & Greene
LOCATION: 4 Westmoreland Place, off N. Orange Grove Blvd., a half block N of Walnut St.
OPEN: Tues. and Thurs. 10–3, first Sun. of month 12–3

A supreme example of quality and craftsmanship in architecture, all the furnishings and fittings for the Gamble House were designed by this famous brother team. Bringing the continuity of a total design concept, the house is considered the architects' finest work. The Gamble House is an example of architecture that has been labeled "The Shingle Style," "Stick Style," and "Bungalow Style." This architectural approach was influenced by the "organic principles" of Frank Lloyd Wright. The Gamble House now serves as a museum and headquarters for the Greene brothers.

PASADENA

The Pasadena Art Museum (Norton Simon Museum)

(1969)

ARCHITECTS: Ladd & Kelsey
LOCATION: 411 West Colorado (corner of Orange)
OPEN: Thursday–Sunday, 12 noon to 6 PM

Arranged in a two-level composition surrounded by inviting outdoor plazas and landscaping, the Pasadena Art Museum uniquely fulfills its function. The galleries, library, auditorium, and other facilities are arranged in "molecule-plan pavilions of varying size and height, which are strung bead-like on a double strand of corridors." (*Progressive Architecture,* Dec. 1969.) The museum, which harmonizes with its residential surroundings, is considered "the best museum of 20th Century Art in the West."

CALIFORNIA

SAN FRANCISCIO

Davies Symphony Hall (1980)

ARCHITECTS: Skidmore, Owings & Merrill
LOCATION: On the corner of Grove and
Van Ness
OPEN: For performances, Tours: Mon.
10:30–2:30, Wed. 1:30 & 2:30, Sat.
12:30–1:30

The handsome new circular Symphony Hall features a circle, within a circle, within a circle plan. This arrangement accommodates perfect acoustics and sound proofing for the structure. The white concrete, glass, and brass building is highlighted on the exterior plaza by a Henry Moore bronze sculpture entitled "Reclining Figures in Four Pieces" especially created for the space. An interior color scheme of pale peach, beige, and rose is carried throughout the complex. A grand staircase encircles the interior space complementing the building's circular plan.

SAN FRANCISCO

580 California Street (1984–)

ARCHITECTS: Philip Johnson/John Burgee
LOCATION: 580 California Street
OPEN: During business hours

Rising 23-stories high, this light gray granite office tower is uniquely topped with a contemporary two-story glass French Mansard roof with cast iron cresting. Three human figures, an extraordinary feature in these times, hover at the base of the roof, functioning as capitals for three soaring slender columns. Shallow bay windows extend to the building's lower levels where decorative grillwork and lanterns create visual interest at the colonnaded extrance. Themes from the past have been surprisingly resurrected in a spirited approach. (See the AT&T Building in New York City.)

SAN FRANCISCO

Ghirardelli Square Redevelopment (1915/1964)

ARCHITECT: Bernardi & Emmons with Halprin Associates
LOCATION: North Point, Larkin, Beach, and Polk Streets

This redevelopment also includes *The Cannery Remodeling* (1895/1969; Joseph Esherick & Associates, located at 2801 Leavenworth St.) *The Ice House Rehabilitation* (1914/1969; Wurster, Bernardi & Emmons, Architects, located at Union Street at Ice House Alley). A superb transformation of a cluster of old buildings by many prominent architects, this ambitious project has proven to be an inviting and economically sound urban renewal development. Facilities throughout provide numerous pleasurable experiences for the visitor including shopping, dining, strolling, and people-watching.

SAN FRANCISCO

Hallidie Building (1917–18)

ARCHITECT: Willis Polk
LOCATION: 130 Sutter Street
OPEN: During business hours

An exquisite example of a glass-curtained wall structure, Hallidie Building is one of the first buildings of its type in America. The building has a facade of glass panels hung three feet in front of the structure. Historians feel the design was a significant link between the Victorian period and the post-war skyscraper. Originally commissioned in 1917 by the University of California as a spec investment, the architectural treasure became an Official Landmark in 1971.

SAN FRANCISCO

Hyatt Regency Hotel (1972–74)

ARCHITECTS: John Portman Assoiates
LOCATION: 5 Embarcadero Center
OPEN: Continuously

John Portman has designed some of the nation's most dramatic hotels and is one of the first architects to depart from traditional hotel design. The vast open atrium, with a mammoth water sculpture, is spectacular. An extraordinary tiered design is executed throughout the complex creating visual excitement from all vantage points.

SAN FRANCISCO

St. Mary's Cathedral (1970)

ARCHITECTS: Pietro Belluschi, Luigi Nervi, and others
LOCATION: Corner of Geary and Gough Streets
OPEN: Daily

Rev. O'Saughnessy said of St. Mary's, "Our bold, assertive Cathedral demands attention and provokes reflection. Like a great white ship that sails across the city skyline, it points to a new horizon." The majestic poured-concrete structure combines the space and spirit of the Gothic Cathedral with the impressive technical abilities of our own age. Vivid stained-glass windows and a striking baldachino composed of thousands of aluminum rods are a few of the creative features. The exterior is sheathed with Italian travertine marble. Nervi, who collaborated on the project, was one of Italy's most prominent early modern architects and engineers.

SAN FRANCISCO

Transamerica Building (1968–72)

ARCHITECT: William Pereira
LOCATION: 600 Montgomery
OPEN: During office hours

Although highly criticized, the piercing needle-nosed "Transam" building is a familiar and fascinating landmark on the San Francisco skyline. The strong design has a heavy trussed based from which the structure soars upward in a pyramid form. The building's unique shape, of course, has lent itself to many descriptive nicknames.

SAN FRANCISCO

V.C. Morris Shop (1948–49)

ARCHITECT: Frank Lloyd Wright
LOCATION: 140 Maiden Lane
OPEN: Now an art gallery, open during business hours

A well articulated exterior facade of brick, the V.C. Morris Shop has no show room windows. Featuring an offset contemporary "Romanesque" arch, the building entices the shopper into the unique interior space. A small red plaque to the left of the entry credits Frank Lloyd Wright as the architect. The interior is a fanciful treatment of ramps and spirals, reflected later on a grand scale at Wright's Guggenheim Museum in New York City. A huge domed skylight and artificial lighting effectively light the gallery's art.

SAN JUAN CAPISTRANO

San Juan Capistrano Regional Library (1983)

ARCHITECT: Michael Graves
LOCATION: 31495 El Camino Real (behind the old Mission)
OPEN: Mon.–Thurs.: 10 AM to 9 PM; Fri. & Sat.: 10 AM to 5 PM

Known for his controversial Post-Modern Portland building in Portland, Oregon, Michael Graves is a leading exponent of this innovative architectural direction. This unique small Regional Library combines stucco and tile in a refreshing interpretation recalling the early mission style. The architect also designed the interior spaces and furnishings carrying out this theme. The abstract plan incorporates lattice reading gazebos and rooms that surround an inner courtyard and fountain. Bold segmental arches over the entrances introduce the visitor to interior spaces. Detailing and lighting throughout are particularly effective.

SAN RAFAEL

Marin County Civic Center

(1959–62/1967–69)

ARCHITECTS: Frank Lloyd Wright & Taliesin Associates
LOCATION: E. off US 101 on San Pedro Rd. 1.5 mi. N of town
OPEN: Mon.–Fri.

Often compared to an ancient Roman aqua-duct, a centipede, and a bridge cutting across the rolling countryside, the Marin County Civic Center was one of Wright's last projects and completed by his Associates ten years after his death. Rhythm by gradation is gracefully planned through a series of oblate arches. A central interior mall with a huge skylight extends the entire length of the Administration Building. The curved form is found everywhere—even down to the furnishings and details.

SANTA ANA

Orange County Court House
(1964–65)

ARCHITECTS: Richard & Dion Neutra with Ramberg, Lowrey & Assoc.
LOCATION: 700 Civic Center Dr. at Flower St.
OPEN: During office hours

Trained by the early modern master architect, Adolf Loos in Vienna, Neutra later became one of California's most illustrious modern architects—known principally for his contribution to modern residential design. The Orange County Court House, with its exterior treatment of vertical louvres, is considered Neutra's finest commercial work.

SANTA CRUZ

University of California at Santa Cruz (1963–)

ARCHITECTS: John Carl Warnecke with others
LOCATION: Bay St. via High St., just N of CA 1, NW of town
OPEN: Daily

An extraordinary campus, The University of California at Santa Cruz boasts a list of impressive modern buildings by many nationally known architects. The various clusters of buildings are uniquely sited within a beautiful natural setting. Each individual college maintains its own identity through placement and design. The *KRESGE COLLEGE* (1972-74) by MLTW/Turnbull Associates and Charles Moore is particularly noteworthy, located off Heller Drive on the west edge of campus. Maps of the campus are available.

ADDITIONAL MODERN STRUCTURES OF INTEREST

ANTELOPE VALLEY

Visitor Center (1980)
ARCHITECTS: The Colyer/Freeman Group
LOCATION: c. 85 miles NE of Los Angeles
in the Mojave Desert

Concrete masonry wall construction blends
beautifully with the surrounding desert for
the plan of this state desert wildflower
reserve.

AUBURN

The Ruck-A-Chucky Bridge (1978)
ARCHITECTS: Skidmore, Owings & Merrill
with T.Y. Lin Int., Eng.
LOCATION: c. 35 miles NE of Sacramento

Superb engineering and fine architectural
design have combined to produce a graceful
bridge consisting of high-strength steel cables
arranged in hyperbolic paraboloid formation.

BALBOA (Newport Beach)

Lovell Beach House (1925)
ARCHITECT: Rudolph Schindler
LOCATION: Thirteenth Street

Although this guide deals primarily with
public buildings, a few famous residential
works are included. The Lovell House, with its
bold vertical and horizontal forms and voids
is considered an important forerunner of the
International Style.

BERKELEY

Berkeley Art Center (late 1950s)
ARCHITECTS: Ratcliff, Slama, Cadwalader,
Architects
LOCATION: Live Oak Park, c. 1 mi. NW of
U.C. campus, 2 blocks N. of Rose St., 1
block E. of Shattuck

A small, inviting structure of pole-supported
construction and natural materials, this pavilion features an interior with an exposed truss
roof and large central skylight.

Environmental Design Building (1965)
ARCHITECT: Joseph Esherick
LOCATION: University of California campus

First Presbyterian Church of Berkeley
(1974)
ARCHITECTS: James Ream and Associates,
Inc.
LOCATION: 2407 Dana Street

**Student Center at the University of
California** (late 1950s)
ARCHITECT: Vernon DeMars with Hardison
and Reay
LOCATION: University of California campus,
South central edge

The design approach to this Student Center is
what the architect calls "action architecture."

BURBANK

Warner Bros. Records, Inc. (1971–75)
ARCHITECT: A. Quincy Jones
LOCATION: 3300 Warner Blvd.

Constructed primarily of wood and glass, this
lowrise building was planned to convey a
feeling of welcome and warmth.

CARMEL HIGHLANDS

Highlands Inn (1983–85)
ARCHITECTS: Shaw Associates, Architects
LOCATION: On Highway 1, 4 miles south of
Carmel

Highlands Inn was originally built in 1916 and
has been extensively renovated and recon-
structed. The sophisticated new complex
affords a panoramic view of the coastline. The
architects have captured an "Arts and Crafts"
feeling through the use of materials and
design motifs.

COLMA

Italian Cemetery Mausoleum #4A (1981)
ARCHITECTS: Botsai, Overstreet &

Rosenberg
LOCATION: 540 F Street, just S. of San Francisco

This earth-bermed cemetery building is constructed of split-faced red Persian travertin tiles on the exterior and red rosoria marble for the interior. The effect of these materials combined with glass and steel is stunning.

CONCORD

Concord Pavilion (1977)
ARCHITECTS: Frank O. Gehry Associates
LOCATION: 2000 Kirker Pass Road (NNE of Berkeley)

CYPRESS

Yamaha Motor Corporation Corporate Headquarters (1979)
ARCHITECTS: William L. Pereira Associates
LOCATION: 6555 Katella Avenue, NW of Garden Grove

This 270,000 square foot complex is designed in three sections that structurally express its own function for production of snowmobiles, sailboats, motorcycles, golf carts, and other machines. The low, rambling white structure interestingly contrasts with its spacious landscaped setting.

EL SEGUNDO

Zerox Building (1966)
ARCHITECTS: Craig Ellwood Associates
LOCATION: 555 Aviation Boulevard at 135th St. (2 miles S of LA International Airport entrance)

FREMONT

Fremont Civic Center (1968)
ARCHITECTS: Fremont Associates (City Hall) Mittelstadt, Griffin & Dalton (Police Building)
LOCATION: 39700 Civic Center Drive (c. 10 miles SSE of San Lorenzo)

The bold concrete forms of the Fremont Civic

Center make a strong impression in its countryside setting.

FRESNO

Fulton Street Mall (1964)
ARCHITECTS: Cesar Pelli and Gruen Associates with Others
LOCATION: Fulton Street

An exhilerating and innovative downtown pedestrian shopping mall covering six blocks, of previously crowded, inconvenient streets.

INDIAN WELLS

The Vintage Club (1983)
ARCHITECTS: Fisher Friedman Associates
LOCATION: SE of Palm Springs, 75000 Vintage Drive West

This unique resort features clusters of pyramids and a network of lattice design.

IRVINE

Corporate Hdqts. For Fluor Corp. & Office Building For Fluor Engineers & Constructors, Southern California Division (1977)
ARCHITECTS: Welton Becket Associates
LOCATION: 3333 Michelson Drive, SE of Santa Ana

These two mammoth structures feature large mushroom shaped towers that soar above the sprawling complex. (Tours not available)

KENSINGTON

First Unitarian Church (1962)
ARCHITECT: William W. Wurster
LOCATION: 1 Lawson Road (Close to Berkeley)

An interesting religious structure designed by one of California's great influential modern architects.

LAFAYETTE

Lafayette-Orinda United Presbyterian Church (1970)

ARCHITECTS: Burton L. Rockwell and
Richard Banwell
LOCATION: 49 Knox Drive (Acalanes exit
from Freeway 24)

Perched on a small hilltop, the shape of this
wooden church relates directly to acoustical
function.

LA JOLLA

La Jolla Women's Club (1913–14)
ARCHITECT: Irving Gill
LOCATION: 715 Silverado

This early work by the famous modern
architect clearly expresses his preference for
simplicity combined with elements of the
Spanish missions he admired.

Library at The University of California, San Diego (1972)
ARCHITECTS: William L. Pereira & Associates
LOCATION: NE edge of campus

This stunning tiered glass and concrete
structure looms above surrounding trees and
landscaped grounds. The unusual library
design has provoked much controversy.

Mandeville Center for The Arts (1968–75)
ARCHITECT: A. Quincy Jones
LOCATION: Central area of campus

Surrounded by well-landscaped grounds and
plazas, this bold sprawling concrete complex
provides numerous facilities including spaces
for music, visual arts, and drama.

Scripps Institute for Oceanography (1908)
ARCHITECT: Irving Gill
LOCATION: 8602 La Jolla Shores Drive (on
ocean front)

This well-known work by California's early
advocate of the modern style combines stark
simplicity of form with functional space.

LARKSPUR

Larkspur Ferry Terminal (1978)
ARCHITECTS: Braccia/De Brer/Heglund
LOCATION: Projects out into Corte Madera
Creek (S of San Rafael)

This striking triangular structure constructed
of white painted steel space frames makes a
strong impression from the freeway.

LIVERMORE

St. Bartholomew's Episcopal Church (mid 1960s)
ARCHITECTS: Mackinlay/Winnacker &
Associates
LOCATION: 678 Enos Way (c. 30 miles SE
of Oakland)

In order to create a sense of unity and
participation by church members, the architects for this "church in the round" were
inspired by the Arthurian Round Table.

LOS ANGELES

Annenberg School of Communications (1972–76)
ARCHITECT: A. Quincy Jones
LOCATION: Campus at University of
Southern California

The well-organized complex was designed to
express a "message" for the new progressive
curriculum.

Beverly Center (1982)
ARCHITECTS: Welton Becket & Associates
LOCATION: 8500 Beverly Boulevard

Pastel panels of porcelain enamel are arranged horizontally and punctuated with an
exterior escalator arrangement.

Broadway Plaza (1973)
ARCHITECTS: Charles Luckman Associates
LOCATION: Broadway Plaza, downtown Los
Angeles

This successful omnicenter is America's first
urban center to combine a retail area, hotel,
and office space into one large structure.

Century Bank (1972)
ARCHITECTS: Anthony Lumsden for DMJM
LOCATION: 6420 Wilshire Boulevard

Century Plaza Towers (1975)
ARCHITECT: Minoru Yamasaki
LOCATION: 2029–2049 Century Park East,
Century City

Stunning towers by the architect of the World Trade Center in New York City.

CNA Building (1972)
ARCHITECTS: Langdon and Wilson
LOCATION: Sixth Street and Commonwealth Avenue

A building with a glass curtain wall designed for maximum energy efficiency.

Coca Cola Building Plant (1936)
ARCHITECT: Robert V. Derrah
LOCATION: 1334 South Central Avenue

One of America's most interesting buildings of the Art Deco period, this red, black, and white building has been faithfully restored. The president of the plant was a boating enthusiast and a nautical theme is used throughout. The structure has been called a "landgoing ocean liner" with its ship's bridge, portholes, and promenade deck.

County Hall of Records (1964)
ARCHITECTS: Richard Neutra and Robert Alexander
LOCATION: 320 West Temple Street

An impressive public building by the great early modern Viennese-born California architect who was known primarily for his residential work.

Crocker Towers (late 1970s)
ARCHITECTS: Skidmore, Owings & Merrill
LOCATION: 333 South Grand, downtown L.A.

A handsome tower sheathed with granite panels from Finland.

E.F. Hutton Building (1973)
ARCHITECTS: Reibsamen, Nickels & Rex
LOCATION: 888 West 6th Street

The handsome E.F. Hutton Building functions as a small office building featuring a curtain-wall skin combined with a sensitive use of other materials combining unique form.

Ennis House (1924)
ARCHITECT: Frank Lloyd Wright
LOCATION: 2607 Glendower Avenue

The Mayan culture is fascinatingly expressed in concrete block designed by America's great modern architect. (Privately owned)

Equitable Building (late 1960s)
ARCHITECT: Welton Becket & Associates
LOCATION: 3435 Wilshire Boulevard

The soaring, 34-story Equitable Building features slender projecting vertical fins of concrete and limestone aggregate.

Federal Aviation Building (1974–75)
ARCHITECTS: Daniel, Mann, Johnson & Mendenhall
LOCATION: Aviation Boulevard at Compton Boulevard

Silver mirror glass wraps the walls and corners of this well planned, six-story complex.

Fritz B. Burns Building, Loyola Law School (1982)
ARCHITECTS: Frank O. Gehry and Associates
LOCATION: Loyola campus, 7101 W. 80th Street

This sculptural building is distinguished by a large hollow central space.

Los Angeles Central Library Building (1925–26)
ARCHITECTS: Bertram Grosvenor Goodhue with C.M. Winslow
LOCATION: 630 W. 5th Street between Flower and Grand

This much photographed building expresses a new direction toward modern architecture with its clean structural surfaces. The staggered forms show the influence of Art Deco design.

Los Angeles County Museum of Art (1964)
ARCHITECT: William Pereira
LOCATION: 5905 Wilshire Boulevard at Genesee in Hancock Park

Three white classic contemporary buildings house an impressive collection of modern art. Open Tuesday through Sunday.

Los Angeles Music Center (1967)
ARCHITECTS: Welton Becket, Edward Durell Stone & others
LOCATION: Broadway, between 1st and Temple

This three-unit complex, which includes the AHMANSON THEATRE, the DOROTHY CHANDLER PAVILION, and the MARK TAPER FORUM are elegantly designed in the classic contemporary approach.

Lovell Health House (1929)
ARCHITECT: Richard Neutra
LOCATION: 4616 Dundee Drive

A revolutionary house employing a steel frame with white concrete walls. The Lovell House is considered one of America's first important dwellings designed in the International Style. (Privately owned)

Office Complex and Plaza (1972)
ARCHITECTS: Edward Durell Stone & Associates
LOCATION: 3731 Wilshire Boulevard

A handsome example of classic contemporary architecture. The twin 11-story buildings are clad with marble and enclose an inviting plaza with fountains and sculpture.

One Park Plaza (1972)
ARCHITECTS: DMJM (Daniel, Mann, Johnson & Mandenhall)
LOCATION: One Park Plaza, on Wilshire Boulevard

A stately steel, concrete, and bronze glass tower.

Tower at 400 South Hope (1970s)
ARCHITECTS: Welton Becket
LOCATION: 400 South Hope

This interestingly angled tower form is clad with Napoleon Red granite from Sweden.

University Research Library (Unit 1, 1964, Unit 2, 1971)

ARCHITECTS: A. Quincy Jones and Frederick E. Emmons
LOCATION: University of California, 405 Hilgard Avenue (near Sunset Boulevard)

This large library facility, surrounded by terraces and gardens, is considered one of Quincy Jones' finest accomplishments. The late architect was known as a "humanist" architect and greatly influenced modern architecture in southern California.

MALIBU

Pepperdine College (1975)
ARCHITECTS: William L. Pereira Associates
LOCATION: Pepperdine College campus

MILL VALLEY

Mill Valley Library (1966)
ARCHITECTS: Wurster, Bernardi & Emmons, Inc.
LOCATION: 375 Throckmorton Avenue

This handsome wood and glass library beautifully fits into its natural setting, an architectural approach this firm is noted for.

MONTEREY

Community Hospital of The Monterey Peninsula (1962)
ARCHITECTS: Edward Durell Stone, Inc.
LOCATION: 23625 W.R. Holman (Highway 68)

This "beautiful" hospital features a large open court and glass dome enclosure designed by Stone, who is known for his classic contemporary architecture.

Monterey Peninsula College (1973)
ARCHITECTS: Edward Larrabee Barnes
LOCATION: Monterey Peninsula College campus

"Our two buildings, the Student Center and Theater, are grouped at the head of a deep ravine that cuts the campus in half. The ravine now becomes an artery instead of a divider and the amphitheater between our buildings is the heart of the campus." (Edward Larrabee Barnes)

NORTHSTAR-AT-TAHOE

(1973)
ARCHITECTS: Eckbo, Dean, Austin & Williams
LOCATION: 6 miles North of Lake Tahoe

A wooded complex designed for snow country and human enjoyment.

OAKLAND

Kaiser Center (1960)
ARCHITECTS: Welton Becket & Associates
LOCATION: 300 Lakeside Drive

This center is dramatized by a sleek, curvilinear, 28-story tower nicely situated on the shores of the lake.

Oakland City Center (The Clorox Tower and Wells Fargo Building) (1973)
ARCHITECTS: Cesar Pelli and Gruen Associates
LOCATION: 1333 Broadway #925

"An economically modest yet quietly brilliant response to the questions of energy, context, and the nature of the wall itself." (*Cesar Pelli,* Watson-Guptill Publications, New York, 1980)

Oakland Temple, Church of Jesus Christ of Latter-Day Saints (1964)
ARCHITECT: Harold W. Burton
LOCATION: 4770 Lincoln Avenue

Nicely landscaped grounds and an information center welcome the visitor. The inspiring religious structure features architectural approaches reminiscent of the Art Deco period. (A panoramic view of the Bay area can be seen from the grounds.)

OJAI

Ojai Valley Inn (Country Club) (1978)
ARCHITECTS: Peter L. Gluck and Associates
LOCATION: Country Club Drive

Terraced down its hillside setting, this inventive and economical complex is constructed of plywood, steel, and concrete. The invitingly designed Inn was planned to withstand occasional earth tremors.

PACIFIC PALISADES

St. Matthew's Parish Church (1983)
ARCHITECTS: Moore Ruble Yudell, Architects & Planners
LOCATION: 1031 Bienveneda Avenue (Just N of Sunset Blvd.)

This unobtrusive religious building was planned to quietly fit into its residential setting. The interior, however, is dramatic, with its strong vertical wood treatment and window placement.

PALO ALTO

All Saints Episcopal Church (Late 1960s)
ARCHITECT: William Guy Garwood
LOCATION: 555 Waverly

The interior of this striking concrete building features a stunning stained glass composition placed at the center of the dome-shaped roof.

Center for Advanced Studies in the Behavioral Sciences (1954)
ARCHITECT: William W. Wurster
LOCATION: Stanford University Campus

A much admired work by one of California's most notable early modern architects.

Medical Center (1959)
ARCHITECT: Edward Durell Stone
LOCATION: Stanford University Campus

A commendable modern building by the late well-known modern architect. Stone also designed the MAIN LIBRARY at Stanford University located at 1213 Newell Road at Parkinson.

Paul Hanna House ("Honeycomb House") (1937)
ARCHITECT: Frank Lloyd Wright
LOCATION: Reservations and maps arranged with Lillian Garner, Educational Services, Stanford Museum of Art, Stanford University

Designed a year after Wright's famous Falling Water, this brick home was donated to Stanford University by Paul and Jean Hanna. The architectural gem is based on a consistent hexagonal form.

The Frederic Emmons Terman Engineering Center (1978)
ARCHITECTS: Harry Weese Associates
LOCATION: Stanford University Campus

PASADENA

Beckman Auditorium (1965)
ARCHITECT: Edward Durell Stone
LOCATION: California Institute of Technology campus

Looking like a "jewel box" or "cupcake," this circular white and gold building is a good example of classic comtemporary architecture.

Plaza Pasadena (1981)
ARCHITECTS: Charles Kober Associates
LOCATION: On Colorado Boulevard

A stunning large brick shopping center that has received national recognition.

Stuart Company (1957–58)
ARCHITECT: Edward Durell Stone
LOCATION: 3300 block, E. Foothill Blvd. at Halstead Street (1 block N of US 66)

Known for his U.S. Embassy in New Delhi, this "pretty" building employs similar properties—including reflecting ponds, grille screens, hanging plants, and fountains.

QUINCY

Feather River College (1973)
ARCHITECTS: Skidmore, Owings & Merrill
LOCATION: c. 100 miles NNE of Sacramento

The redwood-faced buildings of this secluded college in the Sierras is built of 30 foot square prefabricated modules.

RANCHO MIRAGE

Eisenhower Memorial Hospital (1971)
ARCHITECTS: Edward Durell Stone, Inc.
LOCATION: 39000 Bob Hope Drive (Close to Palm Springs)

Built on a desert site donated by Mr. and Mrs.

Bob Hope, this gleaming white four level hospital is centered around a garden courtyard.

REDDING

Convention Center (1969–71)
ARCHITECTS: Van Bourg, Nakamura, Smart & Clabaugh
LOCATION: Auditorium Drive off CA 299

Constructed of concrete forms, this convention center and auditorium accommodates numerous public functions.

REDLANDS

Crafton Hills College (1973)
ARCHITECTS: Williams, Clark & Williams and Jones
LOCATION: Between Redlands and town of Yacaipa in foothills

This stimulating concrete complex of buildings is situated on a challenging steep hillside.

San Bernardino County Museum (1978)
ARCHITECTS: VTN Consolidated, Inc.
LOCATION: 2024 Orange Tree Lane

An interestingly arranged museum facility.

SACRAMENTO

Department of Justice Building (1980s)
ARCHITECTS: Marquis Associates
LOCATION: 4949 Broadway

A stucco, porcelain, and glass structure that houses a training center, crime labs, computer center, and record storage.

Saint Anthony's Church (1970s)
ARCHITECT: Angello-Vitiello
LOCATION: 660 Florin Road

A small, but effectively designed modern religious structure.

State Office Building (Bateson Bldg.) (1981)
ARCHITECTS: Office of the State Architect
LOCATION: 1600 9th Street

A colorful and innovative state office building that departs from traditional modern civic buildings.

SAN BERNADINO

San Bernadino City Hall/Convention Center (1969–73)
ARCHITECTS: Cesar Pelli and Gruen Associates
LOCATION: Civic Plaza, 300 D Street

Raised on bold cylindrical columns, the stunning complex is distinguished by dark glass sheathing. A tiered waterway in the plaza enhances the structure. Gruen Associates also designed the *SECURITY PACIFIC NATIONAL BANK* close by.

SAN DIEGO

First Methodist Church (1964)
ARCHITECTS: Perkins & Will
LOCATION: 2111 Camino Del Rio South

Impressively located on a hillside along the freeway, this gleaming white concrete church features a soaring arched nave pierced with stained glass fenestration.

San Diego Stadium (1966–67)
ARCHITECTS: Frank L. Hope & Associates
LOCATION: Mission Valley, intersection IS 15 with IS 8

Constructed of prestressed and precast concrete, the innovative San Diego Stadium seats over 50,000 spectators and is considered one of the finest structures of its type in the world.

SAN FRANCISCO

Alcoa Building (1965–67)
ARCHITECTS: Skidmore, Owings and Merrill
LOCATION: 1 Maritime Plaza (Washington, Battery, Clay & Sansome)

Similar in design to the dynamic design of SOM's John Hancock tower in Chicago, the unique 24-story Alcoa Building possesses an exo-skeletal system of twelve X-braced supports. The diagonal effect is stunning, especially viewed from the elevated plaza. Note the hemispheric fountain by Robert Woodward of Australia and sculpture by Henry Moore and others in this inviting outdoor space.

American Trust Company, Crown Zellerbach Branch (1960)
ARCHITECTS: Skidmore, Owings & Merrill
LOCATION: 1 Bush Street

This circular bank on a triangular site has been called "a giant sprinkler head." The 20-story tower rises close by.

Bank of America (1968–71)
ARCHITECTS: Wurster, Bernardi and Emmons with Skidmore, Owings & Merrill and Pietro Belluschi
LOCATION: California and Pine Streets between Montgomery & Kearny

Rising fifty-two stories, this handsome tower is distinguished by uniquely angled bays that wrap the entire building, creating a pattern of unity and design focus.

Crocker National Bank (1980s)
ARCHITECTS: Skidmore, Owings & Merrill
LOCATION: Bounded by Post, Sutter, Montgomery and Kearny

The 38-story Crocker National Bank has a regular "graph paper facade" of seemingly square windows. (Actually, they are not) The reddish brown granite sheathing is considered one of the most "elegant skins anywhere." *THE GALLERIA,* with entrances on Post & Sutter, is a delightful pedestrian walkway through what used to be an alley. Two giant arched portals at either end welcome the visitor to a steel and glass, three-story arcade of shops and restaurants. (A great view of the Hallidie Building can be viewed from the Sutter Street entrance).

Four Fifty Sutter Building (1928–29)
ARCHITECTS: Timothy L. Pflueger
LOCATION: 450 Sutter Street

A fine example of the Art Deco period, this twenty-six story building features fenestration recalling the San Francisco bay window. The interior lobby space is particularly striking carrying out the Art Deco theme.

Galaxy Theaters (1983)
ARCHITECTS: Kaplan/McLaughlin/Diaz, Architects
LOCATION: Corner of Van Ness and Sutter

Consisting of four theaters, this glamorous complex principally utilizes a 7 1/2-foot cubical grid. A corner glass tower is the focal point with stepped glass grids descending on either side. The interiors are equally exhilarating.

Golden Gate Bridge (1933–37)
ENGINEERS: Joseph B. Strauss and others
LOCATION: US 101

A graceful red-orange suspension bridge, the Golden Gate has delighted the world. Extending 8,981 feet across the San Francisco Bay, the bridge has two towers soaring 746 feet high and is considered an engineering masterpiece. The trip across the magnificent bridge, whether by foot, bicycle, or vehicle, is a thrilling experience.

Jessica Gunne Sax Headquarters (1938/83)
ARCHITECTS: Hanns Kainz & Associates
LOCATION: 1400 16th

Newly renovated, this 1938 Art Deco building features stunning interiors employing materials, motifs, and lighting remininscent of the 1930s.

Levi's Plaza (1982)
ARCHITECTS: Hellmuth Obata & Kassabaum
LOCATION: Block at E base of Telegraph Hill, NE of downtown

The new corporate low-rise buildings of brick construction for the Levi-Strauss & Co. commendably integrate into the neighborhood setting.

Maritime Museum (1939)
ARCHITECT: William Mooser & Son
LOCATION: Beach Street, just across street W of Ghirardelli Sq.

Inspired by Mendelsohn's famous De la Warr

Pavilion in England, the Maritime Museum is a fine example of the Art Deco period.

Moscone Center (1981)
ARCHITECTS: Jack Young & Associates
LOCATION: 747 Howard Street

Dedicated to the memory of Mayor Moscone, who was killed by an assassin's bullet, this large convention center is constructed of white space frames covering an enclosed area of 650,000 sq. feet.

Neiman-Marcus Store (late 1970s)
ARCHITECTS: Philip Johnson/John Burgee
LOCATION: 150 Stockton

Designed by one of the nation's most illustrious architects, this newly renovated store boasts a striking new exterior and a spacious rotunda topped with a beautiful stained glass composition.

101 California (1980s)
ARCHITECTS: Philip Johnson/John Burgee
LOCATION: 101 California Street

Rising 48 stories, this gleaming circular glass and stone tower is surrounded at its base by an angular concrete plaza that enhances the structure. Built for Gerald Hines Interests, the building is topped with a dazzling sawtooth arrangement. The tower is one of the most spectacular buildings in San Francisco.

Shaklee Terrace (1980s)
ARCHITECTS: Skidmore, Owings & Merrill
LOCATION: 444 Market Street

This handsome tower features an undulating facade of bent glass bands arranged horizontally.

Student Union at San Francisco State University (1974–75)
ARCHITECTS: Paffard Keatinge Clay
LOCATION: Center of campus, W off 19th Ave. via Holloway Avenue

Certainly one of the most provocative buildings of its type in the nation, the sculptural Student Union is distinguished by sharply angled projecting "prows" welcoming the student to unusual interior and exterior spaces.

The Unitarian Center (1970)
ARCHITECTS: Callister, Payne & Rosse
LOCATION: 1187 Franklin

Rough-formed concrete, wood, and glass artfully combine to create a functional complex for worship in an urban setting.

SAN LORENZO

Seabee Chapel (Now The San Lorenzo Community Church) (1946)
ARCHITECT: Bruce Goff
LOCATION: 945 Paseo Grande

This fascinating Navy-SeaBee's quonset hut chapel of 1946, designed by one of the nation's most imaginative architects, now functions as a community church.

SAN LUIS OBISPO

Julian A. McPhee Univerity Union (1973)
ARCHITECTS: Esherick Homsey Dodge & Davis
LOCATION: California Polytechnic State University campus

This lively and inviting structure is student oriented.

SAN MATEO

Bullock's Fashion Island (1981)
ARCHITECTS: L. Gene Zellmer Associates
LOCATION: 2000 West Cape Drive

College of San Mateo (1967–68)
ARCHITECTS: John Carl Warneck & Associates
LOCATION: Off CA 92 (19th Ave) at W Hillside Boulevard

Integrated into a lovely hillside setting overlooking the Bay area, the College of San Mateo features groupings of formal modern buildings around intersecting malls.

Home Office of California-Casualty Insurance Group (1971)
ARCHITECTS: John Carl Warnecke and Associates
LOCATION: 1900 Alameda de las Pulgas

Nicely situated in the suburbs, this ribbed-concrete structure was planned for more flexible office space and a finer new environment for employees. The new building at 2000 Alameda is also noteable.

SAN PEDRO

Cabrillo Marine Museum (1981)
ARCHITECT: Frank Gehry
LOCATION: 3720 Stephen M. White Drive

An innovative "chain link fence" design. The functional chain mesh fence is employed throughout the marine museum.

SANTA CLARA

Administration and Manufacturing Facility for Memorex Corp. (1972)
ARCHITECTS: Leland King & Associates
LOCATION: San Tomas at Central Expressway

A simple, bold, and economical structure in a suburban area, this corporate headquarters with strong horizontal white bands was planned for flexible use of space.

SANTA MONICA

Charles Eames Case Study House (1949)
ARCHITECT: Charles Eames
LOCATION: 203 Chautaugua Boulevard (Pacific Palisades)

A much publicized example of pre-fabricated components used in a residential work. Home of the famous late architect and furniture designer. (Privately owned).

Santa Monica Place (1980)
ARCHITECTS: Frank Gehry
LOCATION: Bounded by Broadway, Second, Colorado Blvd. and Fourth Sts.

Featuring a tall, skylit atrium with a pool and fountain, Santa Monica Place is one of the finest regional shopping centers in southern California.

SANTA ROSA

Bethlehem Lutheran Church (1973)
ARCHITECTS: Duncombe/Roland/Miller
LOCATION: 1300 St. Francis Road

An interesting triangular plan with four banks of pews to provide a sense of "gathering" around the altar.

Santa Rosa Civic Center (1972)
ARCHITECTS: DeBrer/Bell/Heglund & Associates
LOCATION: 100 Santa Rosa Avenue

SANTA TERESA (SAN JOSE)

IBM Santa Teresa Laboratory (1975–77)
ARCHITECTS: MBT Associates (McCue Boone Tomsick)
LOCATION: Bailey Ave. 6 miles S off freeway on US 101, W 1 mile)

Eight four-story office blocks, containing "think tanks," the efficient IBM Lab commendably operates on a low profile basis in the community.

SEA RANCH

The Sea Ranch (1965–)
ARCHITECTS: Moore, Lyndon, Turnbull & Whitaker, Condominiums; Joseph Esherick & Associates; store-restaurant
LOCATION: CA 1, 2.5 miles N of Stewarts Pt., 11 Mi. S of Gaulala (c. 100 mil N of San Francisco)

A thoughtfully planned complex hovering by the sea in an untouched hillside setting, the large cedar wood complex functions primarily as a quiet retreat from busy city life. The ten mile strip of condominiums and private homes is designed to take full advantage of the ocean and sun.

SEASIDE

Seaside City Hall (1966)
ARCHITECT: Edward Durell Stone
LOCATION: 440 Harcourt Avenue

Known for his classic contemporary "pretty" approach to architecture, Stone has created this City Hall in a stately and elegant manner.

SQUAW VALLEY

Cable Car Terminal (1968)
ARCHITECTS: Shepley, Bulfinch, Richardson & Abbott
LOCATION: 2.6 miles W of CA 89, 9 miles S of IS 80

An enlightened building that siezes the opportunity to play up the enormous machinery of the cable car terminal.

STUDIO CITY

St. Michael and All Angels Church (1962)
ARCHITECT: A. Quincy Jones
LOCATION: 3646 Coldwater Canyon Avenue (Los Angeles suburb, NW of Hollywood)

A slender soaring nave opening to skylights distinguishes this church built primarily of wood and glass.

TERRA LINDA

Commerce Clearing House (1970–71)
ARCHITECTS: Marquis & Stoller
LOCATION: W off US 101 via Northgate Drive to Thorndale Drive

Nestled on a hillside just NW of Wright's Marin County Civic Center, this functional facility takes full advantage of its setting to create a beautiful working environment.

THOUSAND OAKS

Thousand Oaks Civic Center (1973)
ARCHITECTS: Robert Mason Houvener
LOCATION: 401 West Hillcrest Drive (N of US 101, between Santa Barbara and Los Angeles)

Looming on a hillside alongside the freeway, this long band of one story structures provides a refreshing departure from civic buildings of the past.

WESTLAKE VILLAGE

Western Home Office, Prudential Insurance Co. of America (1982)
ARCHITECTS: Albert C. Martin and Associates
LOCATION: 111 South Lakeview Canyon Road

This huge granite and glass structure conforms to the slope of its hillside setting and is considered one of the best office buildings of its kind in the state.

YOUNTVILLE

Domaine Chandon Winery (1977)
ARCHITECTS: ROMA Architects
LOCATION: 90 miles NE of San Francisco in Napa Valley

A series of curving roof forms, reminiscent of European traditionalism, is emphasized in this winery. A welcoming Visitor's Center in the rear introduces the winery.

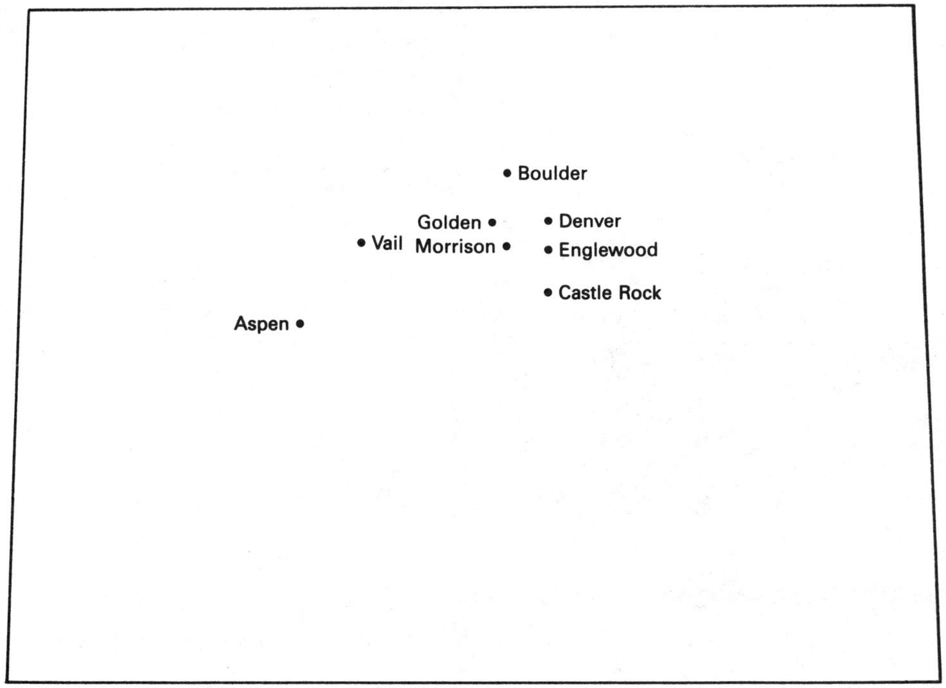

- Boulder

Golden • • Denver
• Vail Morrison • • Englewood
• Castle Rock

Aspen •

Colorado

BOULDER

Engineering Science Center University of Colorado

(1963–66)

ARCHITECTS: W. C. Muchow and
Architectural Associates
LOCATION: Colorado Ave. & Folsom Street
OPEN: During school year

With respect and sensitivity for existing campus buildings and surrounding mountains, Muchow employed local sandstone and red tile roofs to combine with raw concrete surfaces for the design of this admirable Engineering Science Center. The focal point of the complex is the office tower that is flanked by lower lab buildings, a landscaped area of courtyards, benches, and fountains.

BOULDER

National Center for Atmospheric Research

(1965–66)

ARCHITECTS: I.M. Pei and Partners
LOCATION: 2.5 miles SW off Broadway on Table Mesa Road, then NCAR Road
OPEN: Reception area, Mon.–Fri., 8–5

Ten years after Pei designed his highly successful Mile High Center in Denver, he planned this research center complex for five hundred scientists. The complex is nestled on a plateau at the bottom of the rugged Rocky Mountain Range. To capture the spirit and feeling of the surroundings, Pei used unfinished concrete and reddish-brown aggregate that blends with the color of the enveloping mountains.

COLORADO SPRINGS

Air Force Academy (1956–63)

ARCHITECTS: Skidmore, Owings, and Merrill
LOCATION: Off IS 25, 8 miles N of Colorado Springs
OPEN: Daily 7–7, Check in at Visitors Center

A monumental sweeping complex of buildings, the Air Force Academy has been both admired and criticized. The design of the Academy was intended to convey the feeling of "marching in step." The structures have been criticized as endlessly repetitious and lacking human warmth. The geometrically designed chapel, the most popular building on campus, is made up of aluminum clad tetrahedrons suggesting the wings of a plane.

DENVER

Brown Palace Hotel (1889–92)

ARCHITECT: Frank E. Edbrooke
LOCATION: 17th Street at Tremont Place and Broadway
OPEN: Always

A popular landmark in Denver since 1892, this luxury hotel is one of the first architectural expressions in cast iron construction in America. A large, exquisite stained-glass skylight tops a spacious atrium that rises nine stories high. Ornamental bronze panels embellish each balcony in continuous strip panels, and polished onyx lines the first floors. The total design concept was a forerunner for Frank Lloyd Wright's famous Guggenheim Museum in New York City.

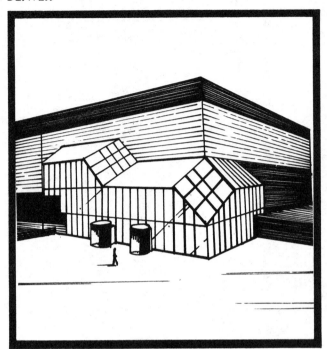

Boettcher Concert Hall

(1976–78)

Helen Bonfils Theater (1980)
ARCHITECTS: Hardy Holzman Pfeiffer,
Boettcher Concert Hall; Roche/Dinkeloo,
Bonfils Theater
LOCATION: 14th Street at Curtis
OPEN: For events and performances

A remarkable four-block super development,
the complex includes the 1907 Auditorium
Theater, a sports arena, an eight-level parking
garage, and the new Helen Bonfils theater.
Boettcher Hall, with its striking exterior glass
facade, is the home of the Denver Symphony
Orchestra. The design of the impressive 730-
seat Bonfils Theater has a curving concrete
wall with window banks of mirror glass that
provides a dramatic entrance.

DENVER

Currigan Exhibition Hall

(1968–69)

ARCHITECTS: Muchow, Ream and Larson
LOCATION: 14th Street between Champa
and Stout
OPEN: During exhibitions and conventions

Mathematically precise, this large steel-pan-
eled structure with 24,000 sections makes an
overwhelming impression. The interior, constructed of a series of space frames, is ideal
for enclosing this vast space. Colorfully
painted light fixtures placed within the
exposed steel framework create an interesting
accent. The Currigan Exhibition Hall combines the finest building materials with the
latest technical advances to create a pleasant
and functional facility.

DENVER

Denver Art Museum (1968–71)

ARCHITECTS: Gio Ponti with James Sudler Associates
LOCATION: 100 West 14th Avenue Parkway
OPEN: Tues.–Sat., 9–5, Sun., 1–5, Wed., also 5–9

Ponti, the great modern architect from Italy, was nearly eighty years old when he designed this six-story museum. Enclosing eleven galleries and a large exhibition hall, twenty-eight sides of the structure are punctuated with a random pattern of windows. The thin walls of the exterior are faced with about one million 2' by 6' pyramidal sections of gray glass tile. Ponti said, "I asked the sun and the light and the sky to help me." An impressive collection of many mediums of art is housed inside.

DENVER

Johns-Manville World Headquarters (1977)

ARCHITECTS: The Architects' Collaborative
LOCATION: Deer Creek Canyon Rd., 23 miles SW of Denver via West Colfax Avenue
OPEN: By appointment. Telephone: (303) 979-1000

The bold 1,100-foot streak of gleaming aluminum used in the construction of this headquarters creates a magnificent contrast against the rugged Rocky Mountain landscape. The complex is located by a ridge of rocks called "the hogbacks." TAC did not want to blend, but rather identify the project as "made by man." Those in praise of the work report that photographs do not give adequate justice to the spectacular design.

DENVER

Mile High Center (1956)

ARCHITECTS: I.M. Pei & Associates
LOCATION: 17th Street & Lincoln
OPEN: During business hours

Pei, the world famous Chinese-born American architect, opened his own firm in Boston in 1955. The twenty-three story Mile High Center was his first important commission, winning the architect national praise. A few years later the May-D & F Department Store was added. The main entry of this complex features a stunning hyperbolic paraboloid shell with large triangular glass walls. A sunken skating rink is surrounded by a landscaped plaza—a popular meeting place and landmark in Denver.

DENVER

Park Central (1973–74)

ARCHITECTS: Muchow Associates
LOCATION: Arapahoe between 15th and 16th Streets
OPEN: During business hours

Park Central is part of a twenty-seven block urban renewal effort that comprises 600,000 square feet of banking, shopping, parking, and office facilities. Park Central, with three towers of varying heights, controlled by city regulations, has a series of modules sheathed with anodized aluminum. The geometric quality of the complex has been admired nationwide.

DENVER

The United Bank Center (1984)

ARCHITECTS: Johnson/Burgee with Morris
Aubry
LOCATION: 1700 Lincoln (across the street
from Mile High Ctr.)
OPEN: During banking hours

Johnson is one of the world's most important
living modern architects. He gained fame with
his much publicized glass house in New
Canaan, Connecticut in 1949. With Burgee, his
partner of fifteen years, Johnson has designed
some of the nation's most spectacular modern
structures.. The new United Bank Center rises
52 stories and features brilliant billowing half-
vault roofs.

MORRISON

Red Rocks Amphitheater

(1941)

ARCHITECT: Burnham Hoyt
LOCATION: 16 miles SW of Denver via US
6, then S on IS 70, S on COL. 26. (Follow
signs)
OPEN: Daily. Summer concerts presented
in evenings

The grandeur of the natural setting of bold
sandstone red rocks for this amphitheater is
awesome and a marvelous acoustical background for the theater. Part of a 13,500 acre
park system the Red Rocks Amphitheater was
created out of a natural cradle providing
around 9,000 seats, a double-decked stage,
and other services.

ADDITIONAL MODERN STRUCTURES OF INTEREST

ASPEN

Main Post Office (1981)
ARCHITECTS: Copland, Hagman, Yaw, Ltd.
LOCATION: Downtown Aspen, 235 Puppy Smith Road

Ribbed-concrete block and aluminum are effectively arranged for the construction of this structure.

Mill Street Plaza (1983)
ARCHITECTS: Hagman Yaw Architects, Ltd.
LOCATION: 434 East Cooper Avenue

"Finger malls" center around a bi-level courtyard featuring an interesting renovation of shops, theaters, and other public facilities.

Pitkin County Airport Terminal (1970s)
ARCHITECTS: Copland Fenholm Hagman Yaw Ltd.
LOCATION: 20292 State Hwy. 82—Sardy Field

The complex design features an efficient post and beam composition of wood and concrete.

BEAVER CREEK

Spruce Saddle Restaurant (1982)
ARCHITECTS: Bull Field Volkmann Stockwell
LOCATION: 10 miles West of Vail

A fascinating structure of wood and glass affording a panoramic view of Gore Range and Vail Mountain.

BOULDER

Boulder Recreation Center (1973)
ARCHITECTS: Nixon-Brown-Brokaw-Bowen
LOCATION: 1360 Gillaspie

Dynamic forms of the Center's roof capture a spirit of the natural surrounding terrain.

First Presbyterian Church (1974)
ARCHITECTS: W.C. Muchow Associates
LOCATION: 1820 15th Street

A strong network of rugged trusses are emphasized in the construction of this dynamic religous structure.

Syntex Chemicals (formerly Arapahoe Chemicals, Inc) (1976)
ARCHITECTS: A. M. Kinney, Inc.
LOCATION: 2075 Arapahoe

This commendable structure won an architectural award for excellence in concrete design.

CASTLE ROCK

Douglas County Administration Building (1983)
ARCHITECTS: Hoover Berg Desmond
LOCATION: Facing downtown Main Street

An austere but stylish building constructed of rugged stone.

COLORADO SPRINGS

Nazarene Bible College (1968/73/77)
ARCHITECTS: Keyes and Holstrup with John Ten Eyck
LOCATION: 1111 Chapman Drive (NE of Academy & Fountain Blvds.)

This stone and red cedar complex captures the spirit of its function and the surrounding Rocky Mountains.

DENVER

Anaconda Tower (1978)
ARCHITECTS: Skidmore, Owings & Merrill
LOCATION: 555 17th Street

A forty-story building with gleaming reflective walls.

Arco Tower (1982) (Marriott Building)
ARCHITECT: Hellmuth, Obata & Kassabaum
LOCATION: 1701 California

This large office-hotel tower of bronze glass is Denver's tallest building, and to date, the most costly.

Auraria Learning Resources Center
(1978)
ARCHITECTS: C.F. Murphy Associates
LOCATION: 1027 9th Street

Simplicity and clarity are demonstrated in this white painted aluminum and glass structure.

Bureau of Reclamation Engineering & Research Center (1967)
ARCHITECTS: Hellmuth, Obata and Kassabaum, Inc.
LOCATION: Federal Center, Building 67

With windows recessed three feet to accommodate Denver's sun glare, this 14-story complex admirably expresses its function.

Cherry Creek Marina, Picnic Shelters, & Beach Facilities (1974)
ARCHITECTS: Cabell Childress and Martha Russell
LOCATION: Cherry Creek Reservoir, near Denver

Bold forms of concrete, providing a sculptural image, were employed for this powerful complex of facilities.

Christian Reformed Church (1976)
ARCHITECT: Jeffrey K. Abrams
LOCATION: 4585 South Chamber Road

The roof of the church and community center features copper solar panels in a steep, sloping arrangement.

Church of The Risen Christ (1970)
ARCHITECT: James A Sudler
LOCATION: 3060 South Monaco Parkway

The soaring main window of this unique religious structure rises 76 feet. The white complex has a cylindrical baptistry connected by an arch.

Colorado National Bank Building (1975)
ARCHITECT: Minoru Yamasaki
LOCATION: 950 17th Street

A stunning white marble and glass building by the architect of the World Trade Center in New York City.

Community College of Denver-North Campus (1977–)
ARCHITECTS: John D. Anderson and Associates
LOCATION: Community College of Denver—North campus

With solar panels slanted and oriented to the sun, the mini-megastructure creates a stunning impression.

City Center IV (1983)
ARCHITECTS: MTY
LOCATION: 1801 California

Staggered forms at varying levels distinguish this soaring tower complex.

Denver-Hilton Hotel (late 1961)
ARCHITECT: I.M. Pei
LOCATION: 1550 Court Place

Denver National Bank Plaza (1980)
ARCHITECTS: Skidmore, Owings and Merrill
LOCATION: 1125 17th Street

A stunning building constructed of aluminum and glass arranged in horizontal bands.

Denver Tech. Center (1980s)
ARCHITECTS: Various architects
LOCATION: South I-25 and Inverness Drive East

A large center made up of many buildings beautifully designed for function and aesthetic appeal.

Energy Center (1981)
ARCHITECTS: Hellmuth, Obata, Kassabum
LOCATION: Downtown Denver on 17th Street

An award-winning design of precast/prestressed concrete by this well-known St. Louis based architectural firm.

The Hotsy Corporation (1981)
ARCHITECT: Richard Crowther
LOCATION: 21 Inverness Way, East, South Denver

A building with special regard for human health and well-being.

Hudson's Bay Centre (1980s)
ARCHITECTS: Skidmore, Owings & Merrill
LOCATION: 1600 Stout

Faced with Pearl Anglais granite from Sweden, this tower has a cut-away design on the corner.

Key Savings & Loan Association (1965)
ARCHITECT: Charles Deaton
LOCATION: 3501 So. Broadway

This fascinating concrete shell is punctuated with unusual window arrangements.

Park Place (1981)
ARCHITECTS: Johnson Hopson & Partners
LOCATION: 3100 Arapahoe

A handsome conversion of a 1953 parking garage into a spacious office complex. A new image is projected through the use of materials and finish.

Amoco Building (1980)
ARCHITECTS: A. Eugene Kohn of Kohn Pedersen Fox
LOCATION: Columbia Plaza

A striking 36-story office complex sheathed with aluminum and reflective glass.

ENGLEWOOD

Harlequin Plaza (1982)
ARCHITECTS: Gensler and Associates
LOCATION: Harlequin Plaza

This dramatic office park is centered around a black and white checkered plaza—giving the Plaza its name. The buildings of reflective glass rest on plinths of maroon quarry tile.

Visitor Center and Park Headqaurters (1965–66)
ARCHITECTS: Taliesin Associates
LOCATION: Rocky Mountain National Park (2.5 miles West of Estes Park on Col. 66) Estes Park, Colorado

GOLDEN

Colorado School of Mines Student Dormitory (1980)
ARCHITECT: John D. Anderson Associates
LOCATION: 18th and Elm Streets

A commendable building. Winner of an A.I.A. Award.

WINTER PARK

West Portal Station (1982)
ARCHITECTS: Muchow, Haller & Larson
LOCATION: Just off Highway 40 at Winter Park Ski Area (c. 60 miles WNW of Denver)

This large, award winning ski facility projects an image of the old historic mine shafts in the area. The building is constructed of black metal siding with an exposed braced wall system.

- Suffield
- Bloomfield
- Torrington
- Avon
- Hartford
- Glastonbury
- Farmington
- Waterbury
- Middletown
- Norwich
- Southbury
- Wallingford
- Danbury
- New London
- Ansonia
- New Haven
- Orange
- Wilton
- Milford
- New Canaan
- Rowayton
- Stamford
- Greenwich

Connecticut

HARTFORD

The Hartford Seminary (1981)

ARCHITECTS: Richard Meier and Partners
LOCATION: 77 Sherman Street
OPEN: 8:30–4:30 Mon.–Fri. (for information call (203) 232-4451)

A building of porcelain clad steel, the dazzling Hartford Seminary is enhanced by the element of light. Purity of expression was the architect's goal achieved through the use of simple geometry combined with functional space planning. The design image projects a new progressive attitude facilitating an inter-denominational theological center—an institute dedicated to furthering religious understanding. The admirable design concept supports this philosophy.

HARTFORD

Unitarian Meeting House

(1963–64)

ARCHITECT: Victor A. Lundy
LOCATION: 50 Bloomfield Ave., off US 44 at CT 189
OPEN: Most weekdays

Beautifully located on several acres of a gently hollow grassy expanse, this dramatic church gives the appearance of an open conduit reaching skyward. Twelve reinforced concrete external support beams come together to form a central circular opening over the sanctuary. The interior is a breathtaking arrangement of supportive steel cables swept upward in tent-like fashion.

MIDDLETOWN

Center for The Arts at Wesleyan University (1972–73)

ARCHITECTS: Kevin Roche/John Dinkeloo & Associates
LOCATION: Wyllys Avenue
OPEN: Gallery open daily from 12–4 and special events

Wesleyan is a neat and inviting campus of about 2,500 students. On the perimeter of the campus is an orderly arrangement of eleven small white limestone clad buildings that are gracefully stepped down the landscape's terrain. The finest facilities for the arts are housed within—including drama, cinema, music, and art units. The cubic structures are all self-contained with repeating connecting walls and entries to break up the blocks.

NEW HAVEN

Art and Architecture Building at Yale University (1961–63)

ARCHITECT: Paul Rudolph
LOCATION: 180 York Street at Chapel
OPEN: During the school year

A highly controversial structure, the Art and Architecture building was designed while Rudolph was the Chairman of the Architecture Department at Yale. The architect tried to meet the challenge of relating the new building to the corner site and to the existing buildings on campus. With a series of bold vertical towers, the textural surfaces, both inside and out, are treated with rough striated concrete—a Rudolph trademark.

NEW HAVEN

Beinecke Rare Book and Manuscript Library at Yale
(1961–63)

ARCHITECTS: Skidmore, Owings and Merrill
LOCATION: High Street and Wall
OPEN: Mon.–Fri. 8:30–4:45, Sat. 8:30–12:15
and 1:30–4:45, Sun. 2–4:45, except
weekends in August

Housing Yale's collection of precious books
and manuscripts, the Beinecke Library is
surrounded by traditional buildings, gaining
prominence with a surrounding dropped
plaza. The exterior grid facade encloses
hundreds of sheer marble panels giving the
structure a uniform and striking appearance.
Many considerations for preserving and maintaining the collections were planned into the
design of the building.

NEW HAVEN

D.S. Ingalls Hockey Rink at Yale University (1956–68)

ARCHITECTS: Eero Saarinen & Associates
LOCATION: 73 Sachem Street at Prospect
OPEN: For hockey games

A delightful mammoth reinforced concrete
parabolic arch with a roof supported on
cables are uniquely incorporated into the
design of this hockey rink. The unusual shape
has been compared by students to an
"inverted boat" and a "giant whale." Close by,
at the North end of Hillhouse Avenue, is
Philip Johnson's commanding *KLINE BIOLOGY
TOWER* (1964–66). This building features a
striking vertical emphasis. Students often refer
to this structure as "the Tootsie Roll."

NEW HAVEN

Ezra Stiles and Morse Colleges at Yale University

(1960–62)

ARCHITECTS: Eero Saarinen & Associates
LOCATION: Broadway at Tower Parkway
OPEN: During school year

Saarinen's challenge was to design these two colleges between two historical buildings on campus. Wanting the structures to have personality and individuality, the concrete buildings were faced with rough masonry. The high level windows and screened slits provide lighting, giving a castle-like quality to the buildings. The half-circular block contains study bedrooms and the central building contains the dining and community facilities.

NEW HAVEN

Knights of Columbus Headquarters (1968–70)

ARCHITECTS: Kevin Roche/John Dinkeloo & Associates
LOCATION: 1 Columbus Plaza (Church Street between George and North Frontage Road)
OPEN: With appointment only

An inventive twenty-six story building, the Knights of Columbus Headquarters is wholly supported by four huge and dominating cylindrical towers—the first building of its type. The towers are sheathed with tile and contain the stairs, restrooms and other service facilities. Window bands are set back five feet for sun protection. The structure has been both praised and criticized.

NEW HAVEN

Veterans Memorial Coliseum

(1970–72)

ARCHITECTS: Kevin Roche/John Dinkeloo & Associates
LOCATION: Between N. Frontage Rd. and George St.
OPEN: During performances and events

Located in the busy downtown area of New Haven, this Coliseum is a surprising solution to providing a large space for entertainment—including an ice rink and parking. Like the Knights of Columbus Building close by, the design concept is unique and efficient. A four-level parking area above the Coliseum has convenient entries and walkways that channel foot traffic to nearby shops, a hotel, and other public facilities.

NEW HAVEN

Yale Art Gallery (1951–53)

ARCHITECTS: Louis I. Kahn with Douglas Orr
LOCATION: Chapel Street at York
OPEN: Tues.–Sat. 10–5, Sun. 2–5

The Yale Art Gallery has the distinction of being the first modern building at Yale University—starting a new building tradition on that campus that now boasts around two dozen structures by some of America's most prominent architects. This four-story structure has invitingly spacious gallery areas with marvelous black-painted tetrahedral ceilings. Twenty years later Kahn designed *THE YALE CENTER FOR BRITISH ART,* a museum, study center, and gallery located across the street. An exterior of pewter-finished stainless steel panels and glass walls are complemented inside with the use of contrasting natural materials. The two museums are well worth a visit.

STAMFORD

First Presbyterian Church

(1956–58)

ARCHITECT: Wallace K. Harrison
LOCATION: 1101 Bedford Street off Hoyt Street
OPEN: Daily, 9–5

A magnificent building, the First Presbyterian Church has a floor plan and elevations in the shape of a fish—an Early Christian symbol. Employing large reinforced concrete panels that function as supports for 22,000 pieces of colored glass, the walls dramatically extend to the roof that in turn slants at ten various angles. The stained glass is arranged in abstract religious motifs, filling the sanctuary with streams of colored light.

WALLINGFORD

Paul Mellon Arts Center

(1970–71)

ARCHITECTS: I. M. Pei & Partners
LOCATION: Christian Street
OPEN: Gallery open Tues.–Sat. 10–5, Sun. 2–5, theater during performances

Serving as a multi-purpose center for the visual and performing arts, this admirable structure consists of two sections housing facilities for a theater, gallery, and teaching units. The curving form of the seat arrangement is repeated in the exterior forms of the enclosing walls. The glass art gallery adjoining is an inviting spacious area for exhibitions.

ADDITIONAL MODERN STRUCTURES OF INTEREST

ANSONIA

Holy Rosary Church (1967)
ARCHITECT: Daniel P. Antinozzi Asociates
LOCATION: Father Salemi Drive

An exposed white quartz surface creates an effective support background for 25-foot-high stained glass windows.

AVON

Memorial United Methodist Church (1971)
ARCHITECTS: Philip Ives & Associates
LOCATION: 867 West Avon Road

Nicely sited on four acres of pasture and surrounded by wooded areas, this conservative, yet interestingly designed church complements its surroundings.

BLOOMFIELD

Cigna Office Building (1984)
ARCHITECTS: TAC (The Architects Collaborative)
LOCATION: 900 Cottage Grove Road

Standards of excellence are carried throughout with emphasis on design from inside to outside to take advantage of lighting.

Connecticut General Life Insurance Co., South Building (1962)
ARCHITECTS: Skidmore, Owings and Merrill
LOCATION: 900–950 Cottage Grove Road

DANBURY

Union Carbide Corporation (1983)
ARCHITECTS: Kevin Roche/John Dinkeloo Associates
LOCATION: Old Ridgebury Road

A wooded setting, an elevated plan, nature walks, and numerous other enjoyable features distinguish this handsome working environment.

GLASTONBURY

Glen Lochen—The Market Place (1975)
ARCHITECTS: Callister-Payne & Bischoff with others
LOCATION: 39 New London Turnpike

A modern shopping facility constructed of wood and arranged in the shape of a boomerang.

EAST HARTFORD

Church of The Blessed Sacrament (1972)
ARCHITECTS: Russell Gibson von Dohlen Inc.
LOCATION: 15 Milbrook Drive

This simple cube constructed of painted white vertical cedar boards is planned for function and highlighted by colorful art.

FARMINGTON

Heublein Corporate Headquarters (1973)
ARCHITECTS: Russell Gibson von Dohlen Inc.
LOCATION: 16 Munson Road (Take Exit 38 or 39 off I84)

Bold projecting forms conform to the hillside through a series of tiered levels for this uniquely designed suburban office building for an international food and beverage marketing corporation.

GREENWICH

American Can Company (1973)
ARCHITECTS: Skidmore, Owings & Merrill
LOCATION: American Lane

This handsome corporate headquarters is situated in a heavily wooded area and was designed as a functional and pleasant environment for over 2,000 employees.

Riviere Du Loup Building (1978)
ARCHITECTS: Johnson/Burgee
LOCATION: 80 Field Point Road (suburb outside Greenwich)

A forceful break with the limitation of the box structure, the Riviere du Loup Building's plan features a unique design that incorporates natural lighting through gabled skylight thoroughfares.

HARTFORD

Civic Center (1975)
ARCHITECT: Vincent Kling
LOCATION: Civic Center Plaza, access from Asylum, Trumbull, & Church St.

A popular and well-planned complex of covered malls, shops, a cafeteria, and lounges, with convention and sports facilities.

Constitution Plaza (1960)
ARCHITECT: Charles Dubose
LOCATION: Market Street

An excellent early example of downtown urban renewal.

Hartford State Company (1978)
ARCHITECT: Robert Venturi
LOCATION: 50 Church Street

An innovative brick exterior treatment.

Phoenix Building (1962–63)
ARCHITECTS: Harrison & Abramovitz
LOCATION: 1 American Row, corner of State & Prospect Sts.

An extraordinary "ship's shape" building of reflective glass.

The Richardson, Renovation
(1875–76/1980)
ORIGINAL ARCHITECT: Henry Hobson Richardson
RENOVATION ARCHITECTS: Stecker/LaBau Architects, Inc.
LOCATION: Cheney Block

The exterior of the Richardson, designed by America's great Romanesque Revivalist and early modern architect, is beautifully preserved. The interior renovation is an entirely different interpretation, planned for office and commercial use in contemporary times.

MILFORD

Milford Jai Alai (Merry Festival) (1977)
ARCHITECT: Herbert S. Newman Associates
LOCATION: 311 Old Gate Lane (Exit #40 I-95)

Created to house facilities for one of the oldest ball games, Jai Alai, of Spanish origin, this bold structure "was designed to create an urbane, festive environment that is colorful and fun." (Herbert Newman, *Arch. Rec.,* April 1978.)

NEW CANAAN

First Presbyterian Church (1970)
ARCHITECT: Philip Ives
LOCATION: 178 Oenoke Ridge Road (W on Main Street)

A dynamic brick and wood church in a lovely setting.

NEW HAVEN

Armstrong Rubber Company, Corporate Hdqts/Research Dev. (1970)
ARCHITECTS: Marcel Breuer and Robert F. Gatje
LOCATION: 500 Sargent Drive

Precast, prestressed concrete with exposed aggregate are the principle building components employed by Breuer for this commanding building.

Center for American Arts (1978)
ARCHITECTS: Herbert S. Newman Associates
LOCATION: Yale University, under Weir Court

This design of clarity and simplicity functions as a new auditorium and exhibition for Yale's Art Gallery.

Dixwell Fire Station (1975)
ARCHITECTS: Venturi & Rauch
LOCATION: Goffe Street at Webster

A highly praised, well-designed structure of red brick.

Engineering/Applied Science Building
(1970)
ARCHITECTS: Marcel Breuer and Hamilton P. Smith
LOCATION: Yale University Campus

This elevated structure boldly dominates its site. An abstract design of precast concrete is featured on the building's facade.

Greeley Memorial Laboratory, Forestry Institute (1957)
ARCHITECT: Paul Rudolph
LOCATION: Yale University Campus

Rudolph's first building at Yale. Other works include a *PARKING GARAGE* of rough-cast concrete (1959) and *MARRIED STUDENT'S HOUSING* (1960).

Jackie Robinson School (1974)
ARCHITECTS: Stull Associates of Boston
LOCATION: 150 Fournier Street

A constroversial building with a high-tech image. Teachers say "You either love it or hate it."

Seeley G. Mudd Library at Yale University (1982)
ARCHITECTS: Roth & Moore
LOCATION: Yale University Campus

A finely detailed structure of masonry with a dintinctive limestone stringcourse treatment.

Teletrack (1981)
ARCHITECT: Herbert S. Newman
LOCATION: 600 Long Wharf Drive

An $8 million structure for video simulcast of thoroughbred racing beamed in from New York State.

Yale School of Organization and Management (1979)
ARCHITECTS: Edward Larrabee Barnes with others
LOCATION: Behind the Hillhouse Avenue villas

An attractive and complementary structure in a unique setting. A building by Skidmore, Owings and Merrill is close by.

NEW LONDON

Congregation Beth El (1973)
ARCHITECT: Paul Rudolph
LOCATION: 660 Ocean Avenue

An imaginative facility featuring strong, bold forms with a roof clad with metal in vertical arrangement.

U.S. Coast Guard Academy Visitor's Information Pavilion
ARCHITECTS: Sturges Daughn Salisbury Inc., of Providence
LOCATION: On Highway I-95, exit 33 on Rt. 32, enter on Tampa St.

An award-winning structure set on a natural plateau of rock. A space frame-covered deck and an enclosed area called "the hull" are featured. Open daily 10–5.

NORWICH

St. Marks Evangelical Lutheran Church (1960)
ARCHITECT: John M. Johansen
LOCATION: 248 Broadway

Eight precast shells enclose the nave and altar of this boldly formed religious structure.

ORANGE

Harvey Hubbell Corporate Headquarters (1966/1972)
ARCHITECTS: Orr-deCossy-Winder Associates with Bruce Campbell Graham
LOCATION: Exit 56 S bound on Wilbur Cross Pkwy. onto Grassy Hill Rd., Turkey Hill Rd., left on Derby-Milford Rd.

A well-planned working space nestled in the woods close to a man-made pond.

ROWAYTON

United Church of Rowayton (1963)
ARCHITECT: Joseph Salerno
LOCATION: 210 Rowayton Avenue

This award-winning religious structure is an extraordinary composition of dynamic swirling forms.

SOUTHBURY

The Bazaar at the Village Green (1970)
ARCHITECTS: Callister and Payne with others
LOCATION: Village Green Shopping Center

Colorful detailing in blue, red, yellow, and green, highlight a background of wood components in the construction of this delightful shopping area.

STAMFORD

Agudath Sholom Synagogue (1965)
ARCHITECTS: Davis, Brody & Associates
LOCATION: 301 Strawberry Hill Avenue

The discovery that this building is a synagogue becomes apparent when coming upon the ark wall and seven gas lamps set in the wall of stained glass.

Harbor Place (1983)
ARCHITECTS: Yankee Planning/Do H. Chung
LOCATION: Off Long Island Sound

This rambling low-rise brick complex was designed to enhance its waterfront setting.

One Champion Plaza (1982)
ARCHITECTS: Ulrich Franzen & Associates
LOCATION: One Champion Plaza

Structures by a number of important modern architects surround the plaza.

Kent Memorial Library (1972)
ARCHITECTS: Warren Platner Associates
LOCATION: 50 North Main Street

This is Platner's first completed work after opening his own office. It is designed for the way "people like to use libraries."

TORRINGTON

Traffic Service Position Systems Building (1974)
ARCHITECTS: Marcel Breuer and Hamilton Smith
LOCATION: Alvord Park Rd., first building on right into the park

This understated and little known work of the famous late architect functions as a facility for the Southern New England Telephone Company.

WALLINGFORD

The Church of the Resurrection (1969)
ARCHITECTS: Russell-Gibson-vonDahlen
LOCATION: 115 Pond Hill Rd. (Rectory: 138 Long Hill Road, close by)

This award-winning religious structure is based on a diagonal emphasis countered by a freestanding bell tower.

WATERBURY

Our Lady of Fatima Catholic Church
ARCHITECT: Alfonso Alvarez
LOCATION: 2071 Baldwin Street

A church that combines the beauty and warmth of wood with the strength of high-pressure lamination.

WEST HARTFORD

St. Peter Claver (1974)
ARCHITECTS: Russell Gibson Von Dohlen
LOCATION: 47 Pleasant

This powerful and yet simply constructed church features seating that fans outward and strong beamed ceiling design.

WILTON

Nabisco Brands Research Center (1979)
ARCHITECTS: Warren Platner Associates
LOCATION: 15 River Road

One of the most elegant and unusual research centers in the nation, this complex features a facade of "silo-like" brick forms.

Richardson–Vicks Corporate Headquarters (1974)
ARCHITECTS: Roche/Dinkeloo and Associates
LOCATION: Ten Westport Road

Constructed of weathering steel, exposed beams, and glass, this impressive ground-hugging structure is beautifully nestled in its wooded site.

St. Matthew's Episcopal/Wilton Presbyterian Church (1971)
ARCHITECTS: SMS Architects
LOCATION: 36 New Canaan Road

This two-sanctuary complex of white-painted brick is nicely located in a wooded area and provides facilities for a school, social activities, and administration space.

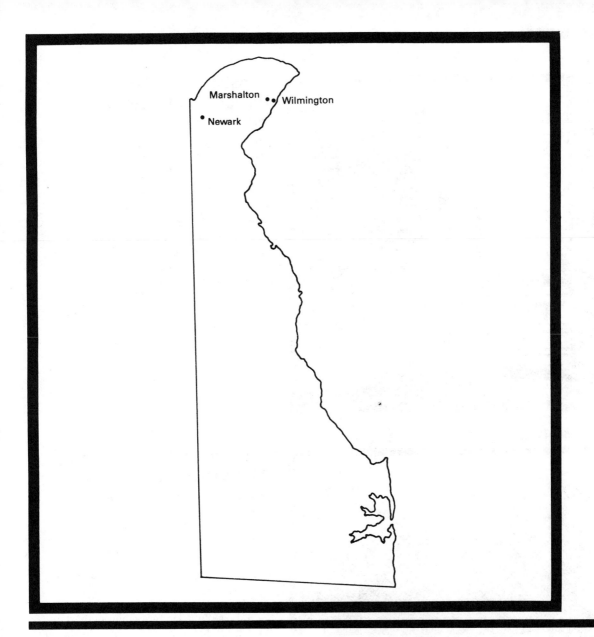

Marshalton

Wilmington

Newark

Delaware

NEWARK

Christiana Towers at the University of Delaware

(1971–72)

ARCHITECTS: The Luckman Partnership
LOCATION: Off DEL 896, .5 miles N of Main Street, enter on Pencader Drive
OPEN: Grounds open daily

Utilizing all the latest technical advantages, the Christiana dormatories and commons are neatly positioned on campus. Aesthetically attractive, the complex admirably functions for the task. Due to economical efficiencies, prefabricated modular units were employed for construction, providing a unified effect. Well equipped and liveable quarters are planned for each student dwelling space.

WILMINGTON

Garden Pavilion at Du Pont Winterthur Museum (1961–66)

ARCHITECTS: Victorine and Samuel Homsey
LOCATION: E off DEL 52, 6 miles NW of Wilmington
OPEN: Mon., 8–2, Tues.–Sat., 8–4, Sun. 11–4

Visitors from all over the United States flock to the Winterthur Museum to see the finest collection of historical rooms in the nation. Set in beautifully landscaped grounds, the Garden Pavilion serves as an introduction and visitor's center to the great estate owned by the Du Pont family. The inviting modern building includes a cafeteria, with lecture and orientation rooms adjoining. Natural building materials combined with large areas of glass windows provide effective lighting and an airy atmosphere.

WILMINGTON

Hercules Incorporated (1983)

ARCHITECTS: Kohn Pedersen Fox Associates
LOCATION: North edge of town bordering riverfront park
OPEN: During business and shopping hours

This fascinating $88 million complex is situated at the north edge of downtown Wilmington bordering the lovely new riverfront park. Smooth granite is employed for the lower levels of the Hercules building, topped in the center with a huge round clock. A gleaming, well articulated arrangement of tinted-glass curtain walls emerge from the lower stone levels creating a surprising impact. The effect is intriguing. The juxtaposition of materials, color, texture, and form are employed to create a unique image. The architects consciously sought to break the confines of the typical corporate tower. Interior features include a shop-lined passageway through the complex connecting the park with downtown Wilmington.

WILMINGTON

The American Life Insurance Building (1971)

ARCHITECTS: I.M. Pei & Partners
LOCATION: Corner of North Market and W. 12th Streets
OPEN: During business hours

This stately 22-story office tower makes a vivid contrast with its surrounding neighbors, especially with the traditional church next door. The concrete structure contains vertical air-distribution shafts that add to the aesthetic effect of the building. An interior 73-foot clear-span floor system is unique, supported by exterior concrete walls. The deep horizontal window voids provide dark shadows that contrast with the vertical shafts contributing to the unity and interest of the building.

ADDITIONAL MODERN STRUCTURES OF INTEREST

MARSHALTON

St. Barnabas Episcopal Church (1963)
ARCHITECTS: Victorine and Samuel
Homsey
LOCATION: 2800 Duncan Road

Nicely sited on a gently rolling surburban
area, this simple and understated church
reflects the spirit of the area.

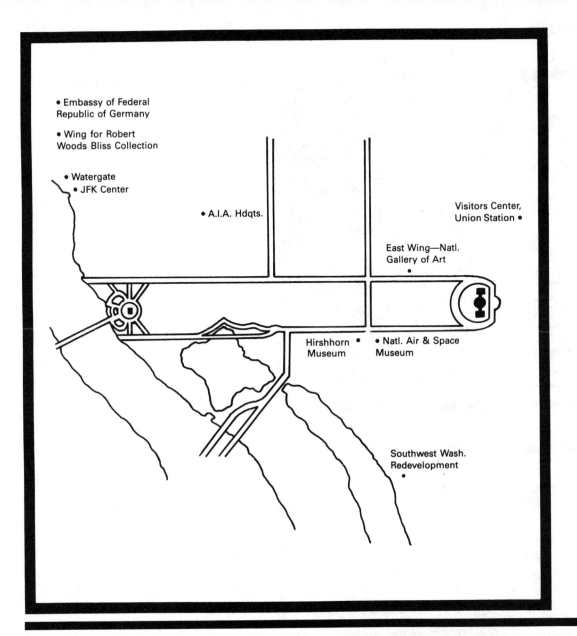

- Embassy of Federal Republic of Germany

- Wing for Robert Woods Bliss Collection

- Watergate
- JFK Center

- A.I.A. Hdqts.

Visitors Center, Union Station •

East Wing—Natl. Gallery of Art

Hirshhorn Museum

- Natl. Air & Space Museum

Southwest Wash. Redevelopment

District of Columbia

East Building—National Gallery of Art (1971–78)

ARCHITECTS: I.M. Pei & Partners
LOCATION: Constitution Avenue at 4th Street
OPEN: Winter, Mon.–Sat., 10–5, Summer, Mon.–Sat., 10–9, Sun., noon–9

This spectacular gallery is composed of a series of unique triangular forms. Connected to the older West Building by means of an underground tunnel, the New Wing features a magnificent arrangement of gallery spaces— some feel the architecture eclipses the exhibitions. Glorious skylights cast streams of light on the various exhibits and surfaces. A huge magnificent Alexander Calder mobile looms over the vast central lobby, setting the tone for the modern art collection.

Embassy of the Federal Republic of Germany (1962–64)

ARCHITECT: Egon Eiermann
LOCATION: 4645 Reservoir Road NW
OPEN: By appointment only

The late Professor Eiermann was one of Germany's foremost post-war modern architects, particularly noted for his Kaiser Wilhelm Memorial Church in Berlin (1963). Maintaining a low profile sympathetic of the surrounding residential neighborhood, Eiermann has utilized a tiered design compatible with the building site. The structure of gray steel, with its open steel network of projecting balconies, gives the building a lightly scaled appearance.

Hirshhorn Museum and Sculpture Garden (early 1970s)

ARCHITECTS: Skidmore, Owings and Merrill
LOCATION: Seventh St. and Independence Ave., S.W.
OPEN: Daily, except Dec. 25

A massive circular structure, the Hirshhorn Museum is flanked by a sunken sculpture garden, reflecting pools, and delightful walkways. Henry Moore's stylized "King and Queen" graces the sculpture garden along with many other modern works by well-known artists. The clean, simple building houses a wonderful collection of some 6,000 paintings and sculptures of the 20th century—bequeathed by financier, Jospeh H. Hirshhorn.

John F. Kennedy Center for the Performing Arts (1971)

ARCHITECT: Edward Durell Stone
LOCATION: 2700 Virginia Avenue, NW
OPEN: Daily and for performances

Beautifully sited on the banks of the Potomac River, the dazzling white classical modern structure contains an opera house, a concert hall, and two large theaters. In honor and tribute to John F. Kennedy, many foreign governments contributed materials for the building. The exterior marble facing and most of the superb chandeliers in the lobby space were gifts from Italy.

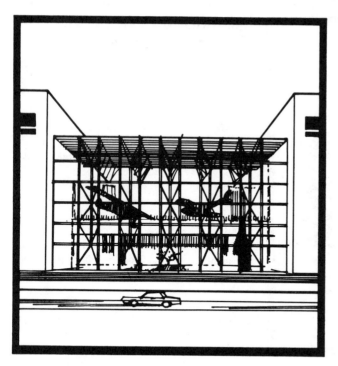

National Air and Space Museum (1975)

ARCHITECTS: Hellmuth Obata & Kassabaum
LOCATION: 7th and Independence SW
OPEN: 10–5:30

Commanding a strong position on the Mall in Washington D.C., the National Air and Space Museum is located alongside some of the nation's most cultural buildings. The bold monolithic structure, clad with pinkish Tennessee marble, has been critized by some as mediocre and lacking imagination, and praised by others as expressive and monumental. The massive building contains some of the most spectacular exhibits in the city, representing America's amazing achievements in air and space exploration.

Southwest Washington Redevelopment (1959–69)

ARCHITECTS: Harry Weese, I.M. Pei and others
LOCATION: South of G Street, East of Maine Ave.

The vast redevelopment project replaced slums surrounding the nation's Capitol Building. Praised as one of the finest urban renewal efforts of its kind at the time, the redevelopment project features many commendable buildings designed by various well-known American architects. Some of the best are Harry Weese's *ARENA STAGE* (1961); Weese's later addition, *THE KREEGER THEATER* (1970); and I.M. Pei's *TOWN CENTER BUILDINGS* (1962). It is a pleasant experience to walk around the development and observe the variety of well-designed structures. Additionally, many older townhouses have been delightfully restored and updated.

Watergate Housing Complex

(1960s)

ARCHITECT: Luigi Moretti and Corning, Moore, Elmore & Fisher
LOCATION: 2500 Virginia Ave. N.W.
OPEN: Commercial spaces open during business hours

Even before the infamous scandal during President Nixon's administration, this large housing project was applauded as an important architectural contribution. For the Watergate buildings, this well-known Italian architect has designed a dynamic curvi-linear plan emphasizing balconies and railings. Surrounded by spacious landscaping and the Potomac River, Watergate makes a commanding outline on the skyline.

Wing for the R.W. Bliss Collection of Pre-Columbian Art (1963)

ARCHITECT: Philip Johnson
LOCATION: Dumbarton Oaks, 1703 32nd Street NW
OPEN: Daily, 2–5, except Mon. Closed in July

The brilliant New Wing for the Robert Woods Bliss Collection of Pre-Columbian Art, with its eight interconnecting circular glass pavilions, adjoins an 1801 Georgian style mansion. Housing a superb collection, the intimate new building is set like a jewel amidst lovely formal gardens and terraces. The interior treatment of marble columns and floors is exquisitely laid out and harmoniously relates to the exterior grounds.

ADDITIONAL MODERN STRUCTURES OF INTEREST

American Institute of Architects Headquarters (1973)
ARCHITECTS: TAC
LOCATION: New York Avenue and 18th Street N.W. (1199 New York)

The new AIA Headquarters wraps around the 175-year-old OCTAGON, creating an exciting juxtaposition of old and new. Landscaping and a plaza further connect the two structures.

Buchanan School Playground (1968)
ARCHITECTS: M. Paul Friedberg, landscape architect with Pomerance & Breines
LOCATION: 13th and E Streets SE

Center for Advanced Study in Visual Arts (1981)
ARCHITECTS: I.M. Pei & Partners
LOCATION: By East Wing of Natl. Gallery of Art

A strong, triangularly-formed building, this center features an interior atrium that soars to a height of 70 feet.

The Design Center (1983)
ARCHITECTS: Keyes Condon Florance
LOCATION: 300 D Street S.W.

This renovated 1920s warehouse with a new reflective glass addition houses showroom space for furniture, carpet, and fabric manufacturers.

Euram Building (1976)
ARCHITECT: George Hartman-Cox of Washington
LOCATION: Dupont Circle

A small, well-designed office building.

Federal Home Loan Bank Board Building (1977)
ARCHITECTS: Max O. Urbahn Associates
LOCATION: 1700 G Street, N.W.

Expressing energy conservation and public accessibility, this new federal building makes a dominant impression.

Federal Office Building No. 7 and the US.S Court of Claims and Court of Customs and Patent Appeals Building (1968)
ARCHITECTS: John Carl Warneck and Associates
LOCATION: Flanking Lafayette Square

These two impressive government buildings are constructed of warm red brick and feature unusual fenestration forms.

H.U.D. (Housing and Urban Development) Headquarters (1963–68)
ARCHITECTS: Marcel Breuer with H. Beckhard and N. Swinburne
LOCATION: 451 Seventh St. SW

Exterior walls of broad-bearing precast panels are supported by rows of sculptural concrete columns. The Y-plan is similar to Breuer's highly acclaimed Uniesco Building in Paris.

Joseph E. Cole Recreational Center (1978)
ARCHITECTS: The Kent Cooper Partnership
LOCATION: Public park at 3030 G Street SE

L'Enfant Plaza (1968)
ARCHITECTS: I.M. Pei & Partners
LOCATION: L'Enfant Plaza

A structural and functional low-rise complex that provides office and retail space.

The Kuwait Chancery (1983)
ARCHITECTS: Skidmore, Owings & Merrill
LOCATION: International Center

This extraordinary structure is an unusual commission for SOM, who also designed the interiors. The building throughout is expressive of the Islamic culture and features a rotating-square principle and symbolic geometric design.

Metro Transit System (1975)
ARCHITECTS: Harry Weese & Associates
LOCATION: Stations at various points throughout the city

One of the finest solutions to functional and attractive underground transportation in the country.

Monetary Fund Building
ARCHITECTS: Vincent G. Kling & Partners with others
LOCATION: 700 19th Street N.W.

This impressive international headquarters building features a dramatic interior atrium space. (This building is not open to the public)

Mount Vernon College (971) Florence Hollis Hand Chapel (1971)
ARCHITECTS: Hartman-Cox and various architects
LOCATION: 26-acre campus located in northwest Washington D.C

The Museum of History and Technology (1964)
ARCHITECTS: McKim, Mead & White
LOCATION: 14th Street and Constitution Avenue

Known for their traditional architecture, the famous architectural team designed this highly criticized building. It is one of the first modern structures of the Smithsonian In-stitute. The story of America's inventions and genius is simply displayed against a structural background.

National Geographic Society Building (1962)
ARCHITECT: Edward Durell Stone
LOCATION: 1145 17 Street N.W.

National Permanent Building (1977)
ARCHITECTS: Hartman-Cox, M. Bioardi, D. Jones
LOCATION: 5250 Mac Arthur Blvd. N.W.

National Presbyterian Church and Center (1969)
ARCHITECT: Harold Wagoner & Associates
LOCATION: 4101 Nebraska Avenue N.W.

This commanding stone religious complex was designed in a contemporary manner reminiscent of the Gothic period.

Park Road Community Church (1972)
ARCHITECTS: Bryant & Bryant
LOCATION: 1019 Park Road N.W.

Studio Theater at the J.F.K. Center for the Performing Arts (1978)
ARCHITECTS: Philip Johnson/John Burgee
LOCATION: 2700 Virginia Avenue, N.W.

Pink, purple, and silver colors were employed for the interiors of this auditorium added to the existing center, conveying an updated Art Deco mood.

1055 Thomas Jefferson Street (1976)
ARCHITECTS: ELS Design Group & Arthur Cotton Moore Associates
LOCATION: 1055 Thomas Jefferson Street

A popular complex with an esplanade along the C & O Canal, 1055 Thomas Jefferson Street, is a marvelous design combination of an old restored 19th century foundry with modern facilities.

Union Station Visitor's Center (1908/1976)
ORIGINAL ARCHITECT: Daniel Burnham
LOCATION: Massachusetts, Louisiana, & Delaware Aves., N.W.

A marvelous renovation for the impressive Beaux-Arts terminal station designed orig-inally by one of America's early modern architects. The traditionally styled building now serves as the National Visitor's Center.

United States Tax Court (1976)
ARCHITECTS: Victor A. Lundy and LBC&W
LOCATION: 400 2nd Street N.W.

Walter Reed General Hospital (1980)
ARCHITECTS: Stone Marraccini and Patterson with others
LOCATION: 6825 16th Street N.W. (principle address)

Situated on an axis with the original 1909 Georgian hospital, the new concrete structure is a technological marvel. The interiors are particularly well planned and visually stimulating.

Vietnam Veterans Memorial (1983)
ARCHITECTS: Cooper-Lecky Partnership,
Architects; Maya Ying Lin, Designer
LOCATION: 21st Street and Constitution
Avenue NW

This bold V-shaped black granite monument
tapers into the earth, creating a feeling of
"infinity, peace, and finality," allowing the
visitor "to interpret the war's meaning in a
deeply personal way." (*Architectural Record*,
May 1984)

**Washington D.C. Temple of the Church
of Jesus Christ of Latter-Day Saints**
(1974)
ARCHITECTS: H.K. Beecher, H.P. Fetzer, F.I.
Markham and K.W. Wilcox
LOCATION: 9900 Stoneybrook Dr.,
Kensington, MD. (off Capitol Beltway)

Faced with 173,000 square feet of Alabama
marble, this Temple makes a striking impression on its hillside setting. Grounds open
daily.

• Tallahassee

Jacksonville

• Gainesville

Orlando •

Tampa • Lakeland

St. Petersburg

• Cape
Kennedy

• Sarasota

Boca Raton •
Fort Lauderdale •
Miami •

Key
Biscayne

Florida

FORT LAUDERDALE

United States Courthouse— Federal Office Building
(1975–79)

ARCHITECTS: William Morgan with H.J. Ross Associates
LOCATION: 299 East Broward Boulevard at Northeast 3rd Ave.
OPEN: Atrium always, offices during business hours

Harmoniously related to downtown surroundings, this remarkable government facility features an inviting 4-story atrium courtyard. Varying levels of walkways, ramps, water fountains, seating, and plantings humanize the environment and add to the citizen's pleasure—a goal outlined by the architects in the initial planning stages. Offices, civil and criminal courts, and other government services are contained within the complex.

GAINESVILLE

Florida State Museum at the University of Florida (1979)

ARCHITECT: William Morgan
LOCATION: Museum Road at Newell Drive
OPEN: Mon.–Sat., 9:30–5, Sun., 1–5

Modelled after the ancient Indian ceremonial grounds of the region, the Florida State Museum is a superb contemporary setting, capturing the spirit of centuries past. Fine exhibits trace the anthropological and biological history of Florida and the Caribbean area from c. 10,000 BC. Designed around the theme "Environment and Man," the plan of the museum has provided spaces for re-created environments for visitors to explore.

JACKSONVILLE

Police Memorial Building

(1974–77)

ARCHITECT: William Morgan
LOCATION: East Bay St. between Liberty and Catherine
OPEN: During office hours, terraces always open

A unique aspect of the Police Memorial Building is the architect's creation of a beautiful and welcoming area for townspeople to enjoy, as opposed to the usual austere and even unfriendly police buildings around the nation. This memorial is dedicated to Jacksonville police killed in the line of duty. Terraces, a pool, a fountain, and seating are all set amidst nicely landscaped areas that function as a public park.

LAKELAND

The Frank Lloyd Wright Buildings—Florida Southern Univ. (1936–59)

ARCHITECT: Frank Lloyd Wright
LOCATION: Via S Florida Ave., E on McDonal St., to Johnson Ave.
OPEN: Daily—maps available at Administration Building

Seven large buildings designed by the great master modern architect are found on this campus—the largest single grouping of structures by Frank Lloyd Wright in the world. These interconnecting structures demonstrate his genius, since he was always concerned with incorporating the building with its surroundings. Although often criticized, the buildings still draw Wright enthusiasts. Particularly interesting is the ANNIE PFEIFFER CHAPEL, with its steel "trellis" tower and colored glass windows. *THE SPIVEY FINE ARTS CENTER* (1970) designed by Nils M. Schweizer, who worked for Wright, is close by the lake just off Johnson Avenue.

MIAMI

Atlantis on Brickell (1982–)

ARCHITECTS: Arquitectonica
LOCATION: Brickell Avenue along Biscayne Bay (2025 Brickell)
OPEN: Lobby and grounds open daily

A fascinating walking tour can be taken beginning at the north side of the building where four huge red columns on white marble stairs introduce the visitor to the exciting design ahead. Gray reflective solar glass and painted stucco concrete block are strikingly accented with powerful contrasting red, yellow, and blue architectural members. Note the enormous red triangular form on top of the complex. This stunning theme is carried throughout the building. Other works by this dynamic architectural team can be seen along Brickell Avenue, including *THE BABYLON, THE IMPERIAL, THE PALACE,* and *HELMSLEY CENTER.*

MIAMI

Art Deco District in Miami Beach (1930s)

ARCHITECTS: Various architects
LOCATION: Southeastern tip of Miami Beach
OPEN: During business and shopping hours

Miami made an important contribution to the Art Deco style during the roaring 20s and 30s in America. A glamorous and romantic feeling was reflected in architecture and interiors with motifs drawn from many exotic sources. One square mile of Art Deco buildings, including hotels, movie houses, a shopping mall, apartment houses, and an ice-cream parlor, have been faithfully restored. Recently made a National Landmark, the Art Deco district is an architectural treasure.

MIAMI

Citizens Federal Savings and Loan Association (1975)

ARCHITECT: Morris Lapidus
LOCATION: 999 Brickell Avenue
OPEN: During business hours

Compared to many of Miami's towering structures, the 11-story Federal Savings and Loan building is small, but fascinating. The structure is constructed of exposed concrete and chrome mirror glass arranged in the form of a star. A spectacular interior lobby rotunda is topped with a twenty-five-foot white illuminated dome. The unique form and design is enhanced by outdoor landscaping and a forty-foot square cascading fountain lit with colored lights. Lapidus has built some of Florida's most unusual buildings.

MIAMI

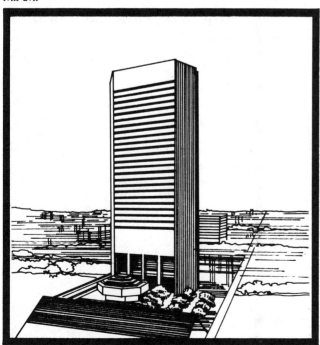

Metro-Dade Administration Center (1981–85)

ARCHITECTS: Hugh Stubbins Associates Collaborative 3
LOCATION: N.W. 2nd Avenue & N.W. 1st Street
OPEN: During office hours

Well known for his impressive structures around the nation, Stubbins taught at Harvard University before devoting his energies to private practice. The Metro-Dade Center towers over a well-planned and unique plaza arrangement. An unusual angled "beehive" building provides a stabilizing effect in the plaza at the base of the tower. A central walk through space at the lower levels contributes to the graceful and airy design image.

MIAMI

Metro Dade Cultural Center
(1984)

ARCHITECTS: Philip Johnson/John Burgee
LOCATION: 101 West Flagler Street
OPEN: Mon.–Wed., 10–6, Thurs., 1–9, Fri.,
10–6, Sat., 10–5, Sun., 12–5

The visitor is introduced to the Dade County Center for the Fine Arts by a raised 33,000 square foot quarry tile plaza that links the building to the new Library and Historical Museum. This outdoor area functions beautifully as an outdoor room reminiscent of the traditional Italian piazza. A terra-cotta tile roof, stucco, and shellstone construction further create a Mediterranean-style atmosphere, but interpreted in a modern approach. The highly criticized, two-level boxy museum building itself boast spacious areas for impressive exhibits.

MIAMI

Southeast Financial Center
(1984)

ARCHITECTS: Skidmore, Owings and Merrill
LOCATION: 200 South Biscayne
OPEN: During business hours

Rising 55 stories above Biscayne Boulevard, Southeast Financial Center, headquarters for Southeast Banking Corporation, is planned to relate to the Bay Front Park across the street. The dazzling towers are topped with a unique cut-away design providing a striking silhouette on the shoreline. The excitement of the building additionally culminates with a vast open air Court between the buildings. The space is paved with an intricate granite stone design and covered with a steel white space frame canopy. The Court is filled with large royal palms that soften the high-tech geometry.

ORLANDO

Epcot Center (1982)

ARCHITECTS: Various architects
LOCATION: Epcot Center Drive
OPEN: Opens daily at 9:00 AM. Closing
time varies from 8:00 to 10:00 PM.

Walt Disney's last dream project opened 16 years after the famed cartoonist's death. "Epcot is a mind-pummeling assault of electronic ingenuity, historical fact, fancy, showmanship, faith, hope, and goo." (*Time Magazine,* Oct. 4, 1982.) A symbol and outstanding structure of the center is the 18-story geosphere called Spaceship Earth. Inside, a moving track shuttle allows visitors to view man's achievements in communications. Another highlight is Kodak's Journey into Imagination. The extraordinary and inventive concept is entertaining and educational and has already become one of the nation's most popular landmarks.

ORLANDO

"Florida Festival" (1980s)

ARCHITECTS: Robert Lamb Hart
LOCATION: 7007 Sea World Drive
OPEN: Daily, 9 AM to 7 PM

A brilliant solution to enclosing large public spaces, the "Florida Festival" complex was designed to provide facilities for entertainment, recreation, and shopping. Orlando's popular Sea World Park is close by, attracting tourists from all over the United States. Swirling translucent fabric coated with "Teflon" hovers over the spaces providing both shelter and light. The innovative idea and festive effect of the structures are inviting. The fiberglass is both durable and economical and has the advantage of low operating costs.

ORLANDO

Orlando Public Library
(1965–66)

ARCHITECTS: John J. Johansen &
Associates
LOCATION: 10 N. Rosalind Ave. at Central
Blvd.
OPEN: Mon.–Fri., 9–9, Sat. 9–6, Sun. 1–5

Known for his expressive Charles Center in
Baltimore, the Mummer's Theater in
Oklahoma, and the Taylor House in Connecticut, Johansen claims he searches for character
in his buildings rather than beauty. This bold
library is composed of startling irregular
forms, constructed of raw striated concrete—a
medium often associated with this architect's
work.

SARASOTA

St. Paul's Lutheran Church
(1959/1968–69)

ARCHITECT: Victor A. Lundy
LOCATION: 2256 Bahia Vista Street
OPEN: Arrangements may be made at
Parish House

Dynamic upsweeping forms dominate the
structural units of St. Paul's Lutheran Church.
Rhythmic expressions of laminated wood
beams create tent-like roofs. These beams are
supported on steel columns sheathed with
coquina. A remarkable cable-suspended roof
is ingeniously supported, adding to the
excitement of the architecture. The statue of
Christ was created by a member of the
church.

SARASOTA

Van Wezel Performing Arts Hall (1968–69)

ARCHITECT: William Wesley Peters of Taliesin Associated
LOCATION: 1 block W of North Tamiami Trail (US 41 at 10th St)
OPEN: During performances. Morning and afternoon tours

Peters, a long time professional associate of the late Frank Lloyd Wright, was selected to design this huge concert hall, theater, and auditorium complex. Dramatically located on the edge of Sarasota Bay, the structures are painted in purple hues—chosen by Mrs. Wright, who still supervises Taliesin West Foundation in Scottsdale, Arizona. With sensitivity for the interior acoustics, the form accommodates that function beautifully. Other facilities were planned for convenience, efficiency, and effect.

TAMPA

Museum of Science and Industry (1981)

ARCHITECTS: Rowe Holmes Associates
LOCATION: N. Tampa, I–275, Fowler Ave., Exit, 3 miles east
OPEN: 10:00 AM –4:30 daily

An extraordinary structure designed to house exhibits in industry, science, and culture, this massive complex makes a bold statement on the city's landscape. The exterior is highlighted with colorful accents. Domed plexiglass skylights flood the interior exhibit spaces with Florida sunlight. Interior planning was arranged for exciting exhibits of all types including sun, weather, electricity, and many hands on experiences for visitors of all ages.

ADDITIONAL MODERN STRUCTURES OF INTEREST

BOCA RATON

Burdine's Department Store (Superstore) (1979)
ARCHITECTS: Walker/Group
LOCATION: 5700 West Glades Road

Six Burdine's department stores in Florida have received national attention for their unique modular grid designs. Other "superstores," as they are now called, are located in West Palm Beach, Miami, St. Petersburg, Fort Myers, and Fort Lauderdale.

IBM Office, Laboratory and Manufacturing Facility (1970)
ARCHITECTS: Marcel Breuer and Robert Gatje
LOCATION: 1000 Northwest 51st Street

Sculptural free tree columns and precast panels characterize the familiar architectural approach of this handsome facility designed by the famous late master architect.

FORT LAUDERDALE

American Express Southern Region Operations Center (1976)
ARCHITECTS: Ferendino/Grafton/Spillis/ Candela
LOCATION: On Cleary Blvd. between Pine Island & University Dr.

Located on a 25-acre site outside of town, this well-planned concrete panel and glass structure was designed for maximum efficiency.

GAINSVILLE

Stephen C. O'Connell Center—University of Florida (1981)
ARCHITECT: Caudill R. Scott
LOCATION: University of Florida campus

Designed with special consideration for the sun's rays, the multi-activity center, with its billowing forms, has been compared to a "pillow and a bubble."

JACKSONVILLE

Florida Community College (1978)
ARCHITECTS: Anthony J. Lumsden of DMJM
LOCATION: Cumberland campus

The sleek horizontally designed Florida Community College is constructed of concrete components arranged in tiers.

Florida Regional Service Center (1977–78)
ARCHITECT: William Morgan
LOCATION: Coast Line Drive just E of US 1/17

An extraordinary tiered plan located on the St. Johns River.

Jacksonville Children's Museum (1970)
ARCHITECT: William Morgan
LOCATION: In St. Johns River Park and Marina

This bold white structure provides marvelous interior spaces for fascinating permanent and changing exhibits particularly geared for children's enjoyment.

Jacksonville Jewish Center (1977)
ARCHITECTS: Freedman/Clements/Rumpel
LOCATION: 3662 Crown Point Road

This modern progressive center was designed for a variety of community services for a conservative congregation. The facility is located in a pleasant 37-acre wooded area.

LAKELAND

Ludd M. Spivey Fine Arts Center
ARCHITECTS: EDG (Environmental Design Group)
LOCATION: Florida Southern College

Bold forms interpreted in concrete and glass create a strong statement for this arts complex.

MIAMI

Barnett Center (1981)
ARCHITECTS: Ferendino, Grafton, Spillis &
Candela
LOCATION: 800 Brickell Avenue

Brickell Key—Phase 1 (1982)
ARCHITECTS: Wilbur Smith & Associates
LOCATION: Claughton Island

Decorative Arts Plaza (1981)
ARCHITECTS: Arquitectonica
LOCATION: 4001 NE 2nd Avenue

Dynamic forms of red, yellow, and blue
appear like giant toys and help attract visitors
to the exciting facility that functions as
furniture showrooms.

Flagship Center (1980)
ARCHITECTS: Hellmuth, Obata, Kassabaum,
Inc.
LOCATION: 777 Brickell Avenue

Fontainebleau Hotel (1954)
ARCHITECT: Morris Lapidus
LOCATION: 4441 Collins Avenue, Miami
Beach

Lapidus also designed the *EDEN ROC* and
AMERICANA hotels along Miami Beach.

Interterra (1982)
ARCHITECTS: Skidmore, Owings and Merrill
LOCATION: 1200 Brickell Avenue

Miami Center (1983)
ARCHITECTS: Pietro Belluschi, Viastimil
Koubek
LOCATION: 100 Chopin Plaza

Miami Dade Community College (1972)
ARCHITECTS: Ferendino/Grafton/Spillis/
Candela
LOCATION: Downtown Miami campus

The Overseas Tower (1981)
ARCHITECTS: Arquitectonica
LOCATION: 9600 Northwest 25th Street

The composition of white planes broken by
tinted glass forms is uniquely arranged. A
surprising cylindrical office space is attached
to the rear of the building.

Note: Miami is undertaking an ambitious and
extensive building program at the present
time. Numerous impressive structures are
listed in publications available at the Chamber of Commerce in Miami.

MIAMI BEACH

Miami Beach Youth Center (1976)
ARCHITECTS: Ferendino/Grafton/Spillis/
Candela
LOCATION: 2700 Sherida Avenue

This colorful and inviting Youth Center
provides a variety of recreational facilities in a
delightful manner.

MIAMI: (KEY BISCAYNE)

The Square at Key Biscayne (1981)
ARCHITECTS: Arquitectonica Architects
LOCATION: 260 Crandon Boulevard, Key
Biscayne

This innovative commercial complex is both
inviting and efficiently planned.

ORLANDO

**Chapel and Religious Education Building
(Stephen L. Rusk Memorial)** (1969)
ARCHITECT: James A. McDonald & Russell
Gustafson
LOCATION: U.S. Naval Training Center

A dramatic hipped roof deisgn with strong
projecting forms.

SARASOTA

East Campus University of South Florida
(1968)
ARCHITECTS: I.M. Pei & Partners
LOCATION: NW edge of Sarasota on US 41
at General Spaatz Blvd.

Plymouth Harbor (1965–66)
ARCHITECT: Frank Folsom Smith
LOCATION: 700 John Ringling Causeway

A brilliantly planned 26-story retirement
complex.

Sarasota Senior High School (1958–59)
ARCHITECT: Paul Rudolph
LOCATION: 1001 South Tamiami Trail

A painted white concrete school, one of Rudolph's early works, that has received national recognition.

The William G. and Marie Selby Public Library (1976)
ARCHITECTS: Skidmore, Owings & Merrill
LOCATION: 1001 Blvd. of the Arts

This admirable library complex with interlocking hexagonals combined with fascinating geometry was designed to invite the public into an intimate "living room" environment.

ST. PETERSBURG

Dali Museum (1980–82)
ARCHITECTS: Harvard, Jolly, Marcet and Associates
LOCATION: 1000 3rd St. So., St. Petersburg

An intriguing modern structure housing an impressive Salvador Dali collection of art. Open Tues., Wed., Fri., Sat., 10–5, Sun. 12–5.

Pinellas County Judical Building (1971)
ARCHITECTS: Anderson-Johnson-Henry-Parrish
LOCATION: 545 First Ave. North. Government complex area, downtown, by lake and park

A series of concrete fluted columns and striated elements throughout distinguish this unusual complex.

TALLAHASSEE

Florida State Capitol (1973–77)
ARCHITECT: Edward Durell Stone
LOCATION: Monroe Street and Alapachee Parkway

A new modern renovation centered around the original 1845 Capitol building.

Tallahassee City Hall (1984)
ARCHITECTS: Heery and Heery
LOCATION: Part of downtown government complex.

The massive new brick and steel City Hall significantly relates to surrounding government buildings and business district without sacrificing a strong identity of its own.

Tallahassee–Leon County Civic Center
ARCHITECTS: Barret, Daffin and Carlen
LOCATION: 505 West Pensacola Street

The Tallahassee District Court of Appeal, First District (1980s)
ARCHITECT: William Morgan
LOCATION: Martin Luther King Boulevard

This gleaming white-painted building with large supportive columns suggests a feeling of the old ante-bellum mansions.

TAMPA

One Tampa City Center (1981)
ARCHITECTS: Welton Becket Associates
LOCATION: One Tampa City Center

One Tampa City Center soars 40-stories and is sheathed with clear silver reflecting glass. A vertical designed emphasis is particularly stunning.

WEST PALM BEACH

Temple Beth El (1976)
ARCHITECT: Alfred Browning Parker
LOCATION: 2815 North Flagler Drive

Spiraling arches the architect calls "spiraloids" create a fanciful expression for this large complex serving a conservative Jewish Community.

• Rosewell

• Marietta

• Doraville

• Decatur

Atlanta •

• Shenandoah

Georgia

GEORGIA

ATLANTA

Atlanta Public Library (Now Fulton County Library) (late 1970s)

ARCHITECTS: Marcel Breuer, Hamilton Smith with Stevens & Wilkinson
LOCATION: Peachtree St., One Margaret Mitchell Square
OPEN: Tues. Wed. Thurs., 9–8, Mon. & Fri. 9–6, Sat., 10–6, Sun. 2–6

The Atlanta Public Library was designed by the late Marcel Breuer, pupil and teacher at the famous Bauhaus design school in Germany. Before the outbreak of World War II, Breuer fled Nazi Germany and assumed a teaching position at Harvard University. The strong design of the Atlanta Public Library appears as a neo-Beuhaus design combined with the dramatic cut-away design of the architect's Whitney Museum in New York City. The library is one of the last completed projects of the architect before his death in 1981.

ATLANTA

Colony Square (1970–78)

ARCHITECTS: Jova/Daniels/Busby, Thompson, Ventulett & Stainback
LOCATION: Peachtree Street at 14th–15th Street
OPEN: During business and shopping hours; hotel always

An impressive multi-use complex, Colony Square is comprised of two office towers, two residential structures, shops, and a hotel. The project is an excellent example of an attractive and convenient urban living-working-shopping-recreation solution.

ATLANTA

Emory University—William R. Cannon Chapel & Religious Center (1980s)

ARCHITECT: Paul Rudolph
LOCATION: Emory University campus, near Decatur
OPEN: During school hours

Precisely formed concrete units with roughly striated texture are unusually arranged in the composition of this religious structure. A series of rounded towers surround the building. A slender soaring form pierced with a cross provides a focal point. A long concrete ramp leading up to the entrance adds additional drama. Spartan interiors are lit with rows of curved clerestory windows accenting the raw concrete surfaces.

ATLANTA

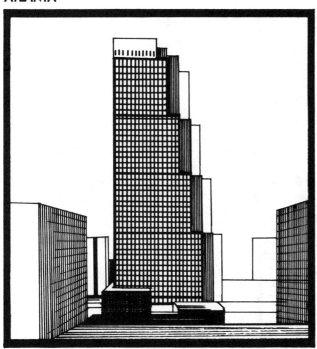

Georgia Pacific Center (1983)

ARCHITECTS: Skidmore, Owings and Merrill
LOCATION: Peachtree St., downtown
OPEN: During business hours

Atlanta boasts three architectural complexes by SOM, the world famous architectural firm—the *EQUITABLE BUILDING* (1968), designed with Finch, Alexander, Barnes, Rothschild & Pachall, located at 100 Peachtree Street NW.; the stunning *SOUTHERN BELL* (1981–82), designed with FABRAP Inc., located at West Peachtree St., (integrating the North Avenue Station of MARTA with a shopping Gallery and the Georgia Pacific Center. The Georgia Pacific Center is one of the firm's best works featuring well planned office and restaurant spaces.

ATLANTA

High Museum of Art (1981–83)

ARCHITECT: Richard Meier
LOCATION: Peachtree and 16th St.
OPEN: Tues.–Sat., 10–5, Sun., 12–5

With a dazzling composition of light and geometry, the new High Museum of Art is a dramatic background for exhibits. A huge wedged skylight looms above the central areas, channeling directions for galleries and offices. The architect has consistently employed a three-foot square module that is repeated throughout in porcelain enamel, granite, and glass. The controversial and unique museum is part of the Atlanta Memorial Arts Center which includes the original High Museum, Symphony Hall, Alliance Theater, and Atlanta College of Art.

ATLANTA

Hyatt Regency Hotel
(1966–67/1969)

ARCHITECTS: John Portman & Associates
LOCATION: 265 Peachtree Street Northeast
OPEN: Always

With a lot of imagination and foresight, Portman developed the nationally acclaimed Peachtree Center. The celebrated Hyatt Regency Hotel with its dazzling cylindrical glass facade and 21-story atrium lobby space is delightful. The interior areas are uniquely executed—completely breaking with old-fashioned ideas of how a hotel should be planned. An exterior elevator rises to the revolving Polaris Restaurant at the top of the complex.

ATLANTA

Omni Coliseum (1970–72),
Omni International (1971–75)
ARCHITECTS: Thompson Ventulett &
Stainback
LOCATION: 100 Techwood Dr., Marietta St.
at Techwood Drive
OPEN: Special events; shops during
business hours

A monumental megastructure, The Omni
complex was designed to provide downtown
Atlanta with a multi-use facility that includes
The Omni—a sports and entertainment coliseum; the Omni International—a hotel, office
space, shops, restaurants, and six movie
theaters around a covered atrium. The many
faceted roof has been compared to a "giant
waffle." The steel framed structure, clad with
Alabama limestone, is considered an engineering masterpiece.

ATLANTA

Peachtree Plaza Hotel (1974–76)

ARCHITECTS: John Portman & Associates
LOCATION: Peachtree Street at International
Boulevard
OPEN: Continuously

Unable to plan another awesome interior
atrium (like his Hyatt Regency) due to lots of
restrictions, the architect used ten huge
cylinders to support the fifty-six floors. The
employment of space, form, and materials is
astounding—with a focal point centered
around refreshing indoor "lagoons." Again,
like the Hyatt Regency, a revolving restaurant
tops the brilliant complex. The Peachtree
Plaza Hotel was voted the city's favorite
building in all categories by the people of
Atlanta in 1982.

ADDITIONAL MODERN STRUCTURES OF INTEREST

ATLANTA

AT & T Long Lines Southern Region Headquarters (1982)
ARCHITECTS: Thompson, Ventulett, Stainback & Associates
LOCATION: Peachtree and 15th Street

Received the Award for Excellence in Architecture in 1982 by GAAIA.

C & S Bank (1968)
ARCHITECTS: Aeck Associates
LOCATION: 603 W. Peachtree St. NE

The Citizens & Southern Bank building is an interesting round tower complex.

Coca-Cola Company Headquarters
ARCHITECTS: FABRAP, Inc.
LOCATION: 310 North Avenue NW

The Coca-Cola building is a favorite industrial building of the people in Atlanta.

Cyclorama (rebuilt in 1982)
ARCHITECTS: FABRAP, Inc.
LOCATION: Grant Park

An innovative building designed to house the Cyclorama of the Battle of Atlanta. Open daily from 9–5.

Flat Iron Building (1897/1976)
ARCHITECT: Bradford Gilbert
LOCATION: Peachtree at Broad St.

Built on a triangular site, the Flat Iron Building is Atlanta's first skyscraper.

Georgia Power Company Headquarters (1981)
ARCHITECTS: Heery & Heery
LOCATION: 333 Piedmont Ave. NE

An admirable solar structure that won the GAAIA Design Award in 1981.

Hartsfield International Airport (1980)
ARCHITECTS: Stevens & Wilkinson
LOCATION: S of Atlanta on I-85

One of the nation's finest airport facilities. The airport is also one of the nation's largest and busiest facilities of its type.

Hilton Hotel
ARCHITECTS: Wong & Tung
LOCATION: 255 Courtland & Harris Streets

A striking complex of white towers with a central lobby core.

IBM Headquarters—General Systems Division (1978)
ARCHITECTS: Thompson, Ventulett, Stainback & Associates
LOCATION: 4111 Northside Parkway NE

This structure won the GAAIA Design Award in 1978.

Lenox Square (1959)
ARCHITECTS: Toombs, Amisano & Wells
LOCATION: 3393 Peachtree Road

An early modern shopping center recently renovated.

Museum of Art & Archeology & Art History Department Renovation (1984)
ARCHITECT: Michael Graves
LOCATION: Emory University campus, near Decatur

The museum of Art & Archeology, Art History Department, and other buildings at Emory University have been interestingly renovated by Michael Graves, one of the nation's most innovative modern architects.

Peachtree Summit (1975)
ARCHITECTS: Toombs, Amisano & Wells
LOCATION: 447 West Peachtree Street

This building received the 1976 GAAIA Design Award.

Robinson Humphrey Building
ARCHITECTS: Smallwood, Reynolds, Stewart & Stewart
LOCATION: 3333 Peachtree Road, NE in Buckhead, Atlanta

Stadium-Atlanta/Fulton County Stadium (1965)
ARCHITECTS: Finch Alexander Barnes Rothschild & Paschal with Heery and Heery
LOCATION: 521 Capitol Avenue SE

Tower Place (1975)
ARCHITECTS: Stevens & Wilkinson
LOCATION: Peachtree and Pedmont Roads

A beautiful development including an office tower, condominiums, a hotel, and shops.

Transit Stations (Marta) (1982)
ARCHITECTS: Various architects
LOCATION: A few notable stations include Art Center Station, Civic Center Station, Decatur Station, Garnett Street Station, Georgia State Station, North Avenue Station, and Peachtree Center Station.

Convenient, functional, and attractive underground transportation design.

Woodruff Medical Center Administration Building (1978)
ARCHITECTS: Heery & Heery
LOCATION: Emory University campus, 1364 Clifton Road

Winner of the GAAIA Design Award in 1978.

Woodruff Library
ARCHITECTS: Toombs, Amisano & Wells
LOCATION: Atlanta University campus, 233 Chestnut Street

Simmons Company Jones Bridge Headquarters (1975)
ARCHITECTS: Thompson, Hancock, Witte, & Associates, Inc.
LOCATION: S of Atlanta, near Airport, overlooking Chatahoochee River

Headquarters for Simmons bedding products; nestled in the woods.

DECATUR

Dana Fine Arts Building (1965)
ARCHITECTS: Edwards and Portman
LOCATION: Agnes Scott campus

The unusual structure for art studies recalls a Gothic theme compatible with surrounding Gothic buildings on campus.

DORAVILLE

Northwoods Presbyterian Church (1974)
ARCHITECT: Jack Durham Haynes

LOCATION: 3330 Chestnut Drive, just off Expressway I-85.

This church, in a rural Georgia community, was sensitively created to combine the old and new images.

MARIETTA

John Knox Presbyterian Church (1965–66)
ARCHITECT: Joseph Amisano
LOCATION: 1236 Powers Ferry Road, E via Roswell Road, C. 2 miles SE of intersection of US 41 and Roswell Road

A charming small church of granite and white painted wood.

ROSEWELL

Herman Miller Rosewell Facility (1983)
ARCHITECTS: Heery & Heery
LOCATION: 20 miles north of Atlanta

Sleek glass and metal components artfully combine for this striking industrial complex. The project was designed with respect for the rolling countryside setting.

SHENANDOAH

Shenandoah Solar Recreation Center (1977)
ARCHITECTS: Taylor & Collum, Inc.
LOCATION: 12032 Amlajack Boulevard, 25 miles SW of Atlanta

Nicely situated in a wooded area, this award-winning recreational complex admirably unites energy and structural consideration. The roof composition is stunning.

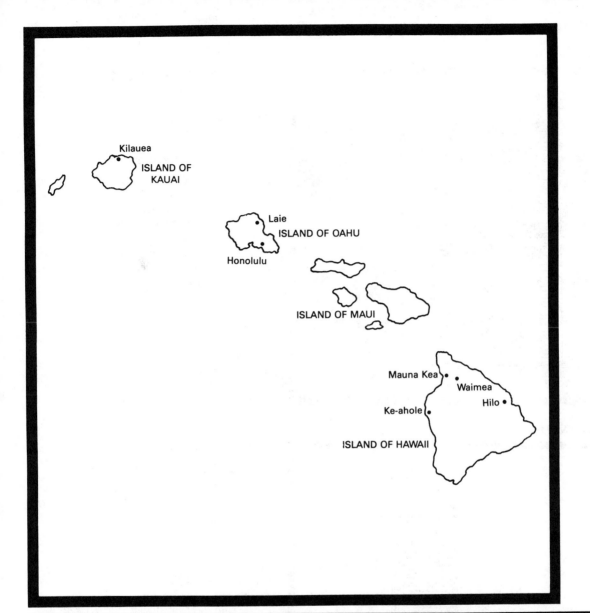

Kilauea

ISLAND OF
KAUAI

Laie

ISLAND OF OAHU

Honolulu

ISLAND OF MAUI

Mauna Kea

Waimea

Hilo

Ke-ahole

ISLAND OF HAWAII

Hawaii

College of Business Administration (1973)

ARCHITECTS: Leo S. Wou & Associates
LOCATION: University of Hawaii, Manoa Campus, North side
OPEN: During school hours

Describing the design concept of the College of Business, *Architectural Record* wrote: "The dumbell-shaped module, consistently used throughout the complex, is not a symmetrical, four-sided unit but by its nature is varied in form and capable of providing the variations which the architect wanted without violating its own integrity. This pattern of modules is arranged on a triangular site and centered around open plazas and courtyards with a series of covered walks, bridges, and balcony corridors." The experience of moving through the complex of spaces and shapes is exhilerating. Other noteworthy buildings on campus by well-known architects are listed under "Additional Modern Structures of Interest."

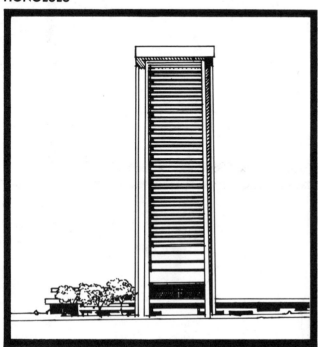

East-West Center at the University of Hawaii (1963)

ARCHITECT: I.M. Pei & Partners
LOCATION: East-West Road, N of Honolulu via University Avenue, E on Dole Street
OPEN: During school year

In 1960, this commendable structure was commissioned by Congress for "the promotion of better relations and understanding among nations and peoples of Asia, the Pacific, and the United States." The large complex utilizes an architecturally advanced support system that sets up an attractive and orderly appearance. The entire complex, with supportive buildings, is beautifully complemented by artistic landscaping.

HONOLULU

State Capitol (1965–69)

ARCHITECTS: John Carl Warnecke &
Associates with Belt, Lemmon, & Lo
LOCATION: Beretania Street between
Richards and Punchbowl
OPEN: Mon.–Fri., 9–5

Responding to the need for radical changes in
the field of architecture, this prominent
California-based architect designed an imaginative and fascinating structure. The
arrangement of space and materials creates a
powerful symbol of government in an historical setting of tropical beauty. The vast central
open atrium of the complex rises four levels
to a marvelous domed skylight.

MAUNA KEA BEACH

Mauna Kea Beach Hotel

(1965–68)

ARCHITECTS: Skidmore, Owings & Merrill
LOCATION: On the coast, S of highway 26,
Island of Hawaii (NW)
OPEN: Continuously

In a resort area that boasts hundreds of
beautifully designed hotels, the Mauna Kea
Beach Hotel is one of the best. SOM, the
world renowned architectural firm, planned
this hotel to establish a close integration with
the lush surroundings and nearby beach. The
goal was accomplished with a stepped design
of balconies and sensitive landscaping. A
masterpiece of space-planning both inside
and out, the hotel is further enhanced by
inviting areas of seating, fountains, pools,
atriums, plantings, and other facilities.

ADDITIONAL MODERN STRUCTURES OF INTEREST

HILO (Island of Hawaii)

C. Brewer & Co., Ltd. Hilo Office (1972)
ARCHITECTS: Ossipoff Snyder, Rowland & Goetz
LOCATION: Hilo Bay, Island of Hawaii

This impressive regional office structure is designed with respect for local venacular.

HONOLULU (Island of Oahu)

Ala Moana Building (1961)
ARCHITECTS: John Graham and Company
LOCATION: 1441 Kapiolani Boulevard

A fascinating feature of this tower is sun shields that automatically open and close as the sun moves around the structure. A rotating restaurant on the top affords a panoramic view of the city.

Buildings at The University of Hawaii at Manoa
ARCHITECTS: Various architects.
LOCATION: University of Hawaii at Manoa campus

Following are some of the buildings on campus designed by nationally known architects (not featured in the text with an illustration): the *BIOMEDICAL SCIENCES BUILDING* designed by Edward Durell Stone; the *CAMPUS CENTER* designed by John Carl Warneke; and the *COLLEGE OF ENGINEERING BUILDING* designed by Skidmore, Owings & Merrill.

Federal Building Complex
Prince Kuhio Federal Building (1970s)
ARCHITECTS: Belt, Lemmon and Lo
LOCATION: 300 Ala Moana Blvd.

The Federal Building Complex is constructed of concrete materials made from coral sand and coral aggregate found in Hawaii. Oval-shaped masonry towers distinguish the 5-story structure.

City Bank of Honolulu (late 1960s)
ARCHITECTS: Walter Tagawa
LOCATION: 810 Richards Street

The award-winning, 10-story Bank of Honolulu features interestingly placed 30' × 30' bays.

The Financial Plaza of The Pacific (late 1960s)
ARCHITECTS: Various architects, including Leo S. Wou and Victor Gruen Associates, Inc.
LOCATION: Bounded by King, Bishop, Merchant, and Fort Streets

This ambitious building development consists of a number of impressive buildings including the BANK OF HAWAII, FINANCIAL PLAZA, and the CASTLE & COOKE BUILDING. It is one of the largest commercial complexes in the United States.

Graduate Research Library (Hamilton Library) (1963–68)
ARCHITECT: A. Quincy Jones, Frederich E. Emmons & Hogan & Chapman
LOCATION: University of Hawaii campus, 2550 The Mall

An excellent library facility by California's nationally-known architect. A. Quincy Jones, with other prominent designers.

Harris United Methodist Church (1962)
ARCHITECTS: Wilson Associates, Inc.
LOCATION: 20 South Vineyard Boulevard

This boldly designed religious structure features a massive shingled roof that wraps the building except for the entrance sides.

Honolulu Academy of Arts (1926–27/1977)
ARCHITECT: Bertram G. Goodhue
LOCATION: 900 South Beretania Street

Invitingly located on "five-within-five," nicely landscaped open courtyards, and a sculpture garden, the Honolulu Academy of Arts is tastefully planned to capture the spirit of the regional venacular. The low structure has a gray tile roof that extends to support thick square columns forming an arcade. Housing an impressive art collection, the structure was finished after the important early modern architect's death in 1924. A new wing, primarily for contemporary art was added in 1977, commemorating the museum's fiftieth anniversary. (Open: Tues.–Sat., 10–4:30, Sun., 2–5)

Hyatt Regency Hotel (1976)
ARCHITECTS: Wimberly, Whisenand, Allison, Tong & Goo with others
LOCATION: Waikiki, Hemmeter Center

The 1,260-room Hyatt Regency Hotel is housed in twin octagonal towers that loom over Waikiki Beach.

Kahala Hilton (1964)
ARCHITECT: Edward Killingsworth
LOCATION: 5000 Kahala Avenue

A luxurious hotel featuring trellises of precast-pre-stressed concrete designed by Killingsworth, a prominent California architect.

Kaiser-Aetna Waterfront Village (1975)
ARCHITECT: David D. Stringer
LOCATION: 7192 Kalanianaole Highway (Near Diamond Head)

A $5 million complex featuring two decks of shops and offices.

Kukui Garden Housing (1969–70)
ARCHITECTS: Daniel, Mann, Johnson & Mendenhall
LOCATION: Liliha Street between No. Vineyard Blvd & Beretania

A superbly designed low-cost housing project that received national acclaim.

Queen Emma Garden Apartments (1964)
ARCHITECT: Minoru Yamasaki
LOCATION: 1519 Nuuanu Avenue (HI 61) at No. Vineyard

A large pleasant apartment complex of three buildings designed by the architect of the World Trade Center in New York City.

U.S.S. Arizona Memorial (1962)
ARCHITECT: Alfred Preis
LOCATION: Pearl Harbor

This dazzling white, award-winning Memorial is boldly formed, capturing the spirit of the sunken ship.

Ward Plaza (1970)
ARCHITECTS: Au, Cutting, Smith and Associates
LOCATION: On Ward Avenue, at Ward Plaza Shopping Center

This four-building complex is unified by connecting bridges, decks, covered walks, and lanais. The structures of strong concrete forms capture the spirit of the casual atmosphere in Hawaii.

KILAUEA (Island of Kauai)

St. Sylvester's (1960)
ARCHITECTS: John H. McAuliffe and Edwin L. Bauer
LOCATION: NNE coast of Kauai

This low budget church in the round is particularly sensitive to its lush surroundings, featuring wood and lava rock construction.

KONA COAST (KE-AHOLE)
Ke-Ahole Airport (1970)
ARCHITECTS: Aotani & Oka, Inc.
LOCATION: NW Coast on Hwy. 19, just N of Kailua,

The uniquely shaped cedar shingle pavilions of the Ke-ahole airport aptly capture the spirit of the local venacular.

LAIE (Island of Oahu)

Hawaiian Temple-Church of Jesus Christ of Latter Day Saints (1919/78)
ARCHITECTS: Hyrum C. Pope and Howard W. Burton
LOCATION: 55-600 Lanihuli Place

Designed in the shape of an ancient Grecian cross and suggestive of ancient temples in South America, the Hawaiian Temple is constructed of concrete made of crushed Hawaiian lava.

- Coeur
  d'Alene

- Moscow

- Boise

- Sun Valley Elkhorn

- Idaho Falls

Idaho

BOISE

Boise Cascade Home Office
(1971–72)

ARCHITECTS: Skidmore, Owings and Merrill
LOCATION: North 11th Street between
Bannock and Jefferson
OPEN: During business hours

SOM's San Francisco office planned this five-story compact glass and steel box in order to keep a low profile compatible with Boise's low skyline rather than to design their more familiar multi-storied skyscraper. By raising the first floor forty feet above street level, loggias were created on all four sides—contributing to the design interest and openness of the building. Uniformity and clarity of design are distinctive elements of the impressive structure.

BOISE

Intermountain Gas Company
(1966)

ARCHITECT: Kenneth W. Brooks
LOCATION: 555 Cole Road at McMullin
OPEN: During business hours

The Intermountain Gas Company is nicely located away from Boise's busy downtown area, making it more accessible for customers. Comprised of four interconnecting units, this admirable architectural project was the recipient of the American Institute of Architects Award of Merit. A welcoming environment greets the customer with well landscaped grounds, large expanses of glass windows, and a convenient arrangement of public facilities.

COEUR D'ALENE

Hagadone Newspapers Corporate Headquarters

(1974)

ARCHITECT: R. G. Nelson
LOCATION: 111 S 1st, on Sherman at
parking entrance to N Shore
OPEN: During business hours

A remarkable 11,000 square foot building, this
newspaper facility is perched on the edge of
a pier overlooking the lake. Complementing
its beautiful natural setting, the boldly designed structure was erected on an existing
1880s railroad pier. Form and space are
uniquely arranged vertically around an airy
atrium. The Hagadone Newspaper Building
won an architectural award for its superb
detailing and imaginative solution to an
unusual problem.

SUN VALLEY

Elkhorn at Sun Valley (1973)

ARCHITECTS: Edward Killingsworth, Brady
& Associates
LOCATION: On Elkhorn Road, a few miles
from Sun Valley (follow signs)
OPEN: Rentals, restaurant, shops, grounds,
daily

Peter Walker, one of the master planners for
this large complex, said "Elkhorn's development is based on the principle of open space
and recreation as primary considerations."
Killingsworth described their approach: "We
wanted it to have as much charm as an Alpine
Village, so we studied European mountain
villages and towns, establishing those basic
elements that are so universally appealing to
people." (*Architectural Record,* January, 1974.)
The design of Elkhorn condominiums and
recreational facilities was determined by
those principles interpreted in a modern
manner.

ADDITIONAL MODERN STRUCTURES OF INTEREST

BOISE

Boise Temple—Church of Jesus Christ of Latter Day Saints (1984)
ARCHITECTS: R. Thurber & Associates
LOCATION: 1111 So. Cole Road

This one-level Temple features three unattached spires. The design is a departure from other "Mormon" temples around the world.

U.S. Court House and Federal Office Building (1967–68)
ARCHITECTS: Hummel, Hummel, Jones & Shawver, with Charles Luckman
LOCATION: West Fort Street at 6th

This uniform and precise building features a grid facade resulting from the architectural treatment of supporting framing and windows.

State Office Building (late 1976)
ARCHITECTS: Hummel, Hummel, Jones & Shawver
LOCATION: 700 West State Street

A strong cube design, the State Office Building is sheathed with energy-efficient reflective glass.

IDAHO FALLS

Idaho Falls Temple—Church of Jesus Christ of Latter Day Saints (1945)
ARCHITECT: Edward O. Anderson
LOCATION: 1000 Memorial Drive

The Idaho Falls Temple is highly suggestive of the temples of ancient Central America interpreted in a contemporary manner.

MOSCOW

University Stadium (1974)
ARCHITECTS: Cline, Smull, Hamill & Associates
LOCATION: University of Idaho campus

The huge trussed-arch roof of this stadium was erected in 26 days.

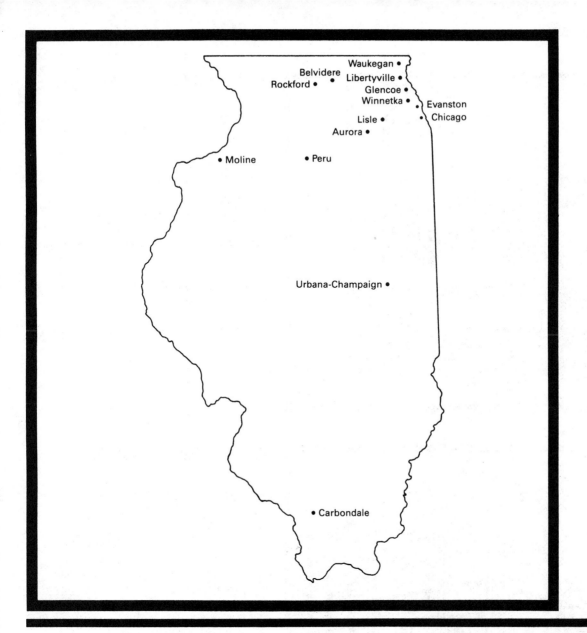

Waukegan •
Belvidere   Libertyville •
Rockford •   • Glencoe •
          Winnetka •   • Evanston
              Lisle •   • Chicago
        Aurora •

• Moline   • Peru

Urbana-Champaign •

• Carbondale

Illinois

Auditorium Building
(1887–89/1967)

ARCHITECTS: Adler & Sullivan, Harry
Weese, Restoration arch.
LOCATION: 430 South Michigan Avenue at
Congress Parkway
OPEN: During performances

Influenced by Richardson's earlier Marshall
Field Warehouse (now destroyed), with its
Romanesque detailing, the Auditorium Building was one of the first multi-use structures in
America. The massive complex, designed by
the famous early modern architectural team,
incorporated a hotel, office space, and an
exquisite theater with Art Nouveau ornamentation. The building was entirely lit by
electricity—an exciting feature for this period.
Recently restored, the Auditorium Building
was made a National Landmark in 1976.

CHICAGO

Carson, Pirie, Scott Store
(1899/1903–4)

ARCHITECT: Louis H. Sullivan
LOCATION: State Street at Madison
OPEN: During shopping hours

Coining the phrase, "form follows function,"
Sullivan felt the design of a building would
naturally unfold, determined by its function.
When ornamentation was planned Sullivan
was a master. The unique corner entrance of
this store is a fantasy of flowing organic forms
in the Art Nouveau style. The rest of the
exterior is structural and functional. Interior
detailing also employs Art Nouveau motifs.

CHICAGO

Federal Center (1963–73)

ARCHITECTS: Mies Van der Rohe, with
Schmidt Garden & Erikson, C.F. Murphy
Associates, & A. Epstein & Son.
LOCATION: South Dearborn, Adams, Clark
Sts. & Jackson Blvd.
OPEN: During office hours

Mies has masterfully designed these three
buildings, in collaboraation with others, comprising a functional Federal Center. A 30-story
unit, a 42-story unit, and a 1-story post office
are artfully arranged around small and large
plazas on a busy, tight location. An exhilerating red art work entitled "Flamingo" by
Alexander Calder adds just the right accent in
the plaza.

CHICAGO

Frank Lloyd Wright Home and Studio (1889–95/1898)

ARCHITECT: Frank Lloyd Wright
LOCATION: 951 Chicago Ave. at Forest Ave.
(Take IS 290 from downtown, Harlem Ave.
exit N), Oakpark
OPEN: Tues., Thurs., 1–2:30, Sat.–Sun., 1–4

With the completion of the Winslow House
and over thirty residential works in Oak Park,
the early modern architect's fame was secure.
During this time he developed his theory of
"organic architecture," experimenting with
many innovative ideas that influenced generations of architects. Many Wright admirers
make the pilgrimage to his home and studio
with interiors and all furnishings totally
planned by the great master architect. (A tape
is available to motorists providing directions
and information on Wright's residential works
in Oak Park).

CHICAGO

Frederick C. Robie House, University of Chicago (1908–10)

ARCHITECT: Frank Lloyd Wright
LOCATION: 5757 South Woodlawn Avenue at 58th Street
OPEN: Through special arrangement. Telephone: (312) 753-4429

Often compared to "a butler balancing trays" and "a ship with many decks," the Robie House is Wright's most important residential achievement during his Oak Park period. The house expresses Wright's view that "a house should grow out of the land." The structure incorporates open planning, large windows, walls opening onto spacious balconies, emphasis on horizontal lines, and a fireplace in the center of a cruciform plan—all Wright trademarks. The Robie House ranks as one of America's most famous modern residential accomplishments.

CHICAGO

Glessner House (1885–87)

ARCHITECT: Henry Hobson Richardson
LOCATION: 1800 South Prairie Avenue
OPEN: Tues., Thurs., Sat., 10–4, Sun., 11–5

Richardson has been called "the father of modern architecture in America." He was one of the first architects to work closely with the engineer and to seek an expression for current times. He felt the medieval Romanesque style, with its rusticated stone, heavy round arches and massive design, reflected the stability and spirit of America. Labeled "the Great Romanesque Revivalist," Richardson made these elements evident in the design of the Glessner House, his last work.

CHICAGO

John Hancock Center (1966–70)

ARCHITECTS: Skidmore, Owings and Merrill
LOCATION: 875 North Michigan Avenue
OPEN: Restaurant & observation areas on
95th floor daily

A striking 1,107-foot skyscraper of dark aluminum and bronze tinted glass, the John Hancock Center dramatically contrasts with its surroundings in downtown Chicago. A bold diagonal "criss-crossing" support system soars the full extension of the structure. Containing shops, apartments, and parking, "Big John," as it is known in Chicago, is like a wonderful mini-city.

CHICAGO

Lake Point Tower (1967–68)

ARCHITECTS: G.D. Schipporeit and John C. Heinrich
LOCATION: 505 North Lake Shore Drive, off Grand Avenue
OPEN: Lobby and grounds always open

Clad with bronze aluminum and tinted glass, Lake Point Tower appears as a magnificent serpentine sculpture on Chicago's shoreline. Nine hundred luxury apartments are contained in the 70-story structure. Many pleasantly designed conveniences for residents are incorporated into the complex, including a parking area, a restaurant, swimming pool, shops, a putting green, and a mini-park. Lake Point Tower is the ultimate in privacy and luxury.

CHICAGO

Lake Shore Drive Apartments (1948–51)

ARCHITECT: Ludwig Mies van der Rohe
LOCATION: 860-880 Lake Shore Dr.
between Chestnut Street and Delaware
Place
OPEN: Lobbies open to public daily

After making a remarkable contribution to modern architecture and furniture design in Europe, Mies left Nazi Germany in 1938, accepting the directorship at Illinois Institute of Technology. Here, in a more accepting climate, Mies was able to develop his brilliant steel and glass skyscrapers—"picking up where the Chicago School left off." Connected by a column-free canopy, these sleek, uniform, box-like units became important prototypes for similar structures around the world.

CHICAGO

Marina City (1960–62)

ARCHITECTS: Bertrand Goldberg Associates
LOCATION: 300 North State Street at
Chicago River
OPEN: Lower floors always open

A familiar landmark on Chicago's skyline, each tower has four hundred and fifty luxurious apartments on the upper two-thirds of the structure. Parking and other convenient services are located below. The distinctive cylindrical design of Marina City, with its repeating rounded form of projected balconies, has been called "Chicago's corn on the cob"!

CHICAGO

McCormick Place (1968–71)

ARCHITECTS: C.F. Murphy Associates
LOCATION: Lake Shore Drive at 23rd Street
OPEN: For a variety of events

An ambitious project, McCormick Place has been admired by critics around the nation for its compatibility with urban planning and landscape. A bold overhanging roof line reveals an intricate network of black-painted steel trusses. An enormous exhibition hall, a 4,451-seat theater and other large public spaces are superbly arranged for flexibility and convenience.

CHICAGO

Reliance Building

(1890–91/1894–95)

ARCHITECTS: Root & Burnham and D.H. Burnham & Co.
LOCATION: 32 North State Street at Washington
OPEN: During business hours

Root and Burnham, two energetic and imaginative architects, are notable for their contribution to the development of modern architecture in America. The Reliance Building, one of the firm's best known works, was an important prototype for skyscraper building. Many contemporary buildings nearby are offshoots of this structure. With its exquisite decorative detailing, the Reliance Building still commands admiration. Burnham, who continued the practice after Root's death, made this inspiring statement: "Make no little plans, they have no magic to stir men's blood."

CHICAGO

Richard J. Daley Center

(1963–66)

ARCHITECTS: C.F. Murphy Associates, Skidmore, Owings & Merrill, and Loebl Schlossman Bennet & Dart
LOCATION: Dearborn, Washington, Clark, & Randolph Streets
OPEN: During business hours

This monumental complex was formerly the Civic Center. When completed in 1966, the vast enclosure had the largest clearspans ever constructed. Measuring 87′ by 48′, the engineering marvel allowed a completely unobstructed floor space. Interiors are brilliantly planned for various functions. A stunning Picasso sculpture entitled "Woman" highlights the surrounding exterior plaza—a gift from the artist "to the people of Chicago." Close by are SOM's *CONNECTICUT GENERAL BUILDING* (1966) and the *BRUNSWICK BUILDING* (1964) on the south side of the Plaza.

CHICAGO

Rookery Building (1886–88/1905)

ARCHITECTS: Root & Burnham, Frank Lloyd Wright (Lobby 1905)
LOCATION: 209 South La Salle Street at Adams
OPEN: During business hours

The birth and early development of the skyscraper evolved in Chicago. Brilliant contributions of the Chicago School helped pave the way for further developments of modern architecture in America. The Chicago School was led by William LeBaron Jenney, (called the Father of the Chicago School), Root and Burnham, Adler and Sullivan, and Frank Lloyd Wright. Opening their office in 1873, Root and Burnham demonstrated a realistic and efficient approach to the problems of office design. The Rookery Building, with its ribbon windows and glass and iron-vaulted inner courtyard was a distinctive innovation for the period. The ground story was remodeled by Wright in 1905.

CHICAGO

Sears Tower (1971–74)

ARCHITECTS: Skidmore, Owings and Merrill
LOCATION: South Franklin, Adams, Wacker,
& Jackson Streets
OPEN: 103rd–floor observation deck,
9–midnight

A masterpiece of engineering ingenuity, the
Sears Building looms above the Chicago
skyline. Revealing the technical possibilities of
our times, the structure soars 110 stories
(1,454 feet)—is the highest structure in the
world. With its series of staggered squared
forms bound together, the tower achieves
lightness and grace. The view from the 103rd
floor is exhilarating.

CHICAGO

S.R. Crown Hall At The Illinois Institute of Technology (1955–56)

ARCHITECT: Ludwig Mies van der Rohe
LOCATION: South State Street at 34th
OPEN: During school hours

Mies was the last director of the internationally famed Bauhaus experimental design
school in Dessau, Germany before Hitler's
stormtroopers closed its doors forever. As
director at I.I.T. Mies spread the Bauhaus
philosophy and design approach, which became an influential direction of architecture in
America. Crown Hall, a masterpiece of steel
and glass construction, epitomizes the well-
known phrase coined by Mies' teacher, Peter
Behrens, at the turn of the century—"Less is
More."

CHICAGO

333 Wacker Drive (1983)

ARCHITECTS: Kohn Pedersen Fox Associates
LOCATION: 555 Wacker Drive
OPEN: During business hours

This commanding complex achieves a perfect combination of form, mass, and correctness. The sleek building is situated on the banks of the river in Chicago's downtown loop. The reflective glass curtain wall is curved, providing a unique dimension to the design. Marble, granite, and stainless steel employed at the entrance level and throughout the complex are striking. The building functions primarily as office space with facilities for retail. The streamlined building has already become a popular landmark in Chicago.

CHICAGO

Tribune Tower (1923–25)

ARCHITECTS: John Mead Howells and Raymond Hood
LOCATION: 435 North Michigan Avenue
OPEN: During office hours

For the design commission of the Chicago Tribune Tower, hundreds of entries from all over the world were received. (An especially notable architect who participated was Eliel Saarinen, the great Finnish designer, who migrated to the U.S. the following year. His entry won second place.) Hood and Howell's winning design, with its traditional overtones, was thought to be the most beautiful and effective skyscraper plan at the time. The building, with its decorative detailing, is one of the last of its type to be built in Chicago. Hood later became a prominent architect of skyscrapers in New York during the Art Deco period.

CHICAGO

Unity Temple—The Universalist Church (1906–08)

ARCHITECT: Frank Lloyd Wright
LOCATION: 875 Lake St. at Kenilworth Ave., Oakpark
OPEN: Tues., Thurs., Fri., 12–3 (Check times in advance)

This church of simplicity and clarity was Wright's first religious work and one of the world's first modern ecclesiastical structures. The Unity Temple, with its structural and functional plan, was a complete break with traditional Christian buildings—no angels, cherubs, or other religious symbols are found—which surprised the world. Interestingly, the congregation sent Wright a telegram on completion of the building, congratulating him on creating a sanctuary of peace and spirituality.

GLENCOE

Chicago Botantic Garden, Visitor's Center (1978)

ARCHITECT: Edward Larrabee Barnes
LOCATION: 1/2 miles E of Edens Highway on Lake Cook Road
OPEN: 9 to sunset, every day except Christmas Day

This complex for the Chicago Horticultural Society is based on a delightful one-story plan featuring a unique series of crystaline tent-like forms. Dazzling textures contrast with surrounding lagoons and garden islands. A magnificent fountain with 49 jets of water greets the visitor at the entranceway. The regular geometry of the design functions admirably with facilities that include an exhibition hall, exhibition spaces, and a restaurant. Wood, glass, and Chicago sewer brick are the principle materials employed, providing a sense of unity and simplicity.

GLENCOE

North Shore Congregation Israel (1970s/1980s)

ARCHITECT: Minoru Yamasaki/Hammond Beeby & Babka
LOCATION: 1185 Sheridan
OPEN: Mon.–Thurs., 10 AM to 4 AM

Yamasaki, who is particularly known for his spectacular skyscrapers around the world, is one of America's most individualistic architects. The expressive Temple Building is an unusual and impressive work. The structure is formed of sixteen dynamic fan vault shells. These vaulted forms have a glazing of translucent amber glass allowing soft streams of light into the interior space.

LISLE

St. Procopius Abbey Church and Monastery (1968–70)

ARCHITECTS: Loebl Schlossman Bennett & Dart
LOCATION: Off Maple Avenue and College Road, SW of town
OPEN: Daily—visitors welcome

One of the most commendable ecclesiastical structures in the nation, this Benedictine church is approximately 28 miles west of Chicago. The starkly simple complex is visually exciting through the use of materials, form, and light. An immense "hidden" clerestory in the nave allows natural light to wash the brick walls. The wooden trusswork is set against Douglas fir strips to create a unique composition.

MOLINE

Deere & Company Administrative Center

(1962–64/1977–78)

ARCHITECTS: Eero Saarinen & Assoc. and Roche/Dinkeloo Assoc.
LOCATION: John Deere Road, c. 7 miles SE of Moline
OPEN: Museum-display bldg. daily. Tours arranged through Administrative Center

Situated on a rolling countryside dotted with trees, this sprawling rural headquarters for Deere & Company was Saarinen's last major commission. The large complex is constructed of gold-tinted mirror glass and a steel alloy that is almost erosion free. The frankly exposed structure also incorporates a brise soleil (sun screen). The Administrative Center is linked to the other buildings by a system of bridges straddling the end of a lake. The new 1978 addition to the center is particularly notable.

URBANA-CHAMPAIGN

Assembly Hall at The University of Illinois (1959–63)

ARCHITECTS: Max Abramovitz of Harrison & Abramovitz
LOCATION: Florida Avenue between 1st and 4th Streets
OPEN: For a variety of special events

A magnificent poured-in-place concrete dome tops this functional multi-purpose Assembly Hall. It is one of the boldest structures of its type in the world. Composed of two enormous roof bowls, each 400 feet in diameter, the complex encloses an astounding interior column free space. *THE KRANNERT CENTER FOR THE PERFORMING ARTS* (1968) by Abramovitz is also located on campus. The huge five-theater structure consists of an open-air amphitheater, a drama theater, a music theater, an orchestral hall, and an experimental theater.

ADDITIONAL MODERN STRUCTURES OF INTEREST

ARGONNE (Lemont, Chicago)

Argonne National Laboratory Program Support Facility (1983)
ARCHITECTS: Murphy/Jahn
LOCATION: 9700 S. Cass Avenue, Lemont, just SW of Chicago

An excellent example of romantic High Tech.

AURORA

The Paramount Arts Centre (1931/1978)
ARCHITECTS: C.W. & G. Rapp, original, Elbasani Logan Severin Frieman
LOCATION: 23 East Galena Boulevard

At one time "Aurora's most precious jewel," this movie house of the Art Deco period has been transformed into a dazzling centre for the performing arts.

BELVIDERE

Pettit Memorial Chapel (1905/1981)
ARCHITECTS: Frank Lloyd Wright and Lisee & Biederman, Ltd.
LOCATION: Corner of Main & Harrison, Belvidere Cemetery, c 60 mi. NW of Chicago

Wright designed this small funeral chapel in 1905 for Mrs. William H. Pettit. After years of neglect, this little-known work by the master architect has been carefully restored.

CARBONDALE

Faner Hall (1975–76)
ARCHITECTS: Geddes Brecher Qualls Cunningham
LOCATION: Southern Illinois University campus (enter at Visitor's Parking Lot by stadium)

CHICAGO

Area 2 Police Center (1982)
ARCHITECTS: City of Chicago Dept. of Public Works with Murphy/Jahn and others
LOCATION: 727 East 111th Street

The color schemes and solid massing of this striking law building project the image of a "cop on his beat."

Art Institute of Chicago—New Wing (1977)
ARCHITECTS: Skidmore, Owings and Merrill
LOCATION: 100,000 sq. ft. addition at S. Michigan and E. Adams

Reflective glass and white blocks are arranged at interesting angles around open courtyards for the design of this new wing.

'BATCOLUMN' (1977)
DESIGNER: Claes Oldeburg
LOCATION: West Madison St. in front of the new Social Security Administration Building

A 100-foot-high baseball bat monument, this steel sculpture, painted gray, is a striking landmark in Chicago.

Central District Filtration Plant (1964–66)
ARCHITECTS: C.F. Murphy & Associates
LOCATION: E. end of Ohio Street on Lake Michigan

Chestnut Place Apartments (1983)
ARCHITECTS: Weese, Seegers Hickey Weese
LOCATION: State Street and Chestnut Place

An unexpected high-rise dwelling tower, Chestnut Place is designed with a flavor of Italy. Especially interesting is the lobby treatment, featuring a painted "trompe l'oeil" design of Florentine architecture by Richard Haas.

Chicago Board of Trade Addition (1982)
ARCHITECTS: Murphy/Jahn/Shaw, Swanke, Hayden, Connell
LOCATION: 141 West Jackson

Added to an existing Art Deco building, this new structure of glass and limestone is a stunning abstract update of the original building.

Equitable Building (1965)
ARCHITECTS: Skidmore, Owings and Merrill
LOCATION: 401 North Michigan

First National Bank (1968–71)
ARCHITECTS: C.F. Murphy Assoc. with
Perkins & Will Partnership
LOCATION: Dearborn, Monroe, Clark, and
Madison Streets

Gateway IV (1984)
ARCHITECTS: Skidmore, Owings & Merrill
LOCATION: 300 South Riverside Plaza

This sleek building, sheathed with reflective
glass, features a deeply undulating facade.

Hyatt Regency O'Hare
ARCHITECT: John Portman
LOCATION: 9300 W. Bryn Mawr, Rosemont,
Illinois

Illinois Regional Library for the Blind
(1978)
ARCHITECTS: Stanley Tigerman
LOCATION: West Roosevelt Road at Blue
Island Avenue

The Joseph Regenstein Library (1972)
ARCHITECTS: Skidmore, Owings & Merrill
LOCATION: The University of Chicago
Campus

This mammoth library of concrete and glass
covers a former athletic field. The geometric
massing is unique.

The Law School, University of Chicago
(1956–60)
Womens' Dormitory and Dining Hall
ARCHITECT: Eero Saarinen
LOCATION: University of Chicago campus

Two interestingly designed buildings by one
of America's most creative architects.

Madison Plaza (1980's)
ARCHITECTS: Skidmore, Owings & Merrill
LOCATION: 200 West Madison

Looming above Chicago's skyline, this metal
and glass tower features a cut-away design on
the corners and roofline.

Malcolm X Community College (1971)
ARCHITECTS: C.F. Murphy Associates
LOCATION: 1900 West Van Buren Street at
Ogden Avenue

Monadnock Building (1889–91/1893)
ARCHITECTS: Root and Burnham
LOCATION: 53 West Jackson Boulevard at
Dearborn Street

An early modern, completely structural building that outraged citizens of Chicago at the
time.

One Magnificent Mile Multiuse Tower
(1983)
ARCHITECTS: Skidmore, Owings and Merrill
LOCATION: Northern end of Michigan Ave.
(980 N. Michigan)

A striking new tower design.

One South Wacker (1980–)
ARCHITECTS: C.F. Murphy/Jahn Associates
LOCATION: One South Wacker

A spectacular new 40-story tower featuring a
3-story atrium and tiered exterior design of
unusual geometrics.

#1 Illinois Center (1971)
ARCHITECT: Ludwig Mies van der Rohe
LOCATION: Across from Wrigley Building,
400 North Michigan

One of the last works by the great early
modern architect.

Onterie Center (1981–)
ARCHITECTS: Skidmore, Owings and Merrill
LOCATION: Corner of Ontario and Erie
(inspired name of Building)

This extraordinarily designed, 58-story tower
is a culmination of the earlier Chicago School
of architecture. A concrete diagonal grid
pattern soars the height of the building.

Pensacola Place (1983)
ARCHITECTS: Tigerman Fugman McCurry
LOCATION: On Lake Michigan to Pensacola
Place

Unusual projecting circular balconies rise the
full length of the stately building, suggesting
huge ionic columns.

Playboy Building (1928–29)
ARCHITECTS: Holabird & Root
LOCATION: 919 North Michigan Avenue at Walton Street

Popular Creek Music Theater (late 1970s)
ARCHITECTS: Rossen/Neumann Associates
LOCATION: 4777 W. Higgins Road, Hoffman Estates (near Chicago)

An enormous outdoor theater created for musical performances, it is the largest facility of its kind in the world. The structure features a steel-tube space frame.

River Forest Women's Club (1913)
ARCHITECTS: L. Guenzal and W. Drummond
LOCATION: River Forest, 526 Ashland Avenue

A boldly designed board and battan arrangement by architects who previously worked for Frank Lloyd Wright.

Second Leiter Building (owned by Sears) (1889–91)
ARCHITECT: William LeBaron Jenney
LOCATION: S.E. corner of Jackson and State Street

An important early example of skeleton construction.

State of Illinois Center (1983–84)
ARCHITECTS: Murphy/Jahn and Lester B. Knight & Associates
LOCATION: Lake and Clark Streets

Although under construction, the striking new State of Illinois Center, with its tiered and sloping glass design, has already been the focus of much attention and anticipation.

33 West Monroe (1980)
ARCHITECTS: Skidmore, Owings & Merrill
LOCATION: 33 West Monroe

A unique stacked atrium design rising 28 stories high and tiered at the top.

Time-Life Building (1970)
ARCHITECT: Harry Weese
LOCATION: East Ohio and Grand Avenue

University of Illinois at Chicago Circle (1965–79)
ARCHITECTS: Skidmore, Owings & Merrill
LOCATION: West Harrison Street at South Halsted

Conveniently located about a mile and a half from Chicago's downtown Loop, the University campus was planned to accommodate up to 20,000 students. Although the buildings and campus have been criticized for an impersonal atmosphere, many of the structures have been admired for their flexibility and functional aspects.

Water Tower Place (1975)
ARCHITECTS: Warren Platner with Loebl, Schlossman Dart & Hackl, & C.F. Murphy Associates
LOCATION: South Dearborn & West Monroe

A stunning new tower complex.

Wrigley Building (1921)
ARCHITECTS: Graham, Anderson, Probst & White
LOCATION: 400 North Michigan

A good example of terra-cotta architecture popular during the early Art Deco period.

EVANSTON

Buildings at Northwestern University (1980s)
ARCHITECTS: Skidmore, Owings and Merrill, and various architects
LOCATION: 910 University Place

SOM has designed a number of admirable buildings on this well-planned campus. (Maps available at the university.) Noteworthy buildings include the *PICK-STAIGER CONCERT HALL*, the *UNIVERSITY LIBRARY*, the *FRANCES SEARLE BUILDING FOR COMMUNICATIVE DISORDERS*, and the *REGENSTEIN HALL OF MUSIC*.

LIBERTYVILLE

Corporate Headquarters, Research & Development Facility, Hollister
ARCHITECTS: Holabird & Root
LOCATION: 2000 Hollister Drive

PERU

Assembly Building for the Benedictine Society of Saint Bede (1974)
ARCHITECTS: Mitchell/Guirgola Associates
LOCATION: 1 mile W of Peru on US 6, take St. Bede turnoff

An interesting addition to an existing monastary.

ROCKFORD

The Unitarian Church (1965–66)
ARCHITECT: Pietro Belluschi and C. Edward Ware
LOCATION: Dawn Avenue & Turner St., N off East State Street

Warm and welcoming, this religious building was designed by the well-known Italian-born American modern architect.

URBANA-CHAMPAIGN

Christian Science Student Center (1967)
ARCHITECT: Paul Rudolph
LOCATION: University of Illinois campus at Urbana–Champaign

Located within the campus on a busy corner site, the Christian Science Center is shadowed by surrounding structures. Rudolph designed the complex, employing heavy concrete that is oriented inward, shutting out the noise of heavy traffic outside. Rough concrete panels were utilized both for exterior and interior walls.

WAUKEGAN

St. Anastasia (1964)
ARCHITECT: I.W. coburn
LOCATION: 1201 Poplar

A series of slender "see-through" arches project above the roofline, suggesting a traditional scheme. Coburn is known for his creative use of contemporary arches.

WINNETKA

Crow Island School (1939–40/1954)
ARCHITECTS: Eliel and Eero Saarinen with Perkins, Wheeler & Will
LOCATION: Willow Road at Glendale Avenue (c. 2 miles E of IS 94)

An early modern work by the famous father/son team.

• Notre Dame
• South Bend
•
Michigan City

Fort Wayne •

• Indianapolis

• Columbus

Bloomington •

• New Harmony

Indiana

BLOOMINGTON

Indiana University Art Museum (1983)

ARCHITECTS: I.M. Pei & Partners
LOCATION: Indiana University campus
OPEN: Daily

Dynamic, and capturing the spirit of contemporary art, the new $10 million Art Museum has been compared to a huge piece of abstract sculpture. The poured-concrete structure contains four galleries with teaching facilities, observation laboratories, and a fine arts library. A four foot square module was employed throughout the complex. Interior spaces are lit by huge angled grid skylights dramatizing strong geometric forms. Occasional punched-out window voids accent smooth flat surfaces, providing an interesting diversion.

COLUMBUS

Cleo Rogers Memorial County Library (1966–69)

ARCHITECTS: I.M. Pei & Partners
LOCATION: 5th Street at Lafayette Avenue (536 Fifth St.)
OPEN: Mon.–Thurs., 8:30 AM–9 PM, Fri.–Sat., 8:30–6

This small, but well-planned library is a contrast in comparison to Pei's more familiar, grandly-scaled structures. For the Cleo Rogers Memorial, he wisely selected a simple and direct design complementing the surrounding environment. The entry plaza, paved with red brick, extends to form the building's wall. A superb sculptural arch by Henry Moore is also found in the entry space.

COLUMBUS

Commons and Courthouse Center (1973)

ARCHITECTS: Cesar Pelli and Gruen Associates, Inc.
LOCATION: Downtown on Fourth and Washington Streets
OPEN: During business hours

Columbus has the flavor of a small town, yet has the distinction of possessing numerous buildings by the nation's leading architects. An ambitious building program was spearheaded and sponsored by J. Irwin Miller and the Cummins Engine Foundation. The results have been extraordinary. The Commons and Courthouse Center was conceived as an indoor town square. The complex is dramatically enclosed with tinted bronze glass creating a strong and appealing contrast with the traditional masonry facades in downtown Columbus. Contained within is a civic plaza and a small shopping mall.

COLUMBUS

First Baptist Church (1969)

ARCHITECT: Harry Weese
LOCATION: 3300 Fairlawn Drive
OPEN: 8–4 Monday through Friday

The First Baptist Church is an early work by the nationally-known Chicago-based architect. Highly influenced by Alvar Aalto of Finland and Eero Saarinen, Weese worked at Cranbrook Academy during its "Golden Age." The combination of rounded and triangular forms employed for this religious structure is immediately intriguing, especially emphasized by a prominent central pyramid-shaped belfry tower.

COLUMBUS

First Christian Church (1940–42)

ARCHITECT: Eliel Saarinen
LOCATION: 531 5th Street
OPEN: Daily, 8–4

Saarinen, the world-renowned Finnish architect and designer, settled in Bloomfield, Michigan where be became affiliated with Cranbrook Academy in 1923. Effectively sited in a garden setting, the First Christian Church ranks as one of the first influential works of the great architect and a significant departure in American religious building approaches. Its bold structural arrangement of forms and materials is admirable and rare during this period of time. The building is one of the first important modern structures erected in the state.

COLUMBUS

Fodrea Community School
(1972–73)

ARCHITECTS: Caudill, Rowlett & Scott
LOCATION: 2775 Illinois Street at Hughes
OPEN: During school hours

In a town boasting some of the nation's finest educational facilities, the Fodrea school is outstanding. An angled projecting roof line revealing a network of space framing, supported by large drum columns, creates a stunning impression. The metal structure, almost windowless, is strongly focused inward featuring an open classroom plan. Architects actually consulted the children during the design process. The inviting environment accomodates up to 640 students.

COLUMBUS

L. Frances Smith Elementary School (1968–69)

ARCHITECT: John M. Johansen
LOCATION: 4505 Waycross Drive, East on 25th Street (IND 46), South on Timbercrest Drive, 1st right
OPEN: During school hours

This elementary school is one of the most fascinating schools in the United States with its unusual network of ramp-tubes that connect various functional units. The experience of touring the complex is memorable and a lot of fun! The elevated library and administrative areas comprise the central core with classroom wings shooting outward. Appearing as a giant sculpture, the school is constructed of steel and concrete. The ramps and tubes are brightly painted.

COLUMBUS

North Christian Church (1963–64)

ARCHITECTS: Eero Saarinen & Associates
LOCATION: 850 Tipton Lane, East off Washington Street
OPEN: Mon.–Fri., 9–5, Sun. service at 10 AM

A well-known landmark in Columbus, by the son of Eliel Saarinen, the North Christian Church is dominated by a sharp needle-like spire that springs from a low-pitched hexagonal roof. The top of the roof contains an open belfry that provides natural lighting for the altar below. Saarinen separated the body of the church from the access that he felt had the quality of symbolically dividing profane from spirituality. The church was the late architect's personal favorite design and completed after his death.

FORT WAYNE

Concordia Theological Seminary (1955–58)

ARCHITECTS: Eero Saarinen & Associates
LOCATION: 6660 North Clinton Street
(1.6 mi. N of US 30)
OPEN: Daily

The bold triangular Kramer Chapel dominates this seminary complex designed for approximately 450 students. Pleasantly located by the lake, the chapel is placed on a raised podium that enhances the building's stature. The interior is artfully lit by a skylight running the full length of the chapel and by skillfully placed windows. Roofs of all the buildings are faced with gray tile, providing a unifying element on the small campus.

INDIANAPOLIS

Clowes Memorial Hall (1962–63)

ARCHITECTS: John M. Johansen and Evans Woollen
LOCATION: West 46th Street at Sunset Ave., at entrance to Butler University
OPEN: For performances and special events

Johansen, whose goal is to create character in his architecture, designed this multi-purpose concert hall and theater to serve both the university community and the townspeople. A dynamic arrangement of vertical rectangular boxes sheathed in limestone make up the complex. The spacious lobby and auditorium are admirable. The strong architectural treatment is executed throughout the interior and exterior spaces.

INDIANAPOLIS

College Life Insurance Company of America (1971–72)

ARCHITECTS: Kevin Roche/John Dinkeloo
LOCATION: 3500 DePauw Boulevard, SE of intersection of IS 465 and US 421., c. 10 mi. NNW of city
OPEN: During business hours

Located in a pleasant countryside setting, this exciting massing of forms reminds one of ancient mammoth Egyptian pyramids on the horizon. The much-photographed complex of buildings features mirrored glass on the sloping side of each unit counter-balanced on the other side with a concrete surface. The interior spaces and lighting are efficiently and aesthetically planned with unique results.

INDIANAPOLIS

Christian Theological Seminary (1965–66)

ARCHITECT: Edward Larrabee Barnes
LOCATION: 1000 West 42nd Street at Haughey Avenue
OPEN: Mon.–Fri., 8–5

A low rambling seminary complex, the Christian Theological Seminary is positioned in a variety of levels providing a distinctive effect. The buildings, constructed of prefabricated pebble concrete panels, are situated in a naturally landscaped hillside above the White River. The interiors are treated simply with wood and plain white plaster, evoking a mood of calm and unpretentiousness.

NEW HARMONY

Roofless Church (1959–60)

ARCHITECT: Philip Johnson
LOCATION: North Main Street at West Worth
OPEN: Daily—early morning to sunset

A decorative gate of golden wreaths introduces this uniquely designed religious structure. Unusually named, the Roofless Church seems, at first glance, to be only a roof! However, the elevated wavy structural form serves as the building's walls. Clad with shingles and supported by strong laminated beams, the inspiring church is enhanced by a surrounding spacious courtyard enclosed with brick walls.

NEW HARMONY

The Atheneum (1979)

ARCHITECTS: Richard A. Meier & Associates
LOCATION: North Street, near Arthur
OPEN: Daily 9–5

This gleaming white, award-winning structure serves as a visitor's orientation center—an "arrival" or "threshold" beginning a tour through the town of New Harmony. The building is based on a white modular unit, typically employed for Meier's structures. Inside, a remarkably interesting history of New Harmony is presented in a 17-minute film. Wood floors and a series of ramps are featured throughout the spartan space. The large complex also functions as a facility for concerts, plays, lectures, and exhibits.

SOUTH BEND

Century Center (1977)

ARCHITECTS: Philip Johnson/John Burgee
LOCATION: On the Saint Joseph River
OPEN: During business hours and for special events

This attractive and inviting complex houses a variety of cultural and civic facilities including a theater, art school, recital hall, convention center, and museum of antique automobiles. Five brick blocks are connected by glass-roofed corridors shuttling traffic to various functions. Dramatically located on the Saint Joseph River, the complex was deisgned to enhance its site. An unusual butterfly-shaped gable creates a focal point at the entrance. The interior village square has a soaring floor to ceiling glass wall that looks over the river, watergate, and waterfall.

SOUTH BEND

First Source Center (1982)

ARCHITECTS: Murphy/Jahn
LOCATION: 100 North Michigan
OPEN: During business hours

First Source Center is a geometric composition of gleaming anodized aluminum and a glass skin. Exposed space frames soar over a dazzling light-filled atrium courtyard connecting a bank, office building, hotel, and garage. This multi-use development occupies an entire block. The steel lattice trusses and aluminum and glass panels, fully exposed, are supreme examples of romantic High-Tech.

ADDITIONAL MODERN STRUCTURES OF INTEREST

BLOOMINGTON

Indiana University Musical Arts Center (1972)
ARCHITECTS: Woollen Associates
LOCATION: Indiana University campus

COLUMBUS

Note: Columbus has been called the "most architecturally advantaged small town in the United States." An efficient way to tour the scores of important modern buildings in Columbus is to begin at the VISITOR'S CENTER located at 506 Fifth Street. In addition to the structures illustrated in the text, some architectural highlights in the city follow:

City Hall (1981)
ARCHITECTS: Charles Basset of Skidmore, Owings & Merrill
LOCATION: 123 Washington Street

Clifty Creek Elementary School (1982)
ARCHITECTS: Richard Meier and Associates
LOCATION: County Road 50 North

Columbus City Hall (1983)
ARCHITECTS: Skidmore, Owings & Merrill
LOCATION: Corner of Washington and Second

The entrance way of triangular building, with its cantilevered 'gate,' steps, and curved, vertical glass-mullioned window wall is the focus of this "restrained" city hall.

Columbus East High School (1970–72)
ARCHITECTS: Mitchell/Giurgola
LOCATION: 230 South Marr Road (SE on State Road, left on Marr)

Columbus Occupational Health Center (1974)
ARCHITECTS: Hardy Holzman Pfeiffer Associates
LOCATION: 605 Cottage Road

The sleek Health Center is based on a split-level scheme that nicely conforms to its spacious setting.

Columbus Post Office (1970)
ARCHITECTS: Kevin Roche/John Dinkeloo and Associates
LOCATION: 450 Jackson Street

Cummins Engine Company Technical Center (1966–68)
ARCHITECTS: Harry Weese & Associates
LOCATION: 1900 McKinley Avenue

Fire Station No. 4 (1967)
ARCHITECTS: Venturi & Rauch
LOCATION: State Road #46, East, 4950 25th Street

Indiana Bell Telephone Company (Electronic Switching Ctr.) (1978)
ARCHITECTS: Caudill Rowlett Scott
LOCATION: Seventh and Franklin Streets

Irwin Union Bank and Trust Company (1954)
ARCHITECT: Eliel Saarinen
LOCATION: 500 Washington Street

Irwin Union Bank and Trust Company and Arcade Addition (1970)
ARCHITECTS: Kevin Roche/John Dinkeloo and Associates
LOCATION: Between Fifth and Sixth Streets on Jackson Street

Irwin Union Bank and Trust Company— Hope Branch (1958)
ARCHITECT: Harry Weese
LOCATION: East Side of Town Square in Hope, Indiana

Irwin Union Bank and Trust Company— Eastbrook Branch (1961)
ARCHITECT: Harry Weese
LOCATION: Twenty-Fifth Street and National Road

Lincoln Center (1958/1975)
ARCHITECTS: Harry Weese/1958, Koster & Associates/1975 addition
LOCATION: 2501 Twenty-Fifth Street

Otter Creek Clubhouse and Golfcourse (1964)
ARCHITECT: Harry Weese, Clubhouse
LOCATION: County Road 50 North

The Republic (1971)
ARCHITECTS: Myron Goldsmith with Skidmore, Owings and Merrill
LOCATION: 333 Second Street

FORT WAYNE

Concordia Senior College (1958)
ARCHITECT: Eero Saarinen
LOCATION: 6600 N. Clinton

INDIANAPOLIS

St. Thomas Aquinas Church (1969)
ARCHITECTS: Woollen Associates
LOCATION: 4600 North Illinois Street

With a goal to modernize this religious structure, the architects have created a spirit of simplicity associated with the early Christian Church. Dramatic colorful forms throughout are theatrical and add effective interest.

MICHIGAN CITY

Public Library (1978)
ARCHITECTS: C. F. Murphy Associates
LOCATION: 4th & Franklin St.

Interior and exterior walls of this main library branch are of fiberglass with a steel frame construction.

NOTRE DAME

Angela Athletic Facility, St. Mary's College (1978)
ARCHITECTS: C. F. Murphy Associates
LOCATION: St. Mary's College campus, near Notre Dame University

An athletic facility that boldly dominates the small campus for the Catholic women's liberal arts college.

St.Mary's College Library (1982)
ARCHITECTS: Woollen, Molzan & Partners
LOCATION: St. Mary's College campus

Complimenting the older buildings on this small college campus, the modern brick clad library features unusual zig-zag bays on the west facade.

Memorial Library (1964)
ARCHITECTS: Ellerbe Architects
LOCATION: University of Notre Dame

The focal point of this structure is an extraordinary 11-story granite mosaic. It is particularly striking when lit.

• Spencer

• Charles City

• Sioux City

• Cedar Falls

Ames •

• Cedar Rapids
• Mount Vernon

Johnston •

• Grinnell

• Iowa City

Des Moines •

• Council Bluffs

Iowa

AMES

The Iowa State Center Iowa State University (1969–75)

ARCHITECTS: Crites & McConnell and Brooks, Borg & Skiles
LOCATION: Lincoln Way or US 30 at Elwood Drive
OPEN: During school hours

A coordinated group of four buildings, this center provides facilities for cultural, recreational, and continuing educational activities. The most prominent and interesting building is the *T. Y. STEPHEN AUDITORIUM* (1969), a composition of raw concrete and tinted glass capped with a massive upswept roof. The *JAMES H. HILTON COLISEUM* (1971), a simple concrete building; the *CARL H. SCHEMAN CONTINUING EDUCATION BUILDING,* a three-storied building used for numerous functions; and a small *J. W. FISHER THEATER* (1974) complete the foursome.

CEDAR FALLS

University Union University of Northern Iowa (1968–69)

ARCHITECTS: Hunter, Rice & Engelbrecht
LOCATION: Off 22nd Street near Merner
OPEN: During school hours

This unique student union building is mostly contained underground. The creative architectural approach provides a centrally located structure easily accessible to students without sacrificing much needed space between existing buildings. A small chapel, a cafeteria, meeting rooms, an auditorium, and other facilities are conveniently arranged within the building. Natural and artificial lighting are brilliantly planned.

CEDAR RAPIDS

St. Paul's United Methodist Church (1913–14)

ARCHITECT: Louis H. Sullivan, initial designer
LOCATION: 1340 3rd Avenue SE
OPEN: Mon.–Fri., 9–12, 1–5 Sun. service

For those interested in the works of Sullivan, the great early modern architect of the Chicago School, St. Paul's United Methodist Church is worth exploring. This little-known building was one of Sullivan's last projects and many finishing details were probably planned by others. It features a 65-foot diameter half-round nave above a sanctuary containing semicircular rows of seating. Recent remodeling has given the church a pleasant up-dated look.

CHARLES CITY

Salsbury Laboratories Research Center (1968–69)

ARCHITECTS: The Perkins & Will Partnership
LOCATION: Off IOWA 14, west of town
OPEN: Grounds and reception areas open during business hours

The Salsbury Center is one of Iowa's most impressive modern buildings. Located in a rural countryside setting, the complex is planned around a nicely landscaped garden and courtyard. Administrative offices, laboratories, a technical library, reception area exhibits, and other areas are neatly arranged around the courtyard. A rotating art exhibit can be viewed in the reception area.

DES MOINES

American Republic Insurance Company (1964–65)

ARCHITECTS: Skidmore, Owings & Merrill
LOCATION: 601 6th Avenue at Keosauqua Way
OPEN: During business hours

The original firm of SOM was formed in 1939 in Chicago and today has offices around the world with over 18 full-time architects. Bunshaft, the principle architect for the American Republic Insurance Company, designed two large structural walls of poured-in-place concrete resting on four prestressed "T" Beams. These beams span 98 feet between walls, allowing a column free space. A marble entrance court features an Alexander Calder stabile.

DES MOINES

Des Moines Art Center and Addition (1948/1968/1985)

ARCHITECTS: Eliel Saarinen, original building; I.M. Pei & Partners, addition
LOCATION: Grand Avenue at 45th Street West
OPEN: Tues.–Sat., 11–5, Sun., 12–5, holidays, 1–5

An admirable older modern building by the late master teacher/architect accents the newer addition by Pei. The two buildings complement the surrounding courtyard and reflecting pool. (Carl Milles' "Pegasus and Bellerophon" grace the pool.) The new addition particularly is oriented to take full advantages of lighting conditions and is a superb background for exhibiting art and sculpture. A gleaming white new addition, designed by Richard Meier, will open in 1985.

DES MOINES

Home Federal Savings & Loan Association (1960–63)

ARCHITECTS: Ludwig Mies van der Rohe & Associates
LOCATION: Grand Avenue at 6th
OPEN: During office hours

A well articulated square structure of tinted glass and darkened metal by one of the world's most notable early modern architects. Expanding on Bauhaus architectural theories, Mies developed the steel and glass skyscraper in America. The Home Federal Savings & Loan Association, although small in comparison to most of Mies' soaring structures, is an excellent example of the master architect's meticulous design.

GRINNELL

Poweshick County National Bank (1914)

ARCHITECT: Louis H. Sullivan
LOCATION: 4th Avenue at Broad Street
OPEN: During business hours

Many admirers of Louis Sullivan seek out the five buildings he designed in Iowa. The Poweshick County National Bank is generally regarded as the best of the five. A burst of ornamentation at the entrance is tempered by plain brick walls—likened to a vault door. The other buildings by Sullivan are the PEOPLE'S SAVINGS BANK in Cedar Rapids, 1911; ST. PAUL'S UNITED METHODIST CHURCH in Cedar Rapids; the ADAMS BUILD-ING in Algona, 1913; and the VAN ALLEN STORE in Clinton, 1915.

ADDITIONAL MODERN STRUCTURES OF INTEREST

CEDAR RAPIDS

All Saints Church (1968)
ARCHITECTS: Leo C. Peiffer and Associates
LOCATION: 724–29th Street S.E.

Exposed white marble aggregate interestingly combines with tinted and stained glass for the design of this modern Mid-Western church.

COUNCIL BLUFFS

Midlands Mall (1977)
ARCHITECTS: Neil Astle & Associates
LOCATION: Broadway at Main

A bold new mall—part of an urban renewel project.

DES MOINES

Mercy Medical Plaza (1981)
ARCHITECTS: Charles Herbert & Associates
LOCATION: 421 Laurel Street

This medical office building, constructed of steel wrapped with foam insulated metal panels, provides a sleek new image to a rundown neighborhood.

Valley National Bank (1932/1978)
ORIGINAL ARCHITECT: Proudfoot Rawson Souers & Thomas
RENOVATION ARCHITECTS: Charles Herbert & Associates
LOCATION: 6th and Walnut

With painstaking care the architects have restored a gem of the modern Art Deco period, preserving the original materials and detailing. The "new look" is striking.

IOWA CITY

Basic Science Building (1973)
ARCHITECTS: Skidmore, Owings and Merrill
LOCATION: University of Iowa campus

The design began with use/relationship diagrams and a separation of program needs. The plan was also inspired by the surrounding Iowa fields.

Carver-Hawkeye Sports Arena (1983)
ARCHITECTS: CRS/Caudill Rowlett Scott
LOCATION: University of Iowa campus

The architects of this award-winning structure "achieved the remarkable feat of making a large-scale, 15,000 seat arena blend harmoniously into its wooded campus setting." (*Architectural Record,* May 1984) The truss roof resting on serpentine glass block walls is stunning.

Library at The University of Iowa (1973)
ARCHITECTS: Skidmore, Owings and Merrill
LOCATION: University of Iowa campus

A modular design plan that intersects on the diagonal.

JOHNSTON

Seed Corn Building (1981)
ARCHITECTS: Charles Herbert & Associates
LOCATION: 7000 Pioneer Parkway

Features a striking curved atrium that soars down the middle of the two-and-a-half-story space.

MISSOURI VALLEY

Desoto Visitor's Center and Refuge (1981)
ARCHITECTS: Astle Ericson & Associates
LOCATION: 6 miles E of Blair and 6 miles W of Missouri Valley

Blending into its natural setting on a waterfront, the Visitor's Center rests on pilings and incorporates passive and active solar systems. The museum houses displays from the Missouri riverboat "Bertrand."

MT. VERNON

Commons Building at Cornell College (Late 1960s)
ARCHITECTS: Harry Weese and Associates
LOCATION: Cornell College campus

With ground level entrances on all three
floors, this structure for a small liberal arts
college is a focal point on campus.

SIOUX CITY

Woodbury County Courthouse (1918)
ARCHITECTS: Steel, Purcell & Elmslie
LOCATION: 620 Douglas Street

A fine example of early Art Deco design in
America.

The Iowa Public Services Company
(1981)
ARCHITECTS: Rossetti Associates with Foss,
Englestad, Heil
LOCATION: 401 Douglas Street

Colorful beams and bands of green and
orange throughout the exterior and interior
of this complex are distinguishing and unique
characteristics.

SPENCER

Trinity Lutheran Church (1969)
ARCHITECTS: The Spitznagel Partners Inc.
LOCATION: 9th Street and 11th Avenue W.

This fortress-like religious structure features a
suspended construction above the interior
altar by Palmer Eide.

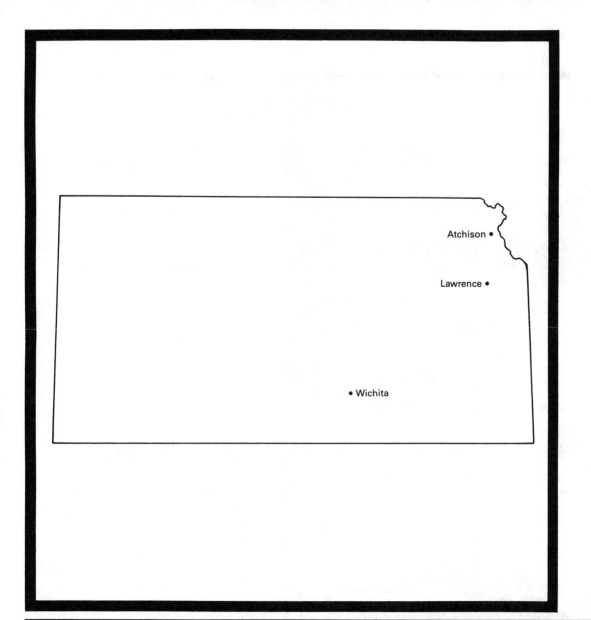

Atchison •

Lawrence •

• Wichita

Kansas

ATCHISON

The Mall (1963–65)

ARCHITECT: Louis J. Krueger
LOCATION: Commercial Street between 5th and 7th
OPEN: Always open

An unusual circumstance brought about this commendable urban renewal project. In 1958 the city experienced disastrous flooding and were recipients of Federal aid. The city took advantage of the opportunity to rebuild a pleasant and convenient mall that in turn helped to stimulate downtown business and activity. A modern arcade integrated with fountains, landscaped areas, seating, and walkways is refreshing and inviting.

WICHITA

Corbin Education Center
(1958–64)

ARCHITECTS: Frank Lloyd Wright and the Wright Foundation
LOCATION: Wichita State University campus
OPEN: During the school year

The Corbin Education Center, consisting of an esplanade and two buildings surmounted with 60-foot light needles, was one of the last projects by Frank Lloyd Wright. Wright completed preliminary planning for the building in April of 1958. The building was constructed and completed after the great architect's death. The graceful brick and concrete structure is highlighted by a polished aluminum and granite sculpture in the esplanade designed by the American artist Ernest Trova.

WICHITA

McKnight Art Center and Edwin A. Ulrich Museum of Art (1974)

ARCHITECT: Charles McAfee
LOCATION: Wichita State University campus
OPEN: During the school year

The award-winning McKnight Art Center consists of two wings connected by bridges spanning a street at the second and third floors. The east wing contains the Ulrich Museum of Art. The south facade of the museum wing features a stunning mosaic mural by the late Spanish contemporary artist Joan Miro. The 28' by 52' mosaic, entitled "Personages Oiseaux," is constructed of one million pieces of colored Venetian glass. The architect's goal was to create a new art center that would relate to the existing buildings and the rolling Kansas prairie. The facility is one of the finest in the nation.

WICHITA

Wichita Museum of Art (1977)

ARCHITECT: Edward Larrabee Barnes with Platt, Adams, Braht & Assoc.
LOCATION: 619 Stackman Drive
OPEN: 10–4:50, Tues.–Sat., Sun. 1–4:50, Tues. eve. 7–9

The original cuboid building designed by Clarence Stein in 1935 has been uniquely preserved. A stunning new cube rotated on a 45 degree angle surrounds the older square structure. Space throughout the new museum has been triangulated, creating exciting and expansive areas for viewing art. Brick, glass terrazzo, metal, wood, and fabrics are beautifully combined both inside and outside the building. "The new Wichita Art Museum is in itself a work of art."

ADDITIONAL MODERN STRUCTURES OF INTEREST

LAWRENCE

University Lutheran Church (1966)
ARCHITECTS: Uel C. Ramy & Jack R. Jones, architects
LOCATION: 2104 West 15th

This award-winning Church of exposed concrete architecturally expresses the heritage and beliefs of its faith.

WICHITA

Allen House (1919)
ARCHITECT: Frank Lloyd Wright
LOCATION: Roosevelt & 2nd Street
(Privately owned)

Farm Credit Bank Building (1972)
ARCHITECTS: Schaffer & Associates
LOCATION: 151 North Main Street

This white marble clad structure rises 10 stories high accented by deeply-set dark tinted windows.

First United Methodist Church (1960–62)
ARCHITECT: Glen E. Benedick
LOCATION: 330 North Broadway

Swirling forms and a stunning stained-glass altar wall highlight the First Methodist Church.

Fourth Financial Center Bank (1974)
ARCHITECTS: Skidmore, Owings, & Merrill
LOCATION: Broadway and Douglas

This handsome structure features an airy, beautifully lit interior atrium.

St. Francis of Assisi Catholic Church (1977)
ARCHITECTS: Thomas G. Sanders, of Hanney-Sanders & Associates
LOCATION: 861 North Socora

This bold stone religious structure makes a strong impression on its hillside setting. The interior spaces are dramatically planned focusing on the central altar.

Wichita Century Two Civic Center
ARCHITECT: John M. Hickman
LOCATION: 225 West Douglas

This massive double-decker concrete structure features conveniently arranged facilities within its circular form.

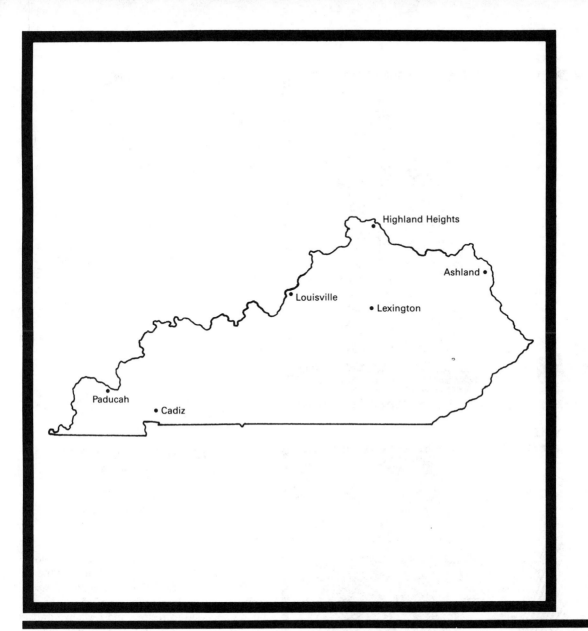

Highland Heights

Ashland •

• Louisville

• Lexington

• Paducah

• Cadiz

Kentucky

LOUISVILLE

Lincoln Income Life Insurance Building (1965)

ARCHITECTS: Taliesin Associated
LOCATION: 6100 Dutchman's Lane, NW off US 60/264 at Breckinridge Lane Intersection
OPEN: During business hours—visitors welcome

This building is one of the most unusual and delightful commercial structures in Kentucky. A lacy exterior of pink and white concrete panels sheath a marvelously constructed suspension frame. Rising 15 stories, the top floors extend beyond the face of the building and function as the supportive anchor. Founded by Frank Lloyd Wright, Taliesin Associated Architects designed this structure six years after the master's death.

LOUISVILLE

Louisville Museum of Natural History and Science (1977–78)

ARCHITECTS: Louis & Henry, Inc.
LOCATION: Main Street West from 2nd
OPEN: Daily

After years of neglect, the city of Louisville has realized the historical heritage of its Old Main Street—an old industrial district of the city. With some of the finest buildings of cast iron facades in the nation, every effort has been expended to restore and revitalize the old structures. Although the exterior of the Museum of Natural History and Science still retains its historical detailing, the effect and treatment of the interior conveys a fine contemporary look and is one of the most admirable rehabilitated buildings on the street.

LOUISVILLE

The Louisville Galleria (1983)

ARCHITECTS: Skidmore, Owings, and
Merrill
LOCATION: Fourth Ave. between Liberty St.
& Muhammad Ali Blvd.
OPEN: 10–6, Mon.–Sat.

Winner of an architectural award, the dazzling
and striking new Galleria is the focus of an
ambitious mixed-use plan incorporating two
office towers, a garage, a department store,
and the landmark 20th-century Kaufman-
Straus Building that has been recently restored. A huge, sharply angled glass atrium
provides an essential and unifying link between the buildings.

PADUCAH

New City Hall (1967)

ARCHITECTS: Edward Durell Stone &
Associates
LOCATION: South 5th Street between Clark
and Washington Sts.
OPEN: During business hours

Located in the western part of Kentucky, this
small, dignified City Hall bears many trademarks of the late architect. Stone, known for
his John F. Kennedy Center for the Performing Arts in Washington D.C., often employed
elements from the past, but in a contemporary and refreshing manner. A peristyle,
columns, atrium, and a lovely skylight compliment the elegant design.

ADDITIONAL MODERN STRUCTURES OF INTEREST

ASHLAND

Kentucky Power Company (1982)
ARCHITECTS: Kevin Roche/John Dinkeloo
LOCATION: 1701 Central Avenue

A lightly scaled structure, the Kentucky Power building has unusual glass awnings arranged on each level. The complex is attractively incorporated into a residential area.

CADIZ

Kentucky State Park Recreational Lodge (1970)
ARCHITECTS: Edward Durell Stone with Lee Potter Smith & Assoc.
LOCATION: On Lake Barkley, near Cadiz

This three-floor cross plan lodge centers on a curved waterfront extending out into Lake Barkley. The main lodge lobby soars 54 feet and is constructed of timber columns and roof beams.

HIGHLAND HEIGHTS

W. Frank Steely Library, Northern Kentucky University (1977)
ARCHITECTS: Fisk, Rinehart, Hall, McAllister, Stockwell
LOCATION: Northern Kentucky University campus

This well-planned and impressive structure has become an important addition to the university community.

LEXINGTON

Buildings at The University of Kentucky (1970–)
ACHITECTS: Johnson-Romanowitz, McCulloch & Bickel and others
LOCATION: University of Kentucky campus

This well-planned campus boasts many impressive buildings including the Patterson Office Tower, White Classroom Building, and the Agricultural Science Building One.

LOUISVILLE

American Life and Accident Insurance Company Building (1971–72)
ARCHITECT: Bruno P. Canterato
LOCATION: Edge of the Plaza at end of Main Street

This impressive building was designed by Canterato who was affiliated with the famous early modern architect Mies van der Rohe.

American Saddle Horse Museum Restoration (1977)
ARCHITECT: Lawrence P. Melillo
LOCATION: 730 West Main Street

This interesting structure was restored in an impressive updated interpretation. The museum is open Mon.–Sat. from 10–4 and on Sun. from 1–5.

First National Bank of Louisville (1970–72)
ARCHITECTS: Harrison & Abramovitz
LOCATION: Across the street from the American Life and Accident Insurance Company at 101 South 5th

This commendable building was designed by the architects of the famous United Nations Secretariat in New York City.

Humana Building (1985)
ARCHITECT: Michael Graves
LOCATION: Corner of 5th and Main Streets

This 27-story high building, clad with granite and marble, features a seven-story "porch" and a barrel-vaulted penthouse.

Riverfront Plaza and Belvedere (1973–74)
ARCHITECTS: Doxiades Associates, later Gruen Associates
LOCATION: Main Street and 5th

An integral addition of the Old Main Street restoration, this two-block elevated park was constructed along the Ohio River—close to where the city was originally founded. Spacious stepped terraces, plazas, seating, pergolas, pools, and plantings are inviting. From the plaza a panoramic view of the river can be seen.

University of Louisville Health Sciences Center (1970)
ARCHITECTS: Smith, Hinchman, & Grylls Associates, Inc.
LOCATION: University of Louisville campus, by Louisville General Hospital

Constructed of concrete elements, this medical-dental school was planned for flexibility and function.

Louisiana

BATON ROUGE

Union Tank Car Repair Facility (1958)
ARCHITECTS: Battey & Childs, Synergetics, Inc. (founded by Richard Buckminster Fuller)
LOCATION: Off US 61 near Alsen, about 12 miles N of city
OPEN: By special appointment—can be seen from gate

Many devotees of the late Buckminster Fuller drive to the gate of the Union Tank Car Company to see one of the world's largest geodesic domes—a mathematical engineering wonder developed by Fuller with a height of 116 feet and a diameter of 384 feet. This was the largest clear-span enclosure in the world at the time. An interior crane ingeniously erected the dome consisting of 321 yellow painted sections with a supportive skeleton of blue pipe framing.

NEW ORLEANS

John Hancock Building
(1960–62)

ARCHITECTS: Skidmore, Owings & Merrill
LOCATION: St. Charles Avenue at Calliope Street
OPEN: During business hours

A sculptural fountain by Noguchi provides a focal point on the outside terrace surrounding the impressive John Hancock Building. Solving the problem of the hot Louisiana sun, SOM created a well-mannered structure featuring an effective wrap around treatment of sun shielding construction—one of the first of its kind in the United States.

NEW ORLEANS

Piazza D'Italia (1976–79)

ARCHITECT: Charles Moore with Allen Eskew and Malcom Heard, Jr.
LOCATION: 400 Block of Poydras Street
OPEN: Outdoor facility always open

In a search to "remake" architecture during the last decade, the Plaza of Italia demonstrates a backlash against purism and functionalism. The innovative design incorporates elements from past architectural styles, but whimsically outlines and highlights them with colorful neon lighting tubes. (Housed inside is a German restaurant with a "deli-order.") A pergola entrance temple is constructed of open-pipe-work and concrete that appropriately introduces the imaginative circular piazza.

NEW ORLEANS

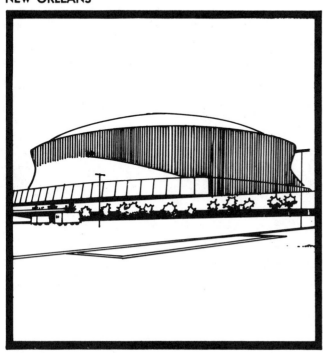

Superdome (1975)

ARCHITECTS: Curtis & Davis
LOCATION: 1500 Block Poydras St. & Sugar Bowl Drive
OPEN: For events and performances

The downtown area of New Orleans has for years maintained the character of a small European city. Today there is an interesting mixture of building types—old and new. By 1970, nearly one out of five buildings standing in the downtown area had been destroyed. The massive circular concrete superdome is a tremendous departure from the early styles and symbolizes the trend of recent modern growth in the city.

ADDITIONAL MODERN STRUCTURES OF INTEREST

BATON ROUGE

The LSU Union (1960–61)
ARCHITECTS: Desmond-Miremont &
Associates, Mathes, Bergman, & Associates,
with Wilson & Sandifer
LOCATION: Tower Drive

LAKE CHARLES

Our Lady Queen of Heaven Church
(1971)
ARCHITECTS: Curtis and Davis
LOCATION: 3939 Lake Street

This white brick, glass, and wood Church is
located in a heavily wooded area and was
designed to express "the union of the people
in social community." (*Progressive Arch.* 12:71)

METAIRIE

Latter Center West (1980)
ARCHITECTS: Skidmore, Owings, and
Merrill
LOCATION: 2800 Veterans Boulevard

An award-winning complex constructed of
prestressed concrete.

NEW ORLEANS

1555 Poydras (1980s)
ARCHITECTS: Sikes Jennings Kelly
LOCATION: 1555 Poydras

An intriguing zig-zag design constructed of
gray bands of concrete and insulating glass.

Louis Armstrong Park (1981)
ARCHITECTS: Robin Riley with Cashio
Cochran & Associates
LOCATION: 800 Block No. Rampart St.

A landscape design and restoration of four
historic buildings for a Jazz Museum. Features
a lagoon, fountains, bridges, Cultural Center
plaza, Aqueduct Fountain, walks, plantings,
restaurants, shops, and performing areas.
Open daily 8–5.

New Orleans Regency (1976)
ARCHITECTS: Welton Becket Associates
LOCATION: At Louisiana Superdome,
Poydras at Loyola Avenue

The extraordinary feature of this hotel complex is the vast interior atrium space.

**Pan-American Life Insurance Company
Building** (1980)
ARCHITECTS: Skidmore, Owings, & Merrill
LOCATION: 601 Poydras

A fascinating atrium-stacked building with a
unique pleated facade.

Tulane University Medical Center (1972)
ARCHITECTS: Caudill Rowlett Scott with A.T.
Kearney & Co., Inc.
LOCATION: Tulane University Medical
Center, downtown New Orleans by Tulane
Avenue

The stunning new Medical Center tower is
sensitively connected to existing medical
facilities.

St. Pius X Church (1966)
ARCHITECTS: Thompson B. Burk and
Associates
LOCATION: 6666 Spanish Fort Boulevard

A kaleidoscope of geometric forms topped
with a lead-coated copper roof distinguish this
unique religious structure.

- Millinockett

- Waterville

Rockport •   Deer Isle

Lewiston •

Brunswick •

Portland •

Maine

BRUNSWICK

Visual Arts Center (1980s)

ARCHITECTS: Edward Larrabee Barnes with others
LOCATION: Bowdoin College Campus
OPEN: During school hours

Situated on the oldest quadrangle of the campus, the sophisticated Visual Arts Center is a fascinating addition to its Neo-Classic neighbors. With great sensitivity to the grand old buildings, the architect has designed the new structure incorporating details that blend beautifully with its surroundings. A focal point features two free-standing Doric columns framing a large studio window and entrance to the building.

DEER ISLE

Haystack Mountain School of Crafts (1962)

ARCHITECT: Edward Larrabee Barnes
LOCATION: Far East end of Deer Isle (Maps available at the Chamber of Commerce)
OPEN: June–Sept, by appointment. Tel: (207) 348-6946

This inviting summer camp-school is artfully tiered down the steep hillside to Penobscot Bay below—beckoning the visitor to experience the walk down the stairway. Simply hewn wood planks are used for the decks and stairs. Cedar shingles are employed for the buildings. The arrangement of materials and form play up a casual and informal atmosphere enhancing the tall pine trees and natural surroundings. The school is a wonderful environment for art and learning.

LEWISTON

Bates College Library (The Ladd Library) (1973)

ARCHITECTS: TAC, Sarah Harkness, architect in charge
LOCATION: Bates College, College St. & Campus Ave.
OPEN: During the school year

The Ladd Library has received a number of architectural awards for excellence in design. Centrally located on the lovely campus, the facility holds more than 416,000 volumes and is an official depository for government documents. An important focus for campus life, the library also has a terrace that is the scene of theater and dance productions.

PORTLAND

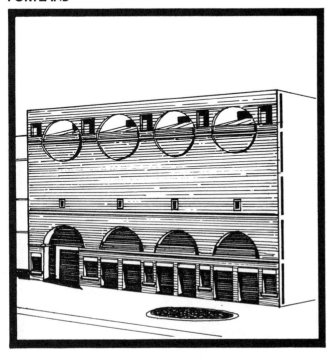

Payson Addition to the Portland Museum of Art (1983)

ARCHITECTS: I.M. Pei & Partners, Henry Cobb, arch. in charge
LOCATION: Seven Congress Square
OPEN: Summer: Tues.–Sat. 10–5, Thurs. 10–9, Sun. 12–5 Winter: Wed.–Sat. 10–4, Thurs. 10–9, Sun. 12–4

Inspired by a gift of Winslow Homer paintings, plans for a new 63,000 square foot addition to the Portland Museum were commenced. The new structure was added to two existing traditional buildings. A facade of exquisite brickwork arranged in dramatic rounded forms and arches creates a powerful image. Four huge circles along the roof's ridge are pierced in half, allowing free flow of space. Interiors are effectively lit, enhancing the exhibits. The gallery floor surfaces are of pine planking inlaid with granite strips.

ADDITIONAL MODERN STRUCTURES OF INTEREST

BRUNSWICK

Coles Tower Bowdoin College (1964)
ARCHITECTS: Hugh Stubbins & Associates
LOCATION: College Street off Maine Street

Rising sixteen stories, the Coles Tower is an admirable complex situated on beautifully landscaped grounds. Facilities for over two hundred students are provided in the dormitory, with interior spaces ingeniously planned for sleeping, studying, lounging, and socializing. Brick and white materials were employed for the building's construction.

MILLINOCKETT

Saint Martin of Tours Catholic Church (1968)
ARCHITECTS: Solomita and Palermo
LOCATION: 18 Colby Street

Inverted, funnel-shaped roofs, windowless walls of masonry, and effectively placed skylights distinguish this religious structure in the suburbs.

ROCKPORT

Samoset Resort Inn (1982)
ARCHITECTS: The Maine Group
LOCATION: On Penobscot Bay

Much of this inviting resort complex was built of wood salvaged from an old grain elevator in Portland, Maine.

WATERVILLE

Colby College Dormitories (1967)
ARCHITECTS: Benjamin Thompson and Associates
LOCATION: West end of campus, via Washington Street

Colby College Dormitories are idyllically arranged in a forest of trees, with the dormitories' windows and balconies taking full advantage of the setting.

Cockeysville • Timonium
Towson
Baltimore •
Clarksburg • Columbia
•

Prince
Frederick •   Calvert Cliffs

Maryland

BALTIMORE

Coldspring New Town (1973–)

ARCHITECTS: Moshe Safdie & Associates
LOCATION: Cold Spring Lane exit W off
Jones Falls Expressway (IS 83), N off first
right onto Springarden Drive.
OPEN: Grounds open daily

Safdie is known for his remarkable Habitat
'67, a multi-unit dwelling of interlocking
blocks, at the Montreal World Fair. For the
development of this uneven terrain west of
Baltimore, he has brilliantly designed a New
Town in a variety of stepped complexes. Set
in a park-like setting, the attractive medium
priced dwellings are surrounded by carefully
planned walkways and landscaping.

BALTIMORE

Inner Harbor Redevelopment (1970–80s)

ARCHITECTS: Wallace, McHarg, Roberts, &
Todd, Planners
LOCATION: West end of Baltimore Harbor

A project applauded as "doing more to
revitalize the Baltimore Harbor than anything
else." It is people oriented, convenient, well
designed, and relates beautifully to the
Harbor. Following are some of the finest
buildings and facilities: *JOSEPH H. RASH
MEMORIAL PARK* (1976), Architects: RTKL
Associates. Located on Key Highway. *MARY-
LAND SCIENCE CENTER* (1976). Architect:
Edward Durell Stone. Located on Light Street
at Key Highway. *CHRIST CHURCH HARBOR
APARTMENTS* (1972). Architects: Don M. Hisaka & Associates. Located across Light Street
from Science Center. (See additional listing at
end of chapter.)

BALTIMORE

Maryland Concert Center
(1982)

ARCHITECTS: Pietro Belluschi and Robert Brannon
LOCATION: 1212 Cathedral Street
OPEN: During performances (special tours available)

A magnificent new $15 million dollar Symphony Hall for the city of Baltimore. Featuring a single immense oval auditorium with 2,400 seats and a foyer, the interior of scalloped balconies projecting from cylindrical forms is stunning. The exterior cap-like structural form is clad with brick and bronzed aluminum. Belluschi migrated from Italy to Oregon in 1924 and has designed many brilliant structures since.

BALTIMORE

Morris A. Mechanic Theater at Charles Center (1966–67)

ARCHITECT: John M. Johansen
LOCATION: Charles Center—off Baltimore Street
OPEN: For performances

"The Mechanics Theater" is a jewel and focal point in Baltimore's Charles Center, an ambitious and successful urban renewal development. Strongly expressed concrete forms and planes are held aloft by concrete piers that spring outwards as the form rises. The Mechanic was "a gift to the city of Baltimore" from a wealthy real estate developer, Morris A. Mechanic, who died six months before the theater opened.

BALTIMORE

Temple Oheb Shalom (1957)

ARCHITECTS: Walter Gropius with TAC (The Architects Collaborative)
LOCATION: 7310 Park Heights Avenue
OPEN: M–F, 9–5, F Services at 8:15 PM, Sat. at 10:30

Gropius, the founder of the famed Bauhaus experimental design school in Germany (1919-1933), came to America before the outbreak of World War II, bringing his design theories to this country. The Temple Oheb Shalom is an intriguing departure from the strict purism of the International Style. (Note: Mies van der Rohe, a later Bauhaus director, designed Highfield House in Baltimore—see end of chapter.)

BALTIMORE

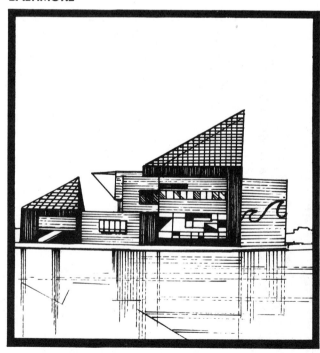

The Baltimore Aquarium Inner Harbor Redevelopment (1979–80)

ARCHITECTS: Cambridge Seven
LOCATION: Pratt Street on Pier 3
OPEN: 10 AM to 5 PM daily, 10 AM to 8 PM Fridays

A spectacular aquarium with a striking glass pyramid rooftop enclosing a tropical forest, that soars over an elaborate multi-level display system of tanks and galleries. Although the aquarium is devoted to water, the structure does not particularly relate to the surrounding waterfront site. The museum plan employs an introverted design and the visitor must go inside to enjoy the aquarium.

BALTIMORE

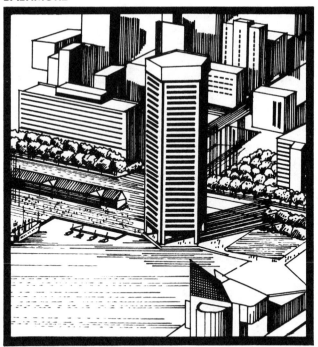

World Trade Center Inner Harbor Redevelopment

(1976–77)

ARCHITECTS: I. M. Pei
LOCATION: Pratt Street between South and Gay Streets
OPEN: During office hours

Dominating the harbor site, this thirty-two story structure is uniquely designed in a pentagonal form, supported by five enormous reinforced concrete piers.

COLUMBIA

Columbia New Town (1966–81)

ARCHITECTS: The Howard Research & Development Corporation Developers; Morton Hoppenfeld, Chief Planner: Various architects
LOCATION: US 29 (about 17 miles SW of Baltimore)
OPEN: Public welcome to browse

Conveniently located between Washington D.C. and Baltimore, Columbia is one of the finest planned communities in the nation. A projected plan of seven "villages" for 110,000 population considering all elements for human well-being and comfort was the goal of the developers. A pleasure to walk around.

ADDITIONAL MODERN STRUCTURES OF INTEREST

ANNE ARUNDEL COUNTY

Baltimore-Washington International Airport (1980)
ARCHITECTS: Ewell, Bomhardt & Associates
LOCATION: On Rt. 46, exit off I 295
Baltimore-Washington Beltway (c. 11 miles SW of Baltimore)

A striking revitalization scheme highlighted by steel space frames and colorful supporting red tile drums.

BALTIMORE

Church of The Redeemer (1958)
ARCHITECTS: Pietro Belluschi with Rogers & Taliaferro
LOCATION: 5603 North Charles Street

Known for his handsome churches of wood and glass, Belluschi has designed this church in a personal and expressive manner.

Community College of Baltiimore (1978)
ARCHITECTS: Anthony J. Lumsden of DMJM
LOCATION: Harbor campus, Inner Harbor Redevelopment Area

Dark reddish brown brick combined with concrete elements are handsomely composed for this college contrasting with traditional buildings close by.

Highfield House (1963–65)
ARCHITECT: Mies van der Rohe
LOCATION: 4000 North Charles Street at Highfield Road

A reinforced concrete structure by the master architect of the International Style. A well articulated and functional design approach.

Inner Harbor Development: Baltimore Convention Center (1977–79)
ARCHITECTS: Naramore, Bain, Brady & Johanson, and Cochran, Stephenson & Donkervoet
LOCATION: Pratt Street at Charles

Inner Harbor Redevelopment— Harborplace (1979–80)
ARCHITECTS: Benjamin Thompson & Associates with James Rouse Co.
LOCATION: Light Street and Pratt

Inner Harbor Redevelopment—Hyatt Regency Hotel (1979–81)
ARCHITECTS: A. Epstein & Sons with RTKL
LOCATION: Light Street and Pratt

Inner Harbor Redevelopment—IBM Building (1975–)
ARCHITECTS: Pietro Belluschi and Emery Roth & Sons
LOCATION: On Light St. across from U.S. Fidelity & Guaranty Co.

Inner Harbor Redevelopment—John L. Deaton Medical Ctr. (1972)
ARCHITECTS: Cochran, Stephenson & Donkervoet
LOCATION: 611 South Charles Street

Inner Harbor Redevelopment—U.S. Fidelity & Guaranty Co. (1971–74)
ARCHITECT: Vlastimil Koubek
LOCATION: 100 Light Street

Walters Art Gallery Addition (1980s)
ARCHITECTS: Shepley Bulfinch Richardson & Abbott
LOCATION: Charles and Center

Form, materials, and composition have been sensitively arranged to compliment the older 1905 structure providing functional exhibit space for one of the nation's finest art collections.

CALVERT CLIFFS (LUSBY)

The Visitors Center, Calvert Cliffs Nuclear Power Plant (1970)
ARCHITECTS: Kamstra, Abrash, Dickerson & Associates
LOCATION: c. 40 miles S. of Baltimore, on MD 2-4, 10 mi. S of Prince Frederich

This center, constructed of barn siding, cedar

shakes, and timber poles, exhibits local and geological historical objects. Open daily, 9–5.

CLARKSBURG

Comsat Laboratories (1967)
ARCHITECT: Cesar Pelli
LOCATION: 22300 Comsat Drive

COCKEYSVILLE

Noxell Office Building (1967)
ARCHITECTS: Skidmore, Owings & Merrill
LOCATION: York Road (MD 45), c. 5 miles
N of IS 695, North of town

OCEAN CITY

The Pyramid Condominum (1975)
ARCHITECTS: William Morgan Architects
LOCATION: Just N. of Ocean City

This high-density housing on the dunes is a complex V-shaped scheme of staggered pyramid structures.

TIMONIUM

John Deere Office and Warehouse
(1967)
ARCHITECTS: RTKL Associates
LOCATION: Near Baltimore, E off IS 83 onto
Padonia Road and Greenspring Drive (2.8
miles N or Beltway-IS 695)

TOWSON

Blue Cross/Blue Shield of Maryland
(1970–72)
ARCHITECTS: Peterson & Brickbauer with
Brown, Guenther Battaglia, Galvin
LOCATION: N of Baltimore at 700 East
Joppa Road.

A commendable building sheathed with reflective glass.

- Williamstown
- Chelmsford
- Andover
- Lincoln
- Salem
- North Hampton
- Amherst
- Arlington
- Cambridge
- Worcester
- Waltham
- Boston
- South Hadley
- Wellesley
- Quincy
- Holyoke
- Weymouth
- Springfield
- North Easton
- Brockton
- North Dartmouth

Massachusetts

AMHERST

University of Massachusetts

(1966–74)

ARCHITECTS: Noted below
LOCATION: North edge of town off MA 116
OPEN: During school year

Initially planned by Pietro Belluschi, the University of Massachusetts now has an enrollment of 25,000 students. Three buildings are particularly noteworthy: (1) *THE SOUTHWEST QUADRANGLE* (1966) by Hugh Stubbins & Associates, at North Hadley Road at University Drive. (2) *THE MURRAY LINCOLN CAMPUS CENTER* (1972) by Marcel Breuer & Herbert Beckhard (illustrated at left). Off Campus Center Way. (3) *THE FINE ARTS CENTER* (1974) by Kevin Roche/John Dinkeloo & Associates, off Massachusetts Avenue. An exhilerating building and dramatic focal point on the campus.

BOSTON

Christian Science Center

(1969–72)

ARCHITECTS: I.M. Pei & partners
LOCATION: Huntington Avenue at Massachusetts Avenue
OPEN: Tours Mon.–Fri. 10–5, Sat.–Sun. 12–5

This prominent Chinese-born American architect came to the United States to study at M.I.T. (1935–39) and later at Harvard. With an enhancing reflecting pool in front of the structure, the attractive Christian Science Center is both a peaceful and pleasant facility on the edge of town. A five-story unit is accented by a soaring twenty-eight story administrative complex. The bold new reinforced concrete facility is designed to harmoniously incorporate the older existing buildings.

BOSTON

City Hall (1963–69)

ARCHITECTS: Kallmann, McKinnell &
Knowles and others
LOCATION: Government Center Square
OPEN: Always open

A structure of staggering lines and forms that still stirs controversy and criticism in Boston. The megastructure features a bold rhythmic repetition of line and form that clearly delineates its various functions: offices at the top, council chamber below, and the mayor's office at a prime point on the side of the building. There are six stories on the plaza side, a popular gathering place, and nine stories on Congress Street. Across the street south of City Hall is the stunning *NEW ENGLAND MERCHANTS NATIONAL BANK BUILDING* (1969) by Edward Larrabee Barnes. I.M. Pei was the chief planner for the urban development project.

BOSTON

Faneuil Hall Marketplace Redevelopment (1978)

ARCHITECTS: Benjamin Thompson &
Associates
LOCATION: Dock Square between North
and South Market Streets
OPEN: Mon.–Fri. 9–5, Sat. 9–12, Sun. 1–5
(Market always open)

One of the finest rehabilitations of its kind in the nation and one of the most popular areas of Massachusetts. The rejuvination of the historical landmark is brilliantly executed. Well designed and inviting shops, restaurants, seating areas, lighting, and landscaping have provided a refreshing contemporary atmosphere (that has been closed off to traffic) that has not disturbed the original feeling and heritage of Faneuil Hall.

BOSTON

Federal Reserve Building

(1974–78)

ARCHITECTS: Hugh Stubbins & Associates
LOCATION: 600 Atlantic Ave. between
Summer and Congress St.
OPEN: Museum and lobby open during
business hours

A handsome and clearly stated thirty-two story structure that is prominently located along the waterfront. A unique facade of horizontal "louvres" adds design interest to the building. Connected to the spacious lobby of the high-rise is an auditorium with 400 seats and a museum. The FRB is visually stabilized through the use of strong vertical corner massing.

BOSTON

John Fitzgerald Kennedy
Library (1977–79)

ARCHITECTS: I.M. Pei and Partners
LOCATION: Columbia Point, SE of Boston
on Dorchester Bay
OPEN: Daily: 9:00 AM to 5:00 PM, except
major holidays

Commanding a prominent position on Columbia Point with a view of the ocean and Boston, this awesome structure seems an appropriate memorial to President John F. Kennedy. (Pei was selected from an impressive list of well-known American architects.) The essence of the building, which is filled with photographs and memorabilia, is its vast openess to space and light— a place that evokes a reflective mood.

BOSTON

John Hancock Building

(1969–76)

ARCHITECTS: I.M. Pei and Partners
LOCATION: Clarendon Street at Copley Square
OPEN: Observation Deck on 60th floor, Mon.–Sat. 9 AM to 10 PM

A majestic structural slab of reflective glass that has become a stunning landmark on the Boston skyline. It interestingly mirrors and contrasts with Richardson's Trinity Church and other historical neighboring buildings. An extreme design, the structure has been naturally attacked by some as insensitive and an intruder to the traditional site. (During a windstorm a few years ago many of the window panes blew out, causing even more concern and criticism.)

BOSTON

New England Aquarium

(1967–69/1971)

ARCHITECTS: Cambridge Seven
LOCATION: Central Wharf-Atlantic Avenue at Central Street
OPEN: Mon.–Fri. 9–5, Sat.–Sun. 10–6

Although the Cambridge Seven are known for their breathtaking Aquarium in Baltimore's new Inner Harbor, the Boston Aquarium's exterior makes a rather plain comparison. The interior, however, is wonderfully planned. A network of walkways and ramps channels the visitor through this engrossing aquatic display—almost like experiencing the depths of the ocean. A giant circular glass water tank with a spiraling ramp is the central focus of the structure.

BOSTON

New West Wing of The Boston Museum of Fine Arts

(1981)

ARCHITECTS: I.M. Pei and Partners
LOCATION: 465 Huntington
OPEN: Tues. 10–5, Wed.–Fri., 10–10. Sat. & Sun., 10–5

Pei, who also designed the new East Wing at the National Gallery of Art in Washington D.C., has designed this monumental new West Wing, adding 80,000 square feet to the historical art gallery of 1909 by Guy Lowell. The outstanding requirement for the architect was to provide aesthetic illumination. (The light fixtures in the central space are architecturally interesting.) The exhibitions areas are enticingly planned.

BOSTON

Public Library Addition

(1969–72)

ARCHITECTS: Philip Johnson/John Burgee
LOCATION: Boylston Street at Exeter
OPEN: Mon.–Fri. 9–9, Sat. 9–6, Sun. 2–6 except summer

A beautiful and compatible addition to McKim, Mead & White's superb Renaissance revival structure of 1888–95. The striking new wing seems like a contemporary continuation of the older building as a result of sensitivity to form and materials.

BOSTON

State Service Center (1971–)

ARCHITECTS: Paul Rudolph, coordinator, with others
LOCATION: Cambridge, Staniford, Merrimac, and New Chardon Streets
OPEN: During business hours

Considered one of Rudolph's most important and expressive projects to date, the entire complex with plazas and building heights of five to seven stories were planned to compliment the traditional urban scale. The interconnecting government buildings are artfully arranged for function and aesthetic appeal. Ramps, plazas, seating, and platings surround and complement the complex.

BOSTON

Trinity Church (1974–77/1897)

ARCHITECT: Henry Hobson Richardson
LOCATION: Copley Square
OPEN: Daily 8–4

Historians call Richardson "the father of modern architecture in America" and "the great Romanesque Revivalist." The two titles seem at odds, especially the former, when looking at the Trinity Church. Every detail of the church bears Richardson's stamp—heavy rusticated stone, Romanesque arches, heavy massive forms, simplification of detail, and an emphasis on the horizontal line. It is considered a masterpiece of early modern architecture in the United States. (The entry was finished after the great architect's death.) (Note the well planned COPLEY SQUARE REDESIGN (1970) in front of the church.)

CAMBRIDGE

Carpenter Center for The Visual Arts, Harvard University (1961–63)

ARCHITECT: Le Corbusier, with Sert, Jackson & Gourley
LOCATION: Quincy Street between Broadway and Harvard
OPEN: Galleries open at special times; ramp always open

His work in the International Style influenced generations of modern architects—Carpenter Center is his only project in the United States. (He was partially responsible for the design of the United Nations building in New York City.) "The structure of glass and concrete is a demonstration of Le Corbusier's theroies and contains a wealth of his lifelong basic ideas: the mutual interpenetration of exterior and interior space, the use of rough concrete, a ramp that connects two streets above the third floor, free-standing structural columns on each of the five floors, and "brise-soleil."

CAMBRIDGE

Crate and Barrel Shop
(1969–70)

ARCHITECTS: Benjamin Thompson & Associates
LOCATION: Brattle Street at Story
OPEN: During shopping hours

An outstanding example of combining advanced building techniques with modern materials. This engaging commercial complex features exterior walls entirely of glass stationed with no visible supports. With a variety of levels and displays, the enormous glass facade creates a giant show-piece allowing visual participation from the outside—especially at night when the interior is lit.

CAMBRIDGE

George Gund Hall (1969–72)

ARCHITECTS: John Andrews, Anderson, Baldwin
LOCATION: Quincy Street between Cambridge and Kirkland
OPEN: During school year

Built amid an onslaught of student protests, faculty opposition, press debates, and battles between the architects, Harvard's new graduate school of design still generates controversy. The strongly expressed stepped structure "trays" of glass, concrete, and steel dominates the area. The concept of the building is admirable—to provide each student with a studio space in a stimulating environment.

CAMBRIDGE

M.I.T. Massachusetts Institute of Technology
(1953–55)

ARCHITECTS: Eero Saarinen & Associates
LOCATION: Off Massachusetts Avenue and Amherst Street
OPEN: Daily from 8–8

With the design of the impressive M.I.T. Chapel, Saarinen wanted to break cubistic confines by designing a drumlike structure. The small brick building is given visual interest with a series of varying low arches around the perimeter that straddle an inside-outside reflecting pool. The focal point is a slender abstract sculpture by Theodore Roszak. The interior is simple and effectively lit. A skylight dome hovers over a shimmering grille by Saarinen's friend and colleague at Cranbrook Academy, Harry Bertoia.

Undergraduate Science Center Harvard University

(1970–73)

ARCHITECTS: Sert, Jackson & Associates
LOCATION: N. of Harvard Yard at Oxford and Kirkland Sts.
OPEN: During school year

While practicing architecture in Spain, Sert was one of the first members of C.I.A.M. (Congres Internationaux d' Moderne)—an avante garde group of modern architects who influenced a new generation of designers. In 1953, Sert was appointed Dean of the Faculty of the Graduate School of Design at Harvard, later opening an architectural practice in Cambridge. For the Undergraduate Science Center, Sert's effective plan to accommodate a variety of science departments relates both to the traditional Yard at Harvard and to the surrounding buildings.

NORTH DARTMOUTH

Southeastern Massachusetts University (1965–72)

ARCHITECTS: Paul Rudolph and Desmond & Lord
LOCATION: Off Old Westport Rd., 1.4 miles S of US 6
OPEN: During school year

The uniquely planned campus was originally intended to be a technical college. Primarily a commuter university, parking lots on the periphery were ingeniously planned by Rudolph. Clustered functional units are arranged around an unusually shaped mall opening up surprising vistas. Use of light, shadow, texture, space and form is engaging.

QUINCY

The Crane Library (1883)

ARCHITECT: Henry Hobson Richardson
LOCATION: 40 Washington
OPEN: Various hours; for information call
(617) 471-2400

In a town that boasts the birthplace and
home of John Quincy Adams is found one of
Richardson's most impressive works—the
Crane Library. Manifesting all the elements of
the great early modern architect's approach,
this building has heavy rusticated stone
construction, a massive (often photographed)
entry arch in the Romanesque style, and low
horizontal emphasis. The effect is one of
simplicity, directness, and clarity.

WORCESTER

R. S. Goddard Library Clark University (1969)

ARCHITECT: John M. Johansen
LOCATION: Downing Street at Woodland
(out on W. Main St.)
OPEN: Exhibition Room, Tues.–Sat. 9–5,
Sun., 1–5

An amazing grouping of various forms and
directions, this reinforced concrete building,
with brick infill panels, is interestingly raised
one story above the ground. The unusual
design, which often provokes comments and
comparisons, is referred to simply as a "box
of books."

ADDITIONAL MODERN STRUCTURES OF INTEREST

AMHERST

Arts Village, Hampshire College (1977)
ARCHITECTS: Juster Pope Associates
LOCATION: Hampshire College campus

This experimental arts complex features interesting solar collectors, earth berms and many innovative design solutions.

ANDOVER

Arts and Communication Center at Phillips Academy
ARCHITECT: Benjamin Thompson
LOCATION: Chapel Avenue

ARLINGTON

Park Avenue Congregational Church (1960)
ARCHITECTS: Pietro Belluschi and Carl Koch & Associates
LOCATION: On Park Avenue and Paul Revere Road

Built on a challenging site and with a low budget, this church is finely detailed and beautifully proportioned.

BOSTON

Back Bay Center (1953)
ARCHITECTS: Belluschi, Bogner, Koch, Stubbins, TAC
LOCATION: Back Bay Center Development Area

The Back Bay Center, designed by numerous impressive architects, has been applauded for its successful design through the years.

The Boston Building (1970)
ARCHITECTS: Pietro Belluschi-Emery Roth & Sons
LOCATION: State & Congress Streets (225 Congress)

This bronzed aluminum tower features cruciform corner columns.

Boston Five Cents Savings Bank (1971–72)
ARCHITECTS: Kallmann & McKinnell
LOCATION: 10 School Street at Washington

Boston University Tower (1965)
ARCHITECTS: Josep Lluis Sert, Jackson & Gourley
LOCATION: Boston University campus

Charles River Park Synagogue (1971)
ARCHITECTS: Childs Bertram Tseckares Associates
LOCATION: 55 Martha Road (Amy Court)

Distinctive fluted masonry blocks both inside and out provide a stunning background for this religious structure.

Copley Square Redesign (1970)
ARCHITECTS: Sasaki Associates
LOCATION: At Copley Square

Earth Sciences Building, M.I.T. (1968)
ARCHITECTS: I.M. Pei & Associates
LOCATION: Massachusetts Institute of Technology campus

A stately and solid tower that adequately functions for its task.

First And Second Church In Boston
ARCHITECT: Paul Rudolph
LOCATION: 50 Fruit Street

Keystone Building (1971)
ARCHITECTS: Pietro Belluschi-Emory Roth & Sons
LOCATION: 99 High Street

This tower features a series of projecting bays.

Long Wharf Marriott Hotel (1982)
ARCHITECTS: Cossuta & Associates
LOCATION: Pier on Great Cove (at waterfront redevelopment)

Dominating its prominent waterfront site, the massive brick structure suggests the prow of a ship.

Mural at Boston Architectural Center
(1977)
DESIGNER: Richard Haas
LOCATION: Visible from turnpike and West Boylston Street

This realistic and striking Beaux-Arts Mural on the west side of the building has become an interesting landmark in Boston. Haas has created a number of trompe l'oeil murals on buildings around the nation.

New England Merchants National Bank Building (1969)
ARCHITECTS: Edward Larrabee Barnes with Emery Roth & Sons
LOCATION: Behind old Faneiul Hall on Washington Street

This handsome thin-skin skyscraper is called "Barnes' Tower."

One Post Office Square (1983)
ARCHITECTS: Jung Brannen Associates
LOCATION: One Post Office Square

A brilliant contemporary office building, this structure is interestingly linked to the refurbished Meridian Hotel.

Residential Complex at the Children's Hospital Medical Center (1968–)
ARCHITECTS: TAC (The Architects Collaborative)
LOCATION: Longwood Avenue at Brookline Avenue

Sixty State Street Building (1979)
ARCHITECTS: Skidmore, Owings & Merrill
LOCATION: Sixty State Street

This granite and glass tower complex handsomely complements its traditional neighbors in downtown Boston.

West Exhibition Building, Boston Museum of Science (1978)
ARCHITECTS: Johnson Hotvedt DeNesco & Associates, Inc.
LOCATION: Science Park

This dynamic new cantilevered wing houses exciting exhibits emphasized by effective lighting and passageways. The new building is linked to the old fifties building by a new lobby.

BRIGHTON (BOSTON)

Brighton Branch Library (1970)
ARCHITECTS: The Architects' Collaborative
LOCATION: 40 Academy Hill Road, Brighton, Boston

This library was especially coordinated through use of materials and color to complement an existing older structure.

BROCKTON

Brockton Art Center-Fuller Memorial (1969)
ARCHITECTS: J. Timothy Anderson & Associates, Inc.
LOCATION: On Oak Street, adjacent to D.W. Field Park (off Rte 27)

The architects of this unique museum carefully designed the sprawling complex to complement the splendid natural wooded site.

CAMBRIDGE

A New "House" or the American Academy of Arts and Sciences
ARCHITECTS: Kallmann, McKinnell & Wood
LOCATION: 955 Massachusetts Ave. between Harvard & Central Sqs.

A gathering place for 2,300 fellows and 400 Honorary Members, this facility was designed as a "quiet country home."

Baker House (1947–48)
ARCHITECT: Alvar Aalto
LOCATION: 362 Memorial Drive

One of two buildings in the United States designed by the internationally known Finnish architect. (The other building is his Library at Mount Angel Abbey in Oregon—see page 325.)

Cambridge Rindge and Latin School (1979)
ARCHITECTS: Eduardo Catalano Associate Architects

LOCATION: Across the street from Harvard Yard

These two public schools are close to Harvard and face each other. A central court, greenhouse, and an arts center are a few of the innovative ideas incorporated into the impressive and functional design.

Cecil & Ida Green Building, Center for Earth Sciences
ARCHITECTS: I.M. Pei & Partners
LOCATION: Harvard University campus

Countway Library of Medicine
(1962/1980s)
ARCHITECTS: Hugh Stubbins & Associates
LOCATION: Harvard University campus

Faculty Office Building & Classroom and Administration Building (1971)
ARCHITECTS: Benjamin Thompson & Associates
LOCATION: Harvard University campus

Adapted to a difficult side, the brick, concrete, and glass structure projects a functional and low profile image on campus.

F.G. Peabody Terrace (Married Students Housing) (1962–64)
ARCHITECTS: Josep Lluis Sert, Jackson & Gourley
LOCATION: Memorial Drive at Sterling Street, N. of Western Avenue, Harvard University Campus

Harvard Graduate Center (1949–50)
ARCHITECTS: TAC (The Architects' Collaborative)
LOCATION: Off Massachusetts Avenue at Everett Street

Hockey Rink and Field House at M.I.T.
(1981)
ARCHITECTS: Davis, Brody & Associates
LOCATION: M.I.T. campus, close to Saarinen's Kresge Auditorium

Holyoke Center at Harvard University
(1960–66)
ARCHITECTS: Josep Lluis Sert, Jackson & Gourley

LOCATION: Massachusetts Avenue, Dunster, Mount Auburn, and Holyoke Streets.

Hyatt Regency Hotel (1978)
ARCHITECTS: Graham Gund Associates
LOCATION: Facing Memorial Drive on the Charles River

Kresge Auditorium (1953–55)
ARCHITECT: Eero Saarinen
LOCATION: Mass. Institute of Tech., by Saarinen's M.I.T. Chapel

Loeb Drama Center (1960)
ARCHITECT: Hugh Stubbins
LOCATION: Harvard University campus, close to Harvard Yard

Office Building at 1050 Massachusetts Avenue (1978)
ARCHITECTS: Cambridge Seven Associates
LOCATION: 1050 Massachusetts Avenue

Simple, yet elegantly designed, this five-story building features a glass-enclosed street level and a stunning glass studio running half the length of the roofline.

Pusey Library (1976)
ARCHITECTS: Hugh Stubbins & Associates, Inc.
LOCATION: Beneath Harvard Yard at Harvard University

Partially buried, this unusual three-level library is covered with landscaping and paths. A black steel Alexander Calder sculpture entitled "Onion" is placed at the entrance.

Rockefeller Hall (1972)
ARCHITECT: Edward Larrabee Barnes
LOCATION: Harvard University campus

Individual and group living have been carefully planned for this small and intimate brick dormitory.

Rowland Institute for Science (1982)
ARCHITECTS: Hugh Stubbins & Associates
LOCATIONS: 100 Cambridge Parkway

An admirable brick and glass complex on the banks of the Charles River, designed for scientific research.

Stratton Student Center (1965)
ARCHITECTS: Eduardo Catalano
LOCATION: At M.I.T., close to Kresge
Auditorium

CHARLESTOWN

Charlestown High School (1979)
ARCHITECTS: Hill Miller Friedlaender
Hollander, Inc.
LOCATION: 240 Medford Street (Part of
Boston, just N. of downtown)

An innovative solution for a contemporary
educational facility.

Constitution Quarters (1983)
ARCHITECTS: Anderson Notter Finegold
Inc.
LOCATION: Charlestown Navy Yard on
Boston Harbor

Tourists come to this national park to see
"Old Ironsides." Of additional interest is the
modern renovation of neo-Georgian buildings
that used to contain a foundry and machine
shop. These handsome buildings are now
recycled rental apartments surrounded by
contemporary landscaping.

CHELMSFORD

Trinity Lutheran Church (1964)
ARCHITECT: Joseph J. Schiffer
LOCATION: 170 Old Westford Road

Reminiscent of Gothic architecture, this small
church sympathetically respects its surroundings and tradition.

EAST WEYMOUTH

Immaculate Conception Church (1960's)
ARCHITECTS: Holmes & Edwards
LOCATION: 1199 Commercial Street

An undulating circular roof tops this unique
religious structure.

HOLYOKE

Holyoke Community College (1976–)
ARCHITECTS: Daniel, Mann, Johnson &
Mendenhall

LOCATION: Holyoke Community College
campus

This mammoth, totally contained superstructure was designed with sensitivity for "people
places."

LEXINGTON

Museum of Our National Heritage (1974)
ARCHITECTS: Shepley Bulfinch Richardson
and Abbott
LOCATION: 33 Marrett Road

Sponsored by the Scottish Rite of Freema-
sonry in the United States to commemorate
the 200th anniversary of the nation's founding,
this museum and library complex is nicely
situated in a neighborhood setting. The
buildings of warm red brick are topped with
steeply pitched roofs allowing for effective
clerestory lighting.

LINCOLN

The Walter Gropius Home (1938)
ARCHITECT: Walter Gropius
LOCATION: Baker Bridge Road

The founder of the Bauhaus and Chairman of
the Department of Architecture at Harvard,
Gropius built this home in the International
Style shortly after his arrival in the U.S.A.
Open by special arrangement. Call (617)
259-8098 for information.

NORTH EASTON

Ames Memorial Library (1877–79)
ARCHITECT: Henry Hobson Richardson
LOCATION: Close to OAKES MEMORIAL
HALL (1879) on Main Street

One of Richardson's first important works in
the neo-Romanesque style.

NORTH HAMPTON

Ainsworth Gymnasium (1980)
ARCHITECTS: TAC (The Architects
Collaborative)
LOCATION: Smith College Campus

Smith College Art Complex
ARCHITECT: John Andrews (Canada)
LOCATION: Smith College Campus

The Art Complex features a roof system of sawtooth skylights.

SALEM

Peabody Museum of Salem (1976)
ARCHITECTS: Philip W. Bourne with Stahl/Bennett, Inc. and others
LOCATION: East India Square

This large addition to the refined Peabody Museum of 1824 sensitively complements the traditional landmark.

SOUTH HADLEY

Willits-Hollowell Center (1976)
ARCHITECTS: Hugh Stubbins & Associates, Inc.
LOCATION: Mt. Holyoke College (Visitors Center)

Constructed of concrete, this low rambling structure was planned to complement the wooded site and stream. The attractive facility serves the school's alumnae, faculty, students, and visitors.

SPRINGFIELD

Sinai Temple (1976)
ARCHITECTS: Warren Platner Associates
LOCATION: 1100 Dickinson Street

A dramatic and elegantly detailed renovation, this religious facility is distinguished by expressively modern interiors.

WALTHAM

Brandeis University (1955–68)
ARCHITECTS: Various architects
LOCATION: Entrance on South Street

Numerous modern buildings of interest are located on this impressive campus. A brochure providing information on the structures is available at the entrance.

WELLESLEY

Mary Cooper Jewett Art Center
(1955-58)
ARCHITECTS: Paul Rudolph, with Anderson, Beckwith & Haible
LOCATION: Wellesley College campus, Jewett Arts Center, W of shopping center downtown on Route 135

Part of an impressive Art Center, the boldly designed structure houses an important collection of art.

Science Center at Wellesley College
(1975–76)
ARCHITECTS: Perry, Dean, Stahl & Rogers
LOCATION: Wellesley College campus, S off Central Street

This controversial structure with its exposed mechanical and structural elements has been compared to the Pompidou Center in Paris.

WILLIAMSTOWN

Sawyer Library (1977)
ARCHITECTS: Harry Weese and Associates
LOCATION: Williams College campus

A simple and direct library of warm brick planned to fit into a small New England campus.

WORCESTER

Downtown Redevelopment (1971–74)
ARCHITECTS: Various architects
LOCATION: Downtown Worcester

Along with Mechanics Hall, a noteworthy building for this project includes *WORCESTER COUNTY NATIONAL BANK* (1971–74) by Kevin Roche and John Dinkeloo located at Worcester Plaza.

Worcester Center (1971)
ARCHITECTS: Welton Becket and Associates
LOCATION: 10 Worcester

A vaulted skylight of white precast concrete arches and steel ribs are highlighted for the design of the brilliant Galleria.

Sault Ste. Marie

Midland •

• Muskegon

• Grand Rapids   Flint •   Port Huron •

• Holland

Bloomfield
Hills
Rochester •
Southfield •   Troy
Kalamazoo •   Ann Arbor •   Warren
Ypsilanti •   Detroit
• Benton Harbor   Dearborn

Michigan

BLOOMFIELD

Cranbrook Academy of Art

(1941–43)

ARCHITECT: Eliel Saarinen
LOCATION: 500 Lone Pine Road (1.1 miles W of US 10)
OPEN: Museum and grounds open Tues.–Sun 1–5

Cranbrook Academy is one of the finest design schools in the nation. Saarinen, the great Finnish designer, settled in the United States in 1923 after winning 2nd place in the Chicago Tribune competition. His principle work in this country is the Cranbrook Academy where he later became the director during its "Golden Age" (40s and 50s), when many prominent designers trained. This example of early modern campus planning with its waterscaping and sculpture is brilliant and had a tremendous impact on American architects.

DETROIT

Calvary Baptist Church (1980)

ARCHITECTS: Gunnar Birkerts & Associates
LOCATION: 1000 Mc Dougall
OPEN: Contact Calvary Baptist Church: phone (313) 567–4575

An award winning structure, Calvary Baptist Church is based on simple, yet dynamic form. Appearing like a superscaled sculpture rising from the surrounding landscape, the exterior treatment is of a bright yellow-orange ribbed metal. A striking interior treatment reflects the bold exterior with an immense many-faceted mirror wall. Simple forms, bright color, and a variety of texture employed within the structure give interest and a "new spirituality" to the Calvary Baptist Church.

DETROIT

Center for Creative Studies

(1974–75)

ARCHITECTS: William Kessler & Associates
LOCATION: John R Street at Kirby (behind Detroit Institute of Arts)
OPEN: During school year

Offering a Bachelor of Fine Arts degree, the Center for Creative Studies is an offshoot of the Society of Arts and Crafts founded in 1906. The building looks like a giant toy that has been assembled by a system of poles, clips, and boxes. The effect of huge concrete columns attached to modular units is bold and evokes a mood of creative activity. Visual communication both within the structure and the surrounding plazas and landscaping is artistically planned.

DETROIT

McGregor Memorial Conference Center Wayne State University (1958)

ARCHITECTS: Minoru Yamasaki & Associates
LOCATION: Ferry and Second Avenues
OPEN: Mon.–Fri. 1:30–4

With an immaculate Japanese garden surrounding the structure, McGregor is a refreshingly styled memorial named in honor of its donors. The large two-story building is superbly lit—in daylight with numerous well-placed windows and at night with artistically placed architectural lighting. The interior treatment complements the exterior with marble floors and classic modern furniture. Yamasaki's College of Education Building on campus is also notable, reminiscent of the "Steamboat Gothic" period. Precast reinforced concrete "trees" were employed throughout the facility (located at 5425 Gullen Mall).

DETROIT

Michigan Consolidated Gas Company; Other Skyscrapers of Griswold Street (1963)

ARCHITECTS: Minoru Yamasaki & Associates
LOCATION: Griswold Street from Jefferson Ave. to Fort Street
OPEN: During business hours

A distinctive building on a street of impressive structures, the Michigan Consolidated Gas Company features slender columns and pre-cast concrete sections that break the monotony of machine precision building. Other noteworthy buildings on Griswold Street include: *GUARDIAN BUILDING* (1929), Griswold-Smith, Hinchman & Grylls, at 500 Griswold; *BUHL BUILDING* (1925) Smith, Hinchman & Grylls, SW corner of Congress Street; *FORD BUILDING* (1909), Daniel Burnham, at 615 Griswold; the *DIME BUILDING*

DETROIT

Renaissance Center (1973–77)

ARCHITECTS: John Portman & Associates
LOCATION: East Jefferson at Brush Street
OPEN: Hotel always opened, others during business hours

Under the sponsorship of Henry Ford II and others, Detroit has been undergoing an ambitious redevelopment program. "RenCen" is a highly successful complex of five reflective glass and steel towers set on an enormous podium. Shops, theaters, restaurants, and the 73-story Detroit Plaza Hotel (the world's tallest hotel) beckon thousands of people each week. The dazzling architectural grouping seems symbolic of the city's future and spirit.

DETROIT

Reynolds Metals Company Building (1959)

ARCHITECTS: Minoru Yamasaki & Associates
LOCATION: 16000 Northland Drive, off Northwestern Highway
OPEN: During business hours

Yamasaki is known for his precise attention to detail. To appreciate this quality one often has to get close to the structure. This is the case with the Reynolds Aluminum Office Building with its lacy aluminum grille facade. The raised building is elaborately constructed and surrounded by a courtyard, pool, and complementary landscaping.

KALAMAZOO

The Cathedral Church of Christ the King (1968–69)

ARCHITECT: Irving W. Colburn
LOCATION: 2600 Vincent Drive
OPEN: Sun. 7:30–5:00. Various times during week

A unique building encircled by attached slender towers functions as a center for worship and the administration of the Diocese of Western Michigan. Almost 12,000 pieces of stained glass arranged in fascinating designs were employed, providing colorful lighting within. The Reverend Canon Don M. Gury nicely sums up the impressive design: "This late 20th century building of brick and glass on structural steel and concrete is a powerful statement of man's faith in God."

MIDLAND

First United Methodist Church (1954)

ARCHITECT: Alden B. Dow
LOCATION: MI 20 (Jerome Street) at West Main Street
OPEN: Mon.–Fri. 9–5:30, Sat. 9–12

A warm and welcoming religious structure, this church has its architectural roots in the organic philosophy of Frank Lloyd Wright. Natural materials compatible with the surrounding landscape are conscienciously planned. Inside, the pews are uniformly arranged facing the altar. The low pitched wooden beamed ceiling runs the length of the nave leading up to and emphasizing the altar. Over the altar, light filters through skylights highlighting the plantings and small cross hung on the wall.

MUSKEGAN

St. Francis De Sales Church (1964–66)

ARCHITECTS: Marcel Breuer and Herbert Beckhard
LOCATION: 2929 McCracken Avenue (West from two on Sherman Boulevard or Norton Avenue)
OPEN: Daily

Bold direction and form are carried throughout this unique religious building. Simple landscaping and a walled atrium harmoniously welcome the visitor into an interior that reflects the strong design of the exterior. An innovative, windowless interior space is given a sense of drama by the light source streaming only from skylights above.

SAULT STE. MARIE

Tower of History Shrine of the Missionaries (1967–68)

ARCHITECTS: Rafferty Rafferty Mikutowski & Associates
LOCATION: 326 East Portage Avenue
OPEN: July–Aug., daily 9–9, late
May–June–Oct., daily 9–6

The huge massive concrete tower is part of a Shrine that includes a church and museum honoring priests who labored in the Michigan area over three hundred years ago. The powerful geometric structure is symbolic of the spirit and courage of these dedicated missionaries expressed in form, space, and materials.

WARREN

General Motors Technical Center (1951–56)

ARCHITECTS: Eero Saarinen & Associates
LOCATION: Mound Road, North of Twelve Mile Road
OPEN: Tours conducted June to Labor Day, 10–5

This facility and Frank Lloyd Wright's Johnson Wax Factory in Wisconsin are excellent early examples of successfully planned industrial complexes in the United States. G.M. has been called "the industrial Versailles of the 20th century." Arranged on a gigantic scale, the buildings are situated around a refreshing 22-acre lake. Advanced curtain walls, complete color coordination, and other innovative design ideas were incorporated into the plan that has substantially influenced architecture in America. This impressive industrial complex was the first important work by the legendary Finnish-born American architect.

ADDITIONAL MODERN STRUCTURES OF INTEREST

ANN ARBOR

Alumni Center (1982)
ARCHITECTS: Hugh Newell Jacobsen
LOCATION: The University of Michigan campus

This fascinating building of brick and concrete block is accented by slender projecting vertical bay windows and varying horizontal bands. The entire building echoes themes of the past.

Concordia Lutheran Junior College—Missouri Synod (1963)
ARCHITECT: Vincent G. Kling
LOCATION: 4090 Geddes Road

This triangular religious structure features a striking central spire and a roof sheathed with steel.

Federal Offices (1978)
ARCHITECTS: TMP Associates
LOCATION: Liberty Street, between downtown and the University

A unique four-step floor plan distinguishes this facility for numerous United States Government functions.

School of Music Building (1964)
ARCHITECT: Eero Saarinen
LOCATION: University of Michigan

This low rambling building by the late inventive architect beautifully conforms to its natural setting.

University of Michigan Law Library Addition (1980s)
ARCHITECTS: Gunnar Birkerts and Associates
LOCATION: University of Michigan campus

A striking new library addition with spectacular glass and steel windows. The design contrasts sharply with traditional buildings close by.

BENTON HARBOR

Lake Michigan College (1974)
ARCHITECTS: Harry Weese & Associates
LOCATION: Lake Michigan College campus

A consistent use of beige brick distinguishes this small college designed for 5,000 students. The peaceful complex is surrounded by large areas of still water.

BIRMINGHAM (DETROIT)

St. Regis Church (1968)
ARCHITECTS: Brown and Deyo Associates
LOCATION: 3695 Lincoln Drive (Corner of Lahser Road) NW suburb of Detroit

Peace and tranquility are conveyed through the use of warm wood and a subtle curving design.

DEARBORN

The Hyatt Regency Hotel (1976)
ARCHITECTS: The Luckman Partnership, Inc. of Los Angeles
LOCATION: Fairlane Town Center (Off Southfield FWY to Michigan Ave.)

Projecting a feeling of welcoming arms, this stunning crescent-shaped building is sheathed with reflective glass panels.

United Technologies Automotive Group (1980)
ARCHITECTS: Rossen/Neumann Associates
LOCATION: 5200 Auto Club Drive

With a consistent use of materials and geometry, this award-winning complex dynamically contrasts with its wooded landscape setting.

DETROIT

Blue Cross/Blue Shield Service Center (1970–71)
ARCHITECTS: Giffels & Rossetti

LOCATION: Lafayette, St. Antoine and Chrysler Freeway

Center for Creative Studies, College of Art & Design (1959)
ARCHITECTS: Minoru Yamasaki & Associates
LOCATION: 245 East Kirby

The exterior of this two-story concrete framed structure is sheathed with an aluminum and glass curtain wall.

Detroit Receiving Hospital Health Care Institute (1979)
ARCHITECTS: William Kessler & Associates
LOCATION: Wayne State University

Bright color and artwork combine with the finest developments in hospital care and design in this functional facility.

Detroit Science Center (1970s)
ARCHITECTS: Ulrich Franzen & Associates, Inc.
LOCATION: 5020 John R.

A fascinating "hands on" center where the public can experience the exhibits. The experience of riding up the interior escalator is worth the visit. (Open Tues.–Fri., 9–4.)

First Federal of Michigan Main Office (1965)
ARCHITECTS: Smith, Hinchman and Grylls
LOCATION: 1001 Woodward Avenue

These handsome towers are constructed of granite and glass in the Miesian approach.

Fisher Administrative Center—University of Detroit (1967)
ARCHITECTS: Gunnar Birkerts and Associates
LOCATION: University of Detroit campus

This striking Administrative Center is constructed of stone and tinted glass and topped with a copper roof, all emphasizing the vertical form.

General Motors Building (1920–22)
ARCHITECTS: Albert Kahn Asociates
LOCATION: West Grand Blvd. between 2nd Ave. and Cass St.

One of the finest and best preserved exam-ples of early industrial building in the United States.

Lafayette Park (1956–63)
ARCHITECT: Ludwig Mies van der Rohe
LOCATION: Lafayette Avenue between Rivard and Orleans Sts.

A finely detailed and well-articulated work by the great early modern architect.

Northland Shopping Center (1954)
ARCHITECTS: Gruen Associates
LOCATION: Eight Mile Road at Northwestern Highway & Greenfield Road.

A well-planned modern shopping center.

Washington Boulevard Improvement Area (1980)
ARCHITECTS: Rosetti Associates
LOCATION: Washington Blvd. to Cadillac Square

Vibrant colors and lively forms combine to create delightful downtown designs on the mall.

CLARKSTON

Pine Knob Music Theater (1973)
ARCHITECTS: Rossen/Newmann Associates
LOCATION: 5880 Waldon Road

Exposed steel reveals the structural design for this outdoor concert building in a meadow setting.

FARMINGTON

Oakland Community College (1970)
ARCHITECTS: Perkins & Will Partnership
LOCATION: 19 miles Northwest of Detroit

An award-winning master plan dealing with space and forms in response to educational programs.

FLINT

Student Union at The University of Michigan (1981)
ARCHITECTS: Ulrich Franzen & Associates with Tomblinson, Harburn, Yurk & Associates
LOCATION: University of Michigan campus

GRAND RAPIDS

Kent County Administration Building (1969)
ARCHITECTS: Skidmore, Owings & Merrill
LOCATION: 300 Monroe, N.W.

This building is particularly famous for its
"Calder-on-the-Roof" artwork, visible from the
tops of surrounding buildings (added in
1974).

Grand River Fish Ladder (1970s)
ARCHITECTS: W.B.D.C., Inc.
LOCATION: 700 Block of Front St., at 5th St.

An award-winning complex designed as an
art form. (Across the street is the Riverfront
Office Bldg—recently renovated from an old
factory.)

St. Jude Catholic Church (1963)
ARCHITECTS: Progressive Design Associates
LOCATION: 3455 Assumption Dr., N.E.

Sharply projecting masonry forms distinguish
this award-winning religious structure.

HOLLAND

Herman Miller—Holland Manufacturing Plant (1980)
ARCHITECTS: CRS
LOCATION: 1401 South Washington

The sleek stainless steel and glass complex is
one of the finest working environments in the
country.

KALAMAZOO

General Headquarters of The Upjohn Company (1961)
ARCHITECTS: Skidmore, Owings and Merrill
LOCATION: Portage Street, c. 2 miles SE of
town

The Kalamazoo Center (1976)
ARCHITECTS: The ELS Design Group
LOCATION: 100 W. Michigan Ave.

PORT HURON

Citizens Federal Building (1979)
ARCHITECTS: Richard C. Cogley
LOCATION: 525 Water Street

Municipal Office Center Building (late 1970s)
ARCHITECT: Richard C. Cogley
LOCATION: 100 McMorran Boulevard

A structure with a diverse variety of forms and
lines.

Times Herald Building (1980)
ARCHITECTS: Roy French Associates
LOCATION: 911 Military

ROCHESTER

Chapel for The University Presbyterian Church (1964)
ARCHITECTS: Linn Smith Associates
LOCATION: On an estate by Oakland
University

The roof of this church interestingly separates
from the brick walls. Although the church
conveys a traditional feeling, the design is
very contemporary.

SOUTHFIELD

B'nai David Synagogue (1966)
ARCHITECTS: Sidney Eisenshtat with Havis-
Glovinsky Associates
LOCATION: 24350 Southfield Road

Distinctive arched walls enclose a large
column-free circular space with 70 stained
glass windows depicting the path from Earth
to Heaven.

Congregation of Shaarey Zedek (1962)
ARCHITECTS: Albert Kahn Associates with
others
LOCATION: 27375 Bell Road

A dramatic religious structure by one of
America's important early modern architects.

IBM Office Building (1977–78)
ARCHITECTS: Gunnar Birkerts and
Associates

LOCATION: 2445 Northwestern Highway at Nine Mile Road

Prudential Town Center
ARCHITECTS: Neuhaus & Taylor of Houston
LOCATION: 3000–4000–5000 Town Center

STERLING HEIGHTS

Nature Interpretive Center (1982)
ARCHITECTS: Straub Associates
LOCATION: 42700 Utica Road, 19 miles N of Detroit

Two separate pavilions with high pitched roofs house a large display room and a 40-seat auditorium. The units are connected by a "greenhouse" entrance. The buildings are brick clad with gray glass and black trim.

TROY

K Mart Corporation International Headquarters (1970–72)
ARCHITECTS: Smith, Hinchman & Grylls
LOCATION: 3100 West Big Beaver Road at Coolidge Highway (North from Detroit on IS 75 to Big Beaver Road, then turn West)

WARREN

The Warren Methodist Church (1959)
ARCHITECTS: Minoru Yamasaki, Leinweber & Associates with others
LOCATION: 5005 Chicago Road

This small church, built on a budget, features a stimulating sanctuary with suspended lighting.

YPSILANTI

Ypsilanti Township Civic Center
ARCHITECTS: O'Dell/Hewlett and Luckenback, Inc.
LOCATION: 7200 S. Huron River Drive

Many facilities contained in one large concrete building connected by a two-story skylit galleria.

ZEELAND

Herman Miller, Inc. (1971–79)
ARCHITECT: A. Quincy Jones
LOCATION: 8500 Byron Road

A number of impressive buildings by well-known architects are located at this complex. Tours by appointment.

• Detroit Lakes (Tamarac Wildlife
Refuge)

• Duluth •

• Moorhead

Collegeville •

St.
Paul
Minneapolis •
•
South Louis Park •
Woodbury

• St. Peter

Mankato • • Owatonna

Minnesota

COLLEGEVILLE

St. John's University Church

(1956–61)

ARCHITECTS: Marcel Breuer, Hamilton P. Smith and Pier Luigi Nervi (of Italy) Structural consultant
LOCATION: N off US 52/IS 94 about 12 miles W of St. Cloud
OPEN: Daily, 7:30 AM –8:00 PM.

A most astounding focal point introduces this innovative church—a mammoth raw concrete bell tower placed in front of the building. The exterior materials of the church are of concrete, granite, and stained glass with the structure located behind a hexagonal concrete grid. A baldachino is centered over the altar surrounded by 1,700 seats. One of America's most remarkable religious structures.

MANKATO

Bethlehem Lutheran Church

(1969)

ARCHITECTS: The Spitznagel Partners
LOCATION: 700 South 2nd Street
OPEN: Mon.–Fri. 8:30–12, 1–5. Sunday Services

A simply-designed brick exterior was selected for the Bethlehem Lutheran Church Building. Located in a busy business district, the church focuses attention inward. Effectively placed skylights flood the space with soft light, especially emphasizing the altar. White plaster, wood, and brick provide a clean, pleasant background. Special and unique highlights on three walls around the nave are rows of saints that have been painted directly on the brick walls by the artist Cyrus Running.

MINNEAPOLIS

Christ Church Lutheran

(1949–50)

ARCHITECTS: Eliel Saarinen with Eero Saarinen, associate
LOCATION: 34th Avenue South at East 33rd Street
OPEN: Mon.–Fri. 9–4:30, Sat. 9–12, Sunday services

A superb example of religious building in America, Christ Lutheran Church has a far-reaching impact on ecclesiastical architecture. The use of simple natural materials, creative lines, form, and direction bear the stamp of the architect's Finnish background. The church, considered one of Saarinen's finest works, was his last work. Across the courtyard is the *EDUCATIONAL AND FELLOWSHIP BUILDING* designed by the architect's son, Eero, in 1962.

MINNEAPOLIS

Federal Reserve Bank (1969–73)

ARCHITECTS: Gunnar Birkerts & Associates and others
LOCATION: 250 Marquette Avenue (Plaza off Nicollet Mall)
OPEN: Tours Mon.–Fri.

Federal Reserve Bank is one of the most innovative and eye-catching structures in Minnesota. The structure gains further attention and prominence by its position—surrounded by a spacious plaza with imaginative seating, effective plantings, sculpture, and fountains. The building features a bold catenary arch that allows the underground level to be free of structural supports. The reflective facade and form of the bank is striking. The organization of the interior is completely geared for the bank's function.

MINNEAPOLIS

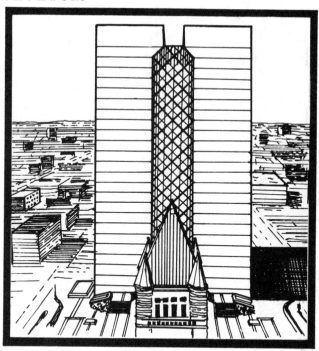

Hennepin County Government Center (1974–75)

ARCHITECTS: John Carl Warnecke & Associates
LOCATION: South 3rd–4th Avenue between 5th and 7th Streets
OPEN: During business hours

Taking a cue from the nearby IDS Crystal Court, the outstanding feature of the Hennepin Center is a brilliantly soaring enclosed interior space with bridges connecting the two units. From the light and airy atrium various government offices are arranged. The twenty-four story structure faced with South Dakota red granite is lightly scaled, achieving a sense of elegant gracefulness.

MINNEAPOLIS

IDS Building and Crystal Court (1969–72)

ARCHITECTS: Philip Johnson and John Burgee with Edward F. Baker
LOCATION: Nicollet Mall, 7th Street, Marquette Avenue, 8th Street
OPEN: Crystal Court, daily. Observation Deck on 51st floor

With the construction of the IDS Center the city was given a stunning visual dimension. Rising fifty-seven stories, the office tower is the tallest building in the state and dominates the skyline. The dazzling IDS Crystal Court provided a new pedestrian life to the city, enclosed in glass to shut out the severe weather. The IDS Building and Crystal Court are marvelous additions to Minneapolis city and have influenced architects around the nation.

MINNEAPOLIS

Minneapolis Skyway System
(1962–)

ARCHITECTS: Edward F. Baker with others
LOCATION: Downtown business and
shopping area
OPEN: Daily

This ingenious architectural system has stimulated shopping in downtown Minneapolis
through a network of enclosed elevated
pedestrian walkways and bridges that now
connect to the second floor of over fifteen
blocks in the central downtown area. Projected to include seventy-six Skyways by 1985,
these enclosed walkways are totally climatized
for comfort and protection. The Skyway
System is a new building challenge for the
architect, providing an airy and inviting means
to shuttle pedestrian traffic in a pleasant
manner.

MINNEAPOLIS

North Western National Life Insurance Company Building
ARCHITECT: Minoru Yamasaki
LOCATION: Plaza off Nicollet Mall
OPEN: During business hours

Yamasaki is internationally known for his
spectacular World Trade Center in New York
City. The North Western National Life Insurance Company, although completely different
in design approach, has been highly praised.
Slender columns form a portico rising eighty
feet high. The simple, clean white structure is
beautifully proportioned and is an excellent
example of the neo-classic modern architectural approach.

MINNEAPOLIS

Orchestra Hall (1973–74)

ARCHITECTS: Hardy Holzman Pfeiffer and
Hammel, Green & Abrahamson
LOCATION: 1111 Nicollet Mall
OPEN: During performances

Orchestra Hall became the new home of the
Minnesota Orchestra in 1974 and has become
one of the state's most appreciated buildings.
The simple unpretentious exterior belies the
brilliance within. Known for its superb
acoustics, the most prominent design feature
is the wall treatment behind the orchestra
that reaches to the ceiling and extends the
full length of the hall—clusters of projecting
cubes and forms. These white on white forms
contrast with the red carpeting and seats.
Orchestra Hall is a remarkable structure in
America and considered one of the finest of
its kind.

MINNEAPOLIS

St. John The Evangelist Catholic Church (1970–71)

ARCHITECTS: Rafferty Rafferty Mikutowski &
Associates
LOCATION: 1428 Preston Lane at Interlachen
Road (S off Excelsior Ave., just W of
Meadowbrook Golf Course)
OPEN: Mon.–Sat. 7:30–6. Sunday services

Located in a quiet residential neighborhood,
the St. John Church is sympathetic with its
surroundings in scale, design, approach, and
materials. The most dynamic impact of the
structure is the play of form and direction
that changes at every turn. Plain and white-
painted brick walls combine with a bold
wood ceiling to carry out the exterior theme.
The lighting is unusual, emphasizing various
functional areas including the clean and
simple raised altar space.

MINNEAPOLIS

Tyrone Guthrie Theater
(1962–63)

ARCHITECTS: Ralph Rapson & Associates
LOCATION: 725 Vineland Place off
Hennepin Avenue
OPEN: For performances

With the completion of this theater, cultural activity in the Twin Cities was stimulated. The bannered glass and steel cube building serves as a symbol to the theater-going society. Consulting with the actor, Sir Tyrone Guthrie, Rapson created an intimate interior space where the audience is never more than 15 seats away from the stage. The entire complex was inspired by ancient Grecian and Shakespearean theater prototypes.

MINNEAPOLIS

Walker Art Center (1969–71)

ARCHITECT: Edward Larrabee Barnes
LOCATION: Vineland Place at Hennepin
Avenue
OPEN: Tues.–Sat. 10–5, Sun. 11–5

Located next to the Guthrie Theater, this new purple brick structure replaces an existing art gallery. The Walker Art Center shares a lobby with the Guthrie Theater, thus linking the two arts. The design scheme of the structure features a helical sequence of galleries terminating in a series of rooftop terraces. White terrazzo floors, white walls, and white ceilings combined with flexible and effective lighting create an excellent background for the art collection.

MOORHEAD

Church of The Good Shepherd (1967–68)

ARCHITECTS: Sovik, Mathre & Madson
LOCATION: 16th Avenue South at South 6th Street
OPEN: Mon.–Fri, 8–12, 1–5. Sunday services

This quiet peaceful religious haven is located close to the Red River and the North Dakota border. The restrained architectural approach is admirable. Simplicity of materials and form are organized in a manner that still evokes visual design interest. Brick walls and a wood beamed ceiling create a harmonious background for maintaining a serene atmosphere. Both artificial and natural lighting are effectively handled.

OWATONNA

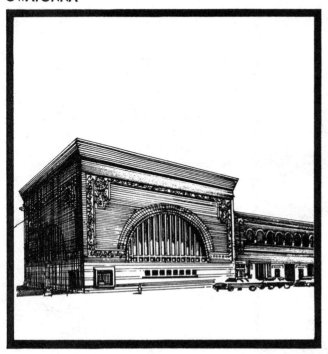

Northwestern National Bank of Owatonna (1907–08)

ARCHITECT: Louis Sullivan
LOCATION: Broadway and Cedar Street
OPEN: During banking hours

Looking like a miniature of Sullivan's famous Transportation Building of 1893 in Chicago, the Northwestern National Bank is a jewel. Located prominently on a corner site, the simple brick facade features a bold arch set within a square with repeating window squares carrying out the theme. A number of Minnesota's architects were trained by the master of early modern architecture and had an important impact in the state.

ST. PAUL

Mount Zion Temple (1950–54)

ARCHITECT: Eric Mendelsohn
LOCATION: Summit Avenue at South Hamline
OPEN: Tours arranged by appointment: Phone (616) 698–3881

An inspiring and serene religious building, Mount Zion Temple was designed by the famous German Expressionist architect who fled Nazi tyranny and settled in San Francisco. Mount Zion Temple is a structure of cubic forms that emphasize the sanctuary's loftiness by means of exterior ribs or buttresses. The copper sheathing of the sanctuary strikingly contrasts with the salmon brick of the lower buildings. The Temple was completed one year after the architect's death.

ST. PAUL

Town Square Park, Town Square and Radisson Plaza
(1970s and 80s)

ARCHITECTS: Various, including BWBR
LOCATION: Between 6th & 8th, and Minnesota & Roberts Sts.
OPEN: Business hours; Plaza always

"The new heart of the skyway system is Town Square Park, a concrete and glass marriage of a pedestrian street mall, a recreation center and a downtown shopping center. Water cascades in controlled streams from the top level park space down three stories past walkways escalators and seating nooks into pools surrounding eating platforms on the food and beverage eating level of the multi-level interior space." AM (*Architecture Minnesota*) April/May 1981. MSAIA Guidebook, These areas provide both visual enjoyment and efficient space planning. The new Town Square Development is connected to the Radisson Plaza Hotel on the second floor.

ADDITIONAL MODERN STRUCTURES OF INTEREST

COLLEGEVILLE
Alcuin College Library (1967)
ARCHITECT: Marcel Breuer
LOCATION: By St. John's University Church

St. John's Preparatory School (1961–62)
ARCHITECTS: Hanson & Michelson
LOCATION: By St. John's University Library
(see illustration at left)

DETROIT LAKES
Tamarac Interpretive Center (Tamarac Wildlife Refuge) (1981)
ARCHITECTS: Leonard Parker Associates
LOCATION: Near Detroits Lake, National Wildlife Refuge

Built for the U.S. Department of the Interior, Fish and Wildlife Service, this structure of natural red cedar siding effectively fits into its heavily wooded site. Inside, space is provided for an auditorium, a theater and offices.

DULUTH
Duluth Public Library (1980)
ARCHITECTS: Gunnar Birkerts & Associates
LOCATION: 520 West Superior Street

EDEN PRAIRIE; MINNEAPOLIS
International Headquarters for Gelco Corporation (1978)
ARCHITECTS: The Leonard Parker Associates
LOCATION: 1 Gelco Road, suburb of Minneapolis

This handsome glass-clad building interestingly tiers down its beautiful countryside setting.

MINNEAPOLIS
Addition to The Minneapolis Institute of Arts (1975)
ARCHITECT: Kenzo Tange (Japan)
LOCATION: 2400 3rd Avenue South

This highly criticized structure is the great modern Japanese architect's first work in the United States. The building of bronze-tinted glass and white-glazed brick functions as a museum, theater, and college buildings.

American Indian Center (1975)
ARCHITECTS: The Hodne-Stageberg Partnership
LOCATION: Franklin and Bloomington

Butler Square (1906/1975)
ARCHITECTS: Muller, Hanson, Westerbeck, Bell
LOCATION: North 1st Avenue at North 6th Street

An interesting rehabilitation project.

Cedar Riverside (1971–80)
ARCHITECTS: Ralph Rapson & Associates
LOCATION: Cedar Ave., between South 4th and 6th Streets

An excellent, large, living facility complex.

Dain Tower (The Old Rand Tower) (1928–30)
ARCHITECTS: Holabird and Root
LOCATION: Corner of Marquette and 6th Street

An outstanding example of Art Deco architecture

The Foshay Tower (1927–29)
ARCHITECTS: Magney & Tusler
LOCATION: 821 Marquette Avenue

This structure, influenced by the ancient Egyptian obelisk, is a good example of the Art Deco period.

Hennepin Center for The Arts (remodelled in 1978–79)
LOCATION: 528 Hennepin and North 6th Street

This newly renovated structure used to be the old Mason Temple.

Lutheran Brotherhood Building (1981)
ARCHITECTS: Skidmore, Owings and Merrill

LOCATION: 4th Avenue between 6th & 7th Streets

A striking staggered bronze tinted glass structure

Nicollet Avenue Mall (1966–68)
ARCHITECTS: Lawrence Halprin & Associates
LOCATION: From Washington Avenue to 10th Street

This well designed pedestrian mall is linked to many of the finest modern structures in Minneapolis.

One Pillsbury Center (1980)
ARCHITECTS: Skidmore, Owings and Merrill
LOCATION: Between 2nd and 3rd Avenue and between 5th and 6th Sts.

A stately travertine and granite tower.

Southdale Center (1954–56)
ARCHITECTS: Gruen Associates
LOCATION: Off MINN 62 at France Ave. and West 66th Street

An impressive, large shopping mall.

Williamson Hall (1975)
ARCHITECTS: Myers and Bennett Architects/ BRW
LOCATION: University of Minnesota Minneapolis campus

An award-winning underground bookstore.

ST. LOUIS PARK

Westwood Lutheran Church of St. Louis (1964)
ARCHITECTS: Sovik Mathre and Madson
LOCATION: 9001 South Cedar Lake Road

Creative use of brick, concrete, quarry tile, and oak building materials are expressed with simplicity and clarity for this award-winning structure.

ST. PAUL

Adult Detention Center (1980)
ARCHITECTS: Wold Association/Gruzen Associates

LOCATION: By Mississippi River by Kellogg Blvd. and Wabasha

One of the finest designed facilities of its type in the nation.

Bethel Theological Seminary (1966–67)
ARCHITECTS: Hammel, Green & Abrahamson
LOCATION: West off MINN 51, South of IS 694 at Valentine Lake

St. John the Baptist Church (1968–69)
ARCHITECTS: Shifflet, Hutchinson & Associates
LOCATION: 812 1st Ave. NW, near IS 694 Interchange with IS 35W in St. Paul (New Brighton)

St. Thomas Aquinas Church (1968–69)
ARCHITECTS: Ralph Rapson & Associates
LOCATION: 9th Avenue at Ashland

Science Museum of Minnesota (1980)
ARCHITECTS: Hammel, Green, and Abrahamson
LOCATION: Between Wabasha and St. Peter Streets, a block and a half North of 8th Street

A marvelous museum featuring many well designed and interesting modern facilities and exhibits.

Town Square (1981)
ARCHITECTS: Skidmore, Owings and Merrill
LOCATION: Bounded by Cedar, Minnesota, Sixth, and Eighth Streets

An admirable mixed-use development covering two major blocks.

(An excellent guide to many new structures in the Minneapolis/St. Paul area has been compiled by *ARCHITECTURE MINNESOTA* at 314 Clifton Avenue, Minneapolis, MN, 55403)

ST. PETER

First Lutheran Church (1963–65)
ARCHITECTS: The Spitznagel Partners, Inc.
LOCATION: 1114 W. Traverse Road, c. 60 miles S. of Minneapolis

This admirable church, designed by the well-known South Dakota firm, features an interesting brick bas-relief by Robert Aldern on the altar wall.

WINONA

Merchants National Bank (1911–12)
ARCHITECTS: Purcell, Feick & Elmslie
LOCATION: Lafayette Street at 3rd

An important work by these architects who trained with Louis Sullivan in Chicago.

WOODBURY

Western Life Insurance Headquarters (1980)
ARCHITECTS: Ellerbe Associates
LOCATION: Suburb SE of St. Paul

This commendable office complex is energy efficient and nicely located in a wooded area on the outskirts of town.

Clinton •
• Jackson

Biloxi •

Mississippi

BILOXI

Biloxi Public Library and Cultural Center (1976–77)

ARCHITECTS: MLTW/Turnbull Associates
LOCATION: 217 Lameuse Street
OPEN: Mon.–Wed., 9–8:30, Thurs.–Sat., 9–5:30

The San Francisco firm of MLTW/Turnbull Associates was selected to design the city's new library and museum. The innovative exterior design recalls the simple Spanish Colonial style of the past in an updated fresh contemporary manner. The approach is particularly apparent at the entrance archway. The interior spaces are superbly arranged in a series of unfolding forms and angles throughout the complex.

BILOXI

Broadwater Beach Marina (1965)

ENGINEER: T. M. Dorsett, Jr.
LOCATION: On US 90 opposite Broadwater Beach Hotel
OPEN: Daily

Today Biloxi attracts many tourists who enjoy Mississippi's historical past. A number of new buildings have been designed during the past decade that are particularly noteworthy. Of interest is the Broadwater Beach Marina, an inviting and delightful area of pavilions surrounding three sides of a square inlet of water. The design is light and graceful with functional facilities for boats conveniently located. The Marina has 136 berths, most of them covered, and with electrical outlets.

JACKSON

Dormitories and Library at Tougaloo College (1971–73)

ARCHITECTS: Gunnar Birkerts & Associates
LOCATION: County Line Road (West off Tougaloo exit off IS55), about 9 miles N of Jackson at Tougaloo
OPEN: During the school year

Part of an ambitious building program on campus, the L. Zenobia Coleman Library is situated between the two dormatories. The architects wisely employed similar architectural features to unify the entire string of buildings. Reinforced concrete piers not only support the structures, but become an attractive design element. Landscaping and walkways conveniently link the campus to the new structures adding to the existing harmony.

JACKSON

State Office Complex (1970–72)

ARCHITECTS: Barlow & Plunkett
LOCATION: High Street at President
OPEN: During business hours

Situated across from the State Capitol (built in 1903, and patterned after the nation's Capitol in Washington D.C.), the new State Office Complex is a complete design departure. Simple, direct, and uniform, the modern buildings consist of the twenty-story Walter Sillers State Office Building and the lower structure housing the State Supreme Court. The complex is attractively set on a raised plaza physically linking the dignified buildings.

ADDITIONAL MODERN STRUCTURES OF INTEREST

CLINTON

Christ Community Church (1981)
ARCHITECTS: Goodman & Mockbee
LOCATION: 1704 Old Vicksburg Road

Farm buildings and barns inspired the design
approach of this simply and interestingly
formed religious structure.

Kirksville •

• Kansas City

Jefferson City •

St. Louis •

Missouri

KANSAS CITY

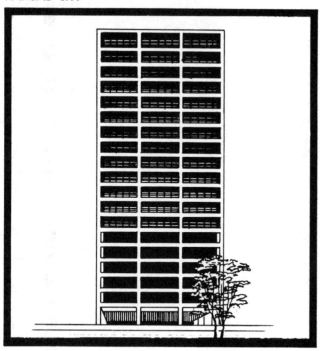

Business Men's Assurance Company Building (1962–63)

ARCHITECTS: Skidmore, Owings and Merrill
LOCATION: Penn Valley Park, SW Trafficway at 31st Street
OPEN: During business hours

A nineteen-story skyscraper by SOM's Chicago office, this building is regarded as one of their strongest and finest projects. With an open, see-through ground floor space, the structure gains lightness and airiness. Dominating a lofty hillside in the city, the marble framed structure has a consistent grid design framing dark windows set back six feet. This feature not only provides a bold contrast but functions as a sun shield as well.

KANSAS CITY

Crown Center (1967–83)

ARCHITECTS: Edward Larrabee Barnes with others
LOCATION: Pershing Rd. between Main St. and Gilham Rd.
OPEN: During shopping and business hours; hotel always

Initially planned by Cesar Pelli and Gruen Associates, Crown Center is one of the best and largest developments of its kind in the nation. Geared to bring new life back to the downtown area, the successful complex includes inter-related spaces for a number of office buildings, shopping, condominiums, an impressive hotel by Harry Weese & Associates (note the waterfall and garden in the lobby), and other public facilities. The rooftop restaurant interior is spectacular. (CRYSTAL PAVILION and Warren Platner's AMERICAN RESTAURANT are additional highlights.)

ST. LOUIS

Gateway Arch, Jefferson National Expansion Memorial
(1962–68)

ARCHITECTS: Eero Saarinen & Associates with Severud-Elstad-Krueger Associates, structural engineers
LOCATION: At the foot of Chestnut, Market, and Walnut Sts.
OPEN: Daily

President Jefferson made the Louisiana Purchase in 1803 and by this act opened the path for the great Westward Expansion. The magnificent Gateway Arch was created with prefabricated steel sections rising 630 feet and symbolizing the great Westward Expansion. Ranking as one of the world's great architectural feats, the sculptural hollow arch has a system of moving seats that shuttle tourists to an observation point. One of the nation's most exciting monuments!

ST. LOUIS

General American Life Insurance Company (1977)

ARCHITECTS: Johnson/Burgee
LOCATION: 700 Market
OPEN: During business hours

Close to Saarinen's famous arch, this headquarters building is small but dynamically planned. Clusters of brick and glass architectural forms are locked together highlighted by a vast cylinder that rises 107 feet. A sharply angled corner projection is supported by slender steel drums. The six-story interior galleria is equally dramatic with brick clad sculptural staircases and stacked elevator lobbies.

ST. LOUIS (CREVE COEUR)

Priory of St. Mary and St. Louis and St. Louis Priory School (1962)

ARCHITECTS: Hellmuth, Obata & Kassabaum
LOCATION: c. 18 miles W of St. Louis on US 40, N .4 miles on Mason Road c. 3 miles W off IS 244
OPEN: Daily, 9–5

An imaginative, and much photographed circular structure, this Priory features a tiered treatment of undulating parabolas. The lower arches rise to thirty-two feet, and the second row to twelve feet. This double row of arches is capped with a central belfry tower and cross reaching up another thirty-two feet. The sprayed concrete texture makes a stunning contrast for the dark window treatment. A stained-glass screen inside by Emil Frei highlights the Celebrants seat.

ST. LOUIS

Terminal Building, St. Louis Airport (1957/1965)

ARCHITECTS: Minoru Yamasaki with Hellmuth & Leinweber
LOCATION: NW of downtown on IS 70 (Mark Twain Expressway)
OPEN: Continously

This trend-setting terminal is one of the first thin shell concrete structures in America. The structure boasts three pairs of span barrel vaults that soar one-hundred-twenty feet. The result is an interior that is spacious and bright, conveying a spirit of loftiness. The pioneering engineering effort experienced in this airport seems an appropriate and fitting enclosure for Charles Lindberg's airplane "the Spirit of St. Louis," that is prominently displayed inside.

ST. LOUIS

The Climatron Missouri Botanical Garden (Shaw's Garden) (1960)

ARCHITECTS: Murphy & Mackey, with Synergetics, Inc. Richard Buckminster Fuller, Structural Engineers
LOCATION: 2315 Tower Grove Ave. at Flora Place
OPEN: May–Oct., daily 9–6, Nov.–Apr., 9–5

Fuller is known throughout the world for his development of the geodesic dome. A logical and brilliant design, enclosing a large space for plants, The Climatron is a marvelous network of aluminum supports and plastic panes based on Fuller's ingenious architectural geometry. The interior was created for full enjoyment of plants, with walkways on many levels meandering through the gardens. Air conditioning is perfectly controlled. The architects received the R.S. Reynolds Memorial Award for the project in 1961.

ST. LOUIS

Wainwright Building
(1890–91/1974)

ARCHITECTS: Louis Sullivan with Dankmar Adler
LOCATION: Chestnut Street at 7th
OPEN: During business hours

St. Louis is the home of one of America's first and most important skyscrapers designed by one of the nation's most famous pioneer architects. With the panel design different on each of its nine floors, the Wainwright Building was an exceptionally light and lofty structure for the time. Sullivan, who felt "form follows function," planned the building in a rational manner allowing the "function to dictate the design." Restoration and additions were designed by Hastings & Chivetta and Mitchell/Giurgola Associates.

ADDITIONAL MODERN STRUCTURES OF INTEREST

JEFFERSON CITY

Central Motor Bank (1962)
ARCHITECTS: Skidmore, Owings and Merrill
LOCATION: 500 Madison Street

KANSAS CITY

Boley Clothing Co. (1908–9)
ARCHITECTS: Louis S. Curtiss
LOCATION: 12th and Walnut Streets

An exceptional building for its time, this little known pioneer structure is the world's first example of steel-mullioned strip-windows and metal spandrels facade.

City Center Square (1976)
ARCHITECTS: Skidmore, Owings & Merrill
LOCATION: City Center Square, 1100 Main

Angled and tiered design distinguishes this impressive retail and office development that rises 30 stories.

Executive Plaza for Tower Properties (1975)
ARCHITECTS: Hellmuth, Obata & Kassabaum, Inc.
LOCATION: 720 Main

A dazzling cubistic complex sheathed with reflective glass.

H. Roe Bartle Exhibition Hall (1974–76)
ARCHITECTS: Convention Center Associates
LOCATION: 12–14th Streets, Central and Broadway.

Across the street from this impressive hall is the *MUNICIPAL AUDITORIUM* (1934–36) by Alonzo H. Gentry and others, and is an interesting example of Art Deco design.

Kansas City International Airport (1968–72)
ARCHITECTS: Kivett & Myers
LOCATION: c. 18 miles NW of the city on IS 29

A highly admired airport planned for efficiency and function. Four three-quarter circular structures provide services for up to nineteen airplanes at one time.

Kemper Arena (1974–75)
ARCHITECTS: C. F. Murphy Associates
LOCATION: 17th Street and Genesee

The arena features a bold steel tube space-frame construction.

Mercantile Tower (1975)
ARCHITECTS: Harry Weese and Associates
LOCATION: 1101 Walnut

A striking painted steel exterior with a unique system of liquid-filled columns.

The New Sanctuary for Congregation B'nai Jehudah (1967)
ARCHITECTS: Kivett and Myers
LOCATION: 712 East 69th Street

This marvelous Sanctuary addition to an existing structure features a swirling tent-like glass ceiling. Many symbolic features are incorporated and interpreted in contemporary terms.

Penn Towers (1971–72)
ARCHITECTS: Peckham/Guyton/Albers/Ziets
LOCATION: 31st and Broadway

This well designed complex is sheathed with reflective glass.

South Central Patrol Division (1977)
ARCHITECTS: Patty Berkebile Nelson Associates
LOCATION: 1880 E. 63rd Street

Nicely located for public accessibility, this new police facility projects a new image for a law building.

KIRKSVILLE

First Christian Church (1971)
ARCHITECTS: Anselevicius/Rupe/Associates
LOCATION: c. 200 miles NW of St. Louis

Responding to its small town environment, this commendable religious structure is simple and direct. Natural lighting washes the interior walls creating a unique effect.

ST. LOUIS

CBS-Gateway Tower (1969)
ARCHITECTS: Hellmuth, Obata and Kassabaum
LOCATION: 1 Memorial Drive

This handsome tower complex commands a sweeping view of the river and Gateway Arch, functioning as a facility for radio and television studios.

Community Federal Center (1977)
ARCHITECTS: Hellmuth, Obata & Kassabaum
LOCATION: Ballas Road at Manchester (outside of St. Louis)

This suburban office building is uniquely arranged with interesting staggered units beautifully related to the surroundings.

Environmental Systems Building, Emerson Electric Company (1971)
ARCHITECTS: Hellmuth, Obata & Kassabaum, Inc.
LOCATION: 8000 West Florissant

Nicely situated in a park-like setting on the outskirts of the city, this six-story building is constructed of projecting reflective glass bands and a weathered steel frame.

Forest Park Community College (1967–69)
ARCHITECTS: Harry Weese & Associates
LOCATION: West on US 40 at US 67, West on Oakland Avenue

McDonnell Douglas Automation Company (McAUTO) (1981–1983)
ARCHITECTS: Hellmuth, Obata & Kassabaum, Inc.
LOCATION: 270 & Brown Rd. (McDonnell Blvd. by airport)

Bright blue and red panels and red circles interestingly combine with gleaming steel for the design of the world's largest computer center.

McDonnell Planetarium (1962–63)
ARCHITECTS: Hellmuth, Obata, & Kassabaum
LOCATION: Off Clayton Road, SE corner of Forest Park (Exit off US 40 at Hampton Avenue)

Monsanto Company Cafeteria (1968)
ARCHITECTS: Vincent G. Kling & Associates
LOCATION: 800 N. Lindbergh Boulevard

This below-ground employee cafeteria takes advantage of form, color, and light to create fascinating interior spaces.

Mercantile Tower (1975)
ARCHITECTS: Sverdrup & Parcel and Associates
LOCATION: One Mercantile Center (7th and Washington)

The strong design of the Mercantile Tower features vertical trusses providing a striking image. The corners are cropped to provide more sunlight surrounding the tower. The design provides effective wind bracing.

Monsanto Environmental Health Laboratory (1980)
ARCHITECTS: Holabird & Root
LOCATION: 800 N. Lindbergh Blvd.

A curtained wall exterior of insulated metal panels and insulated glass—"a highly refined solution to a very high-tech complicated program."

Neiman-Marcus, Frontenac Fashion Center (1975)
ARCHITECTS: John Carl Warnecke, Architects
LOCATION: Plaza Frontenac, Clayton Road & Lindbergh Blvd.

A visually exciting focal point is a huge rotunda and dome.

One Centerre Plaza (1980s)
ARCHITECTS: 3/D International
LOCATION: Market St. between 8th & 9th Streets

A stunning high-rise and low-rise skyscraper complex constructed of reflective glass and aluminum.

Pet Plaza
ARCHITECTS: A.L. Aydeiott & Associates
LOCATION: 400 S. 4th Street

Surrounded by plazas, the building is faced with four different colors and textures of granite and crushed limestone. Above the complex is an observation balcony.

Raeder Place (1874/1978)
ARCHITECTS: Original architect: Frederick W. Raeder Renovation: Kimble A. Cohn & Associates
LOCATION: 727 North 1st Street

An excellent example of early cast-iron construction in America. Beautifully and sensitively renovated.

St. Louis Art Museum Restoration (1978)
ARCHITECTS: Hardy Holzman Pfeiffer
LOCATION: Forest Park

Cass Gilbert's original Beaux Arts building has been admirably updated and lit.

Wainwright Tomb (1892)
ARCHITECT: Louis H. Sullivan
LOCATION: Prospect Avenue, SE corner of Belleefontaine Cemetery (Enter at 4947 West Florissant Avenue)

Ellis Wainwright, owner of the great Wainwright Building commissioned Sullivan to design a tomb for his beloved wife, who died at an early age, and for himself.

ST. LOUIS (CREVE COEUR)

Religious Facilities for Congregation Temple Israel (1962)
ARCHITECTS: Hellmuth, Obata & Kassabaum, Inc.
LOCATION: 10675 Ladue Road

An outstanding feature of this flexible Synagogue is the roof structure composed of a series of diagonal beams forming a network of hexagons and triangles.

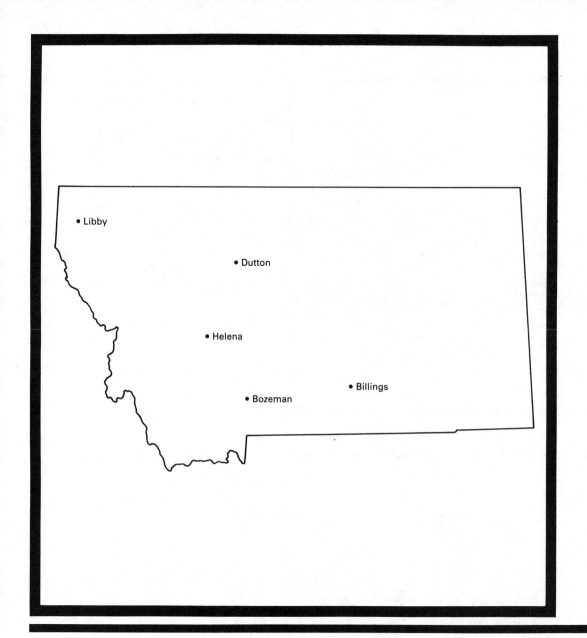

- Libby
- Dutton
- Helena
- Billings
- Bozeman

Montana

BILLINGS

Fortin Educational Center at Rocky Mountain College

(1968–69)

ARCHITECTS AND ENGINEERS: CTA
LOCATION: Just off Rimrock Road, East of 17th Street West
OPEN: During the school year

An interesting arrangement of forms, this center is suitable to the particular function required. The designers were especially sensitive to scale when planning these facilities to house a 2,400 seat gymnasium, a large swimming pool, a small auditorium, classrooms, a medical clinic, and offices. The Fortin Center brilliantly encloses all of these functional spaces without sacrificing unity and aesthetic appeal.

BOZEMAN

Gallatin County Detention Center (1983)

ARCHITECTS: RS Architects & BGS Architects with others
LOCATION: 615 South 16th
OPEN: Closed to public

One of the most unique structures of its type in the nation, the new Gallatin County Detention Center was erected next to a nineteenth century jail of the Old West. (The old jail and original gallows are now part of a museum.) The massive new complex is highlighted by a rhythmic series of arched pavilions that relieve the somewhat austere feeling of the concrete and grout-filled block building. The correctional facility achieves a strong sculptural effect enhanced by its simple meadow setting.

HELENA

Power Block on Last Chance Gulch (1889)

ARCHITECTS: Shaffer & Read
LOCATION: #58, #60, and #62 Last Chance Gulch
OPEN: During business hours

Enjoying a sudden burst of wealth when prospectors found gold in 1864, Helena witnessed a brief building spurt of impressive structures. One of the best is Power Block, a building clearly based on the Romanesque design principles of America's great early modern architect, Henry Hobson Richardson. The building features rusticated stone, round arches, simple detailing, and an emphasis on heavy, low massing.

LIBBY

Libby Dam (1964–75)

ARCHITECTS: Paul Thiry ENGINEERS: U.S. Army Corps of Engineers
LOCATION: 18 miles East of Libby on MT 37

This spectacular dam reaches 2,200 feet across the Kootenai River. The dam was dedicated by President Ford in 1964. Libby Dam is one of over 50 similar projects designed by the U.S. Army Corps of Engineers and is considered one of their most impressive works. Thiry was commissioned to work with the Corps, providing a successful pooling of expertise to create this engineering marvel.

ADDITIONAL MODERN STRUCTURES OF INTEREST

DUTTON

Bethany Lutheran Church (1965)
ARCHITECTS: Davidson and Kuhr
LOCATION: c. 35 miles N. of Great Falls,
take Dutton exit off I-15 (just N.E. of town)

This award-winning religious structure is
simply and functionally designed through use
of basic form and materials.

Schuyler •

Omaha•

Grand Island•

Lincoln •

Kearney •

Nebraska

GRAND ISLAND

Stuhr Museum of The Prairie Pioneer (1966–67)

ARCHITECT: Edward Durell Stone
LOCATION: 4 miles N of IS 80 (take Grand Island exit) Junction of US 34 and US 281
OPEN: Mon.–Sat. 9–5, Sun. 1–5; times change on holidays

LIke an oasis in the prairie, the Stuhr Museum is surrounded by a moat and fountains. The simple modern structure, with its classical overtones, is typical of the late architect's work, and provides an effective backdrop for the many fascinating exhibits and displays of America's early forefathers. The interior space is flooded with sunlight, providing a refreshing and inviting atmosphere throughout the intimate museum.

LINCOLN

Nebraska State Capitol (1922–32)

ARCHITECT: Bertram Grosvenor Goodhue
LOCATION: 14–16th Sts. between H and K
OPEN: Mon.–Fri. 9–5, Sat. 10–5, Sun. 1–5

The State Capitol is one of Nebraska's most interesting landmarks and a great example of modern eclecticism. Built during the Art Deco period, the style of the State Capitol is in step with the times, featuring a sleek, staggered form culminating in a dome. Advanced technology and a creative use of materials, especially with the interior treatment, have made the building an important trend setter. Goodhue died a few years after the initial commission and building period. The structure was completed by his partners.

LINCOLN

Sheldon Memorial Art Gallery (1962–63)

ARCHITECT: Philip Johnson
LOCATION: University of Nebraska, No. 12th St. at R
OPEN: Tues. 10–10, Wed.–Sat. 10–5, Sun. 2–5

Sheathed with smooth Italian travertine, the Sheldon Memorial Art Gallery illustrates the architect's adaptive use of classical modern forms. Repeating columns become pilasters flanking each side of the arched entrance. The sculptural effect of the facade is carried into the interior spaces, creating an exciting and engaging background for art. Interior walls are windowless with artificial light providing the only illumination. Materials throughout the gallery, auditorium, and teaching spaces are fascinatingly combined.

OMAHA

W. Dale Clark Library (1975–77)

ARCHITECTS: Hellmuth, Obata & Kassabaum with John Latenser & Sons
LOCATION: 215 South 15th Street
OPEN:: Mon.–Fri. 9–8:30, Sat. 9–5:30

A superb example of library design, this facility was organized for function and efficiency. The five-story structure has a cutaway facade of tinted glass windows arranged in horizontal bands. The roof is topped with forty-eight skylight domes that flood the interior spaces with light. A catwalk extends over a sunken area, adding interest as well as convenient accessability.

ADDITIONAL MODERN STRUCTURES OF INTEREST

KEARNEY

Windy Hills Elementary School (1981)
ARCHITECT: Lynn Bonge
LOCATION: 4211 20th Avenue

An intriguing example of new directions in
architecture, this educational facility features
an earth berm, passive solar design.

LINCOLN

**First Plymouth Congregational Church
Addition** (1966)
ARCHITECTS: Davis-Fenton-Strange-Darling
LOCATION: 20th and "D" Streets

Beautifully relating and enhancing an older
church, this new addition features solid walls
of masonry with asymmetrically placed
arches.

National Bank of Commerce (1977)
ARCHITECTS: I.M. Pei & Partners with others
LOCATION: Northwest corner of "P," "O,"
and 13th

Occupying a prominent downtown site, this
long concrete bank commendably complements its neighbors and provides Lincoln with
a first-rate example of modern architecture.

OMAHA

The Bemis Company Inc. (1977)
ARCHITECTS: Bahr Vermeer & Haecker
LOCATION: 3514 South 25 Street

Providing warehouse and factory facilities for
a packaging firm, this large manufacturing
complex was planned for conservation and
efficiency without sacrificing aesthetic appeal.

SCHUYLER

Benedictine Mission House (1979)
ARCHITECTS: Astle Ericson & Associates
LOCATION: R.R. 1, 4 miles N. of Schuyler on
Hwy. 15

This superbly planned complex for a unique
function artfully blends into the Nebraska
landscape.

• Reno

• Carson City

Las Vegas •

Nevada

LAS VEGAS

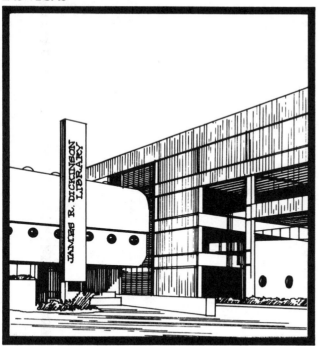

James R. Dickenson Library
(1981)

ARCHITECTS: Jack Miller & Associates, Inc.
LOCATION: University of Nevada Campus
OPEN: During school hours

This stunning new university library is a study in constrasts, with smooth and rough surfaces, shiny and dull textures, muted and bold colors, and straight and curved forms. These elements create a striking architectural image. The stimulating structure is a unique focal point at this desert campus. The entry composition of bright red forms introduces functional and airy interior spaces.

LAS VEGAS

The Strip (1950s–)

ARCHITECTS: Various architects
LOCATION: Las Vegas Boulevard South
OPEN: Most buildings continuously

There is no other conglomeration of architecture concentrated in one area as there is on the famous strip in Las Vegas, the popular adult entertainment center of the world. The architecture amazes, delights, stimulates, and evokes a myriad of feelings. The Strip, with its variety of architectural styles, ranging from Greco-Roman to Persian, competes to attract the visitors' patronage. The atmosphere may be gawdy and flashing, but it never fails to fascinate.

LAS VEGAS

Vocational-Technical Center of Southern Nevada (1966–68)

ARCHITECTS: William Blurock & partners with Julius Gabriele (first phase) William Blurock & Partners with James Brooks McDaniel (second phase)
LOCATION: Maple Avenue at Russell Road, SE edge of Las Vegas

The architects of this commendable "Trade-Tech" center have sought to provide students with a plan that is both functional, convenient, and pleasant. Educational facilities provide planned spaces for numerous classes extending from a large central corridor that channels traffic effectively throughout the complex. Almost 2,000 students attend the school that is nicely located away from the activity of the city in an attractive park setting.

RENO

Washoe County Library (1966)

ARCHITECT: Hewitt C. Wells
LOCATION: Between East Liberty and Ryland on Center Street
OPEN: Mon.–Fri. 9–8:50, Sat. 9–5:50, Sun. 1–5

A modern library facility that truly invites the patron into its spacious interior through the artful arrangement of varying levels lush with plantings and greenery. A break from the usual greeting of necessary library trappings that tend to be impersonal and business-like, this library design is a refreshing approach. Seating, fountains, and spacious areas add to the welcoming environment. The innovative plan also conveniently functions in an efficient manner.

ADDITIONAL MODERN STRUCTURES OF INTEREST

CARSON CITY

Carson City High School (1970)
ARCHITECTS: Caudill Rowlett Scott with
Selden and Stewart
LOCATION: 1111 No. Saliman Road

This "school community" emphasizes a "main
street." The flexible structure is planned in
the hope that "the school will become society
and society will become a school." (*Arch.
Record,* January 1971.)

LAS VEGAS

Summa Office Building (1982)
ARCHITECTS: Archisystems International
LOCATION: 3260 South Industrial Road

Sharply projecting roofs characterize the
design of this building that is clad with bright
blue and green metal panels.

RENO

**Charles and Henrietta Fleischmann
Atmospherium Planetarium** (1968)
ARCHITECTS: Raymond Hellman
LOCATION: University of Nevada campus

This dramatic small structure features unusual
forms interpreted through concrete and glass
construction.

- Hanover

Concord •   Durham •

Manchester •   Exeter •

New Hampshire

CONCORD

Dance Studio and Music Performance Hall (1981)

ARCHITECTS: Hardy, Holzman, Pfeiffer Associates
LOCATION: St. Paul's School
OPEN: During school hours

The unique modern barn-like studio is conveniently situated on a hillside in the center of campus. Brick, corrugated cement-asbestos paneled walls are accentuated with a copper roof providing an interesting interplay of textures. The plan suggests a feeling of the state's architectural heritage interpreted in a contemporary outlook. The exposed frame, ducts, metal stairs, and balustrades recall the modern age. Simple shaker furniture enhances the structural background.

EXETER

Physical Education Facilities (1967–69)

ARCHITECTS: Kallmann & McKinnell
LOCATION: The Phillips Exeter Academy. Court Street at Gilman
OPEN: During game events

The Physical Education Facilities at this Academy for young men, boasts one of the finest buildings of its type in the nation. Well planned halls and other passageways invitingly channel traffic throughout. Spaces are arranged for basketball courts, a pool, hockey rinks, a gymnasium and squash courts. The modern complex harmoniously adjoins an existing traditional styled building. Kallmann & McKinnel are the architects of the highly controversial Boston City Hall.

EXETER

The Phillips Exeter Academy Library (1969–71)

ARCHITECT: Louis I. Kahn
LOCATION: Front Street between Elm Street and Tan Lane
OPEN: During school hours

Ranking as one of the states' most important modern hallmarks, the Phillips Exeter Academy Library is deceivingly simple from the exterior. The interior, however, is dynamically treated. The lighting is particularly impressive and superbly handled for maximum effect. The late architect (d. 1974) was especially fond of the play of light on natural textures. Lighting floods and highlights the geometric surfaces of concrete. Library facilities are artfully arranged without interfering with convenience.

MANCHESTER

The Currier Gallery Art Expansion (1982)

ARCHITECTS: Hardy Holzman Pfeiffer Associates
LOCATION: 192 Orange Street
OPEN: Tues., Wed., Fri., Sat. 10–4, Thurs. 10–10, Sun. 2–5

Constructed of pale yellow brick, this handsome new structure adjoins an existing 1929 Beaux Arts Museum. Two expansion wings are beautifully integrated to the old through the use of simple structural columns recalling the original design. The spacious airy wings house the museum's permanent collections and special exhibits against the simple, well lit background. Wood strip flooring provides warmth against the pure white walls.

ADDITIONAL MODERN STRUCTURES OF INTEREST

CONCORD

Conservation Center (1983)
ARCHITECTS: Banwell White & Arnold with Peter Lovell
LOCATION: Above the Concord and Merrimack Rivers

This clapboard structure was designed for the Society for the Protection of New Hampshire Forests, functioning as a reception area with office and lecture spaces. The architects have created a design that admirably fits its purpose and surroundings. New England spruce is employed throughout the complex.

The Second Congregational Society in Concord (Unitarian) (1960)
ARCHITECTS: Hugh Stubbins and Associates, Inc.
LOCATION: 274 Pleasant Street

The architects were charged with creating a church that related to the New Hampshire countryside and was reminiscent of traditional Unitarian worship. Both goals were beautifully accomplished.

DURHAM

Christensen, Williamson, and Philbrook Halls (1969–72)
ARCHITECTS: Ulrich Franzen & Associates
LOCATION: University of New Hampshire, S. off Main Street on Mill Road, SW edge of campus

The sensitive arrangement of these stately buildings in relation to the campus is commendable. The excellent use of form and materials is planned for efficiency and function.

EXETER

Fisher Theater (1974)
ARCHITECTS: Hardy Holzman Pfeiffer Associates
LOCATION: Phillips Exeter Academy

This pre-engineered building, built on a low budget, was designed for flexibility and to harmonize with its natural setting.

HANOVER

Hopkins Center (1964)
ARCHITECTS: Harrison & Abramovitz
LOCATION: Dartmouth College campus

This impressive building functions as a facility to expose the students to all the Creative Arts and to provide a place for social activities.

Sherman Fairchild Physical Sciences Center (1974)
ARCHITECTS: Shepley Bulfinch Richardson & Abbott
LOCATION: Dartmouth College campus

This new glass and concrete tower unifies the entire science complex.

MANCHESTER

New Hampshire College (1972–)
ARCHITECTS: Huygens and Tappe
LOCATION: New Hampshire College campus (15 min. from downtown)

This new college was designed as a "townscape," which is evident throughout the campus.

Wayne ●   Paterson
           ●
Parsippany ●
         Englewood ●
Livingston ●

Peapack-Gladstone ●
        Newark ●
        Jersey City

Raritan ●

● Princeton
   ● Plainsboro   Holmdel
Lawrenceville

● Trenton
      Lakewood ●
● Moorestown
● Mt. Laurel

Pomona ●

New Jersey

ATLANTIC CITY

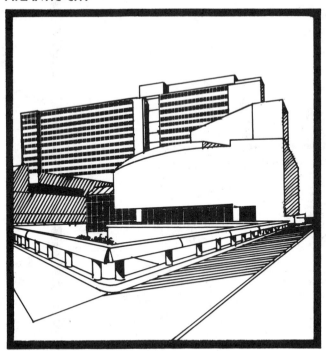

Harrah's Marina Hotel Casino
(1980)

ARCHITECTS: BWB Associates
LOCATION: Shore of Absecon Bay, 1 1/2 mi.
N of Atlantic City
OPEN: Continuously

Harrah's is one of the finest casino hotels in this popular seaside resort. The stunning complex, with its twelve-story hotel tower, neatly fits into a wedge-shaped site and was deisgned to enhance its shoreline position. A three-story triangular wing houses the dramatically designed 46,000-square-foot casino. In addition there are conference rooms, a full-size theater, restaurants, bars, and a "fun center" for children and teens. A space frame arcade throughout creates an atmosphere of spaciousness, flooding the interior spaces with light.

LAWRENCEVILLE

E. R. Squibb & Sons World Headquarters (1970–72)

ARCHITECTS: Hellmuth, Obata &
Kassabaum
LOCATION: On US 206, 3 miles South of
Princeton, 2.2 miles North of Lawrenceville
OPEN: Art gallery and pharmaceutical
museum during business hours and on
Thurs. until 9 PM, Sun. 1–5

A rolling grassy site leads up to the well-articulated complex for the well-known pharmaceutical corporation. Consisting of eleven three-story units, the facilities are well planned for administrative and research activities for 2,000 employees. Interconnnecting passageways allow easy access from one module to the other. Interiors are pleasantly executed including lively color accents denoting various functions. An interesting museum and art gallery are provided for the general public.

LIBERTY STATE PARK (BY JERSEY CITY)

The Environmental Education Center (1983)

ARCHITECT: Michael Graves
LOCATION: Exit 14B off New Jersey
Turnpike (I-95). Follow signs.
OPEN: Daily, Mon.–Sat., 8–8, Sun., 8–10 PM.

This unique museum center directs visitors through the park. Exhibits along the way provide information on wildlife and the environment. Grave's supportive pavilion brings added drama and interest to the visitor's visual experience. The architect's very personal and identifiable style is evident throughout the complex. The award-winning facility's pitched-roof pavilions surround a tall, central space. An open-air orientation pavilion aids the visitor and introduces the design concept.

POMONA

Stockton State College
(1973–76)

ARCHITECTS: Geddes Brecher Qualls
Cunningham
LOCATION: Exit 44 off Garden State
Parkway, S to College Dr.
OPEN: During school hours

The basic layout for this admirably designed College is totally geared for student convenience and enjoyment. Traffic effectively and naturally flows through the central two-story building pleasantly decorated with well-placed furniture and colorful artwork. The area has become an inviting meetingplace on campus. Additional building units adjoin the main structure. Surrounded by well-land-scaped grounds and courtyards, the campus is both interesting and visually pleasing.

PRINCETON

Biochemistry Lab (1980)

ARCHITECTS: Davis, Brody and Associates
LOCATION: Princeton University campus
OPEN: During school hours

A strongly expressed building, the new Biochemistry Lab has already become an important landmark on Princeton's campus. Although bold in its statement, the building beautifully relates to the older structures on campus. Research, teaching, and office spaces are logically composed with plans to accommodate future expansion. Dynamic forms are skillfully tempered with horizontal wraparound window bands.

PRINCETON

Scanticon—Princeton (Conference and Training Ctr.) (1980s)

ARCHITECTS: Friis & Moltke (Denmark)
LOCATION: 100 College Road East
OPEN: Year around. Open by appointment only

Few firms have contributed more to the Danish influence in international architecture than Friis and Moltke. Their successful training centers in Munich, Germany and Jutland, Denmark have been highly praised. Scanticon–Princeton Training Center is beautifully situated on twenty-five acres of natural forest park. The welcoming complex is basically Danish in its architecture, constructed primarily of brick, wood, and glass. The interior spaces in the large complex are planned to provide physical or visual contact with the outdoors. Scanticon has stimulated interest in similar facilities around the nation.

SHORT HILLS (NEWARK)

Temple B'nai Jeshurun (Children of the Upright)
(1968)

ARCHITECTS: Pietro Belluschi and Gruzen and Partners
LOCATION: 1025 South Orange Avenue, 7 miles W. of Newark in Millburn
OPEN: Most evenings at 8:30. Times vary each year.

Surrounded by well-landscaped grounds, this handsome brick structure is topped with a copper roof. A twelve-foot skylight spans the roof and a stunning stained-glass window soars eighty feet to the full height of the building. Beautiful works of art, symbolic to the Jewish faith, are emphasized through the sensitive use of materials, form, and light. The focal point of the interior space is the Holy of Holies, the Ark of the Covenent, which is surrounded by the thousand-seat Sanctuary. The Temple admirably reflects the spirit of "oneness with God."

TRENTON

Bath House for The Jewish Community Center (1958)

ARCHITECT: Louis I. Kahn
LOCATION: 999 Lower Ferry Road, West Trenton
OPEN: 9 AM–10 PM., Mon.–Thurs., 9–5, Sun., 9–4 Fri.

Kahn's phrase of "serving spaces and served spaces," was first applied in the Trenton Community Bath House. Four massive masonry squares surround a central square capped by a pyramidal roof. The smaller square, or "servant" space provides an entrance or storage area, and the larger "served" space as the communal area. The great Russian-born American architect was knighted by Queen ELizabeth II of England.

ADDITIONAL MODERN STRUCTURES OF INTEREST

ENGLEWOOD

Nature Center, Flat Rock Brook Center for Environmental Studies (1980)
ARCHITECTS: Ballou-Levy-Fellgraff
LOCATION: 443 Van Nostrand Avenue

The architect's goal for this complex was "to provide a reintroduction of the public to the environment." The center is oriented to the sun and to its surroundings.

HOLMDEL

Bell Telephone Corporation: Research Laboratories (1957–62)
ARCHITECT: Eero Saarinen
LOCATION: Crawfords Corner, off N.J. Parkway 114

A complex of four rectangular buildings designed to house 4,000 scientific workers, the complex features huge curtain walls of glazed reflective glass.

Garden State Arts Center (1968)
ARCHITECT: Edward Durell Stone
LOCATION: Telegraph Hill Park by Garden State Parkway

This handsome center, built for the New Jersey Highway Authority, is nicely located in a rolling green hillside by the highway, conveniently accessible for visitors.

LAKEWOOD

Synagogue of The Congregation Sons of Israel (1964)
ARCHITECTS: Davis, Brody & Associates
LOCATION: 6th Street and Madison Ave.

Numerous changes in the copper roof design, accented by the use of battens, highlight this expressive religious building.

LIVINGSTON

Temple Beth Shalom (1968)
ARCHITECT: C. J. Wisniewski
LOCATION: 193 E. Mount Pleasant Avenue

Dramatic use of vertical concrete bays inset with glass provide a beautiful view of the surroundings.

MT. LAUREL

Zurich American Insurance Company (1973)
ARCHITECT: Cesar Pelli
LOCATION: St. Hwy. 38, Marter Rd.

An example of early "high-tech" architecture by Pelli.

MOUNTAINSIDE

Union County Nature and Science Museum (Trailside Museum) (1980s)
ARCHITECT: Michael Graves
LOCATION: Watchung Reservation, Union County Park, 11 mi. SW of Newark

The Nature and Science Museum is innovatively planned to heighten its function and complement the surrounding natural setting.

NEWARK

Pavilion Park Apartments (1960 to present)
ARCHITECT: Ludwig Mies van der Rohe
LOCATION: 351–381 Broad Street

Anodized aluminum curtain walls, classically unified, demonstrate the great master architect's design philosophy of "less is more."

PATERSON

Calvary Baptist Church (1972)
ARCHITECTS: J. Robert Gilchrist &Associates
LOCATION: 575 East 18th Street

Constructed of red brown masonry walls, wood beams and exposed concrete systems of modular components, this structure is part of an ambitious Urban Renewal Project. Amber windows provide soft colored light to flood the interior spaces.

PARSIPPANY

The Evans Partnership Building and Offices (1979)
ARCHITECTS: Gwathmey-Siegel & Associates
LOCATION: 4 Wood Hollow Road, off Route 80

Functioning as a headquarters for a New Jersey firm of builders and real estate developers, this complex features combinations of materials and form that are visually stimulating.

PEAPACK/GLADSTONE

Beneficial Center (1982)
ARCHITECTS: The Hillier Group, Architects
LOCATION: 300 Beneficial Center

This office village complex is interestingly designed in a contemporary version of styles from the past.

PLAINSBORO

Enerplex (1982)
ARCHITECTS: Skidmore, Owings & Merrill
LOCATION: Princeton University Forrestal Center

This huge office complex is admirably designed for energy efficiency.

PRINCETON

Administration Building at Princeton University
ARCHITECT: Edward Larrabee Barnes
LOCATION: Princeton University campus

A smooth concrete finished square complex with a contrasting deep window arrangement.

Academic Building and Dining Hall (1970–71)
ARCHITECTS: Geddes Brecher Qualls Cunningham
LOCATION: Institute for Advanced Study, Princeton Univ. campus; West end of Nassau Street, SW on Mercer, S on Olden

Gordon Wu Hall (1982)
ARCHITECTS: Venturi, Rauch and Scott Brown
LOCATION: Princeton University campus

Wu Hall is constructed principally of brick and glass. The innovative building admirably demonstrates a variety of forms, yet is sensitive to surrounding buildings on campus.

L. Stockwell Jadwin Gymnasium (1966–68)
ARCHITECTS: Walker O. Cain & Associates
LOCATION: Off Washington Road, SE edge of campus

One of the best facilities of its kind in the nation.

Stanley P. Jadwin Hall (1968–69)
ARCHITECTS: Hugh Stubbins & Associates
LOCATION: E off Washington Road, opposite Palmer Stadium

A superior modern facility that houses the Physical Laboratory.

Spelman Halls (1973)
ARCHITECTS: I.M. Pei & Partners
LOCATION: Princeton University, University Place at College Rd.

An award-winning complex designed for energy conservation and compatibility with existing buildings.

Woodrow Wilson School at Princeton University
ARCHITECT: Minoru Yamasaki
LOCATION: Princeton University campus

A rather precise modern neo-classic structure befitting the prevailing Gothic-styled buildings at Princeton. The complex houses the School of Public and International Affairs.

RARITAN

The Thomas & Betts Building (1978)
ARCHITECTS: Gwathmey & Siegel
LOCATION: 920-Route 202

A bold complex clad with granite aggregate panels. An emphasis on lighting is stressed throughout the building, featuring a long central skylit gallery.

TINTON FALLS

Luther Memorial Lutheran Church (1965)
ARCHITECT: Jules Gregory; Allan M. Blauth,
Associate in charge
LOCATION: 818 Tinton Avenue

The exciting nave of laminated wood beams
is supported by a circular wall of concrete
block. A narrow window band between the
two components, combine with a central
skylight to provide unique lighting into the
space.

TRENTON

Trenton State College Student Center
(1978)
ARCHITECT: Caudill Rowlett Scott
LOCATION: Trenton State College campus

A unique center serving both commuter and
resident students. The angled brick building
is topped with a large and airy mirrored glass
skylight.

WAYNE

Union Camp Headquarters (1969–70)
ARCHITECTS: Schofield & Colgan
LOCATION: 1600 Valley Road (via IS 80, S
on NJ 62, W on NJ 46, N on Riverview and
Valley Roads.

This well-designed corporate headquarters
blends nicely with the natural wooded site.

BERNARDS TOWNSHIP

Pingry School (1983)
ARCHITECTS: Hardy Holzman Pfeiffer
Associates
LOCATION: c. 5 miles S of Bernardsville,
Close to Liberty Corner (c. 30 mi. WSW of
Newark)

Located in a rural area, this prep school
incorporates refreshing new ideas with traditionalism. An eye-catching two-story-high
portico clad with aqua terra-cotta introduces
the sprawling educational facility. Interiors are
excitingly arranged.

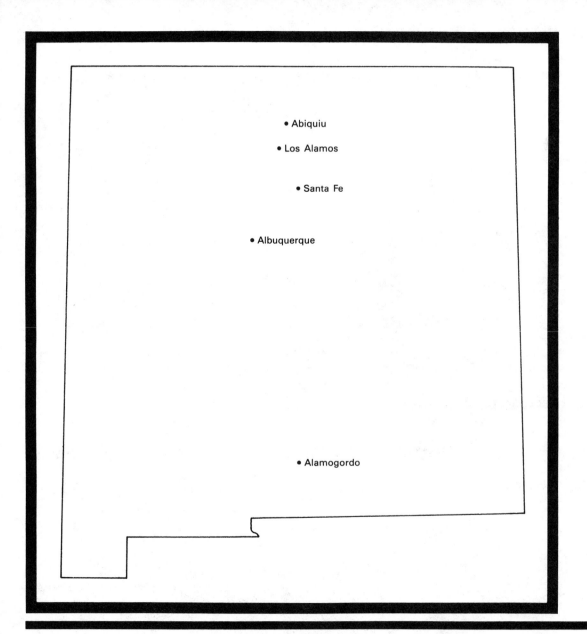

- Abiquiu
- Los Alamos
- Santa Fe
- Albuquerque
- Alamogordo

New Mexico

ALAMOGORDO

International Space Hall of Fame (1976)

ARCHITECT: Charles E. Nolan Jr. & Associates
LOCATION: Top of Highway 2001, follow posted signs
OPEN: 9 AM to 6 PM daily, except Christmas Day

The extraordinary aspect of the bold and dazzling cubistic structure is its desert wilderness setting. The building was designed to reflect the pioneering spirit of the space age, and it honors all nations who have explored the universe for mankind. Exhibits of the world's space story are displayed inside and out. The five-story structure features a cube of reflective glass seemingly clamped by huge concrete monoliths. The surprising contrast with its surroundings is eye-catching and yet symbolic of the advancements of the space age.

ALBUQUERQUE

First National Bank Building (1974)

ARCHITECTS: Harry Weese and Associates
LOCATION: Between 2nd and 3rd, Copper & Tijeras
OPEN: During business hours

This enormous banking complex was influenced by Le Corbusier's work, incorporating a mixed-use underground galleria with a restaurant and arcades opening to the street side. The structure was designed to "wrap" around a refreshing outdoor fountain and pool—a most welcome feature in the hot desert climate. In keeping with New Mexico's Spanish-Indian architectural roots, desert beige masonry similar to adobe clay was employed. First Plaza, as it is known, has become a popular meeting place in downtown Albuquerque.

SANTA FE

Outdoor American Indian Theater (1970)

ARCHITECTS: Paolo Soleri with Pacheco & Graham
LOCATION: Cerrillos Road (US 35) at Teseuque Drive
OPEN: Mon.–Fri., 10–5

Certainly one of the most imaginative and visionary architects in America, Soleri was commissioned by the Institute of American Indian Arts to create this intriguing theater. Bold concrete forms were cast on the earth with earthmoving equipment and finished by hand. When the concrete was cured, the earth was skillfully removed from beneath. Soleri's amazing cities in the Arizona desert are similar in design. (See the Chapter on Arizona)

SANTA FE

The Santa Fe Opera House (1967)

ARCHITECTS: McHugh & Kidder, Burran, Wright
LOCATION: c. 6 miles N of Santa Fe off US 64, 84, and 285
OPEN: Performances in summer from Jul.–Aug., 9:00 PM

The Santa Fe Opera House is a marvelous composition of flowing concrete forms that hover over the audience. The innovative structure features many technical advancements suited for an outdoor theater of this type. Surrounding mountains, combined with a view of the stars and the city in the background, provide a very memorable theater-going experience.

ADDITIONAL MODERN STRUCTURES OF INTEREST

ABIQUIU

Dar Al-Islam Foundation Islamic Village Center (1983)
ARCHITECT: Dr. Hassan Fathy
LOCATION: 42-acre plateau overlooking the Chama River, Northern N. Mexico

In this small community made famous by the artist Georgia O'Keeffe is this religious center serving America's first Islamic village. The modern structural design is reminiscent of the traditional Islamic mosque.

ALBUQUERQUE

The Albuquerque Museum (1979)
ARCHITECTS: Antoine Predock
LOCATION: 2000 Mountain NW

The exterior, courtyards, gallery, and exhibit areas of the museum recall traditional regional archiecture with exposed beams, plastered walls, and stucco construction.

Buildings At The University of New Mexico
ARCHITECTS: Various architects listed
LOCATION: UNM main campus

Many buildings on the UNM campus are reflective of the traditional vernacular of the Southwest Adobe. Following are some of the outstanding structures: *ALUMNI MEMORIAL CHAPEL* (1954–60) Holien, Buckley; *HUMANITIES BLDG.* (1974), W.C. Kruger; *OLD ZIMMERMAN LIBRARY* (1936) John Gaw Meem.

Mountain Bell Building (La Compana) (1982)
ARCHITECTS: Caudill, Rowlett & Scott with Stevens, Mallory Pearl & Campbell
LOCATION: 400 Tijeras NW

Featuring bold forms sheathed with reflective glass, this structure makes a strong impression. A number of interestingly designed modern structures are published in a pamphlet prepared by the Albuquerque Chapter, American Institute of Architects. Additional buildings of interest are: *FIRST UNITARIAN CHURCH* (1964), by Harvey Hoshour at 3701 Carlisle NE; *FAITH IN CHRIST LUTHERAN CHURCH* (1981), Schlegel & Lewis, located at Chelwood & Indian School NE; *OFFICE BUILDING ("JAWS")* (1973), Bart Prince, located at SW corner of Zuni & Louisiana; *SAINT PAUL'S LUTHERAN CHURCH* (1971), Flatow, Moore, Bryan, 1100 Indian School NE; *PUBLIC SERVICE OF NEW MEXICO BUILDING* (1980), Boehning, Protz, Cook & Pogue, 414 Silver SW.; the *RIO GRANDE NATURE CENTER* (1982), Antoine Predock, 2901 Candelaria NW; and the *SANDIA SAVINGS BANK* (1975), G. Stanton Mason, 4400 Lead SE.

New Mexico Union, University of New Mexico (1978)
ARCHITECTS: Antoine Predock with others
LOCATION: University of New Mexico campus (middle)

An admirable renovation with modern interiors designed for student needs. A good example of regionalism.

The University Center at The University of Albuquerque (1960s)
ARCHITECT: Wybe J. van der Meer
LOCATION: University of Albuquerque campus

Bold concrete forms repeating across the facade highlight this uniformly designed Center.

COCHITI

Cochiti Lake Recreation Center (1973)
ARCHITECTS: Frank O. Gehry and Associates
LOCATION: Just north of Albuquerque on the Indian Reservation

This Center, the first building of the New Town, is reflective of the rugged surroundings and hot climate.

LOS ALAMOS

Immaculate Heart of Mary Church (1972)
ARCHITECTS: Pacheco & Graham
LOCATION: 3700 Canyon Road

Featuring a dramatic "swirling" effect of wood beams and a ceiling pierced with skylights, this church combines a spirit of traditional building styles of old New Mexico. The building is open from 8–5, Monday through Friday.

Plattsburg

• Potsdam

• Canton

Lake Placid •

Rochester

Syracuse Utica •

• Lewiston

Clinton •

Saratoga Springs

• Niagara Falls

Schenectedy • • Albany

• Buffalo

Aurora • Hamilton •

Troy •

Ithaca •

New
Paltz

• Fredonia

Corning • Binghamton • Kerhonkson •

Poughkeepsie

West Point
•

Harrison

Armonk
White Plains
Yonkers
New York City

• Goshen Port Chester

Great Neck

Flushing

New York

ALBANY

The Gov. Nelson A. Rockefeller Empire State Plaza (1979)

ARCHITECTS: Harrison & Abramovitz with others
LOCATION: Albany Mall
OPEN: Free tours conducted daily on the hour, 9–4

The extraordinary Governor Nelson A. Rockefeller Empire State Plaza is a government center, a performing arts center, and site of the world's largest publicly-owned contemporary art collection. Although highly criticized, the complex of buildings is exciting and perhaps amusing to tour. The most astounding structure is "The Egg," an oddly shaped structure that has been compared to "a futuristic Italian bidet." The huge concourse, beautifully landscaped, is flanked with glass and marble towers. The $2 billion project was spearheaded by the late Governor of New York.

BINGHAMTON

First City National Bank (1971–72)

ARCHITECTS: Ulrich Franzen & Associates
LOCATION: 2 Court Street at Hawley
OPEN: During banking hours

With a sensitive awareness of the aesthetic potential of the Chenango River, the First City National Bank was designed to enhance and incorporate this element. Situated along the river by an extended pedestrian walk, the building is planned in a tiered arrangement, built around terraces and fountains. The complex is an admirable addition to Binghamton's downtown rehabilitation program.

BUFFALO

Prudential (Formerly The Guaranty) Building (1895–96)

ARCHITECTS: Dankmar Adler and Louis H. Sullivan
LOCATION: Church Street at Pearl
OPEN: Louis Sullivan Museum open at various times; lobby open during business hours

Along with the Wainwright Building in St. Louis, the Guaranty Building is considered Sullivan's finest work. One of America's great pioneer developers of the skyscraper, Sullivan coined the phrase "form follows function"— now a battle cry for modernists. The Prudential Building, with its combination of arches and ornamentation, has an intimate charm still admired today.

BUFFALO

Albright-Knox Art Gallery Addition (1962)

ARCHITECTS: Skidmore, Owings and Merrill
LOCATION: 1285 Elmwood Avenue
OPEN: Tues.–Sat., 10–5, Sun., 12–5

The impressive Albright-Knox Art Gallery Addition features a fascinating value contrast created through the use of gleaming Vermont marble on the ground floor of the structure topped with dark reflective glass over the auditorium. The juxtaposition of the existing dignified Greco-Roman styled museum of 1900 with the new addition strikes a complementary contrast.

CORNING

The Corning Museum of Glass (1980)

ARCHITECTS: Gunnar Birkerts & Associates
LOCATION: Centerway
OPEN: Daily, 9–5, including Sunday

A dazzling undulating glass museum, this striking complex has been compared to an irregular flower with wing expansions radiating out from the center. The rambling design springs outward from an existing complex of offices. Shiny surfaces and curving forms are a perfect background for its function. A marvelous collection of glass is displayed in the interior spaces, highlighted by effective lighting.

GOSHEN

Orange County Government Center (1968–70)

ARCHITECTS: Paul Rudolph, with Peter P. Barbone
LOCATION: 265 Main St. Between Erie St. and Scotchtown Ave.
OPEN: 9–5, Mon. through Fri.

This imaginative design concept has incorporated three buildings loosely connected by a raised courtyard. The sensational effect is like walking into a three-dimensional painting by Mondrian. Concrete block surfaces are vertically striated—a favored textural treatment employed by the architect—which also helps control staining and weathering. The interior echos the exterior finishes. Bold orange carpeting employed for interior floor coverings contrasts with the concrete surfaces.

ITHACA

Bradfield Agronomy Building Cornell University (1968)

ARCHITECTS: Ulrich Franzen & Associates
LOCATION: New York State College of
Agriculture on Tower Rd.
OPEN: During the school year

Rising like a monument to science, the
Bradfield Building is brilliantly expressive.
The windowless structure is clad with fine
brickwork with the massiveness relieved by
varying vertical projections and indentations.
The entire design concept was geared to
provide the best facilities for agronomical
research. Franzen also designed the *RE-
SEARCH LABORATORY* at Cornell University
in 1973 for the College of Veterinary Medi-
cine. Located at the east end of Tower Road
(illustrated at left).

ITHACA

Herbert Johnson Art Building at Cornell University

(1975)

ARCHITECTS: I.M. Pei & Partners
LOCATION: Cornell University Campus,
inquire: 110 Day Hall
OPEN: During the school year, 10–5,
Tues.–Sat.

A strong silhouette on campus, the Museum
of Art was constructed at the top of a sloping
hillside affording a spectacular view of the
surroundings. The structure and shell are of
poured-in-place concrete with an exposed
board finish. Critics have said of this teaching
museum that "there is in this musuem an
appropriate use of unusual form in that the
building acts as a 'window,' the solids the
frame for the view."

KERHONKSON

Holy Trinity Ukrainian Catholic Church (1981)

ARCHITECTS: Radoslav Zuk with Groman, Mixon & Blood (Canada)
LOCATION: Foorde More Road
OPEN: May–Sept., afternoons, Oct–Apr. by appointment; Sundays, year around

Spiralling around a central tower, this dramatic church is based on a plan of triangles. The spiral form chosen for the church originated when the congregation met under the trees in spiral arrangement to worship. The structure is beautifully situated in the woods and serves a congregation for a large Ukrainian summer resort area in the Catskill Mountains. Primarily constructed of wood, the exterior is clad with shingles. This commendable church has meaning combined with tradition.

NEW YORK CITY

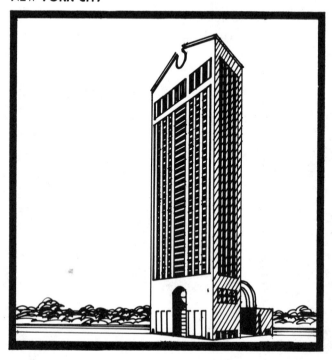

American Telephone and Telegraph Headquarters (1979–83)

ARCHITECTS: Philip Johnson/John Burgee
LOCATION: 550 Madison Avenue
OPEN: During business hours

The AT&T Building is a highly controversial "do you or don't you like it" structure of surprising design. An abstractly interpreted neo-classic granite curtain wall is topped with a stylized pediment. Of the building's design, Burgee says, "we're breaking the rules for the same kind of building that they were written for." With an entry that rises sixty feet high, the soaring building has been nicknamed "Ma Bell's Cupboard." It is decidedly the most interesting new building in New York. "The International Style is over!" (Philip Johnson, 1982.)

NEW YORK CITY

Cast Iron Buildings (c. 1840–1900)

ARCHITECTS: James Bogardus and various architects
LOCATION: SoHo District: South of Houston St., North of Canal between Broadway and West Broadway
OPEN: Some lobbies open during business hours

Bogardus made a sizeable contribution to the evolvement of modern architecture when he developed an iron grid system making the skyscraper feasible. Employing a cast iron skeleton Bogardus built "skyscrapers" up to eleven stores! He even envisioned that people would one day live in these multi-storied dwellings. Cast iron as a building material for large structures was ushered in with the Industrial Revolution. Bogardus, along with others, designed a number of admirable structures of this type in New York City. These are some of the best.

NEW YORK CITY

CBS Building (1963–65)

ARCHITECTS: Eero Saarinen & Associates
LOCATION: 51 West 52nd St. at Ave. of the Americas
OPEN: Restaurant, bar, & bank during business hours

Saarinen said of the CBS Building, "It is the simplest skyscraper in New York." The facade features strongly emphasized vertical forms reaching 491 feet in height. The vertical emphasis is coupled with the use of tinted glass. Vertical triangular sculptured concrete columns, containing the utilities, are faced with dark granite. They soar from a base five feet below ground level. The building incorporates numerous inventive engineering feats.

NEW YORK CITY

Chase Manhattan Bank

(1957–61)

ARCHITECTS: Skidmore, Owings & Merrill
LOCATION: 1 Chase Manhattan Plaza:
Nassau Street between Pine, Liberty and
William

Marine Midland Building

(1967–68)

ARCHITECTS: Skidmore, Owings & Merrill
LOCATION: 140 Broadway between Cedar
and Liberty Streets

One Liberty Plaza (1970–72)

ARCHITECTS: Skidmore, Owings & Merrill
LOCATION: 165 Broadway at Liberty Street

These innovative and influential towers by the
internationally respected firm of SOM are in
close proximity. The stately buildings are
enhanced by landscaping, fountains, plazas,
and sculpture.

NEW YORK CITY

Chrysler Building (1928–30)

ARCHITECT: William van Alen
LOCATION: Lexington Ave. between 42nd
and 43rd Streets
OPEN: During business hours

The gleaming stainless-steel-clad Chrysler
Building still remains a shining monument of
the Art Deco style. This design period was
officially launched at the 1925 Paris Exposition
Internationale des Arts Decoratifs. The popular sunburst motif, borrowed from ancient
Egypt, crowns the billowing top ending in a
sharp "needle nose" spire. Eagle gargoyles
radiate outward from the corners. Everywhere
are automotive symbols. The unique building
still amuses and delights the spectator today.

NEW YORK CITY

Citicorp Center and St. Peter's Lutheran Church

(1971–77)

ARCHITECTS: Hugh Stubbins & Associates
LOCATION: Lexington Ave. between 53rd and 54th Streets
OPEN: During business hours; market 10–10 daily

The shining steel and glass Citicorp Center is a marvelous addition to downtown Manhattan. The light and spacious seven-story interior atrium of the tower incorporates shops, restaurants, and lounging spaces on the lower level that has become a popular meeting place. Citicorp Center is an extraordinary well-planned commercial space on very expensive property. The sleek modern St. Peter's Lutheran Church is brilliantly integrated on one corner of the center.

NEW YORK CITY

Daily News Building (1929–30)

ARCHITECTS: Raymond M. Hood with John Mead Howells
LOCATION: 220 East 42nd Street
OPEN: During business hours

Hood's streamlined cut-away design for the Daily News Building heralded in a new epoch in his career. Earlier he won the now famous Chicago Tribune international competition with a Gothic design. Soon afterward, the country became emerged in the new modernistic period of Art Deco. Traditional approaches were now outdated. Close by are two more important works by Hood—the striking gold and black brick *AMERICAN RADIATOR BUILDING* (1923–24) at 40 West 40th Street, and the *MCGRAW-HILL BUILDING* (1930–31) at 330 West 42nd. This structure, sheathed with blue-green terra-cotta, is called "the Green Building."

NEW YORK CITY

Empire State Building (1929–31)

ARCHITECTS: Shreve, Lamb & Harmon
LOCATION: 350 5th Ave., between 33rd
and 34th Streets
OPEN: 9:30 AM to midnight—observation
decks open daily on 86th and 102nd floors

The skyscraper that dazzled the world, the
Empire State Building is still one of the most
remarkable and best known structures in the
United States. At the time it was built, it was a
symbol of strength and faith for the future
following the stock market crash. For four
decades it was the world's tallest building,
rising 102 stories with a 222-foot spire
surmounting the tower. Faced with Indiana
limestone and granite, the stately building is
visited by millions of people and is one of the
nation's most popular landmarks.

NEW YORK CITY

Flatiron Building (1901–03)

ARCHITECTS: Daniel H. Burnham &
Company
LOCATION: 175 5th Avenue, 949 Broadway,
at 23rd Street
OPEN: During business hours

Built on an unusual corner site by the famous
Daniel Burnham of the Chicago School, this
building was fashioned in the form of a
household iron. The exciting structure was
one of the tallest buildings in New York City
at the time. Burnham, who was enamoured
with classical Greco-Roman architecture, covered the steel-framed Flatiron Building with
ornamental detailing. Today the "little landmark" is overshadowed by its towering
successors.

NEW YORK CITY

Ford Foundation (1966–67)

ARCHITECTS: Kevin Roche & John Dinkeloo
LOCATION: 320 East 43rd Street
OPEN: During working hours

A marvelous enclosure of space providing visual pleasure for hundreds of employees, the Ford Foundation has become a trendsetter for similar design concepts. The atrium garden, full of lush plants, rises the full height of the structure, terminating in glass skylights. Virtually all the offices open onto the sunlit atrium. A palette of natural colors was employed as background material to enhance the garden. The design and arrangement of this complex have made a substantial contribution to the working environment.

NEW YORK CITY

Guggenheim Museum (1956–59)

ARCHITECT: Frank Lloyd Wright
LOCATION: 1071 5th Avenue between 88th and 89th Streets
OPEN: Tues., 11–8, Wed.–Sun. and holidays, 11–5

Wright's fascination with circles and spirals expressively culminated in this dynamic work completed the year of the great architect's death. Breaking the confines of museum buildings of the past—viewing art in boxy rooms—Wright entices the patron to view modern paintings on a spiralling ramp. An appropriate and innovative background for art, the building itself is like a giant sculpture.

NEW YORK CITY

Lehman Wing at The Metropolitan Museum (1975)

ARCHITECTS: Kevin Roche and John Dinkeloo
LOCATION: 5th Avenue at 82nd Street
OPEN: Tues., 10–8:45, Wed.–Sat., 10–4:45, Sun., 11–4:45

The brilliant new wing of the Metropolitan Museum is "set like a jewel in the Met's crown." The sleek glass and limestone complex is a direct contrast to the original neo-classic museum. The vast interior of the new wing features a two-tiered cascade of skylights enclosing a magnitude of space. An ensemble of smaller additions and courtyards welcomes the visitor. Although the addition has been criticized as unsympathetic of McKim, Mead, & White's original structure, the exhibits, lighting, spaciousness, and design delight the museum-goer.

NEW YORK CITY

Lever House (1950–52)

ARCHITECTS: Skidmore, Owings & Merrill
LOCATION: 390 Park Avenue between 53rd and 54th Streets
OPEN: During business hours, exhibition area on ground floor

A trend-setting skyscraper in America, the Lever House is a building of uniformity and strength. SOM designed the structure providing a refreshing integration of walkways and an inner courtyard—a first attempt to humanize the base of a high-rise tower. Today it still reigns as a respected "old hallmark of modern architecture." The *MANUFACTUERS HANOVER TRUST COMPANY* (1953–54) on 5th Avenue at 43rd Street is another interesting structure by America's early modern architectural firm.

NEW YORK CITY

Lincoln Center for The Performing Arts (1959–68)

ARCHITECTS: *AVERY FISHER HALL* (1962), Max Abramovitz, later remodelled by Philip Johnson; *NEW YORK STATE THEATER* (1964), Philip Johnson and Richard Foster; *VIVIAN BEAUMONT THEATER* (1965), Eero Saarinen & Associates; *METROPOLITAN OPERA HOUSE* (1966), Wallace K. Harrison; *JUILLIARD SCHOOL OF MUSIC,* Pietro Belluschi, Eduardo Catalano and Westermann & Miller.
LOCATION: 62nd–66th Sts. at Columbus Ave. (Broadway) and Amsterdam Avenue

The Lincoln Center is surely the nation's most brilliant complex of buildings for the performing arts. Designed by some of the most prominent modern architects in the country, Lincoln Center is invitingly arranged around a spacious plaza.

NEW YORK CITY

Museum of Modern Art

(1938–39)
Sculpture Garden (1953/64/84)
ARCHITECTS: Edward Durell Stone & Philip L. Goodwin, Philip Johnson, and Cesar Pelli and Gruen Associates.
LOCATION: 11 West 53rd Street
OPEN: Mon.–Tues., 11–6, Thurs. 11–9, Fri.–Sat. 12–6

MoMA is simply designed, but engagingly geared as an effective background for modern art and design. It is one of the first and finest museums of its kind in the nation. The visitor is immediately encompassed with an intriguing collection of art from the first step through the door. An exquisitely designed sculpture garden enclosed by a high gray brick wall contains a fine modern sculpture display. The new reflective glass tower addition (mostly residential units) enhances the museum's efficiency and appeal.

NEW YORK CITY

Pan-Am Building (1963)

ARCHITECTS: Walter Gropius and The
Architects' Collaborative & others
LOCATION: 200 Park Avenue (48th St.)
OPEN: During business hours

During his chairmanship for the Department
of Architecture at Harvard University, Gropius
continued his professional practice. He later
formed TAC, The Architects' Collaborative, in
1945. The highly criticized and praised Pan
Am Building, with its unusual shape, is a
familiar landmark—some say "intrusion"—at
the end of Park Avenue. The glass wrapped
structure, with the letters PAN AM boldly
integrated into the design, contrasts consider-
ably with its neighbors, particularly the
decorative Grand Central Station close by.

NEW YORK CITY

Rockefeller Center (1931–40)

ARCHITECTS: Reinhard & Hofmeister;
Corbett, Harrison & MacMurray; Hood &
Fouilhoux
LOCATION: 5th Ave., Ave. of the Americas,
48th–51st Streets
OPEN: RCA Building Observation Roof
open daily

The Art Deco craze in America was in full
swing when this center, comprising thirteen
buildings, was erected. The structures are
flanked alongside a beautiful and inviting
pedestrian mall leading up to a sunken plaza
surrounded by colorful flags from all nations.
The golden "Prometheus" sculpture creates a
striking focal point. The RCA BUILDING and
the recently restored RADIO CITY MUSIC
HALL are notable examples of Art Deco
design and popular attractions in New York
City.

NEW YORK CITY

Seagram Building (1954–58)

ARCHITECTS: Ludwig Mies van der Rohe
and Philip Johnson
LOCATION: 375 Park Avenue (between
52nd and 53rd Streets)
OPEN: Four Seasons Restaurant and lobby
open during business hours

Undoubtedly Mies' finest and most admired
work, the Seagram Building, like the Lever
House across the street, has become an
important prototype for skyscrapers around
the world. The well-articulated bronzed glass
structure is set back from the street to allow
welcome space for a slightly raised granite
plaza. The detailing of the structure is
perfection and the Four Seasons Restaurant
on the first floors by Philip Johnson pure
elegance.

NEW YORK CITY

TWA Flight Center John F. Kennedy International Airport (1958–62)

ARCHITECT: Eero Saarinen
LOCATION: via Van Wyck Expressway,
Queens
OPEN: Continuously

Desiring to capture the spirit and feeling of
flight, Saarinen designed this rhapsody in
concrete. Bold, flowing concrete forms surely
capture the drama of air travel. The expressive structure consists of four interconnected
barrel vaults supported on four Y-shaped
columns. The huge concrete shell is fifty-feet
high and three-hundred-fifteen feet long. The
design concept is carried throughout the
interior spaces right down to the departure
and arrival screens.

NEW YORK CITY

United Nations Plaza Hotel

ARCHITECTS: Roche/Dinkeloo & Associates
LOCATION: One United Nations Plaza
OPEN: Continuously

Coupled with the United Nations Building across the street, the United Nations Plaza Hotel makes a vivid silhouette on Manhattan's skyline. The well-articulated complex, with its reflective glass skin, gains interest through dramatically sloping level changes at three points. The approach breaks the confines of the "traditional" boxy modern Miesian skyscrapers. A protective and inviting glass and metal canopy at the base of the building makes a nice transition between the street and the soaring tower.

NEW YORK CITY

United Nations Secretariat Building (1947–50)

ARCHITECTS: W.K. Harrison, M. Abramovitz, Le Corbusier, S. Markelius, O. Niemeyer, and N.N.D. Bassov
LOCATION: 1st Avenue between 42nd and 48th Streets
OPEN: Daily tours: 9:15–4:45 of the UN complex

A strong outline on New York's shoreline, the United Nations Building has become a shining symbol of international cooperation and world peace. Appropriately, an international team of architects contributed to the design concept; Niemeyer from Brazil, Markelius from Sweden, Le Corbusier from France, and Harrison and Abramovitz from the United States. Wrapped in green tinted glass, the building is dignified and solid, incorporating innovations unheard of when it was built. Unquestionably, the UN Building is still an admirable landmark.

NEW YORK CITY

Trump Tower (1983)

ARCHITECTS: Swanke Hayden Connell &
Partners
LOCATION: 725 Fifth Avenue, corner of
56th Street

The dazzling new Trump Tower looms over
Fifth Avenue and is already considered one of
the city's most exciting new structures.
Staggered forms on the upper sections of the
slim tower adds to the building's visual
appeal. A skin of dark tinted glass is
contrasted at the entrance by a stunning entry
of gleaming brass. An interior sculpture in the
entry lobby in the form of embracing "T's"
identifies the building. A red stone fountain
with projecting forms cascades down into an
interior atrium space creating pleasant audio/
visual experience.

NEW YORK CITY

Whitney Museum of American Art (1964–66)

ARCHITECTS: Marcel Breuer and Hamilton
Smith
LOCATION: 945 Madison Avenue at 75th
Street
OPEN: Tues. 11–9, Wed.–Sat. 11–6, Sun. &
Holidays noon to 6

It is hardly possible to walk by this fascinating "upside-down ziggarat" museum without
wanting to cross over the catwalk hovering
over a sunken sculpture garden and explore
the premises. In fact, the outdoor sculpture
garden, a full story below street level, is the
extraordinary feature of the structure. The
interior areas continue the expression of
unusual form and space. After his Bauhaus
experience in Germany, Breuer had an
opportunity to develop his individualistic
approach.

NEW YORK CITY

Woolworth Building (1911–13)

ARCHITECT: Cass Gilbert
LOCATION: 233 Broadway at Park Place
OPEN: During business hours

An extraordinary engineering feat for the time, and the world's tallest structure until 1930, the Woolworth Building delighted the public. It is a skyscraper in the Gothic style that Frank Woolworth loved. He commissioned Gilbert to design his fifty-eight-story office building employing a feeling from Europe's medieval Gothic cathedrals and London's Parliament buildings. The building was a success—both technically and aesthetically. The spectacular lobby, renovated in 1978, is open to the public.

NEW YORK CITY

World of Birds at The Bronx Zoo, World of Darkness

(1971–72)

ARCHITECTS: Morris Ketchum, Jr. & Associates
LOCATION: Pelham and Bronx River Parkways, Bronx Park
OPEN: Mon.–Sat., 10–5, Sun., 10–5:30

These two engaging structures of innovative modern design are located in a park setting at the Bronx Zoo. The World of Birds is an imaginative design complex for the task of "housing" instead of "caging" birds. Hundreds of species fly freely in the cavernous spaces. Visitors meander through the natural habitat that is completely climate controlled. Informative screens are placed along the way. The World of Darkness is a fascinating reverse environment from the lightness of the World of Birds. It was created to let the visitor experience an animal's world at night. Both buildings are beautifully expressive of their functions.

NEW YORK CITY

World Trade Center (1966–80)

ARCHITECTS: Minoru Yamasaki & Associates
with Emery Roth & Sons
LOCATION: Church Street between Liberty
and Vesey
OPEN: Observation deck in Tower 2 open
daily; restaurant at top of Tower 1 open
daily

The tallest skyscrapers in New York City, the
110-story structures required the development
of new technology to allow construction.
Seventy-foot high lobbies welcome the visitor
and feature large cathedral-like modules with
glass infils. The elevator ride to the top of the
towers and the panoramic view of the city is
exhilarating. The Windows of the World
Restaurant, on the 107th floor, was planned by
the prominent designer Warren Platner.

NIAGARA FALLS

Niagara Falls Convention Center (1974)

ARCHITECTS: Philip Johnson/John Burgee
LOCATION: End of Rainbow Center Mall
OPEN: Special events and performances

The splendid Convention Center is part of an
ambitious urban renewal effort for Niagara
Falls. In an attempt to attract tourists to one of
the nation's most spectacular sights, the city
fathers commissioned many superb new
buildings in the downtown area. The huge,
domed structure is placed at the end of a
15,000 foot-long mall, thus creating an effective link with the Falls.

NIAGARA FALLS

Winter Garden and Rainbow Center Mall (1975–77)

ARCHITECTS: Cesar Pelli and Gruen Associates
LOCATION: Just off Rainbow Boulevard
OPEN: 10–10 daily

With its interestingly angled forms, this lacy superstructure seems to suggest powerful shifts in the earth's surface. The pattern of red-painted trusses reveals the composition of a dazzling complex. The effect of the glass structure at night has been described as "a space filled with clear, yet thickly refractive liquid" and as "a form carved from a huge block of crystal."

PORT CHESTER

Kneses Tifereth Israel Synagogue (1956)

ARCHITECT: Philip Johnson
LOCATION: 575 King Street
OPEN: During services or by special appointment; tel: (914) 939-1004

Simple, small, yet intriguing, this synagogue was designed a few years after the architect's famous glass house in New Canaan, Connecticut. Contrasting with its country setting, the stark white walls of the building are pierced with slender vertical slits of colorful stained glass, providing interest and fenestration. The rectangular shape of the main structure is broken by a sculptural oval vestibule that introduces the visitor into the spiritual space.

PURCHASE

Purchase Campus—State University of New York (1971–78)

ARCHITECTS: Edward L. Barnes & others
LOCATION: Exit 28 off Hutchinson River Pkwy., N on Lincoln Avenue, R on Anderson Hill Road
OPEN: Museum: Tues–Sat., 11–5, Sun., 1–5

Purchase campus boasts a marvelous concentration of structures designed by some of America's leading architects. Some of the best are: the *LIBRARY* (1974), by Edward Larrabee Barnes; the *HUMANITIES BUILDING* (1974), by Venturi and Rauch; the *ROY R. NEUBERGER MUSEUM OF ART* (1972), by Johnson/Burgee; the *NATURAL SCIENCE BUILDING* (1975), by Paul Rudolph; the *DANCE INSTRUCTIONAL FACILITY* (1976), by Gunnar Birkerts; the *SOCIAL SCIENCE BUILDING* (1978), by Venturi & Rauch; the *MUSICAL INSTRUCTION BUILDINGS* (1978), by Edward Larrabee Barnes; and the *VISUAL ARTS INSTRUCTIONAL BUILDING* (1977), by the Architects' Collaborative.

ROCHESTER

First Unitarian Church (1961–63)

ARCHITECT: Louis I. Kahn
LOCATION: 220 Winton Road South
OPEN: Sunday service; Mon.–Fri., 9–5

Kahn was particularly fond of employing brick as a building material. With the design of this religious structure, the architect, through brilliant use of form, light, and materials, has created an enticing complex. The central congregational area is topped with an enormous concrete roof in the shape of a Greek Cross that totally dominates the interior space.

SYRACUSE

Everson Museum of Art

(1966–68)

ARCHITECTS: I.M. Pei
LOCATION: 401 Harrison Street at South State Street
OPEN: Tues.–Fri., Sun. 12–5

The intriguing arrangement of four cantilevered forms comprising the Everson Museum appears as a great piece of sculpture. Constructed of concrete and red aggregate throughout, the complex houses galleries, hung with modern art, an auditorium, and administrative areas. A bold Henry Moore sculpture, placed near the entry, introduces and captures the spirit of the strongly expressed museum.

UTICA

Munson-Williams-Proctor Institute (1960)

ARCHITECTS: Philip Johnson Associates
LOCATION: 310 Genesee Street
OPEN: Tues.–Sat. 10–5, Sun. 1–5

Fascinating structural components draw the visitor through the interior spaces of this powerfully designed museum of stone and glass. The box-shaped structure is punctuated with four vertical slabs extending above the roof line. A traditional Victorian home close by interestingly contrasts with the dramatic museum. The interior features a vast exhibit space topped with a grid of over a hundred domed skylights that flood the area with light. Walls around the perimeter of the first floor and mezzanine are lined with an impressive modern art collection.

WHITE PLAINS

The General Foods Corporate Office (1983)

ARCHITECTS: Kevin Roche/John Dinkeloo Associates
LOCATION: Ryebrook, White Plains, just off Pkwy. 287
OPEN: Tours: Mon.–Fri. 10 AM and 2 PM

The sprawling new Corporate Offices for General Foods is beautifully situated in a wooded area stradlling a meandering pond. The gleaming glass and white aluminum clad structure has been likened to a Renaissance palace. Noble and stately, the building is one of a few trend-setting structures in the United States with a design based on themes recalled from the past. The integration of traditional and modern concepts is fascinating and refreshing.

YONKERS

Hudson River Museum

(1967–68)

ARCHITECTS: The SMS Architects
LOCATION: Trevor Park, 511 Warburton Avenue
OPEN: Tues.–Sat. 10–5, Sun. 11–5

Built on a steep slope, the modern Hudson River Museum was planned around an existing 1877 house that functioned as the former museum space. The contrast is engaging— arranged around a courtyard full of abstract sculpture. Three separate concrete units contain a library, museum, planetarium, teaching areas, and other facilities for the arts.

ADDITIONAL MODERN STRUCTURES OF INTEREST

The state of New York boasts thousands of modern buildings designed during the past century. The following structures were selected based on their architectural importance, national and international recognition, and unique qualities most interesting to the public.

ALBANY

Albany Campus Center (1983)
ARCHITECTS: Architectural Resources Cambridge
LOCATION: Russell Sage College

City Hall (1881–82)
ARCHITECT: Henry Hobson Richardson
LOCATION: Across Academy Park on Eagle Street

An early work by the great "Romanesque Revivalist" demonstrating a modern direction towards structural architecture.

ARMONK

I.B.M. Corporation (1957–61)
ARCHITECT: Eero Saarinen
LOCATION: Old Orchard Road

A simple and direct architectural expression of functionalism by one of America's foremost modern designers.

AURORA

Louis Jefferson Long Library (1968)
ARCHITECTS: Skidmore, Owings & Merrill
LOCATION: Wells College campus, NY 90

A clear and functional library facility by one of the nation's most prominent architectural firms. A fascinating interior plan.

BINGHAMTON

Ely Park Houses (1971)
ARCHITECTS: TAC (The Architects Collaborative)

LOCATION: N off US 17 on Glenwood Rd., NW of town

"Townhouses" of cedar uniquely planned around irregular terrain.

Science Complex, Suny (1972–74)
ARCHITECTS: Davis, Brody & Associates
LOCATION: Vestal Parkway E (S off NY 434)

Beautiful handling of spacial relationships. Three new buildings incorporate and connect older structures on a challenging hillside.

BUFFALO

Ellicott Square Building (1895–96)
ARCHITECT: Daniel Burnham
LOCATION: 295 Main Street

A building, not as well known, by America's great pioneer modern architect.

Kleinhans Music Hall (1938)
ARCHITECT: Eliel Saarinen
LOCATION: Symphony Circle

A functionally designed and acoustically superb music hall by the great Finnish born American architect.

M & T Bank Building (1964–66)
ARCHITECT: Minoru Yamasaki
LOCATION: Main and N. Division Streets

This bank building was designed by the architect of the World Trade Center in New York City. Note the Harry Bertoia sculptural fountain in the plaza.

Shoreline Apartments (1973–77)
ARCHITECT: Paul Rudolph
LOCATION: Niagara Street between Caroline and West Mohawk

Close to Lake Erie, the plan features staggered rows of dwellings creating a feeling of individuality.

Temple Beth Zion (1966–67)
ARCHITECTS: Harrison and Abramovitz
LOCATION: 805 Delaware Avenue

Ten scalloped panels representing the Ten Commandments enclose the temple.

CANTON

Addition to Owen D. Young Library in Honor of Arthur Starratt Torrey (1980)
ARCHITECTS: Don Hisaka & Associates
LOCATION: St. Lawrence University campus

CLINTON

Kirkland College (1968–72)
ARCHITECTS: Benjamin Thompson & Associates
LOCATION: Off College Street, 1.6 miles W of town

Constructed of concrete frames and walls, these three story structures house classrooms, dormitories and public areas. Designed for low maintenance on a limited budget.

CORNING

Corning Community College (1964)
ARCHITECTS: Warner Burns Toan Lunde
LOCATION: E on Dennison Parkway (NY 17), S on Chemung Street (c. 2.8 miles S of town)

A nicely planned commuter college for about 2,000 students.

W.C. Decker Engineering Building (1980)
ARCHITECTS: Davis, Brody & Associates
LOCATION: Corning Glass Works, Centerway

FLUSHING

New York State Pavilion (1964)
ARCHITECT: Philip Johnson
LOCATION: Queens Theater in the Park (visible from freeway)

The spectacular Pavilion, designed for the 1964 World's Fair, now functions as a theater in the park.

FREDONIA

SUNY (State University of New York at Fredonia (1970–)
ARCHITECTS: I.M. Pei and Partners
LOCATION: SUNY campus at Fredonia

One of the most interestingly designed of SUNY's 23 campuses. The Daniel Reed Library is just one of the many fine buildings on campus.

GREAT NECK

Chase Manhattan Bank (1960s)
ARCHITECTS: Benjamin Thompson
LOCATION: 22 Grace Avenue

GARDEN CITY

Adelphi College Library (1957–63)
ARCHITECT: Richard Neutra
LOCATION: Adelphi College campus, on South Avenue

A work by the great California pioner modern architect.

Endo Laboratories (1962–64)
ARCHITECT: Paul Rudolph
LOCATION: 1000 Stewart Avenue

Finished with Rudolph's typical rough striated concrete texture, Endo Laboratories is considered one of the finest industrial complexes in the nation. Inspired by the medieval fortress.

HAMILTON

Creative Arts Center—Colgate University (1963–66)
ARCHITECT: Paul Rudolph
LOCATION: Colgate University campus

This innovative Arts Center was designed a few years after Rudolph's controversial Art and Architecture Building at Yale University.

HARRISON (PURCHASE)

Pepsico, Inc. World Headquarters (1971)
ARCHITECTS: Edward Durell Stone & Associates
LOCATION: 700 Anderson Hill Road

A handsome corporate complex designed by Stone, known for his "beautiful" modern architecture.

ITHACA

Center Ithaca (1980s)
ARCHITECTS: Werner Seligmann & Associates
LOCATION: Tioga Street close to State Street

Elm Street Housing (1971–73)
ARCHITECTS: Werner Seligmann & Associates
LOCATION: Elm Street at West Village Place

The nicely laid out, low-rise housing units are interestingly terraced on a hillside setting.

The Ithaca College Performing Arts Center (1969)
ARCHITECTS: Tallman & Tallman, Prof. Thomas Canfield, designer
LOCATION: Ithaca College campus

LONG ISLAND

Library-Learning Center (1975)
ARCHITECTS: Davis, Brody & Associates
LOCATION: Long Island University campus

Stony Brook Campus (SUNY) (1981)
ARCHITECTS: Damaz, Pokorny, Weigel, William Kessler and others
LOCATION: State University of New York campus at Stony Brook

A campus design that has received much favorable publicity.

NEW YORK CITY

Aaron Davis Hall, Leonard Avis Ctr. for The Performing Arts (1979)
ARCHITECTS: Abraham W. Geller & Associates
LOCATION: City College of NY, c. 3 1/2 miles N of downtown

ABC Broadcast Facilities (1979)
ARCHITECTS: Kohn Pedersen Fox
LOCATION: 30 West 67th Street

This nationally prominent firm is known for their stunning architectural approach.

Apartment Tower (1978)
ARCHITECTS: Gruzen & Partners
LOCATION: 265 East 66th Street

A sleek tower of dark glass nicely positioned on a corner lot.

Banque Nationale De Paris (1980s)
ARCHITECTS: I.M. Pei & Partners
LOCATION: 499 Park Avenue

Clad with a black glass skin, this banking tower makes a striking outline on Park Avenue. Interior treatments carry out this bold theme.

Bronx Developmental Center (1973–77)
ARCHITECTS: Richard Meier & Associates
LOCATION: 1200 Waters Place, Hutchinson River Parkway from Manhattan, E to Westchester Avenue exit

This admirable development has received considerable national attention. Buildings are standardized, utilizing module panels. The complex is well planned for human activities and enjoyment employing the latest technical advancements.

Brooklyn Bridge (1869–83)
ENGINEERS: John Augustus Roebling & Washington Roebling
LOCATION: City Hall Park in Manhattan, Cadman Plaza in Brooklyn

Recently celebrating its 100th birthday, the extraordinary bridge still evokes amazement as an engineering marvel.

Brooklyn Children's Museum (1970s)
ARCHITECTS: Hardy Holzman Pfeiffer
LOCATION: 145 Brooklyn Avenue, Brooklyn

A delightful complex and playground geared for children's enjoyment.

Chem Court (1982)
ARCHITECTS: Haines Lunberg Waehler
LOCATION: 277 Park Avenue

A visually appealing and inviting "tack on" facade constructed of space frames providing a large interior space full of greenery and a fountain.

Continental Illinois Center (1980s)
ARCHITECTS: Swanke, Hayden Connell
LOCATION: Madison Avenue between 53rd
and 54th Streets

Faced with red granite, the streamlined new
Center splays outward on the lower levels.

Continental Insurance Building (1980s)
ARCHITECTS: Poor, Swanke, Hayden &
Connell
LOCATION: 180 Maiden Lane

A stunning tower of tinted glass, space frames
and a spacious interior plaza.

Corning Glass Building (1959)
ARCHITECTS: Harrison & Abramovitz
LOCATION: 717 Fifth Avenue

A still handsome building displaying exquisite
Stueben glass.

1001 Fifth Avenue Facade (1979)
ARCHITECTS: Philip Johnson/John Burgee
LOCATION: 1001 Fifth Ave. (across street
from Metropolitan Museum)

Designed with consideration for neighboring
buildings, this praised and criticized facade of
stone and soaring vertical bands of dark glass,
creates an "historical allusion."

Galleria (1975)
ARCHITECTS: David Kenneth Specter with
others
LOCATION: 115 East 57th Street

A clearly functional tower employing simple
form and materials.

General Motors Building (1971)
ARCHITECT: Edward Durell Stone
LOCATION: 767 5th Avenue, between 58th
and 59th Streets

Slender soaring white forms are accented by
slivers of dark glass creating a striking effect.

George Washington Bridge Bus Station
(1963)
ARCHITECT: Pier Luigi Nervi (Italy)
LOCATION: East end of the George
Washington Bridge

This large concrete structure straddles the
end of a 12-lane Expressway. Designed by
Italy's most famous early modern architect.

Hammarskjold Tower (1980s)
ARCHITECTS: Gruzen & Partners
LOCATION: 240 East 47th Street

A simple tower interestingly angled to create
"non-boxy" apartment plans.

Headquarters of The Asia Society (1981)
ARCHITECTS: Edward Larrabee Barnes
Associates
LOCATION: 725 Park Avenue

Sheathed with stone, the Asia Society building
is visually simple, the entrance way functioning as a focal point.

I.B.M. Tower (1980s)
ARCHITECT: Edward Larrabee Barnes
LOCATION: Corner of 57th Street and
Madison Avenue

Clean and direct, this functional tower features an attractive large interior space full of
lush plants.

Irving Trust Company (1930–31/1966)
ARCHITECTS: Voorhees, Gmelin & Walker
(1931) Smith, Smith, Hains, Lundberg &
Waehler (1966)
LOCATION: 1 Wall Street at Broadway

This handsome building, with additions sensitively incorporated, features well planned
and designed interior spaces.

Kips Bay Plaza
ARCHITECTS: I.M. Pei & Partners
LOCATION: 300 East 33rd

Nicely arranged tower dwellings planned for
human enjoyment in a city atmosphere.

Lecture Hall at New York University
(1961)
ARCHITECT: Marcel Breuer
LOCATION: New York University Bronx
campus

A strong and expressive lecture hall constructed of raw concrete.

Lehman College Center for The Arts
(1981)
ARCHITECTS: Todd/Pokorny with others
LOCATION: Bronx Community College
campus

Manufacturers Hanover Trust Company
(1953–54)
ARCHITECTS: Skidmore, Owings & Merrill
LOCATION: 5th Avenue at 43rd Street

Designed a few years after their famous Lever House on Park Avenue, this small 4 1/2 story bank was one of the first to be designed in non-historic terms.

Mercedes Benz Showroom (early 50s, Renovation 1970s)
ARCHITECT: Frank Lloyd Wright/Taliesin Associates
LOCATION: Corner of Park Avenue and 56th Street

This little known work by Wright has recently been restored to its original design featuring a spiralling ramp resembling that at the Guggenheim Museum.

One Federal Plaza (1984)
ARCHITECTS: Philip Johnson/John Burgee
LOCATION: Maiden Lane at Nausau

One of the firms latest works suggesting historic forms interpreted in modern terms. The narrow tower is sandwiched in a crowded section of the Wall Street area.

100 William Street Building (1980s)
ARCHITECTS: Davis Brody & Associates with Emery Roth & Sons
LOCATION: 100 William Street

Located in a dense area of the Wall Street area, this nicely angled, dark glass tower, makes a vivid impression.

101 Park Avenue Tower (1980s)
ARCHITECTS: Eli Attia Architects
LOCATION: 101 Park Avenue

The combination of materials, including granite and dark glass, contribute to this tower's striking image.

1199 Plaza (1971–75)
ARCHITECTS: The Hodne/Stageberg Partners, Inc.
LOCATION: 1st Avenue between 107th and 111th Streets

Operations Center for Irving Trust Co.
(1981)
ARCHITECTS: Skidmore, Owings & Merrill
LOCATION: 101 Barclay Street

Although located close to the base of the spectacular World Trade Center, this sleek staggered Center makes a dynamic impression. The soaring interior atrium space is breathtaking.

Park Avenue Plaza (1980s)
ARCHITECTS: Skidmore, Owings & Merrill
LOCATION: 55 East 52nd (just off Park Avenue)

A stately and dignified tower designed for function and efficiency.

Pepsi Cola Company (1959)
ARCHITECTS: Skidmore, Owings & Merrill
LOCATION: 500 Park Avenue (at 59th Street)

This low-rise, simply designed structure, demonstrates SOM's emphasis on clean functional architecture.

Philip Morris Corporate Headquarters
(1979–82)
ARCHITECTS: Ulrich Franzen
LOCATION: Park Avenue, entry at 41st Street

Wrapping the entire corner, this sleek building incorporates a small branch of the Whitney Museum of Modern Art. The clean surfaces are an ideal backdrop for the modern art.

Police Plaza (1968–73)
ARCHITECTS: Gruzen & Partners
LOCATION: Centre Street at Manhattan at end of Brooklyn Bridge

This admirably planned plaza and surrounding buildings have been incorporated into a busy downtown section. The new buildings compliment the surrounding older structures, especially McKim, Mead & White's historic Municipal Building close by.

Solo Building "Avon Building" (1970s)
ARCHITECTS: Skidmore, Owings & Merrill
LOCATION: 9 West 57th Street

Sheathed with travertine, a bold contrasting section of dark glass soars upward through the structure. The building splays outward on the bottom levels adding to the drama. A huge orange sculptural figure "9" on the sidewalk is a highlight. The GRACE BUILDING (1970) located at 1114 Avenue of the Americas is also designed by SOM and a twin to the Solo building.

Starrett-Lehigh Building (1921–31)
ARCHITECTS: Russell G. and Walter R. Cory
LOCATION: 26th–27th Streets between 11th and 12th Avenues

The Starrett-Lehigh Building was considered one of the most significant industrial structures of the time. The design, typical of the Art Deco period, employs bands of glass and spandrels.

The Richard Feigen Gallery (Now Hanae Mori International) (1969)
ARCHITECT: Hans Hollein (Austria)
LOCATION: 27 East 79th Street

This small stunning building, now a clothing store, was designed by Austria's internationally known architect. Stark white surfaces are broken with gleaming metal cylinders.

University Plaza (1966)
ARCHITECTS: I.M. Pei & Partners
LOCATION: 100 and 110 Bleecker Street, 505 W. Broadway

These three identical towers are nicely arranged around a plaza enhancing the thirty story, simply designed structure.

Verrazano-Narrows Bridge (1962)
ENGINEERS: Ammann and Whitney
LOCATION: Hwy. 278 East Staten Island spanning Lower New York Bay to Brooklyn

Considered one of the finest new bridges in New York.

Wang Building (1980s)
ARCHITECTS: Skidmore, Owings & Merrill
LOCATION: 780 Third Avenue

Stark simplicity of this tower is made interesting through the use of red granite sheathing

and a series of humorous black vertical sculptural forms.

Waterside (1970–74)
ARCHITECTS: Davis, Brody & Associates
LOCATION: FDR Drive at 25–30 Streets (Take 23rd Street exit southbound)
OPEN: Public plaza open daily

A highly commendable housing development consisting of four towers, townhouse duplexes, and a shopping area, Waterside is situated on the waterfront of New York's east side Manhattan. The complex of 1,471 apartments is a private and comfortable retreat from the city atmosphere. The towers radiate outward surrounded at the base by plazas and pleasant landscaping. The design concept, according to the architects, was to seek a more "convenient, humane, exciting, and attractive place."

World Financial Center (1983–)
ARCHITECTS: Cesar Pelli and others
LOCATION: Lower Manhattan, Battery Park City on the Hudson River

NEW PALTZ

Concourse Development, SUNY (1963–68)
ARCHITECTS: Ballard Todd Associates with Davis, Brody & Associates and others
LOCATION: Off Maine St., (NY 299), W off S. Chestnut St. (NY 208)

One of the finer designed State University campuses in the state boasting many well planned facilities.

NIAGARA FALLS

Earl W. Brydges Public Library (1973–74)
ARCHITECT: Paul Rudolph
LOCATION: 1425 Main Street between Pierce and Lockport

Projecting forms, raw striated concrete surfaces and superb space planning distinguish this library facility.

NORTH TARRYTOWN

IBM World Trade Americas/Far East Corporation Hdqts. (1975)
ARCHITECTS: Edward Larrabee Barnes and Associates
LOCATION: Rockwood Rd., Rt. 9, a few miles NW of White Plains

PLATTSBURG

Student Union at State University (1975)
ARCHITECTS: Mitchell/Giurgola
LOCATION: Rugar Street

POTSDAM

Buildings at State University of New York at Potsdam (1971–)
ARCHITECT: Edward Larrabee Barnes
LOCATION: State University of New York (SUNY) campus

POUGHKEEPSIE

College Center at Vassar College (1977)
ARCHITECTS: Shepley Bulfinch
LOCATION: Routes 44/55 to Raymond Ave. (S, almost to Rt. 376)

ROCHESTER

Manhattan Square Park (1974)
ARCHITECTS: Lawrence Halprin Associates
LOCATION: Manhattan Square Park, SE Loop section of the city

A welcoming plaza-fountain under a space-frame, surrounded with delightful landscaping has provided downtown Rochester with a new identity.

Rochester Institute of Technology (1968–)
ARCHITECTS: Anderson, Beckwith & Haible, Corgan & Balestiere, Edward Larrabee Barnes, Roche/Dinkeloo, Hugh Stubbins, and Harry Weese.
LOCATION: Jefferson Town Line Rd. at East River Rd., SW of city

This new campus of modern buildings has been designed by some of the nation's most illustrious architects.

Temple and School B'rith Kodesh (1963)
ARCHITECT: Pietro Belluschi-Waasdorp, Northrup & Austin
LOCATION: 2131 Elmwood Avenue

An impressive religious structure designed by the famous Italian-born American architect.

SARATOGA SPRINGS

New Campus of Skidmore College (1966)
ARCHITECTS: Ford, Powell & Carson
LOCATION: Third Street, West of Broadway

Saratoga Performing Arts Center (mid 1960s)
ARCHITECTS: Vollmer Associates
LOCATION: Saratoga Springs Park, off Route 50

The steel-framed Performing Arts Center is located in a 150,000 sq. ft. wooded area, and features a pleated fan-shaped amphitheater.

SCHENECTEDY

The First Unitarian Church (1964)
ARCHITECT: Edward Durell Stone
LOCATION: 1221 Wendell Avenue

SYRACUSE

Building II at Syracuse University (1972–73)
ARCHITECTS: Skidmore, Owings & Merrill
LOCATION: Waverly Avenue at University Avenue

May Memorial Unitarian Church (1965)
ARCHITECTS: Pietro Belluschi and Pederson Hueber Hares & Glavin
LOCATION: 3800 East Genesee Street

Belluschi is particularly known for his warm and sensitively planned religious structures throughout the nation.

Onondaga County Civic Center (1978)
ARCHITECTS: Mc Afee, Malo/Lebensold, Affleck, Nichol & others
LOCATION: 421 Montgomery Street

St. Mary's Complex (1966–68)
ARCHITECTS: Sargent-Webster-Crenshaw & Folley
LOCATION: Van Buren Street facing IS 81

This interesting complex of buildings was erected over a no longer existing cemetery site. The 24-story TOOMEY ABBOTT TOWER houses dwellings for the aged and the other buildings provide facilities for students at Syracuse University.

S.I. Newhouse School of Public Communications, Building I (1962–64)
ARCHITECTS: I.M. Pei & Partners
LOCATION: Syracuse University, University Place at University Ave.

University Union at Syracuse University (1973)
ARCHITECTS: Cambridge Seven Associates
LOCATION: Syracuse University campus

TROY

Snell Music Building and William Moore Dietel Library (1969)
ARCHITECTS: Edward Larrabee Barnes-Noel Yauch
LOCATION: Emma Willard School Campus

This building demonstrates Barnes clear and direct approach to architecture.

Uncle Sam Atrium, Shopping Mall & Garage (1981)
ARCHITECTS: Geoffrey Freeman Associates
LOCATION: Third & Fourth Streets, downtown Troy

One of the state's most warm and interestingly arranged shopping malls.

WEST POINT

Eisenhower Hall (1975)
ARCHITECTS: Welton Becket & Associates
LOCATION: West Point Military Academy, Bldg. 655 between Ruger and Pitcher Roads

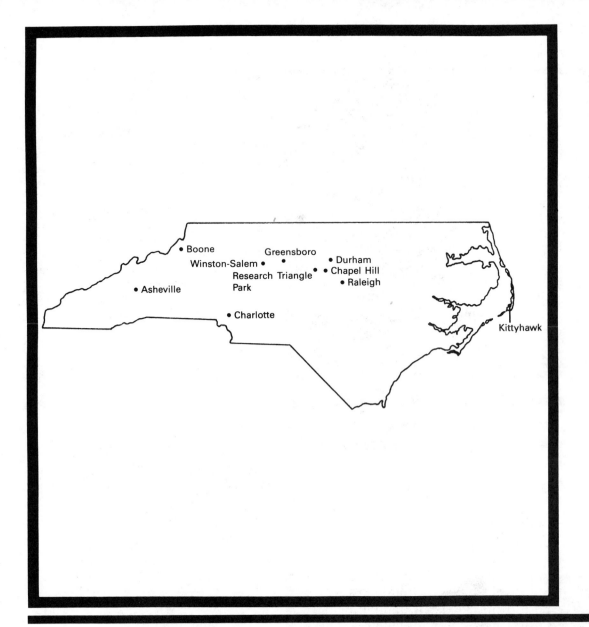

Boone

Greensboro

Winston-Salem •

• Durham

Research Triangle

• Chapel Hill

Park

• Raleigh

• Asheville

• Charlotte

Kittyhawk

North Carolina

CHAPEL HILL

North Carolina Blue Cross/ Blue Shield (1971–73)

ARCHITECTS: Odell Associates
LOCATION: Chapel Hill–Durham Boulevard, 2 miles E of town
OPEN: Tours Friday at 2:30

With the challenge of keeping construction costs to a minimum, this well-known North Carolina architectural firm designed a sleek structure with a curtain wall of reflective glass. Not only is the glass attractive, but it has the ability to reduce heat loss during winter and control heat gain during summer. The fascinating geometrically angled cantilever structure is flanked on one side by two water sculptures.

CHARLOTTE

Charlotte Museum of Science and Technology Discovery Place (1980)

ARCHITECTS: Clark, Tribble, Harris and Li
LOCATION: 301 North Tryon Street
OPEN: Weekdays 9–5, Sat. 9–6, Sun. 1–6

In association with the prominent architectural firm of Venturi and Rauch and other experts, the design of the Museum of Science and Technology is a tremendous success. An excellent floor plan and exhibit spaces provide the visitor with an intriguing experience. Sam Granger, the designer and illustrator of Spider Man, has created a popular booklet for the museum's tourists.

CHARLOTTE

Radisson Plaza Hotel (1977)

ARCHITECTS: Odell Associates with Thompson, Ventulett, Stainback & Associates
LOCATION: Two NCNB Plaza
OPEN: Always open

Streamlined and dazzling, the Radisson Hotel makes an impressive contribution to Charlotte's skyline. The hotel and plaza are connected by a convenient skyway system to the Civic Center and Belk Department Store. The complex includes a rooftop swimming pool, a ballroom, and an indoor shopping mall. With its unique bold form, the hotel has been compared to "the prow of a ship."

CHARLOTTE

Spirit Square & People's Place (1980)

ARCHITECTS: Hardy Holzman Pfeiffer Associates
LOCATION: 110 East 7th Street
OPEN: During business hours

In an attempt to promote business in downtown Charlotte and create a place for people to enjoy, this admirable arts program was instigated by the city fathers and local businessmen. Four older structures that previously belonged to a church were refurbished and dramatically linked to the new modern People's Place. The architects have sensitively incorporated the old and new through the use of materials and detailing. The result is intriguing. Facilities are provided for a theater, workshops, offices, and a restaurant, with plans continuing for further activities.

GREENSBORO

Governmental Center (1968–73)

ARCHITECT: Eduardo Catalano
LOCATION: Greene Street at Sycamore
(between Washington and Market)
OPEN: During business hours

The new Government Center is compatible and even complementary to the adjoining Old Guilford Court House. The new building prominently stands on its own through the use of bold modular planes and materials. A sunken plaza surrounded by plantings and seating ties the complex together and welcomes the visitor.

RALEIGH

State Legislative Building
(1961–63)

ARCHITECTS: Edward Durell Stone
Associates
LOCATION: Halifax Street at Jones,
Salisbury, and Wilmington
OPEN: June–Aug., Mon.–Fri. 8–5;
Sept.–May, Mon.–Fri. 8:30–5:30, Sat. 9–5,
Sun. 1–5

The State Capitol was designed a few years after Stone's highly praised US Pavilion at the 1958 Brussels' World Fair. He was one of the first American architects to break with the European International Style. With overtones of classicism, Stone's work is elegant, "pretty," and beautifully proportioned. The interior furnishings were also planned by the architect. A rich red carpet invites the visitor into the interior spaces.

RALEIGH

Temple Beth Or (1979)

ARCHITECT: Michael Landau
LOCATION: 5315 Creedmoot Road
OPEN: 9–4, Mon.–Tues.; 9–1 Fri., 8 PM–9 PM
on Fri.

This dramatic new synagogue features a bold curving ceiling reminiscent of the synagogues of Eastern Europe. When students of architecture at N.C. State University were asked to select a local building that best exemplified post-modernism, the Temple Beth Or was the most popular choice. Local cedar shakes were employed for the roof and brick for the walls. Uniquely fashioned glass windows are employed throughout, creating a special effect.

RESEARCH TRIANGLE PARK

Burroughs Wellcome Company (1970–72)

ARCHITECT: Paul Rudolph
LOCATION: 3030 Cornwallis Road, On I-40 between Durham & Raleigh
OPEN: Lobby and grounds during business hours

A dynamic and expressive design was created for this administrative headquarters. Rhythm and space are achieved through the use of strong external forms arranged in a contemporary "ziggarat fashion." Lighting within the interior spaces effectively adds to the building's design. The interaction of bold forms with the rolling hillside is intriguing as well as harmonious. The Burroughs building is one of its kind in the nation.

ADDITIONAL MODERN STRUCTURES OF INTEREST

ASHEVILLE

Mountain Area Health Education Center
(1979)
ARCHITECTS: Six Associates of Asheville
LOCATION: 501 Biltmore Avenue

A mountainous setting emphasizes the strong design of this health educational facility.

BOONE

Council of Governments Building (1983)
ARCHITECTS: McMurray, Abernathy and Poetzsch
LOCATION: Blowing Rock Road

A simple and uniform building labeled "Breuer-esque."

CHARLOTTE

Carmel Presbyterian Church (1976)
ARCHITECTS: Wheatley/Whisnant Associates
LOCATION: 2048 Carmel Road

This large church is topped with a distinctive pyramidal roof of steel sheathed with pine decking. The interior treatment is particularly well planned.

Charlotte Civic Center (1973)
ARCHITECTS: A. G. Odell and Associates
LOCATION: 101 S. College Street

A four-level complex featuring a dramatic series of white pyramids.

Colvard Building (1980s)
ARCHITECTS: Wolf Associates
LOCATION: University of North Carolina campus

Two commendable buildings by Wolf Associates complement the existing buildings. Brick, glass, and steel building materials were employed for construction.

Equitable Life's Regional Headquarters
(1979)
ARCHITECTS: Wolf Associates
LOCATION: 6301 Morrison Blvd.

A dramatic building of glass sheathing that is energy efficient.

Mecklenburg County Courthouse
ARCHITECTS: Wolf Associates
LOCATION: 600 E. Trade Street

A functional and practical building of reinforced concrete, the Mecklenburg County Courthouse is one of the finest structures of its type in the nation.

Slug's 30th Edition Restaurant (1981)
ARCHITECTS: Wolf Associates
LOCATION: 2900 First Union Tower

A dazzling use of materials, especially the interior treatment, this restaurant, part of the complex, features black marble and black lacquered columns with black stone walls.

DURHAM

Durham City Hall (1978)
ARCHITECTS: John D. Latimer and Associates
LOCATION: 101 City Hall Plaza

The Durham City Hall is a building that takes on various facets from different angles fitting nicely into a complex downtown setting.

GREENSBORO

Burlington Corporate Headquarters
(1971)
ARCHITECTS: Odell Associates
LOCATION: Friendly Road at Hobbs Street, WNW of downtown

A unique exposed skeletal steel frame with bronzed glass windows, the complex greatly contrasts with its country setting.

KITTYHAWK

The Visitor Center—Wright Brothers National Memorial (1960)
ARCHITECTS: Mitchell/Giurgola Associates
LOCATION: Mile Post 7, 158 By-pass, Kill Devil Hills

Many tourists make a pilgrimage to Kittyhawk to view the place where the Wright brothers made their historic flight. Effectively housed inside the Visitor's Center is a replica of the famous original airplane design by these pioneer aviators. The architect's goal was to convey the spirit of this first flight and to create spaces for various related activities. Expansive windows and soaring architectural forms create this environment. (Open daily, summer: 8:30–7:00, Winter: 9–5.)

RALEIGH

Cate Student Center at Meredith College (1979)
ARCHITECTS: Nelson Benzing
LOCATION: 3800 Hillsborough Street

Dramatically placed scoop windows provide a focal point for this well-designed student center.

Civic Center (1976)
ARCHITECTS: Odell Associates, Inc.
LOCATION: 500 Fayetteville Street Mall

This boldly designed 100,000 square foot facility functions for numerous events including trade shows and expositions.

Our Lady of Lourdes Roman Catholic Church (1978)
ARCHITECT: Roger H. Clark
LOCATION: 2912 Anderson Drive

An innovative design, this new church breaks with over 2,000 years of traditional religious architecture.

RESEARCH TRIANGLE PARK

National Humanities Center (1978)
ARCHITECTS: Hartman-Cox with TUCASI
LOCATION: On I-40 between Durham & Raleigh

An elaborate glass entrance is emphasized on this facility for Duke University, North Carolina State, and the University of North Carolina.

WINSTON-SALEM

Fine Arts Building—Wake Forest University (Scales Fine Arts Museum)
ARCHITECTS: Caudill Rowlett Scott
LOCATION: On Wake Forest Drive on campus at Reynolds Station

A bold modern design utilizing the potential of brick as a building material.

Integon Headquarters (1980s)
ARCHITECT: Welton Becket
LOCATION: 500 West Fifth Street

R.J. Reynolds' Headquarters (1979)
ARCHITECTS: Odell Associates
LOCATION: 1100 Reynolds Blvd.

A dramatic corporate structure designed for flexibility, energy conservation, and function. Also of interest is the restoration of Reynold's 1929 Art Deco building designed by Shreve & Lamb, architects of the Empire State Bldg.

Sawtooth Center for Visual Design (1970s)
LOCATION: By Winston Park

The building was once a textile mill, then a car dealership. Recently renovated by The Arts Council, the building now provides facilities for exhibit space, two galleries, a restaurant, and classrooms.

Stevens Center (1930s/1982)
LOCATION: 405 W. Fourth Street

An interesting renovation of an Art Deco movie house.

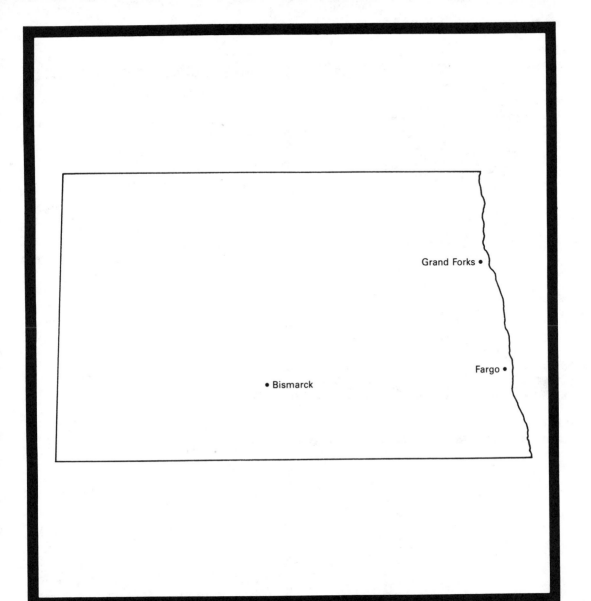

Grand Forks •

Fargo •

• Bismarck

North Dakota

BISMARCK

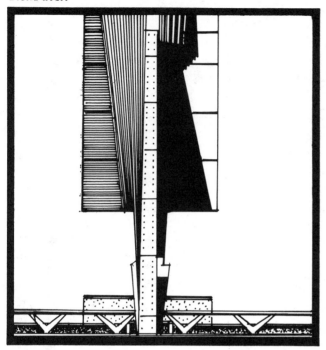

Annunciation Priory (1959–63)

ARCHITECTS: Marcel Breuer and Hamilton Smith
LOCATION: c. 7 miles S of Bismarck via 9th St. on ND 1804
OPEN: Guided tours daily. Chapel open daily

On an open, rugged, grassy plateau overlooking the Missouri River, the Annunciation Priory is one of Breuer's many successful projects. The structures of the Benedictine convent are clustered within an enclosed rectangular "island" with courtyards between the buildings. The 100-foot-high bell tower, constructed of raw concrete with an indented cross, looms above the complex, creating a spectacular focus for the sprawling buildings.

BISMARCK

North Dakota State Capitol
(1933–34)

ARCHITECTS: Joseph Bell de Remer and W.F. Kurke with Holabird & Root
LOCATION: Capitol Park
OPEN: Tours Mon.–Fri, on the hour 8–11 AM, 1–4 PM, also in summer, Sat. 9–4, Sun 1–4

Built to replace the previous state capitol destroyed by fire in 1933, the stately Capitol Building is not what people generally expect a building of this type to look like. A crisp, streamlined multi-story structure was designed, reflecting the popular design of the Art Deco period when modernistic skyscrapers were still in an experimental stage. The building makes a sleek and stately silhouette against its sloping hillside setting.

BISMARCK

The Mary College (1965–68)

ARCHITECTS: Marcel Breuer, Hamilton
Smith, & Tician Papachristou
LOCATION: Apple Creek Road, c. 7 miles S
of Bismarck via 9th St. on ND 1804
OPEN: Grounds open during school year

Close by the Annunciation Priory and an
affiliate of that institution, Mary College is
part of an ambitious building program. This
unified and commendable complex of buildings is pleasantly nestled on a sloping green
hillside. Breuer efficiently grouped buildings
around a U-shaped plan. Deeply set windows
framed by pre-cast concrete units with
splayed support braces constitute the design
theme.

GRAND FORKS

Edmond A. Hughes Fine Arts Center (1975)

ARCHITECTS: Seifert & Staszko
LOCATION: The University of North Dakota
campus
OPEN: During school hours

Constructed of pre-cast concrete and glass,
the Edmond A. Hughes Fine Arts Center
sensitively respects the beautifully landscaped
topography of its setting on campus. The
rambling, low-rise complex is in "keeping
with the concern for function and the future,
which is inherent in the fine arts community
and its work." Excellent facilities are found
throughout the Center providing functional
spaces for numerous activities.

ADDITIONAL MODERN STRUCTURES OF INTEREST

FARGO (WAHPETON)

Gate City Savings and Loan (1980)
ARCHITECTS: Hunter-Grobe
LOCATION: 802 Dakota Avenue, Wahpeton

The challenge of creating an attractive building, despite limited space program requirements, is nicely demonstrated in this small bank. The structure incorporates heating/cooling solar panels on the second level, providing about 60% of the energy requirements.

Toledo •

Cleveland
• Painesville
• Euclid
• Shaker Heights

•
Parma

Oberlin •

Kent •

Akron •

• Marion

Toronto •

• Wapakoneta

• Sidney

• Brownsville

• Columbus

• Dayton

• Oxford

Cincinnati
•

Ohio

AKRON

Edwin J. Thomas Performing Arts Hall (1971–73)

ARCHITECTS: Dalton, Van Dijk, Johnson & Partners with Caudill, Rowlett, Scott
LOCATION: Center Street at Hill
OPEN: For performances

A structure that is literally compelling—beckoning the visitor into the spaces. Mullion-free expanses of glass are dazzling against bold geometric forms of the structure. The lobby area features twenty-seven steel cylinders that serve as a functional support and as an attractive sculpture as well. Innovative features are found throughout the complex, creating one of the most advanced theater designs in the country. The complex is particularly beautiful at night when lit.

BROWNSVILLE

Flint Ridge Museum (1968)

ARCHITECT: E. A. Glendening
LOCATION: IS exit 55 eastbound, 56 westbound, off OH 668 3 miles N of town
OPEN: Mar.–Nov., Tues.–Sun. 9:30–5; Dec.–Feb., Sun.

Located in a green shady wooded area, the Flint Ridge Museum is constructed of cedar wood complementing its natural surroundings. A fascinating collection of Indian arrowheads and artifacts are artfully displayed. The most exciting focal point, however, is a well lit open recessed area showing two figures mining a deposit of Indian wares. The museum was constructed on one of America's richest sources of Indian relics—the building plan highlights this treasure.

CINCINNATI

Cincinnati Union Terminal
(1929–33/1980s)

ARCHITECTS: Fellheimer & Wagner
RENOVATION: Schofeld & Schofeld
LOCATION: W end of Ezzard Charles Drive
OPEN: Daily

The marvelous Cincinnati Union Railroad Terminal is one of the most unique examples of Art Deco in the nation. The interiors, recently and faithfully renovated, are particularly striking and dazzling. Strong geometric forms and colors, with typical motifs from the 1920s and 30s period are admirably employed. A semicircular drive and beautifully landscaped grounds emphasize the structure's distinctive characteristics.

CINCINNATI

Riverfront Stadium (1968–70)

ARCHITECTS: Finch-Heery with Alexander, Barnes, Rothschild & Paschal
LOCATION: 2nd Street, US 52 at Suspension Bridge
OPEN: During events

This marvelous engineering feat, the Queen City's "crown," is sandwiched in between the Ohio River and downtown Cincinnati. The cost for the structure was astounding. It is used for many sports events, and the functional requirements for each are masterfully planned. Resting atop a podium with parking below, the white-painted steel complex has greatly contributed to the revitalization of the downtown area.

CLEVELAND

Blossom Music Center

(1967–68)

ARCHITECTS: Schafer, Flynn & Van Dijk
LOCATION: About 5 miles S of exit 12 off
IS 80 (30 miles from Cleveland)
OPEN: For performances, June through
September

Rising 200 feet and spanning an area 400 feet wide, the obliquely angled composition of the Blossom Music Center makes a commanding impression. Nestled in a rolling grassy field, the exposed steel structure seats 4,642 people in a partially opened space with huge overhangs for protection from weather. Parking, gates, and ticket offices are located away from the building so as not to disturb the aesthetics of the design concept.

CLEVELAND

Metropolitan Campus of Cuyahoga Community College (1968–69)

ARCHITECTS: The Outcalt-Guenther Partners
LOCATION: Community College Ave.,
Woodland Ave. at 30th St.
OPEN: Daily

This commendable commuter college on the southeast outskirts of Cleveland has received national recognition for its fine design concept and plan. The campus is invitingly centered away from the noise and activity of the city. A sunken plaza with fountains, seating, and plantings is flanked by the principle buildings in a tiered composition. Interiors are pleasantly and conveniently designed, entirely geared to student life.

CLEVELAND

The Cleveland Arcade
(1888–90)

ARCHITECTS: John M. Eisenmann, George H. Smith
LOCATION: 401 Euclid Avenue, and Superior Avenue
OPEN: Daily

The light and airy Cleveland Arcade is a splendid example of early glass and trussed arch construction in America. Lined with shops and offices, the Arcade is an important mid-block link between two major streets. The effect of the design concept is exhilerating—similar in feeling to The Arcade (1827–28) in Providence, Rhode Island. The tiered levels further dramatize the space. The brilliant structure, recently renovated, is considered a national architectural treasure.

CLEVELAND

The New Cleveland Playhouse (1983–)

ARCHITECTS: Philip Johnson/John Burgee
LOCATION: 8500 Euclid Avenue
OPEN: For performances; tours Mon.–Fri. 10–4

At first glance this cluster of buildings echoes themes drawn from the Romanesque period of the Middle Ages. On closer inspection the fascinating complex is more contemporary and structural with a fresh interpretation. The buildings on the left, about one-fifth of the total composition, were built in 1924 by Small & Rowley. Johnson and Burgee have brilliantly incorporated the existing landmark into the new addition. Dark red brick has been extensively employed, providing a nice unity. Arches, domes, parapets, columns, pediments, and hipped roofs contribute to the building's interest. Johnson said of this project, "This is the first time I have ever copied Bernini."

COLUMBUS

Wyandotte Building (1897–98)

ARCHITECTS: Daniel H. Burnham & Co.
LOCATION: 21 West Broad Street
OPEN: During office hours

Those interested in the early modern Chicago School of architecture during the latter half of the 19th century make a pilgrimage to the Wyandotte Building to view the work of one of America's great early pioneer modern architects. Although not as well known as other buildings by Burnham, this commendable small skyscraper is well worth the visit. (Burnham's partner, John Root, died in 1891). The building features unique decorative bays that undulate across the facade, extending the full length of the 11-story structure.

DAYTON

Air Force Museum Wright-Patterson U.S. Air Force Base (1983)

ARCHITECT: Kevin Roche
LOCATION: 6 mi. NE Of Dayton, Route 4, follow signs
OPEN: Weekdays, 9–5, Sat. & Sun., 10–6

A stupendous architectural undertaking that beckons the visitor to explore the building. The dynamic structure conveys the spirit of flight and man's achievements in aviation history. Fascinating exhibits are housed within. Roche, whose well-known partner, John Dinkeloo, died in 1982, said of this technically advanced building: "The goal was to create a place that would fill the visitor with a sense of awe and pride at man's achievement."

OXFORD

Miami University Art Museum
(1979)

ARCHITECTS: Skidmore, Owings & Merrill
LOCATION: Miami University
OPEN: During school hours

The new Art Museum is pleasantly sited on a gently sloping hillside on campus. Display areas of the enticing one-story barrier-free facility open outward to take advantage of viewing the lovely pond and wooded area beyond. There are a number of galleries throughout the interior spaces—many with large skylit areas. A glass-enclosed entry vestibule introduces the visitor to the facilities that include studios, media centers, classrooms, and display areas. Exhibits include paintings, sculpture, folk art, glass, furniture, and graphics.

SIDNEY

People's Federal Savings & Loan Association (1917–18)

ARCHITECT: Louis Sullivan
LOCATION: SE corner of Ohio and Court Streets
OPEN: During banking hours

Looking like a miniature of Sullivan's famous Transportation Building designed for the Columbian Exposition of 1893 in Chicago, this building is superbly executed. Making use of a massive, intricately decorated arched entry, the feature serves as the facade's main interest. The side wall is also exquisite. The structure is considered one of the master pioneer architect's finest works. Sullivan died a few years later—a lonely and broken man.

ADDITIONAL MODERN STRUCTURES OF INTEREST

AKRON

Akron Art Musuem (Renovation) (1981)
ARCHITECTS: Dalton, van Dijk, Johnson &
Partners
LOCATION: 70 East Market Street

After years of neglect, the historic Post Office
Building erected in 1889 has been carefully
restored and the interiors modernized.

CINCINNATI

Atrium One (1980)
ARCHITECTS: Skidmore, Owings & Merrill
LOCATION: 201 E. 4th Street

An unusual architectural approach, this building features four stacked atriums and a tiered
design at the top of the structure.

Carew Tower (1930s)
ARCHITECTS: Walter Ahlschlazer with
Delano & Aldrich
LOCATION: 441 Vine Street

Carew Tower is one of the city's first
important skyscrapers. The 48-story structure
is designed in the Art Deco style.

Central Trust Tower & Center
ARCHITECTS: Skidmore, Owings & Merrill
LOCATION: 3–5 W. 4th Street and 201 E.
5th Street

Two streamlined high-rise commercial
buildings.

Dubois Tower
ARCHITECTS: Harrison and Abramovitz
LOCATION: 511 Walnut Street

This simple rectangular structure features a
slender pin-stripe design.

Federated Building (1982)
ARCHITECTS: RTKL Associates
LOCATION: 7 West 7th Street

Bold horizontal and diagonal forms arranged
in a dramatic cut-away composition, the
Federated Building makes a strong impact.

Fountain Square (1980s)
ARCHITECTS: Abramovitz–Harrison–
Kingsland
LOCATION: Fountain Square, downtown

Part of a redevelopment plan, the complex is
made up of a series of towers employing
strong horizontal forms.

Procter & Gamble World Headquarters
(1983)
ARCHITECTS: KPF, A.E. Kohn, architect in
charge
LOCATION: 301 East 6th Street

This new corporate headquarters is a streamlined update of original Art Deco building
complexes.

Riverband Concert Pavilion (1984)
ARCHITECTS: Michael Graves
LOCATION: Old Coney Park, Off Kellogg
Blvd.

This pleasantly designed outdoor pavilion
serves as a summer concert facility for the
Cincinnati Symphony Orchestra. The steel
frame structure, located on the banks of the
Ohio River, seats 5,000 patrons, with surrounding earth berming planned for
additional outdoor seating.

CLEVELAND

The Ameritrust Company Headquarters
(1972)
ARCHITECTS: Marcel Breuer and Hamilton
Smith
LOCATION: 900 Euclid Avenue

A pre-cast building constructed to preserve an
existing landmark bank of 1907 close by.

**B'nai Jeshurun (Formerly Temple of The
Heights)** (1980)
ARCHITECTS: Don M. Hisaka & Associates
LOCATION: 27501 Fairmount, Pepper Pike,
Cleveland

This large white complex coveys simplicity
and order, functioning as a flexible Jewish
center.

Cleveland Clinic (1980)
ARCHITECT: Cesar Pelli
LOCATION: 9500 Euclid Ave.

A structure featuring a striking reflective glass skin.

The Cleveland Museum of Art, Education Wing Expansion (1970)
ARCHITECTS: Marcel Breuer and Hamilton Smith
LOCATION: 11150 East Boulevard

Unity and clarity are exemplified in the treatment of light and dark gray alternating bands of granite for this arts facility by the famous Bauhaus designer.

Ecumenical Center (1973)
ARCHITECTS: Richard Fleischman Architects, Inc.
LOCATION: Case Western Reserve University campus

A church that suitably expresses the changing values of a new society.

John F. Kennedy Recreation Center (1973)
ARCHITECTS: Whitley-Whitley Inc.
LOCATION: 17300 Harvard

1111 Superior Square (1983)
ARCHITECTS: Skidmore, Owings & Merrill
LOCATION: 1111 Superior Square

Clad with gleaming reflective glass, this tower is highlighted by a cut-corner composition.

University Center (1974)
ARCHITECTS: Don M. Hisaka & Associates with others
LOCATION: Cleveland State University campus, downtown Cleveland

This multi-purpose student center has been designed to function as "a living room for the whole campus."

COLUMBUS

Hyatt Regency (1980)
ARCHITECTS: Patrick & Associates
LOCATION: 350 North High

Bold concrete forms support a dazzling

reflective cube placed at an angle with the adjacent complex.

Ohio Historical Center Library/Archives (1972)
ARCHITECTS: Ireland/Associates, Inc.
LOCATION: 1982 Velma Ave., at 17th Ave. & I–71

This bold superstructure soars over a base housing the museum and lobby. The massive concrete complex is a favorite museum for children, with full-size replicas, theaters, a Hall of Fame, and other marvelous exhibits.

St. Margaret of Cortona Church (1970)
ARCHITECTS: Pietro Belluschi
LOCATION: 3388 Trabue Road

A warm and welcoming church designed by the famous Italian-born American architect.

DAYTON

Arcade Square (1902–04/1980)
ARCHITECTS: Lorenz & Williams, Inc. (Original architect: Frank Andrews, Third Street Building)
LOCATION: Third Street to Courthouse Square

This delightful and airy complex incorporates existing masonry walls with stone ornaments, new storefront walls, glass, and aluminum. The huge rotunda of glass and metal is particularly interesting.

Library Resource Center (1974)
ARCHITECTS: Don M. Hisaka & Associates
LOCATION: Wright State University campus, just outside Dayton

This impressive building of poured-in-place concrete and glass serves as an important center for the university community.

NCR Corporate Headquarters (1976)
ARCHITECTS: Lorenz and Williams, Inc. and others
LOCATION: 1700 South Patterson Blvd.

Creating a low profile image, this horizontally-arranged complex features a reflective glass wall on the entrance side with a huge circular entrance driveway and grounds.

Propylaeum (1982)
ARCHITECTS: Levin Porter Associates, Inc.
LOCATION: Dayton Art Institute

The Propylaeum is a monumental new gateway and entrance to the classically designed museum of 1928.

EUCLID

Lake Shore Christian Church (1982)
ARCHITECTS: Robert A. Barclay
LOCATION: 28010 Lake Shore Blvd.

This award-winning religious structure is uniquely designed with simplicity and clarity of form.

Sanctuary Addition—Lake Shore Christian Church (1980)
ARCHITECTS: William A. Blunden, Robert A. Barclay Associates
LOCATION: 28010 Lake Shore Blvd.

This complex is an impressive new 3,600 square foot addition to an existing church.

KENT

School of Art—Kent State University
ARCHITECTS: Ross, Yamane Architects
LOCATION: Just off Terrace Dr. by Van Deusen Bldg.

This new art facility is based on a 25-foot square expandable modular bay system of steel. Most of the building is clad with standard units of prefabricated fiberglass panels.

MARION

Howard Swink Advertising Inc. Office Building (1984)
ARCHITECTS: Don M. Hisaka and Associates
LOCATION: 333 East Center

This work has been described as "clean, direct, straightforward, and uncomplicated."

OBERLIN

Allen Memorial Art Museum at Oberlin College
ARCHITECTS: Venturi and Rauch
LOCATION: South Main at East Lorain Street

This bold new modern wing was designed to complement the traditional existing building by Cass Gilbert.

Warner Concert Hall (1964)
ARCHITECTS: Minoru Yamasaki and Associates
LOCATION: Oberlin College campus

Simple, classical design was employed to create an excellent facility for music.

PARMA

Holy Family Catholic Church (1964)
ARCHITECTS: Conrad and Fleischman
LOCATION: 7367 York Road

Concrete modules are expressively arranged in a composition of arches, bold sweeping curves, and diagonal forms for the design of this impressive church.

PLAINESVILLE

James F. Lincoln Library (1966–67)
ARCHITECTS: Victor F. Christ-Janer and Associates
LOCATION: Lake Erie College. Mentor Avenue (US 20), W of town

This fascinating library complex resembles giant stacked toy building blocks.

SHAKER HEIGHTS

Tower East (1968)
ARCHITECTS: Walter Gropius and The Architects' Collaborative Inc.
LOCATION: 20600 Chagrin Blvd.

This 12-story commercial office building by the founder of the Bauhaus in Germany is a focal point in its park setting in downtown Shaker Heights.

TOLEDO

The Fiberglas Tower Owens-Corning Fiberglas Corp. (1970)
ARCHITECTS: Harrison & Abramovitz
LOCATION: Jefferson and St. Clair Streets

Planned to effectively display the image of Owens-Corning Fiberglas, the architects have designed a handsome 30-story steel and glass tower.

Toledo Trustcorp Inc.
ARCHITECTS: Samborn Steketee, Otis & Evans, Inc.
LOCATION: 3 Seagate

WAPAKONETA

The Neil Armstrong Air and Space Museum (1972)
ARCHITECTS: Don M. Hisaka & Associates with others
LOCATION: Cleveland State University campus, downtown Cleveland

The earth is mounded up to the roof line of the poured-in-place concrete museum. The visitor experiences many unusual architectural sensations while viewing the aircraft and space hardware.

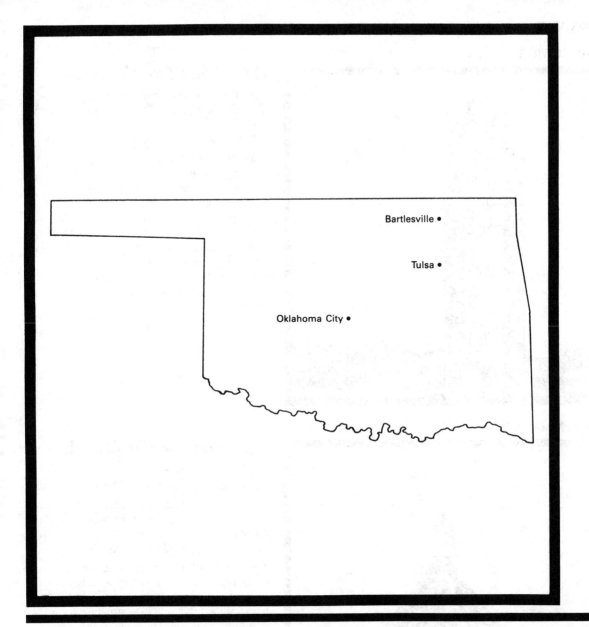

Bartlesville •

Tulsa •

Oklahoma City •

Oklahoma

BARTLESVILLE

H.C . Price Tower (1954–55)

ARCHITECT: Frank Lloyd Wright
LOCATION: East 6th Street at South Dewey
Avenue
OPEN: During business hours

The Price Tower is Wright's first and last skyscraper—although he had plans on the drawing board for a mile-high structure before his death in 1959. A far cry from the sleek glass and steel skyscrapers popular today, the tower is an unusual arrangement of outward angled projections. Gold tinted glass, tan masonry, copper, and concrete are the principle materials employed. The engaging exterior design theme is also carried into the interior spaces.

OKLAHOMA CITY

Hopewell Baptist Church
(1953)

ARCHITECT: Bruce Goff
LOCATION: 8 miles W of US 77 (Broadway Express) via 3rd St.; W in Edmond (N of the city)
OPEN: Sunday and various other days

Associated with unique and creative structures, particularly in residential design (his Bavinger House of 1957 is most notable), Goff has designed this religious structure for a small congregation. The imaginative form of the church, with its accompanying steel supports, has evoked symbolism of the state's Indian teepee heritage and of the Oklahoma oil well, thus creating a common bond with the people and their place of worship.

OKLAHOMA CITY

McGee Tower (1973)

ARCHITECTS: Frankfurt-Short-Emery-
McKinley with Pietro Belluschi
LOCATION: 123 R.S. Kerr Avenue
OPEN: During business hours

Surrounded by thoughtfully planned landscaping, the McGee Tower features an inviting garden entry. The structure looms over the adjacent buildings, dominating the area. A strikingly unusual window design immediately captures the viewer's attention—fenestration that enlarges through consecutive levels. The soaring box with its unique design concept achieves interest and uniformity. The Robert S. Kerr Park, close by is also notable for its refreshing layout.

OKLAHOMA CITY

Oklahoma Theater Center
(1969–70)

ARCHITECT: John M. Johansen
LOCATION: 400 West Sheridan (between Hudson and Walker Aves.)
OPEN: For performances

Originally the Mummers Theater, this spectacular building generates interest through a cluster of boxes connected by a series of ramps, stairs, bridges, and ducts. White, black, and gray components are accented with bright red, blue, and yellow, recalling the design approach of the Dutch de Stijl group. In his work, Johansen attempts to create character—the Oklahoma Theater certainly achieves this goal.

OKLAHOMA CITY

St. Patrick's Church (1962)

ARCHITECTS: Murray Jones Murray with
Felix Candela
LOCATION: 2021 North Portland Avenue
OPEN: Daily from 9:15–5

Numerous unique ideas have been incorporated into the design of this impressive
church, especially the creation of a glass wall
within a concrete wall. Fascinating geometric
angles are integrated into the exterior and
interior spaces of the structure, providing
movement and interest through the expert
use of materials and light.

TULSA

Boston Avenue United
Methodist Church (1927–29)

ARCHITECTS: Rush, Endacott & Rush
LOCATION: South Boston Avenue at 13th
Street
OPEN: Daily from 9–5

Built during the modernistic Art Deco period,
this flamboyant religious structure with Gothic
overtones makes a stunning silhouette against
the horizon. Elongated stylized figures (including the founders of the Methodist church)
line the roof's perimeter. The effect is
stunning. The unique theme carries into the
interior spaces, creating an effect of unity and
interest. The building is regarded as one of
Tulsa's most important architectural treasures.

TULSA

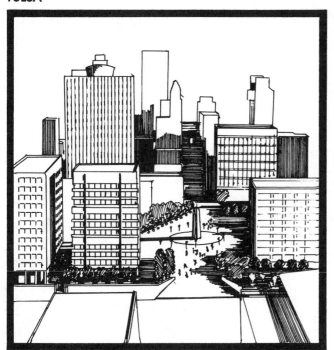

Central Tulsa Pedestrian System (1976–78)

ARCHITECTS: Hudgins, Thompson, Ball & Associates
LOCATION: Main Street and 5th Street
OPEN: Continuously

Central Tulsa Pedestrian System, comprising seven blocks in the downtown area, is a marvelous example of urban planning. Design that welcomes the visitor is employed everywhere, enhanced by beautiful landscaping. Underground malls are skillfully integrated and geared for the convenience and pleasure of the pedestrian. The project is typical of many similar urban redevelopment programs around the nation and is one of the most successful.

TULSA

Oral Roberts University (1947–)

ARCHITECTS: Various architects
LOCATION: 7777 South Lewis
OPEN: During school hours, Sunday services

Although critics of this university's buildings have not always been kind, people from all over the United States make pilgrimages to see the unusual structures on the campus. Planned for 4,000 students, Oral Roberts University boasts numerous modern buildings of striking design. Often called "modern baroque architecture" by critics, the Christ's Prayer Tower is particularly expressive and serves as a central symbol of the popular religious university's spirit and mission.

ADDITIONAL MODERN STRUCTURES OF INTEREST

OKLAHOMA CITY

The Chapel (1968)
ARCHITECT: Pietro Belluschi
LOCATION: Oklahoma City University
campus, NW 23rd & Blackwelder

This admirable chapel was designed by one
of the nation's foremost architects of religious
structures.

Continental Federal Savings and Loan
(1976)
ARCHITECTS: Noftsger, Lawrence, Lawrence,
and Flesher
LOCATION: 101 Park Avenue

This modern office building was once an
aging hotel. It has been given a facelift
employing reflective insulating glass.

TULSA

Assembly Center (1960s)
ARCHITECT: Edward Durell Stone
LOCATION: 100 Civic Center (bounded by
4th and 6th Streets on north and south,
and Houston Avenue on west)

A dignified and well-planned building by the
late nationally-known modern architect.

Bank of Oklahoma Tower (1976)
ARCHITECT: Minoru Yamasaki
LOCATION: North end of Boston Avenue,
between 1st and 2nd Streets

This soaring 51-story tower is part of an
extensive nine-square-block building program.
The center also has a performing arts
building, an enclosed shopping mall, restaurants, a hotel, and park.

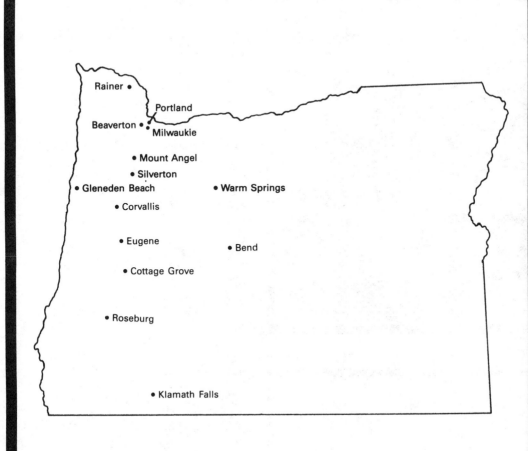

Rainer •

Portland

Beaverton • •
Milwaukie

• Mount Angel

• Silverton

• Gleneden Beach   • Warm Springs

• Corvallis

• Eugene   • Bend

• Cottage Grove

• Roseburg

• Klamath Falls

Oregon

COTTAGE GROVE

First Presbyterian (1950–51)

ARCHITECT: Pietro Belluschi
LOCATION: 216 South 3rd Street at Adams Avenue
OPEN: Sunday services, weekdays at various times

Located in a lovely wooded and garden area, the First Presbyterian Church is the best known of Belluschi's many religious structures. Belluschi soon became an architectural leader in the northwest after his arrival to the states from Italy. Developing a regional style still widely copied, the architect often employs wood, glass, and plain white plaster in attractive forms—demonstrated in this structure. A large boulder at the entrance is inscribed with a scripture welcoming the visitor. The interior design treatment and lighting are superb.

EUGENE

City Hall (1962–64)

ARCHITECTS: Stafford, Morin & Longwood
LOCATION: Pearl Street between 7th and 8th Avenues
OPEN: During office hours

Architecture that was literally built around an existing ninety-year-old walnut tree, the City Hall was brilliantly planned for the tree to become a pleasant focus. The entire block is raised on a platform accommodating parking spaces beneath. Numerous innovative ideas are incorporated into the facility at every turn. The council chamber is interestingly stationed over a pool!

EUGENE

Hult Center for the Performing Arts (1982)

ARCHITECTS: Hardy Holzman Pfeiffer
LOCATION: One Eugene Centre
OPEN: Daily tours at 12:00 and 1:15, and performances

A series of steep metal clad roofs and glass walls distinguish this $24 million Performing Arts Center. An awesome interior four-tiered lobby space with its forest of wooden supports and flowered carpet has been compared to a walk through the Oregon landscape. The large Silva Concert Hall is extraordinary. A ceiling composition of largely scaled woven bands was inspired by holding a peach basket upside-down to the sun. The effect is stunning. Another focal point is the stage curtain, decorated with stylized blackberry bushes and clouds—the work of two local women artists.

MOUNT ANGEL

Library—Mount Angel Abbey (1967–70)

ARCHITECTS: Alvar Aalto (Finland), with DeMars & Wells
LOCATION: c. 20 miles NE of Salem, on hill E of Mount Angel
OPEN: During school year

Known as the "humanist architect" because of his great concern for human comfort and well-being, this famous Finnish architect designed only two structures in America. (The other work is Baker Dormitory at M.I.T. in Cambridge, Mass.) The unpretentious library for the Benedictine Abbey is constructed of brick and wood blending harmoniously with its hillside setting. The interior spaces, lighting, surface treatments, and other elements are superbly handled—typical of the architect's masterful approach.

PORTLAND

Auditorium Forecourt Fountain (1970)

ARCHITECTS: Lawrence Halprin & Associates
LOCATION: Southwest 2nd & 3rd Aves. between Clay & Market
OPEN: Fountains run from 11 AM–10 PM

Halprin, one of Oregon's most esteemed architects, has developed a distinctive architectural tradition during the past decades. This full block fountain is a wonderful contribution to downtown Portland. Activated at 11:00 AM daily, 13,000 gallons of water per minute flow through artfully positioned sculptural concrete forms. Water sprays and cascades everywhere, allowing the visitor to experience a unique sight and sound of the enveloping water fountains.

PORTLAND

Equitable Building (now the Commonwealth Building) (1947–48)

ARCHITECT: Pietro Belluschi
LOCATION: Southwest 6th Ave. between Stark & Washington Sts.
OPEN: During business hours

The advanced construction and technology employed for the Commonwealth Building were revolutionary at the time and contributed to the development of the skyscraper in America. The blue-green glass and aluminum covered concrete tower still seems fresh and sophisticated today. Belluschi received national attention for his *NEW WING OF THE PORTLAND ART MUSEUM* in 1932, located close by the Equitable Building at 1219 Southwest Park Avenue.

PORTLAND

Memorial Coliseum (1960)

ARCHITECTS: Skidmore, Owings and Merrill
LOCATION: 1401 North Wheeler
OPEN: Special events and performances

Portland's dramatic Memorial Coliseum, designed by the nation's internationally renowned architectural firm, is a marvelous engineering achievement. Especially at night, while brilliantly lit, the expressive forms of steel and glass can be fully appreciated. The highly praised Coliseum was a challenging departure for the firm, known for their fine commercial tower designs.

PORTLAND

Portland Building (1983)

ARCHITECT: Michael Graves
LOCATION: SW 5th Avenue at Main
OPEN: During office hours

Graves, with his highly personal style, is considered one of the nation's most inventive architects. The Portland Building occupies a prominent site in the downtown area, greatly contrasting with its architectural neighbors. The building, with its unusual color combinations, unique forms, and arrangement has provoked much comment in architectural circles. The architect's work is both masterful and complex—an approach that often suggests anthropomorphic metaphors! This extraordinary Post-Modern structure, along with the new *KOIN CENTER* by Zimmer Gunsul Frasca (see page 331), is considered Portland's most exciting new modern landmark of architecture.

PORTLAND

Portland Center Project
(1966–68)

ARCHITECT: Skidmore, Owings and Merrill
LOCATION: Southwest Harrison Street at 1st
Avenue
OPEN: Shopping center daily

A brilliant downtown renewal solution, the
Portland Center Project incorporates an excellent layout plan for apartment blocks and a
shopping center. Close by is SOM's *BOISE
CASCADE BUILDING* of 1968 and the *BLUE
CROSS BUILDING* of 1969—both located north
of the Center. *LOVEJOY PARK AND FOUNTAIN,*
designed in 1966 by Laurence Halprin Associates, are located at the corner of 4th Avenue
at Southwest Hall Street. The fountain is
especially delightful and a forerunner of
Halprin's marvelous Auditorium Forecourt
Fountain.

PORTLAND

Portland Community College
(1967–69)

ARCHITECTS: Wolff-Zimmer-Gunsul-Frasca-
Ritter
LOCATION: 12000 Southwest 49th Avenue,
S of IS 5 and US 99W via Capitol Highway
exit
OPEN: During school year

Pleasantly positioned in a countryside setting
on the outskirts of Portland, this two-year
College ingeniously incorporates architectural
forms with educational innovations. The plan
is arranged in an open and inviting composition with facilities conveniently available to
the student. Construction materials of wood,
concrete, glass, and brick are effectively
combined throughout the complex. Views of
the rolling hills from various vantage points
add to the architectural charm.

PORTLAND

Willamette Center, Headquarters for Portland General Electric Co. (1979)

ARCHITECTS: Zimmer Gunsul Frasca
Partnership, Pietro Belluschi
LOCATION: 121 S.W. Salmon
OPEN: During business hours

A dazzling space frame entry introduces this unique mixed-use high rise tower and buildings located by the Willamette River in downtown Portland. The architects have created a "people place" on the waterfront through the use of inviting space planning. Shops and restaurants line the L-shaped complex. A covered arcade constructed of glass is supported by white-painted trusses providing protection from weather and adding a unique design dimension. The 500,000 square foot facility is a sensitive and innovative addition to the city.

ROSEBURG

Douglas County Museum (1969–79)

ARCHITECTS: Backen, Arragoni & Ross and WE Group
LOCATION: Fairgrounds exit off IS 5 SW of Roseburg
OPEN: Daily 9:30–5

Nestled in a hillside setting, the Douglas County Museum is constructed of vertically placed cedar, recalling local barn design. The complex is interestingly clustered into three units connected by convenient passageways. The museum functions as a display center for the historical heritage of Douglas County. (Douglas County was named after Stephen A. Douglas.) Striking arrangements of fenestration flood the interior spaces with light. Close by is Douglas Hall (1970) by the same architects and used principally as a multipurpose center.

ADDITIONAL MODERN STRUCTURES OF INTEREST

BEAVERTON

Oregon Regional Primate Center
ARCHITECTS: Skidmore, Owings and Merrill
LOCATION: 505 NW 185th Avenue

BEND

Sunriver Lodge and Community (1969–)
ARCHITECTS: George T. Rockrise &
Associates
LOCATION: 2.5 miles W of US 97, c. 15
miles S of Bend

An admirably planned resort community
carefully built among the trees. The lodge,
constructed of lava and wood, is surrounded
by a shopping center, condominiums, and
private single unit houses.

CORVALLIS

Corvallis Aquatic Center
ARCHITECTS: Broome, Oringdulph, O'Toole,
Rudolph Associates
LOCATION: 1940 N.W. Highland Drive

This fascinating modern aquatic center is
open from 6 AM to 9 PM weekdays, Sat., 7–9
and Sun., 1–9.

EUGENE

**Recreational Facilities, University of
Oregon**
ARCHITECTS: Unthank Seder Poticha
LOCATION: Information Desk in Oregon
Hall at 13th Ave. and Agate Street

The facility features an unusual roof that
effectively covers a large recreational building.

GLENEDEN BEACH

Salishan Lodge and Residences
(1962–65)
ARCHITECTS: Skidmore, Owings and Merrill
with John Storrs
LOCATION: On US 101

Breathtakingly located on three miles of the
Pacific Ocean, this community has been
skillfully planned to preserve the natural
beauty of its setting.

KLAMATH FALLS

Oregon Institute of Technology (1972)
ARCHITECTS: Skidmore, Owings & Merrill
LOCATION: Campus Drive—north edge of
town

This stunning low-rise structure features reflective glass and enameled surface panels
that contrast interestingly in its natural setting.

MILWAUKIE

St. John The Baptist Church (1966)
ARCHITECTS: Stearns, Mention & Morris
LOCATION: 10955 S.E. 25th Avenue

PORTLAND

Central Lutheran Church (1948)
ARCHITECT: Pietro Belluschi
LOCATION: 2104 NE Hancock

Inspired by the Northwestern state's redwood
barns, this structure of wood clearly expresses
the Italian-born American architect's design
philosophy. The church is a building of
restraint and simplicity. The employment of
the vertical line is strongly expressed through
the arrangement of slender wood supports
and a soaring bell tower topped with a simple
cross.

Columbia Tower
ARCHITECTS: Zimmer Gunsul Frasca
LOCATION: SW 2nd Avenue at Columbia

Japanese Pavilion
ARCHITECTS: Skidmore, Owings and Merrill
LOCATION: Washington Park

Justice Center (1983)
ARCHITECTS: Zimmer Gunsul Frasca

LOCATION: By Chapman Park, between SW Madison & SW Main Sts.

Portland's stunning new Justice Center compliments Michael Grave's controversial Portland Building across the park. The new 15-story concrete structure is distinguished by a gleaming concave geometric glass design at the entrance created by Ed Carpenter.

Justice Service Center
ARCHITECTS: Zimmer Gunsul Frasca
LOCATION: SW 3rd Avenue at Main

Koin Center (1984)
ARCHITECTS: Zimmer Gunsul Frasca
LOCATION: Bounded by Jefferson, Clay, 1st & 2nd Aves.

Portland's newest, and one of the finest, modern landmarks. KOIN Tower rises thirty stories— "a lofty ziggurat with a pointed crown" (*Architectural Record*, Nov. 1984). The structural design recalls the Art Deco period of the 1920s.

Koinonia Center
ARCHITECTS: Fletcher & Finch
LOCATION: SW Broadway and Montgomery

Lloyd Center
ARCHITECT: John Graham
LOCATION: NW Wiedler at 9th

Oregon Historical Society (1967)
ARCHITECTS: Wolf-Zimmer/Pietro Belluschi, consultant
LOCATION: 1230 SW Park Avenue

Pacific Northwest Bell (1977)
ARCHITECTS: Zimmer Gunsul Frasca Partnership
LOCATION: 4th Avenue by Lovejoy Fountain

A sleek, partly underground facility of polished aluminum and glass. The building was planned so as not to intrude on the Halprin's Lovejoy Fountain area.

Pac-West Building (1983)
ARCHITECT: Hugh Stubbins
LOCATION: SW Broadway

Performing Arts Center
ARCHITECTS: Broome, Oringdulph, O'Toole
LOCATION: SW Broadway at Main

Pettygrove Park
ARCHITECTS: Lawrence Halprin & Associates
LOCATION: SW 4th and Market

Pioneer Square
ARCHITECTS: Will Martin of Martin-Soderstrom-Matteson
LOCATION: SW Broadway at Alder

Portland Plaza (1970)
ARCHITECTS: Anthony J. Lumsden and others
LOCATION: Flanking the Civic Auditorium Forecourt Plaza

Strong triangular towers of gray heat-resistant glass and aluminum, Portland Plaza towers are set diagonally on raised plazas.

Portland State University Library
ARCHITECTS: Skidmore, Owings and Merrill
LOCATION: SW Harrison at 10th Avenue

Reed College Library Addition (1963)
ARCHITECTS: Harry Weese & Associates with others
LOCATION: SE Woodstock

Other interesting buildings at Reed College are the *REED COLLEGE SPORTS CENTER* by Weese; the *REED COLLEGE VOLLUM CENTER* (1982), by Neil Farnham; and the *ARTS CENTER*.

Saint Thomas More Church
ARCHITECT: Pietro Belluschi
LOCATION: 3525 S.W. Patton Road

One of Belluschi's best known religious structures.

Transit Mall Bus Shelters (1974)Transit Mall (1979)
ARCHITECTS: Skidmore, Owings & Merrill
LOCATION: Shelters located throughout the city

One of the beautifully planned downtown malls, the loop consists of 22 blocks. Attractive bus shelters along the way contribute to the well-designed environment.

U.S. Bancorp Tower
ARCHITECTS: Skidmore, Owings and Merrill
LOCATION: West Burnside at 5th Avenue

Portland Art Museum (1932–39)
ARCHITECT: A.E. Doyle & Associates/Pietro Belluschi, Designer
LOCATION: 1219 SW Park Avenue

Portland Hilton (1964)
ARCHITECTS: Skidmore, Owings & Merrill
LOCATION: 921 S.W. Sixth Avenue

Zion Lutheran Church
ARCHITECT: Pietro Belluschi
LOCATION: 1015 S.W. 18th

This church features a dynamic central nave reminiscent of medieval Gothic forms.

RAINIER

Visitors Information Center (Trojan Energy Plant) (1975)
ARCHITECTS: Wolff Zimmer Gunsal Frasca
LOCATION: 71760 Columbia River Hwy, 42 miles NW of Portland

Owned by Portland General Electric Co., this interesting building features a large, open two-level lobby topped with a white space frame. Fascinating exhibit areas are reached by ramps.

ROSEBURG

St. Joseph's Parish Church (1969)
ARCHITECTS: Wolff, Zimmer, Gunsal, Frasca, Ritter & Pietro Belluschi
LOCATION: 800 West Stanton

This award winning church was designed to welcome people and convey a feeling that God is to be understood, not feared.

SILVERTON

Immanuel Lutheran Church (1979)
ARCHITECT: Pietro Belluschi
LOCATION: 303 North Church

This powerfully expressed church features wood arches and geodesic intersections in a soaring 80-foot high sanctuary.

WARM SPRINGS

Kah-Nee-Ta Lodge (1971)
ARCHITECTS: Wolff Zimmer Gunsul Frasca Ritter
LOCATION: c. 11 miles N of Warm Springs on Hwy. 3 then Hwy. 8 (Follow signs)

Nestled on a rolling hillside, this tourist resort, built of wood and concrete, is in the middle of an Indian Reservation.

• Wilkes Barre

Nanticoke •

Easton •

Allentown •

• Pittsburgh • Loretto

• Greenburg

Harrisburg •

Philadelphia

Lancaster •

Newton
Square •

• Ohiopyle

Gettysburg •

Swarthmore

Pennsylvania

ALLENTOWN

Fine Arts Center (1977)

ARCHITECTS: Johnson/Burgee with Coston, Wallace & Watson
LOCATION: Muhlenberg College Campus
OPEN: During school hours

Containing a theater, recital hall, art studios, gallery, classrooms, and offices, the central feature of the Fine Arts Center is a 200-foot-long skylit promenade lined with a row of long colorful banners. The plan of the white-painted brick structure is intriguing, with floors that tier down a grassy sloping hillside. The inviting complex, commissioned by the Lutheran-sponsored coeducational school, has become a popular student gathering place for many activities.

OHIOPYLE

Fallingwater (1936 –37)

ARCHITECT: Frank Lloyd Wright
LOCATION: PA 381, 3.5 miles N of Ohiopyle
OPEN: Apr.–mid Nov., Tues.–Sun. 10–5, reservation required; telephone: (412) 329-8501

Considered a masterpiece of modern residential design, Fallingwater incorporates many of Wright's theories of "organic architecture." Canti-levered concrete terraces are positioned over the waterfall, taking full advantage of the setting. Stone, concrete, and glass are employed throughout the home enclosing a fascinating arrangement of space. Edgar Kaufmann Jr., son of the owners, gave this architectural treasure to the Western Pennsylvania Conservancy in 1963. The *GUEST HOUSE* by Wright and the *VISITOR'S CENTER* (1978) by Paul Mayan and others are also notable.

PHILADELPHIA

Alfred Newton Richards Medical Research Building

(1957–61) and Biology Laboratory (1962–64)
ARCHITECT: Louis I. Kahn
LOCATION: Hamilton Walk, next to Medical School
OPEN: Ground floor open to public

Kahn's theory of "served" and "serving" spaces is well expressed with the dramatic grouping of exterior service towers for this complex. The large structure of brick, Kahn's favorite building material, is considered one of the architect's most important works. The prominent designer was also recognized as one of the great writers, teachers, and philosophers of modern architecture.

PHILADELPHIA

Beth Sholom Synagogue (House of Peace) (1959)

ARCHITECT: Frank Lloyd Wright
LOCATION: Old York Road just N of Church Road, c. 11 miles N of downtown Philadelphia
OPEN: Tues., Thurs. 1–3, 12–4; services Fri. 8:30 PM, Sat. 9:30 AM

The dynamic triangular forms, line, and direction of the Synagogue create a strong impression. Dominating the hillside, the geometric detailing of the roof line accentuates the design concept. The structure, designed when Wright was in his mid-eighties, expresses the master architect's fascination with new interpretations of form and space.

Franklin Court (1975–76)

ARCHITECTS: Venturi & Rauch, with John Milner and The National Heritage Corporation
LOCATION: Market St. between 3rd & 4th
OPEN: Daily 8:30–5

The creation of Franklin Court is a brilliant "impression" of Benjamiin Franklin's house and print shop torn down in 1812. Constructed on the site, the architects have spacially evoked an illusion of the house rather than attempting to rebuild a precise replica of the former structure. A large museum and theater are located under the mauve-painted steel tube frame.

PHILADELPHIA

Glass Palace, New Market (1976)

ARCHITECT: Louis Sauer
LOCATION: Society Hill, facing Front Street
OPEN: During shopping hours

Society Hill has been called Philadelphia's most exciting place and the "Glass Palace" the most exciting structure there. The dazzling arrangement and construction of glass cubes has been compared to Joseph Paxton's famous Crystal Palace of 1851 in London. The huge glass-cubed complex clusters around a "water plaza," providing an inviting gathering area that effectively channels traffic.

PHILADELPHIA

INA Tower (1974–75)

ARCHITECTS: Mitchell/Giurgola
LOCATION: Arch Street at 17th, W of
Kennedy Plaza
OPEN: During business hours

Combining architectural construction with the sun's potential, the architects have ingeniously created an energy efficient office tower. A predominantly glass facade on the north side contrasts wth deeply set horizontal window strips on the south. The 27-story structure is clad wth enameled-aluminum that harmonizes with the green-tinted glass fenestration. The INA Tower makes a striking contrast with Independence Hall close by.

PHILADELPHIA

Penn Mutual Tower (1976)

ARCHITECTS: Mitchell/Giurgola
LOCATION: 508 Walnut Street
OPEN: During office hours

Located amidst one of America's most important historical areas, close to Independence Hall, Penn Tower is a handsome addition to an insurance company's office complex. The 21-story Tower uniquely incorporates the facade of an existing Egyptian styled building designed in 1835. The 4-story Egyptian facade creates a strong contrast and focal point for the steel, concrete, and tinted glass tower. Broken massing, sensitive use of materials, and unusual fenestration are additional distinctions of this award-winning structure.

Philadelphia Saving Fund Society Building (1929–32)

ARCHITECTS: George Howe and William Lescaze
LOCATION: Market Street at South 12th
OPEN: During business hours

One of America's first important tall skyscrapers, the Philadelphia Saving Fund Society Building is also one of the nation's first great office buildings designed in the International Style. The structure's design is brilliant with its frankly exposed frame and cantilevered slabs. Narrow window strips are emphasized by vertical and horizontal bands, giving the building a streamlined appearance.

PHILADELPHIA

Robin Hood Dell West

(1975–76)

ARCHITECTS: John H. MacFadyen and Alfredo de Vido
LOCATION: Parkside at 52nd Drive
OPEN: For performances

Beautifully and conveniently located in a rolling grassy hillside, Robin Hood Dell West is the Philadelphia Orchestra's summer home. Thousands of music lovers can be seated under the huge roof or on seats or slopes outside the complex under the stars. The unique roof itself, sheathed with 80,000 square feet of shining stainless steel, creates a gigantic sculptural effect that contrasts significantly with the natural surroundings.

PHILADELPHIA

Visitor Center, Independence National Historical Park (1976)

ARCHITECTS: Cambridge Seven
LOCATION: At Third and Chestnuts Streets
OPEN: 9 AM to 5 PM daily (except Christmas & New Years)

The massive brick, steel, and glass structure is build around a sizable belfry originally intended to house the treasured Liberty Bell, but oppostion to the idea cancelled the plan. The function of the large complex is to provide a convenient point of arrival and orientation for visitors to Independence National Historical Park. Open barrel-vaulted skylights, a steel space frame, ramps, bridges, and seating all contribute to the tourist's comfort and enjoyment. The belfry now accommodates a bell presented to the United States as a gift.

PITTSBURGH

Allegheny County Jail and Court House (1884–88)

ARCHITECT: Henry Hobson Richardson
LOCATION: 436 Grant St. between 5th Ave. and Forbes Ave.
OPEN: Mon.–Fri., 8:30–4:30

The Allegheny County Court House and Jail is considered one of Richardson's most influential and important works. An early pioneer of modern architecture, he helped to unite the architect and the engineer and has been called "the father of modern architecture in America." Richardson's love of employing medieval Romanesque themes earned him another title—"the great Romanesque Revivalist." This great landmark with rusticated stone walls, arches, and towers, was completed after the architect's death.

PITTSBURGH

Equibank (1975–)

ARCHITECTS: Skidmore, Owings and Merrill
LOCATION: Oliver Plaza
OPEN: During business hours

Like a sparkling jewel in downtown Pittsburgh's Golden Triangle, the striking Equibank is an impressive addition to the area. Slender twin towers wth 14 facets are sheathed with reflective insulating glass. Surrounded by other skyscrapers and tradtional buildings of an earlier building, the complex is harmoniously unified with its neighbors through effective placement of plazas and landscaping.

PITTSBURGH

PPG World Industries Building (1983–)

ARCHITECTS: Philip Johnson/John Burgee
LOCATION: Market Square area, downtown Pittsburgh
OPEN: During business hours

Designed with careful consideration and respect for existing buildings and environment, the gleaming mirrored-glass PPG Building is the principal focus of the Market-Stanwix urban renewal area of downtown Pittsburgh. Like the architect's controversial AT&T Building in New York City, with its traditional pediment, this stunning new structure also has design overtones from the past. Stylized Gothic spires top the building, providing a distinctive and unique element.

PITTSBURGH

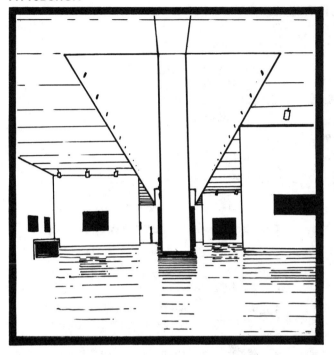

Sarah Scaife Gallery (1974)

ARCHITECT: Edward Larrabee Barnes
LOCATION: Adjoining Carnegie Institute,
4400 Forbes Ave.
OPEN: Tues.–Sat., 10–5, Sun., 1–5

The brilliant glass exterior wall of the Scaife Gallery creates a striking impression and contrast with its traditional neighbors. The wall is braced only with glass and extends to a height of forty feet. The bold structure's north entrance is tempered by fountains and a splendid sculpture by Louise Nevelson.

PITTSBURGH

U.S. Steel Building (1970)

ARCHITECTS: Harrison & Abramovitz and Abbe
LOCATION: 600 Grant Street
OPEN: Top of the Triangle Restaurant on 62nd Floor open for lunch and dinner, Mon.–Sat. ·

It seems fitting that a building for U.S. Steel would feature an innovative architectural approach—its frankly exposed frames of steel are filled with water and antifreeze to satisfy building codes for fire protection. Many technical details were worked out to accommodate the brilliant design of the structure. The glass windows are set back and arranged in a modular arrangement that is further emphasized by the modular composition of the steel frame.

ADDITIONAL MODERN STRUCTURES OF INTEREST

BRYN MAWR (PHILADELPHIA)

Erdman Dormitories (1962–65)
ARCHITECT: Louis I. Kahn
LOCATION: Merion Avenue at Bryn Mawr
College (W. suburb of Philadelphia)

MDRT Hall, American College of Life Underwriters (1971)
ARCHITECTS: Mitchell/Giurgola Associates
LOCATION: Bryn Mawr campus (West
suburb of Philadelphia)

This geometric structure of German red tile
and heat-reflecting glass has been called "a
machined abstraction in the landscape."

EASTON

Easton Data Center Equitable Life Insurance (1974)
ARCHITECTS: Kahn and Jacobs/Hellmuth,
Obata & Kassabaum
LOCATION: 300 Morrison Avenue

This unique loft-type building serves as a
computer center for Equitable Life Insurance
Society.

GETTYSBURG

College Library (1982)
ARCHITECT: Hugh Newell Jacobsen
LOCATION: Gettysburg College Campus

The new brick College Library is a surprising
and entriguing composition of forms.

Gettysburg Visitor's Center & Cyclorama Building (1962)
ARCHITECTS: Richard J. Neutra & Robert E.
Alexander, Thaddeus Longstreth
Association
LOCATION: Gettysburg National Military
Park

This poured concrete structure with vertical
flutings was designed by Neutra, the late
famous California architect, who contributed
much to the modern movement.

GREENSBURG

Tribune Review Building (1958)
ARCHITECT: Louis I. Kahn
LOCATION: Cabin Hill Drive

An early work of the great modern architect.

HARRISBURG

City Government Center (City Hall) (1981)
ARCHITECTS: Murray/Savrann Associates
LOCATION: 10 North Market Square

Olivetti Corporation of America Factory (1970)
ARCHITECT: Louis I. Kahn
LOCATION: 2800 Valley Rd., S side of IS 81,
just E. of Progress Avenue exit

Strawberry Square (Late 1970s)
ARCHITECTS: Mitchell/Giurgola with Lawrie
& Green
LOCATION: Strawberry Sq. on east bank of
Susquehanna River, 3rd & Walnut

A decisive yet flexible complex, Strawberry
Square is a successful solution to an am-
bitious development plan for downtown
Harrisburg—restaurants, stores, offices, etc.

LANCASTER

Lancaster Neighborhood Center (1977)
ARCHITECTS: Friday Architects/Planners
LOCATION: 630 Rockland Street

LORETTO

Southern Alleghenies Museum of Art (1920s/1970s)
ARCHITECTS: Roger Ferri and L. Robert
Kimball
LOCATION: St. Francis College campus (SW
Pa., 5 miles ENE of Ebensburg)

Located on a grassy tree-lined mall, the
museum is an original 1920s gymnasium
interestingly converted into a small art
museum.

NANTICOKE

Conference Center (1982)
ARCHITECTS: Bohlin Powell Larkin Cywinski
LOCATION: Luzerne County, Community
College

This well-planned facility functions as a
conference center and important gateway to
the small campus.

NEWTON SQUARE

Arco Chemical Company Research and Engineering Center (1980s)
ARCHITECTS: Davis, Brody & Associates
LOCATION: 3801 Westchester Pike (Open
by special arrangement only)

Located in a lovely meadow setting, this huge
complex for Richfield Company makes a vivid
contrast with its natural surroundings. Masonry, steel, and glass are uniquely combined.

PHILADELPHIA

8 Penn Center (1982)
ARCHITECTS: A. Eugene Kohn with Arthur
May
LOCATION: 8 Penn Center

This structure, sheathed with mirrored glass,
wraps around a curved corner site. Vertical
and horizontal lines create a strong con-
strasting effect.

Guild House (1960–63)
ARCHITECTS: Venturi & Rauch with Cope &
Lippincott
LOCATION: Spring Garden Street near 7th
Street

Institute for Scientific Information (ISI) (1979)
ARCHITECTS: Venturi, Rauch and Scott
Brown
LOCATION: University City Science Center,
Market Street West

ISI is the largest for-profit organization of its
type in the world. The colorful 4-story
building is punctuated with a "punchcard"
decoration of white, black, blue, and orange,
relieving an otherwise monotonous structure.

1600 Market Street (1980s)
ARCHITECTS: Skidmore, Owings & Merrill
LOCATION: 1600 Market Street

Utilizing gleaming reflective glass, this clustered tower complex is acutely cut at the
corners.

One Logan Square (1983)
ARCHITECTS: Kohn Pederson Fox Associates
LOCATION: One Logan Square

This award winning, mixed-use complex rises
400 feet (a limit imposed by the city), and
contains both a 350-room hotel and a 30-story
office tower.

Philadelphia Stock Exchange (1982)
ARCHITECTS: Cope Linder Associates
LOCATION: Market Street between 19th
and 20th Sts.

A large landscaped atrium under a 15,000-
square-foot skylight distinguishes this "people
oriented" building. Horizontal tiered strips of
reflective glass windows and a cut-away
corner entrance add to the stunning exterior
appearance.

Rohm and Hass Building (1964)
ARCHITECTS: Pietro Belluschi and George
Ewing & Co.
LOCATION: Southwest corner of 6th and
Market Streets

Society Hill Apartments and Town Houses (1962–64)
ARCHITECT: I.M. Pei
LOCATION: 2nd and Dock Streets

Boldly situated on Philadelphia's historic
waterfront, the Society Hill development
replaced a previous slum. The architect
sensitively restored and preserved old townhouses on the site, integrating three stately
modern apartment towers. The pleasing solution, combined with well-planned
landscaping, has been admired throughout
the nation.

Student Activity Center (1981)
ARCHITECTS: Friday Architects
LOCATION: Temple University

The design of this new Student Center employs an Art Deco theme in a delightfully contemporary manner.

The United Fund Building (1971)
ARCHITECTS: Mitchell/Giurgola
LOCATION: Benjamin Franklin Parkway at Logan Square

A unique building that employs a concrete sunscreen on its western wall, and an exposed concrete wall on the south.

PITTSBURGH

"The Cathedral of Learning"
ARCHITECT: Charles Klauder
LOCATION: University of Pittsburgh campus

This highly praised and criticized tower was built during the Art Deco period and designed to house a whole university in a single structure. The effect, with its Beaux Arts approach, is awesome.

Community College of Allegheny County (1973)
ARCHITECT: Tasso Katselas
LOCATION: 800 Block of Ridge Ave., Northside district of Pittsburgh

Compared to a work of sculpture, the assertive Allegheny Community College is a complex of cantilever, cylinders, deep recesses, triangular windows, and diagonal escalators.

Dravo Tower (1981)
ARCHITECTS: Welton Becket Associates
LOCATION: Steel Plaza

Featuring a stunning exposed steel-wall system, the 54-story skyscraper is an engineering marvel.

Mellon Square (1956) and the Alcoa Building (1952)
ARCHITECTS: Harrison & Abramovitz (Alcoa Building)
LOCATION: William Penn Place, Oliver Avenue, Smithfield Street, and 6th Avenue

The stately Alcoa Building was one of Pennsylvania's first important office towers.

The Oxford Center (1980s)
ARCHITECTS: HOK Architects
LOCATION: Grant Street

A magnificent horizontal banded tower design in a clustered arrangement, this center facilitates both office and retailing space.

Pittsburgh Plan for Art (PPA), Gallery 407
ARCHITECTS: Daminos & Pedone
LOCATION: 407 S. Craig St., Oakland Area

Interesting exhibit space for 70 artist members of PPA.

St. Sebastian's Catholic Church (1964)
ARCHITECTS: Gerard & McDonald-M.W. Stuhldreher Associates
LOCATION: North Hills, Pittsburgh

The triangular form is strongly expressed throughout this striking church, featuring sliced roof composition.

Student Union (1967)
ARCHITECT: Paul Schweikher
LOCATION: Centennial Walk at Duquesne University

U.S. Steel Workers of American Building (1963)
ARCHITECTS: Curtis & Davis
LOCATION: 5 Gateway Center

This lacy building features an exposed system of steel trusses—one of the first buildings of its type in the world.

RADNOR

Sun Oil Company Headquarters (1977)
ARCHITECTS: John Carl Warnecke
LOCATION: One Radnor Corporate Center, 12 miles NW of Philadelphia

A handsome office complex surrounded by lovely landscaping and a wildlife preserve.

SPRINGFIELD

Shelly Ridge Girl Scout Center (1983)
ARCHITECTS: Bohlin Powell Larkin Cywinski
LOCATION: Springfield Township, close to Springfield

This much publicized complex of four shin-gle-clad buildings, "is refreshingly witty and imaginative.. an atmosphere of fun through the use of color, columns, and gables.." (*Architectural Record,* May 1984)

STRAFFORD

Tredyffrin Public Library (1978)
ARCHITECTS: Mitchell/Giurgola
LOCATION: 582 Upper Gulph Rd., Strafford
Wayne

SWARTHMORE

Dining Hall at Swarthmore College (1964)
ARCHITECTS: Vincent G. Kling and others
LOCATION: Swarthmore College campus

With some Gothic overtones, this wood and stone structure captures the spirit of the rolling wooded countryside and venacular architecture.

Swarthmore College Music Building (Lang Music Hall) (1974)
ARCHITECTS: Mitchell/Giurgola
LOCATION: Swarthmore College campus

WILKES-BARRE

Coal Street Park, Pool, and Ice Rink (1973)
ARCHITECTS: Bohlin Powell Larkin Cywinski
LOCATION: Coal Street, between "The East End" and "The Heights"

This recreation complex is one of the finest public recreational facilities in the state.

Downtown Renewal Program Featuring Bohlin Powell Brown's Clock Tower— South Main Street/Public Square Urban Developments: (1972–)
ARCHITECTS: Bohlin Powell Larkin Cywinski
LOCATION: Downtown, South Main Street area, I-80, Public Sq.

This delightful downtown development was instigated after the disastrous Hurricane Agnes Flood in 1972. Many features, some amusing, entice the visitor. A striking glazed canopy links and "contains" the diverse architecture.

- Woonsocket
- Providence
- Warwick
- Bristol
- Portsmouth
- Newport
- Kingston

Rhode Island

BRISTOL

Herreshoff Yachting Museum

(1970s)

ARCHITECT: Evan L. Schwartz
LOCATION: 18 Burnside Street
OPEN: May through October, Wed. and
Sun., 1–4

Nicely situated on the waterfront, this unique 21,500 square foot maritime museum was built on the former location of the original Herreshoff boatworks destroyed in 1938 by a hurricane. Two large wedge-shaped forms intersect, creating fascinating entrance and exhibition spaces. An outdoor plaza is tiered down to the waterfront flanked by the building's colonnaded facade. Exhibits are interestingly displayed under sailcloth ceilings with beams and columns of bright yellow.

PORTSMOUTH

Church and Monastery for Portsmouth Priory (1961)

ARCHITECT: Pietro Belluschi
LOCATION: W. off RI 114 via Cory's Lane
OPEN: During school year

Belluschi, the well-known Italian-born American architect, has designed a number of noteworthy religious structures—particularly in Oregon. In all of his designs the architect has attempted "to create an atmosphere where the basic elements of light, materials, and proportion may play their unifying roles." Overlooking the bay, this Benedictine complex nicely exemplifies Belluschi's design theories. The Monastery and Priory are primarily constructed of concrete, redwood, Rhode Island fieldstone, and copper.

PROVIDENCE

Computing Laboratory at Brown University (1959–60)

ARCHITECT: Philip Johnson
LOCATION: At the corner of Brook and George Streets
OPEN: During school hours

Thought of as a "gem" on Brown's campus, the building's design was described by the architect: "I conceived the Brown Computing Laboratory as a porticus-porch to emphasize its importance as a technical center, its unique setting in the cityscape, and its dignity as a memorial building. Though neo-Classical, therefore, in conception, the materials and the design of the columns are quite contemporary. Only precast stone could have been used to form the Xs of the entablature; only plate glass could render the porch usable in New England. By use of the red granite chips I thought to harmonize the Laboratory with the 19th Century that surrounds it." Johnson also designed the ALBERT AND VERA LIST ART BUILDING on campus (see page 350).

PROVIDENCE

Geology-Chemistry Research Building at Brown University (1982)

ARCHITECTS: Davis, Brody & Associates and Russo & Sonder
LOCATION: Brown University campus
OPEN: During school hours

The new "giant" Geology-Chemistry Research Building has created a prominent point on Brown University's campus. Constructed of warm red-brick, the five-story structure is topped with a sloping copper roof. The mammoth building, containing facilities for the Geology and Chemistry departments, was described by one professor as a building "designed for the twenty-first century."

ADDITIONAL MODERN STRUCTURES OF INTEREST

KINGSTON

Housing for the University of Rhode Island (1964)
ARCHITECTS: Pietro Belluschi with Sasaki Walker & Associates
LOCATION: Just off The University of Rhode Island campus

The outstanding focus of this housing project is its compatibility with nature. The design of simple 4-story housing units is arranged around pleasant landscaping of trees, turf, rocks, and water.

NEWPORT

Sheraton-Islander Inn (1970)
ARCHITECTS: Warner Burns Toan Lunde
LOCATION: End of Goat Island in Narragansett Bay

This sharply-angled design of pitched roofs was inspired by local shingle-style houses in the area.

PROVIDENCE

Brown Sciences Library (1972)
ARCHITECTS: Warner Burns Toan Lunde
LOCATION: Brown University campus

An impressive tower library, it is one of the first to combine all its science departmental collections into a single structure.

Pembroke Dormitories (1975)
ARCHITECTS: MLTW/Moore, Lyndon, Turnbull
LOCATION: Brown University campus

With exterior walls faced with colorful brick, the Pembroke Dormitories are fascinating compositions of form and direction.

Roger Williams Park Zoo (1979)
ARCHITECTS: The Architects Design Group
LOCATION: Entrance to Zoo on Elmwood Avenue

This award-winning Zoo is particularly imaginative and an excellent facility for children's appreciation of animal life.

The Albert and Vera List Art Building (1971)
ARCHITECTS: Philip Johnson with Samuel Glaser and Partners
LOCATION: Brown University campus

The controversial List Art Building was planned to respect the surrounding buildings and community. A row of bold jagged skylights top the concrete cubistic building. Protruding balcony offices, sun shades, and other forms distinguish this "work place for artists."

The Arcade (1827–29)
ARCHITECTS: J.C. Bucklin and Russell Warren
LOCATION: 130 Westminster St. and 65 Weybosset

An admired pioneer of early glass and iron roof construction in the United States.

WARWICK

L.L. Evan Restaurant (1982)
ARCHITECTS: Warren Platner Associates
LOCATION: Parking lot of Apex Shopping Center

This colorful white and yellow restaurant was designed on a budget by one of the nation's most prominent designers.

WOONSOCKET

Congregation B'Nai Israel Temple (1962)
ARCHITECTS: S. Glaser Associates
LOCATION: 224 Prospect Street

Constructed of white concrete precast units, this Temple incorporates colorful stained glass design enclosed in bold triangular forms.

Woonsocket Harris Public Library (1974)
ARCHITECTS: William D. Warner, Architects and Planners
LOCATION: 303 Clinton Street

This handsome monochromatic building demonstrates a sensitive handling of materials and form created for function.

• Clemson

• Columbia

Charleston •
• Kiawah Island

South Carolina

CHARLESTON

Charles Towne Landing Exposition Park (1970)

ARCHITECT: Harlan McClure
LOCATION: c. 6 miles NW of Charleston on IS 26, then 2.7 miles SW on SC 7 and SC 171 (follow signs)
OPEN: Apr.–Sept. Mon.–Sat., 9–6: Sun., 9–7:Oct.–Mar., Daily 9–5

Built to commemorate the three hundreth anniversary of South Carolina's founding, the Charles Towne Land Exposition is a delightful modern complex. Consisting of a cluster of pavilions housing fascinating exhibits of history and development of the area, the Park is effectively landscaped and inviting. The buildings themselves feature an intricate lacy system of truss supports housing interesting exhibits of the history of the site itself.

CHARLESTON

The Charleston Museum (1980)

ARCHITECTS: Crissman and Soloman Architects, Inc.
LOCATION: 360 Meeting Street
OPEN: Seven days a week, 9 AM –5 PM

In a town that loves its heritage and old buildings, this new modern facility had to "respect the scale, materials, and mood of this area of town." (*Arch. Rec.,* Jul. 1981.) The beauty of this museum unfolds upon entering the courtyard spaces. Four 2-story rectangles are joined by glass corridors. The low-profile building is clad with warm brown brick sensitively complementing the historic Adam styled Manigault House of 1803 close by—a primary goal of the architects.

CLEMSON

Keowee Toxaway Visitors' Center (1969–78)

ARCHITECTS: Freeman, Wells & Major
LOCATION: Duke Power Company Nuclear Station, W. of Clemson on US 123, N. on SC 130
OPEN: Mon.–Sat., 9–5; Sun., 10:30–6

The design concept of the Keowee Toxaway Visitors' Center is an exemplary plan demonstrating the architect's sensitivity to the mountainous location. The building superbly houses administrative facilities, a space with a sweeping view of the area, and a station with an innovative exhibit depicting "The Story of Energy."

COLUMBIA

U.S. Post Office (1964–66)

ARCHITECTS: Lyles, Bissett, Carlisle & Wolff
LOCATION: Assembly Street at Taylor
OPEN: During office hours

The site of this impressive U.S. Post Office was planned for maximum efficiency for the task. The 4-story structure (two below ground level) is landscaped with a surrounding plaza full of plantings, greatly enhancing the downtown district. A uniform colonnade accents dark tinted glass windows. Bold letters identifying the building create an eye-catching focal point. The complex admirably states the dignity and dependability of the postal service.

ADDITIONAL MODERN STRUCTURES OF INTEREST

GREENVILLE

Textile Hall (1964–66/1969/1977)
ARCHITECTS: J.E. Sirrine & Co.
LOCATION: Exposition Ave., S of
intersection IS 385 and SC 291 Greenville,
South Carolina

A gigantic one-and-a-half-storied structure
dedicated to the progress of textiles.

KIAWAH ISLAND

Windswept (1982)
ARCHITECTS: Sandy & Babcock
LOCATION: East Beach Village, oceanfront

Windswept Condominiums complex blends
nicely into its sandune setting at this popular
resort community. (Open only to resort
guests and property owners.)

South Dakota

SIOUX FALLS

McKennan Health Center

(1973–76)

ARCHITECTS: The Spitznagel Partners and Caudill, Rowlett and Scott
LOCATION: 7th Avenue at 22nd Street
OPEN: Public areas daily 9–5

Sensitively planned to harmonize and complement the quiet residential setting, the McKennan Health Center rises only three stories. The complex, providing 240 patient beds, is constructed of concrete and brick divided by ribbons of glass that accent the horizontal line and enhance the surrounding landscaping. Efficient patient care influenced all aspects of interior space planning.

SIOUX FALLS

St. Mary's Church (1958–59)

ARCHITECTS: The Spitznagel Partners
LOCATION: 5th Avenue at 29th Street
OPEN: Daily 9–5

The principle attraction of this admirable religious structure is the art and its placement within the interior space. The slightly arched beamed ceiling of dark wood combined with light flooding the area create a dramatic focal point for the white ceramic tile altar wall. A large slender black cross is flanked by a mosaic depicting Mary and Child by Robert Harmon and a smaller white cross. Stained glass and enamel designs add to the pleasing atmosphere.

STURGIS

Meade County Court House
(1965)

ARCHITECTS: Gay and Gass
LOCATION: 5th Street at Sherman
OPEN: During office hours

Located on a small site in downtown Sturgis, this commendable structure, built on a limited budget, is an attractive addition to the small town of less than five thousand inhabitants. Constructured of precast concrete panels set within a white concrete frame, the low 1-story building is capped with a copper roof. Vertical lines are emphasized moving from the column supports upward to the roof height.

WATERTOWN

Holy Name Church (1967–68)

ARCHITECTS: The Spitznagel Partners
LOCATION: 10th Avenue at Sky Line Drive
OPEN: Daily 8–7

An intimate atmosphere permeates this Roman Catholic church through the thoughtful use of materials, form, and space. Warm red brick is employed everywhere, beginning with the inviting courtyard. The interior walls are also sheathed with brick, including the altar wall. This texture, enhanced by soft lighting, provides a unifying background for the simple pulpit and lectern.

ADDITIONAL MODERN STRUCTURES OF INTEREST

RAPID CITY

St. John's School of Nursing (1968–69)
ARCHITECT: Robert B. Gay
LOCATION: 11th Street at South

SIOUX FALLS

Christ The King Church (1978)
ARCHITECTS: The Spitznagel Partners
LOCATION: 1501 West 26th Street

This unusually shaped church is constructed
of sheet metal, masonry, and glass.

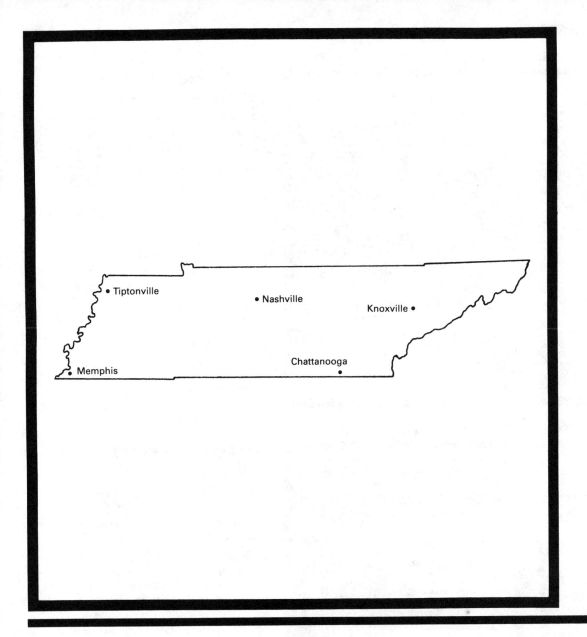

Tennessee

CHATTANOOGA

Hunter Museum of Art Extension (1974–75)

ARCHITECTS: Derthick & Henley
LOCATION: 10 Bluff View Avenue
OPEN: Tues.–Sat., 10–4:30, Sun., 1–4:30

With a challenge to complement the large 1904 neo-Colonial house close by, the architects did not attempt to compete with the old brick structure. Rather, in uncompromising terms, the new Hunter Museum contrasts interestingly. Cascading down the slope toward the Tennessee River, the exhibit areas have been artfully arranged to enhance the setting.

KNOXVILLE

Art and Architecture Building (1982)

ARCHITECTS: McCarty Bullock Holsaple, Inc.
LOCATION: University of Tennessee campus
OPEN: During school hhurs

A unique building composed of modular sections, the Art and Architecture building is built around a central atrium that functions as a throughfare. The striking building forms an important link with existing buildings—both old and new. Natural lighting floods the interior spaces, providing an airy and pleasant meeting place for students. Facilities within creatively function for many activities.

KNOXVILLE

Clarence Brown Theatre for The Performing Arts (1968–69)

ARCHITECTS: Bruce McCarty & Associates
LOCATION: University of Tennessee, 1714 Andy Holt Avenue
OPEN: For performances

An architecturally spirited building design, the Clarence Brown Theatre admirably conveys the essence of the performing arts. With the difficult task of creating the building's own identity, the architects have successfully combined a variety of angles and rounded forms, that complement the brick and concrete construction. The auditorium is a superior design for its purpose and function.

MEMPHIS

Commercial & Industrial Bank (1970–72)

ARCHITECTS: Gassner-Nathan-Browne
LOCATION: 200 Madison Avenue
OPEN: During business hours

The four-story sloping skylight of this bank's facade creates drama and attention in comparison with the surrounding buildings in downtown Memphis. The effect inside is equally dazzling, with light flooding the terraced levels. Seven-thousand square feet of glass was employed to provide the effect. Terraced levels accommodate the various banking functions in open and spacious areas. Poured-in-place concrete and a yellow welded steel space-frame were used for the building's construction.

ADDITIONAL MODERN STRUCTURES OF INTEREST

CHATTANOOGA

Chattanooga Choo-Choo (1906–8/1973)
ARCHITECT: Donn Barber, of original station
LOCATION: South Market Street between
Alabama and 14th

Instead of destroying an old obsolete train
station, a unique plan to transform the
building resulted in a delightful renovation.
With careful consideration for the Chattanooga Choo-Choo building, the old brick
arches and trackside have been preserved and
incorporated into the new plan. Restaurants,
shops, and other commericial enterprises are
attractively set up within the spaces.

KNOXVILLE

Laurel Church of Christ (1968)
ARCHITECTS: Yearwood & Johnson
LOCATION: 3457 Kingston Pike

Beautifully situated on a sloping hillside, this
small church features a steeply pitched wood
beam nave.

1982 Expo Buildings (1982)
ARCHITECTS: Various architects, Bruce
McCarty, executive
LOCATION: Expo Fair Grounds

Many fascinating structures were designed for
the spectacular 1982 Expo. Particularly noteworthy is the U.S. Pavilion with its interesting
sloping exterior sections.

United American Plaza (1978)
ARCHITECTS: Carry Cooper Associates
LOCATION: United American Plaza

This soaring reflective banking tower features
a unique 5-story sloping atrium springing
from the lower levels of the structure.

MEMPHIS

**The Brooks Memorial Art Gallery
Addition** (1973)
ARCHITECTS: Walk Jones with Francis May,
Inc.

LOCATION: In Overton Park

The subtle exterior of this new addition
belies its explosive interior exhibition spaces.

First Tennessee Bank of Memphis (1964)
ARCHITECTS: Walk C. Jones Jr.
LOCATION: 165 Madison Ave.

This 25-story tower of aluminum and gray
glass is designed in the Miesan approach.

Hyatt Regency at Ridgeway (1970s)
ARCHITECTS: Walk Jones and Francis Mah,
Inc.
LOCATION: Ridgeway, Memphis, 939 Ridge
Lake Blvd.

Memphis Metropolitan Airport Terminal
(1964)
ARCHITECTS: Mann & Harrover
LOCATION: 2491 Winchester

A series of gracefully designed concrete
mushroom-shaped pillars distinguish this airport facility.

**Memphis Publishing Company (The
Commercial Appeal)** (1977)
ARCHITECTS: Walk Jones & Francis Mah,
Inc.
LOCATION: 495 Union Ave.

This new 5-story office building for two
newspaper firms features a striking undulating glass wall composition.

The Riverfront Redevelopment (1974–)
ARCHITECTS: Marcou, O'Leary &
Associates, Inc.
LOCATION: Court Square

This long-range program for downtown
Memphis includes designs for restored buildings, a visitor's center, pedestrian walkways,
and other interesting buildings and activities
tiered down to the Mississippi River.

Mud Island Park (1980s)
ARCHITECTS: Roy P. Harrover & Associates
and others
LOCATION: Island at the confluence of the
Mississippi and Wolf Rivers.

This new recreational and educational park has become one of the state's most popular tourist attractions. "All major towns and cities along the river are depicted by slate blocks within stainless steel streets complete wth street names." (*Progressive Architecture,* March 1983.) This small model of the Mississippi, called the "River Walk," is flanked by a Pavilion, Museum, Amphitheater, restaurant. Pedestrian bridge/monorails, Observation towers, and other public facilities. This marvelous architectural project allows the visitor to walk along a miniature composition of the Mississippi River. The island is accessible by monorail or bicycle.

Temple Israel (1976)
ARCHITECTS: Gassner/Nathan & Partners
LOCATION: 1376 East Massey

This admirable sprawling complex is set in a wooded area. The new synagogue features a glass-covered garden and skylit gallery.

NASHVILLE

Hickory Hollow Mall (1981)
ARCHITECTS: Cooper, Carry & Associates, Inc.
LOCATION: On Hickory Hollow Parkway

This light and airy, award-winning shopping mall features a lacy network of space frames combined with spacious areas of glass.

One Commerce Place and Radisson Plaza Hotel (1981)
ARCHITECTS: Thompson, Ventulett, Stainback & Associates
LOCATION: One Commerce Place, downtown square

These two outstanding triangular high-rise structures are interestingly placed on the block with a pedestrian walkway diagonally cutting through the block area.

OPRYLAND

The Grand Ole Opry (1973)
ARCHITECTS: Welton Becket and Associates
LOCATION: 10 miles NE of downtown Nashville

This handsome brick, wood, and glass structure houses the world's largest radio and television broadcasting studio.

TIPTONVILLE

Airpark Lodge (1973)
ARCHITECTS: Gassner/Nathan/Browne
LOCATION: Reel foot Lake State Park, Far NW end of state

An interesting wooden complex built around a swampy wilderness lake with effort to preserve the natural beauty.

- El Paso
- Lubbock
- Irving
- Fort Worth
- Dallas
- San Angelo
- Navasota
- Orange
- Austin
- Spring
- Houston
- San Antonio
- Corpus Christi

Texas

AUSTIN

Lyndon Baines Johnson Library (1968–71)

ARCHITECTS: Skidmore, Owings & Merrill
LOCATION: Just off I–35, University of Texas campus
OPEN: 9 AM –5 PM daily

The powerful design of the LBJ Library creates a commanding impression in its spacious, well-landscaped grounds and plaza. The building, sheathed with cream colored travertine, is a monument to the late President of the United States. The interior spaces were especially planned to house Johnson's books, writings, and other memorabilia. The building has received both praise and criticism. Its unusual form has been compared to a "giant printing machine" and an "Egyptian tomb."

CORPUS CHRISTI

Art Museum of South Texas (1970–72)

ARCHITECTS: Philip Johnson/John Burgee
LOCATION: 1902 North Shoreline Drive
OPEN: Tues.–Sat., 10–5, Sun., 1–5

Boldly located on the edge of a hillside, the stark-white, hard edged forms of this superb museum seem to slice the blue sky. The building is small and built on a limited budget, but the finest concrete was employed throughout the complex and one of the nation's most prestigious architectural teams received the commission for its design. The enticement of the museum begins as one approaches the dazzling bright building and continues into the interior spaces. A haven from the hot Texas sun, the interior areas house an impressive art collection.

DALLAS

Hyatt Regency and Reunion Tower (1976–78)
ARCHITECTS: Welton Becket Associates
LOCATION: 300 Reunion Boulevard at Stemmons Freeway
OPEN: Continuously

The brilliant effect of the silvered reflective glass towers of the Hyatt Regency is stunning. Steel plate wall construction provides a safety feature from high winds. The cluster of staggered forms is counterbalanced by the Reunion Tower looming 564 feet above the hotel complex and housing a restaurant and observation deck. The interior spaces contain 956 guest rooms centered around a 200-foot-high square atrium. The entire complex makes a striking silhouette on the skyline and is considered one of the finest facilities of its kind in the nation.

DALLAS

John F. Kennedy Memorial (1970)
ARCHITECT: Philip Johnson
LOCATION: Main, Market, Elm, and Record Streets
OPEN: Always

Seventy-two precast concrete slabs comprise the construction of this expressive memorial to America's 35th President, who was assassinated a few hundred yards away. Eight of these slabs function as leg supports elevating the simple hollow cube structure. A break in the vertical composition accommodates a long slender entry. The symbolic building evokes feelings of life, death, and fate.

DALLAS

Kalita Humhreys Theater
Dallas Theater Center (1958–59)

ARCHITECT: Frank Lloyd Wright
LOCATION: 3636 Turtle Creek Blvd., SW off
Blackburn Avenue
OPEN: Daily tours and performances,
Telephone: (214) 526-8210

Demonstrating Wright's interest in rounded
forms, the Kalita Humphreys Theater was
completed the year of the great modern
architect's death and was his first public
theater design effort. Artfully sandwiched into
its hillside park setting, the complex offers
theatergoers many innovative design experiences. Wright himself was an avid supporter
of the performing arts.

DALLAS

One Main Place (1967–68)

ARCHITECTS: Skidmore, Owings & Merrill
LOCATION: Main Street at Griffin
OPEN: During business hours

This elegant 34-story skyscraper is one of the
first significant modern structures in Dallas.
An inviting sunken plaza with a large fountain
in front of the building enhances the crowded
downtown area, providing a spacious and
pleasant gathering place. The concrete and
glass tower is uniformly designed and its
skeletal frame frankly exposed.

DALLAS

Thanks-Giving Square (1977)

ARCHITECTS: Philip Johnson/John Burgee
LOCATION: Pacific Street at Ervay
OPEN: Mon.–Fri., 10–5, Sat.–Sun., 1–5

Situated on a tiny, neatly landscaped triangle in downtown Dallas, this Chapel and garden were planned to commemorate world thanksgiving. The garden itself is a symphony of geometric forms employing grass, concrete, aggregate and water. The dazzling white spiral chapel is the focus of the square, inspired by a ninth-century minaret. The simple interior space is highlighted by a dramatic spiraling stained-glass composition arranged in a webbed design—the only light source within. The colors reflected on the stark white walls are stunning.

DALLAS

The Dallas Municipal Building
(1975–78)

ARCHITECTS: I.M. Pei & Partners; Harper & Kemp
LOCATION: Off Young Street between Akard and Ervay
OPEN: During office hours

Located at the head of a spacious plaza, the City Hall boasts a remarkable step-back design. The Municipal Building has been declared "easily the nation's most dramatic seat of local government since the Boston City Hall." The block-long cantilever structure "interlocks urban space with civic structure." The symbolic building was called "a gift of space," by Pei. The angular structure of finely crafted concrete was created to express the city and people of Dallas.

DALLAS

The Dallas Museum (1983)

ARCHITECT: Edward Larrabee Barnes
LOCATION: Bounded by Woodall Rodgers
Freeway and Ross, Routh and St. Paul.
OPEN: Tues., Wed., Fri., Sat., 10–5, Thurs.
10–10, Sun., 12–5

Barnes' sprawling Art Museum dominates
downtown Dallas in what is known as the
new "Art District" comprising 60 acres. The
massive structure's facade is covered with
immense blocks of pale Indiana limestone.
Extending over an entire city block, Barnes
said of the design, "I didn't want an elevator
building, I wanted lots of horizontal space."
The city of Dallas is delighted to have this
monumental museum moving into a previously dying neighborhood. It is projected
that by the year 2000, the entire Arts District
will be completed. In 1987, I.M. Pei's spectacular new *SYMPHONY HALL* will be
completed.

FORT WORTH

Amon Carter Museum

(1961/1978)

ARCHITECT: Philip Johnson
LOCATION: W. on Lancaster Ave. to 3501
Camp Bowie Blvd.
OPEN: Tues.–Sat., 10–5, Sun., 1–5:30

A striking value contrast of five slender
sculptural arches and dark tinted glass introduce the visitor to a remarkable collection of
American Art owned by Amon Carter. The
museum's floors are tiered down a gently
rolling slope adding to the drama of the
building's design. Interior galleries and detailing are sensitively planned by the architect to
enhance the exhibits of art. The museum is
like a fine jewel in its beautifully landscaped
setting.

FORT WORTH

Kimbell Art Museum (1969–72)

ARCHITECT: Louis I. Kahn
LOCATION: Will Rogers Road West between
West Lancaster Avenue and Camp Bowie
Boulevard
OPEN: Tues., 10–9, Wed.–Sat., 10–5, Sun.,
1–5

Located in an inviting park setting, the
expressive Kimball Art Museum plays up a
simple rhythmic design derived from the
repetition of cycloid, vaulted shapes. The
exhibition rooms are approached through
unique open vaults. The design concept has
been praised as a superb use of space, light,
and form. Considered one of America's finest
museum interiors, materials include beautifully finished oak, travertine, concrete, and
stainless steel.

FORT WORTH

The Water Garden (1974)

ARCHITECTS: Philip Johnson/John Burgee
LOCATION: 12, Commerce, Lancaster, and
Houston Streets
OPEN: Always

This refreshing and welcoming oasis in a
usually hot climate is an innovative and
admirable attempt to humanize the city
environment. Situated in the middle of a park,
the sunken water garden descends four
stories, creating a central focus. This extraordinary creation was commissioned by the
Amon Carter Foundation and projects an
image of miniature landscapes of mountains,
forests, and lakes on a contour map. Layers of
concrete allow water to cascade from all sides
into a center pit. The experience of walking
around the Water Garden is exhilerating.

FORT WORTH

Visual Arts and Communications Building
(1982)

ARCHITECTS: Kevin Roche/John Dinkeloo
LOCATION: Texas Christian University
campus
OPEN: During school hours

This outstanding new facility is one of the latest projects of the prominent New York firm of Roche/Dinkeloo. Surrounded by Georgian styled buildings, the new Visual Arts and Communications Building additionally functions as an important gateway to the campus. The arrangement of glass, concrete, and brick is interestingly angled to complement its unusual site and existing buildings. A network of white space-frames add to the visual excitement of the complex, bringing an airy and light atmosphere.

HOUSTON

Alley Theatre (1967–68)

ARCHITECTS: Ulrich Franzen & Associates
LOCATION: 615 Texas Avenue between
Smith and Louisiana
OPEN: Performances Oct–June; tours
Tues.–Fri. 12:45; summer; open July–Sept.

The Alley Theatre has been praised by critics as a "brilliant theatrical event and a striking work of architecture—a bold and confident plastic expression—the interior spaces have been skillfully designed to enhance the excitement of theatergoing." The project consists of two theaters—the larger has 800 seats, and the smaller, 300 seats for in-the-round performances. The boldly designed theatre in its urban setting is part of a previously planned civic center development.

HOUSTON

Best Products Showroom

(1976)

ARCHITECTS: Site Inc.
LOCATION: W. of Almeda Mall, off IS 45/US
75, c. 13 miles S. of Houston
OPEN: During shopping hours

Provoking a wide range of comments, due to the "unfinished" design image, the Best Products Showroom ingeniously draws customers. Appearing as if some sort of disaster has struck, the crumbling gaps and jagged roofline is the principle focus of the remarkable building's facade. Best Products Showroom buildings are found across the nation—many exhibiting similar design concepts found on this unique structure.

HOUSTON

Contemporary Arts Museum

(1973)
Museum of Fine Arts (1958/1974)
ARCHITECTS: Gunnar Birkerts & Associates/
Mies van der Rohe
LOCATION: Montrose Boulevard at Bisonnet
Avenue
OPEN: Tues.–Sat., 10–5, Sun., 1–5; MFA:
Tues.–Sat. 9:30–5, Sun., 12–6

The dynamic triangular shaped CAM consists of 17,500 square feet of exhibit space. The steel and concrete museum's slotted entrance opens into an intriguing wedge-shaped lobby. The spacious interior exhibit areas are entirely lit artificially. Diagonal forms also dominate the interior spaces through placement of walls, partitions, and ceiling grids. Mies van der Rohe's formal Museum of Fine Arts with its new additions is also an important landmark and complements the Contemporary Arts Museum close by.

HOUSTON

Interfirst Bank (1981)

ARCHITECTS: Skidmore, Owings and Merrill
LOCATION: 1100 Louisiana
OPEN: During office hours

Each level of the brilliant First International Plaza is dramatically stepped back fifteen feet as it soars to its full height. The structure, with its exterior tube, composite steel frame, contains 22,000 square feet of rentable office space. The extraordinary building is situated on a small grid lot artfully landscaped to dramatize the building's unique design.

HOUSTON

Jesse H. Jones Hall (1965–66)

ARCHITECTS: Caudill, Rowlett, Scott
LOCATION: 615 Louisiana Street between Texas and Capitol
OPEN: For performances. Inquire about tours

The elegant Jesse H. Jones Hall functions as a facility for the Performing Arts. Modern classicism is expressed through slender structural columns supporting the massive roof. Entirely sheathed with Italian travertine, the exterior exudes a feeling of dignity and restraint. The interior space is highlighted by 870 bronze hexagonal panels providing emphasis and interest. Numerous inventive technical and design features have been incorporated into this admirable theater complex.

HOUSTON

Penzoil Plaza (1974–76)

ARCHITECTS: Philip Johnson/John Burgee
LOCATION: Louisiana, Capitol, Milan, and
Rusk Streets
OPEN: During business hours

One of Johnson/Burgees' most spectacular and photographed work, Penzoil Plaza makes a distinctive silhouette on Houston's skyline. The striking wedge-shaped twin towers rise 36 stories and end sliced at a 45 degree angle. The glass towers are attached at the base by a vast high-tech galleria of glass and white space frames appearing much like a giant "erector-set" composition. The spacious interior galleria is filled with trees, flowers, and sunlight—a popular meeting place in downtown Houston.

HOUSTON

Post Oak Central (1976)

ARCHITECTS: Johnson/Burgee with S.I.
Morris Associates
LOCATION: 2000 Post Oak Boulevard
OPEN: During business hours

Recalling the suave "Art Deco" and "Art Moderne" period of the 1920s and 30s, the new suburban galleria office complex is one of Houston's most interesting additions. The stunning black and silver materials are arranged in strong horizontal bands that wrap the corners. The stepped design breaks at the 12th and 22nd floors, adding to the building's drama. The architects have drawn upon the most elegant features of the Deco Style. Surrounding the bases of the structures is gray slate that is carried into the lobby that is lined with gray marble.

HOUSTON

Republic Bank Center (1983–)

ARCHITECTS: Philip Johnson/John Burgee
LOCATION: 700 Louisiana
OPEN: During business hours

The astounding new Republic Bank is clad with red Swedish granite and is one of the latest Johnson/Burgee buildings to appear on Houston's downtown skyline. Drawing inspiration from sixteenth-century Holland, the structure emphasizes a distinctive crows-step gable design dramatically tiered three times. The building, along with other recent structures across the nation by this internationally famous design firm, heralds a new epoch in skyscraper planning.

HOUSTON

The Allied Bank Plaza (1983)

ARCHITECTS: Skidmore, Owings & Merrill
LOCATION: 1000 Louisiana
OPEN: During business hours

This exhilarating new tower's unique design consists of two quarter-circles offset fifteen feet from one another. Clad with a curtain wall of dark green reflective glass, the building's base is treated with contrasting polished black granite. Allied Bank tower soars 71 stories and is 985 feet tall—the ninth tallest building in the world. Sleek and stately, the structure embodies the philosophies of the machine esthetic. Interior spaces are equally stunning. "For all its height and bulk, Allied Bank is Houston's "skyscraper." (*Architecture*/ April 1984)

HOUSTON

The Rothko Chapel (1970–71)

ARCHITECTS: Howard Barnstone and
Eugene Aubry
LOCATION: Yupon Street between Branard
and Sul Ross
OPEN: Noon to 8 PM daily

This octagonal-shaped structure with an octagonal skylight is a center for all religions—devoted to the creations of a single artist—Mark Rothko. Fourteen immense paintings, called Rothko's "supreme achievement," hang on walls of muted gray cement. Tragically, Rothko committed suicide one year before the chapel was dedicated. In front of the Chapel is a fascinating twenty-six foot high steel sculpture entitled, "Broken Obelisk,"—dedicated to the memory of Martin Luther King.

HOUSTON

Transco II (1983–)

ARCHITECTS: Philip Johnson/John Burgee
LOCATION: 2800 Post Oak Blvd.
OPEN: During business hours

Philip Johnson, describing the impact of this building, wrote, "This will always look like the tallest building in the world." The 65-story tower, visible for miles, looms above surrounding low-rise buildings emphasizing its height. The sculptural building has been likened as the "Empire State Building—Texas style." The cutaway treatment of the structure's exterior treatment is reminiscent of the popular Art Deco period of the 1920s and 30s in America—the period when the Empire State Building was constructed.

ADDITIONAL MODERN STRUCTURES OF INTEREST

AUSTIN

First Federal Plaza (1977)
ARCHITECTS: 3D/Brooks Barr Graeber White
LOCATION: 200 E. 10th

Texas Law Center (1978)
ARCHITECTS: Kenneth Bentsen Associates
LOCATION: 1 block from State Capitol Bldg.

Surrounded by a large plaza this impressive complex is constructed of concrete, red granite and tinted glass.

Special Events Center at The University of Texas (1980)
ARCHITECTS: Crain/Anderson, Inc.
LOCATION: 1701 Red River

DALLAS

Arco Oil & Gas Company (1983)
ARCHITECTS: I.M. Pei & Partners
LOCATION: 1601 Bryan Street

This 49-story corporate headquarters building features a triangular design with horizontal bands of gray polished granite between strips of reflective glass fenestration.

Brookhollow Plaza (1971)
ARCHITECTS: Paul Rudolph and Harwood K. Smith and Partners
LOCATION: Stemmons Freeway at Mockingbird Lane

A 16-story precast concrete office tower.

Collin Creek Mall (1981)
ARCHITECTS: RTKL Associates
LOCATION: Plano, Dallas

Dallas Central Library (1982)
ARCHITECTS: I.M. Pei & Partners
LOCATION: Wood, Young, and Evray

Dallas/Fort Worth Airport (1968–73)
ARCHITECTS: Hellmuth, Obata & Kassabaum; Brodsky, Hopf & Adler
LOCATION: Via TEX 114 or 183, 21 miles from Dallas

Employees Casualty Building (1984)
ARCHITECTS: Burson, Henricks and Wall
LOCATION: 423 South Akard

The dramatic exterior wall, framed with bold concrete forms, encloses a 13-story atrium. The new complex is a vast extension to an existing building.

Magnolia Building (1921)
LOCATION: 1401 Commerce

This Dallas hallmark of architecture, topped with a flying horse, was the tallest building (33 stories) west of the Mississippi. It has been renovated and functions as an office building.

Mountain View College (1970–71)
ARCHITECTS: Harrell & Hamilton/Chan & Rader
LOCATION: Illinois Avenue at Duncanville Road, S of Dallas-Fort Worth Turnpike, E on Loop Road

One Dallas Center (1981)
ARCHITECTS: I.M. Pei & Partners
LOCATION: One Dallas Center, downtown

In a town full of reflective glass towers, One Dallas Center is one of the finest. A triangular theme is employed throughout the granite and reflective glass tower.

Stemmons Towers (1962–67)
ARCHITECT: Harold A. Berry
LOCATION: 2710 Stemmon Freeway

Temple Emanuel (1955–56)
ARCHITECTS: Howard R. Meyer and Max M. Sandfield
LOCATION: Hillcrest Road at Northwest Highway

Note: A marvelous "Walking Tour of Downtown Dallas" is available from the Chamber of Commerce at 1507 Pacific, guiding the tourist to many outstanding architectural treasures.

EL PASO

Mills Building (1976–80)
ARCHITECTS: Greener & Sumner
LOCATION: 303 North Oregon Street

A 65-year-old landmark building with a new facelift and renovation.

FORT WORTH

City Center Tower (1983)
ARCHITECT: Paul Rudolph
LOCATION: 301 Commerce Street

Paul Rudolph's first glass building. (Known for his raw concrete designs.) The imposing structure has been nicknamed "Darth Vader."

Continental Plaza Building (1980–82)
ARCHITECTS: Jarvis Putty Jarvis Firm
LOCATION: Seventh and Main Streets

First United Tower (1981–1983)
ARCHITECTS: Geren Associates with Skiles Jennings Kelly
LOCATION: 801 Cherry Street

Fort Worth Municipal Building (1971)
ARCHITECT: Edward Durell Stone
LOCATION: 1000 Throckmorton Street

Fort Worth National Bank (Now Texas American Bank/Fort Worth (1974)
ARCHITECT: John Portman
LOCATION: 500 Throckmorton Street

An interesting Alexander Calder sculpture in front is called "the Eagle."

The Sid W. Richardson Physical Sciences Building (1971)
ARCHITECTS: Paul Rudolph with Preston M. Geren and others
LOCATION: Texas Christian University

This large 5-story building features bold horizontal forms of masonry broken with huge cylinders. The windows seem to be hidden by the deeply recessed walkways.

Tarrant County Junior College (1976)
ARCHITECTS: Geren Associates
LOCATION: Northwest Campus, Fort Worth

A unified and interesting "one-building" complex designed with student input.

HOUSTON

Art School of The Museum of Fine Arts (Alfred C. Glassel, Jr., Art School) (1978)
ARCHITECTS: S.I. Morris Associates
LOCATION: 5101 Montrose

This dazzling structure of Corning glass block is accented with a huge arched central entrance and hallway.

Astrodome (1965)
ARCHITECTS: Wilson, Morris, Crain & Anderson
LOCATION: Kirby and South Loop 610

Bates College of Law (1966–67)
ARCHITECTS: Freeman & Van Ness
LOCATION: University of Houston, Gulf Freeway (IS45) at Calhoun

Cypress Creek Christian Church and Community Center (1978)
ARCHITECTS: Clovis Heimsath
LOCATION: 6823 Cypresswood Drive

Episcopal Church of The Epiphany (1975)
ARCHITECTS: Clovis Heimsath Associates, Inc.
LOCATION: 9600 South Gessner

The most emphatic feature of this church is a bold roof form pierced with a round stained glass window.

First City National Bank (1961)
ARCHITECTS: Skidmore, Owings and Merrill
LOCATION: 1021 Main Street

Four Leaf Towers (1982)
ARCHITECTS: Cesar Pelli
LOCATION: 5100 San Felipe Blvd.

The top levels of these soaring twin towers are interestingly sloped, providing visual variety.

Four Oaks Towers (1982)
ARCHITECTS: Cesar Pelli
LOCATION: Post Oak Road

Galleria (1978)
ARCHITECTS: Hellmuth & Obata
LOCATION: 5015 Westheimer

A large, impressive complex containing facilities for shopping, offices, and a hotel.

Greenway Plaza (1970–73)
ARCHITECTS: Lloyd Jones Brewer & Associates
LOCATION: Southwest Freeway; take Buffalo Speedway exit N, about 4 miles SW of Houston

A well-planned shopping complex with office and office-living spaces.

Gus. S. Wortham Theater Center (1984–86)
ARCHITECTS: Morris Aubry Architects
LOCATION: 550 Prairie Avenue

This stunning new theater design is under construction and is projected for completion in 1986.

Houston Central Library (1978)
ARCHITECTS: S.I. Morris Associates
LOCATION: 500 Mc Kinney Street

This bold new granite and glass structure adjoins the older library. The entrance to the new library addition is particularly stunning.

Houston Intercontinental Airport (1966–69)
ARCHITECTS: Golemon & Rolfe with Pierce, Goodwin, Alexander
LOCATION: N on US 59 (Eastex Freeway), W on N Belt Rd, N on Kennedy Blvd.

Hyatt Regency Hotel (1972)
ARCHITECTS: JVIII Koetter, Tharp & Cowell; Caudill Rowlett, Scott, & others
LOCATION: 1200 Louisiana

This huge multi-use hotel features a huge atrium interior space with facilities especially geared for public activities.

Miller Outdoor Theatre (late 1960s)
ARCHITECTS: Eugene Werlin & Associates
LOCATION: In Hermann Park, off Main Street

An outstanding example of exposed truss construction, the Miller Memorial Theatre boasts a dynamic shell-type roof.

Neiman-Marcus Store (1983)
ARCHITECTS: Hellmuth, Obata & Kassabaum, Inc.
LOCATION: 10615 Town and Country Way

Strong concrete forms combine in a functional and direct approach for the new Neiman-Marcus Store in Houston.

Newman Hall-Texas Southern University (1969)
ARCHITECTS: Clovis Heimsath Associates
LOCATION: Texas Southern University campus

Relating effectively to the campus, this small complex of diverse shapes houses spaces for relaxation, worhsip, and information.

One Shell Plaza (1971)
ARCHITECTS: Skidmore, Owings & Merrill
LOCATION: near SOM's First City National Bank

One of the tallest reinforced-concrete structures in the nation.

Gulf Tower-III Houston Center (1983)
ARCHITECTS: CRS
LOCATION: 1301 Mc Kinney

This handsome metal and glass tower provides visual interest through varying planes.

IBM Building (1981)
ARCHITECTS: CRS
LOCATION: 2 River Way

This tower won an energy efficiency award.

Robert Herring Hall at Rice University (1984)
ARCHITECTS: Cesar Pelli
LOCATION: Rice University campus

St. Cecilia Catholic Church (1982)
ARCHITECTS: Charles Tapley, Associates
LOCATION: 11730 Denise

An intimte and welcoming modern religious design constructed of brick, copper, and wood. A coffered barrel vault inside is particularly interesting.

School of Architecture at Rice University (1977)
ARCHITECT: James Stirling (Great Britain)
LOCATION: Rice University campus

Esteemed as one of England's finest modern architects, James Stirling was the recipient of the prestigious international Pritzker Architecture Prize. Many of his structures have dazzled the world. His design renovation for the School of Architecture at Rice University seems conservative in comparison. The building of brick construction features a series of arches that commendably blend with existing buildings on campus. The structure draws many visitors interested in the great English architect's work.

Southwest Houston Office Facility for Brown & Root
ARCHITECTS: Morris Aubry
LOCATION: 3535 1/2 Sage Road

Massive concrete drums march across the three-sided facade of this stately building. A slender arched entry rises above the roofline providing a focal point for the complex.

Superior Oil Research (1967)
ARCHITECTS: Todd Tackett Lacy
LOCATION: W from Houston on Westheimer Road

Tenneco Building (1962–63)
ARCHITECTS: Skidmore, Owings & Merrill
LOCATION: 1010 Milam Street between Lamar and McKinney

The 33-story Tenneco Building was one of the first high-rise commercial buildings to appear on the Houston skyline, and is among SOM's most admirable projects. Tinted glass windows are set back within a uniformly designed white frame providing efficient sun control and design interest.

Texas Commerce Bank Building (1982)
ARCHITECTS: I.M. Pei & Partners
LOCATION: Bounded by Texas, Capitol, Travis, and Milam

An inspiring skyscraper highlighted with a Joan Miro sculpture entitled "Personage with Birds" at the entrance. The granite tower is cut at the corners.

Warwick Post Oak Hotel
ARCHITECTS: I.M. Pei & Partners
LOCATION: 2001 Post Oak Blvd.

A building that makes use of unusual geometric shapes.

YWCA Masterson Branch and Metropolitan Office (1980s)
ARCHITECTS: Taft Architects
LOCATION: 1600 Louisiana

This building features colorful stucco and ceramic tile artfully arranged in a flat composition but giving the illusion of depth and architectural detailing.

IRVING

Soundstage (1982)
ARCHITECTS: Martin Growald
LOCATION: 1 Dallas Communications Complex, Los Colinas suburb

Soundstage, with its 72-foot-high space, is topped by a copper-sheathed barrel vault with huge round windows at each end. The bold structure is a first stage development for the Dallas Communications Complex—a video and film industry.

LUBBOCK

Texas Tech University (1969–70)
ARCHITECTS: Various architects
LOCATION: Bordered by 4th, 19th Streets and Univ. & Quaker Avenues

A campus boasting many fine buildings by a number of prominent architects. Of particular note is the Tech Library.

NAVASOTA

Camp Allen Episcopal Camps and Conference Center (1981)
ARCHITECTS: Charles Tapley Associates
LOCATION: S on HWY 6, L on Rd 2 (Lynn

Grove), R on FM 362, continue for 3 miles, follow signs (about 17 miles SW of Navasota)

A pleasant camp and conference center operated by the Episcopal Diocese of Texas. Excellent facilities for meetings, summer camp, and retreats.

ORANGE

Stark Museum of Art (1977)
ARCHITECTS: Page Southerland Page
LOCATION: 700 W. Green Ave.

An impressive collection of art is housed in a clean, "stark" structural complex.

SAN ANGELO

Central High School (1957–58)
ARCHITECTS: Caudill, Rowlett, Scott
LOCATION: West Harris Ave. at Cottonwood

The innovative space planning for this school influenced educational facilities around the nation and was this well-known architectural firm's first important building.

SAN ANTONIO

Laurie Auditorium and Communications Center (1971)
ARCHITECTS: Ford, Powell, & Carson: Bartlett Cocke & Assoc., Inc.
LOCATION: Trinity University, 715 Stadium Drive

Lone Star Brewery Converted into The New San Antonio Museum of Art (1981)
ARCHITECTS: Cambridge Seven Associates, Inc.
LOCATION: 200 West Jones Avenue

One of the most intriguing museums of art in the nation, this new Art Museum was formerly a brewery complex.

Ruth Taylor Theater (1965–66)
ARCHITECTS: Ford, Powell & Carson: Bartlett Cocke & Assoc., Inc.

LOCATION: Trinity University on Stadium Drive

San Antonio Hyatt Hotel (1983)
ARCHITECTS: Thompson, Ventulett, Stainback & Associates, Inc.
LOCATION: Along the "Paseo del Rio"

Situated along San Antonio's beautiful "Paseo del Rio" riverwalk, this 16-story hotel was designed to complement the low-rise buildings, lush gardens, and terraces surrounding the hotel's small site. An outstanding feature of the hotel is the "Paseo del Alamo," a pedestrian waterwalk through the lobby, that has become a popular attraction for the city.

Tower of the Americas (1967–68)
ARCHITECTS: Ford, Powell & Carson
LOCATION: HemisFair Grounds, South Alamo Street

An admirably engineered tower designed for the San Antonio HemisFair of 1968, this tower features a revolving restaurant that accommodates up to 500 people.

United Services Automobile Association Office (1976)
ARCHITECTS: Benham-Blair & Affiliates, Inc.
LOCATION: 9800 Fredericksburg Road

One of the world's largest office buildings, the USAA building is uniquely planned for functionalism and expansion.

University of Texas at San Antonio (late 1975–)
ARCHITECTS: Ford, Powell & Carson
LOCATION: NW of city, 2 miles W of intersection IH 10 and Loop 1604

This small campus is centered around an inviting courtyard plaza featuring a pleasant colonnaded sunshade.

SPRING

Christ The Good Shepherd Catholic Community (1981)
ARCHITECT: Spencer Herolz Architects
LOCATION: Outside of Houston, 18511 Klein Church Road

This dynamic new circular church building features bold exposed laminated beams and bands of stained glass.

THE WOODLANDS

Lord of Life Lutheran Community Church (1981)
ARCHITECTS: Clovis Heimsath Associates
LOCATION: 3801 South Panther Creek

The design of this handsome religious structure complements its surroundings and welcomes the visitor.

The Woodlands Visitors Center (1980s)
ARCHITECTS: Bennie M. Gonzales, Inc., with others
LOCATION: 28 miles N of downtown Houston, 2120 Buckthorn Place

Known for his boldly expressed structures with a flavor of the old Southwest venacular, this well-known Arizona-based architect has admirably met a new challenge with the organic design of the new town of The Woodlands Visitors Center. Located by a lake in a wooded area, the center is part of a projected 20-year development plan sponsored by Mitchell Energy Development Corporation.

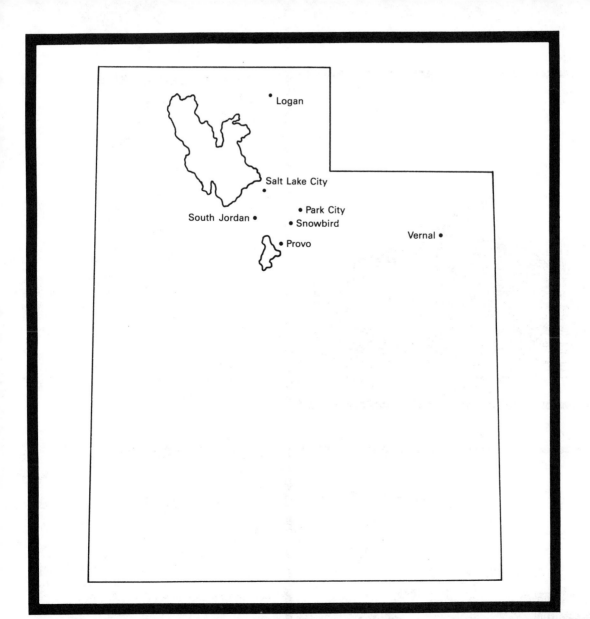

Utah

LOGAN

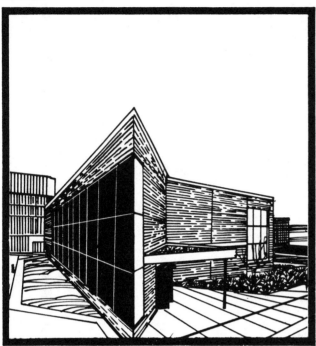

Fine Arts Center at Utah State University

(1967–68/1980/1982)

ARCHITECTS: Burtch W. Beall, Jr./Edward Larrabee Barnes
LOCATION: Off 700 North Street at 1100 East
OPEN: Mon–Fri., 10:30–4:30, Sat., 2–5, and during performances

Clearly expressing its function, the Fine Arts Center provides facilities for an art gallery, a theater, concert halls, studios, and classrooms. Brick, concrete, and glass are the basic construction materials employed, effectively arranged for maximum efficiency. The latest wing houses the Nora Eccles Harrison Museum of Art and was designed by the nationally prominent architect, Edward Larrabee Barnes, known for his handsome museum plans in numerous cities throughout the United States.

PARK CITY (DEER VALLEY)

Deer Valley Resort (1983)

ARCHITECTS: Esherick Homsey Dodge and Davis
LOCATION: 1351 Deer Valley Drive, 2 miles E of Park City
OPEN: Daily

Located in one of the finest ski areas of the United States, the Silver Lakes and Snow Park Center lodges comprise the first phase of the new Deer Valley Resort. A rustic, heavy timber-joined-by-steel-connector structural system was employed. Local sandstone, Douglas fir logs, and other natural materials grandly combine to capture the spirit of the surrounding pine forests and rugged slopes.

SALT LAKE CITY

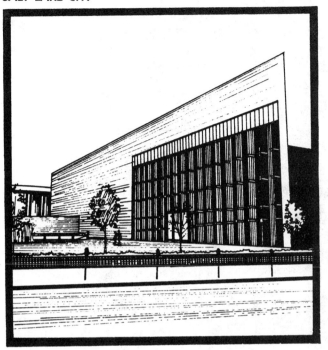

Salt Lake Symphony Hall and Art Center (1979)

Exhibition Center (1983)
ARCHITECTS: Fowler Ferguson Kingston Ruben; Symphony Hall and Art Center, Edwards & Daniels & Associates: Exhibition Center
LOCATION: West Corner of South & West Temple
OPEN: Hall tours: Tues., and Thurs., 1–2:30
Art Center: Tues.–Sat., 10–5, Fri., 10–9, Sun. 1–5

These impressive additions to the downtown urban development program were planned to relate to historic Temple Square across the street. The bold triangular plan of the hall is positioned toward the block to the northeast. Visual emphasis is created by the huge glass entry facade, further dramatized by the fountains in the outdoor plaza. The new post-modern "machine for exhibition" center, west of the hall, is a horizontally emphasized, tiered structure, constructed of light-weight aluminum panels spanning an underpass over 2nd West Street.

SALT LAKE CITY

Special Events Center at The University of Utah (1967–69)

ARCHITECTS: Young & Fowler; H.C. Hughes (Structural Engineer)
LOCATION: South Campus Drive, off 5th South Street
OPEN: During sports events, performances, and other events

Constructed of laminated wood, the dome of the Special Events Center is the world's second largest structure of its type. Effectively positioned into the sloping hillside, this large circular complex provides excellent facilities for physical education, sports, performances by leading entertainers, and other special events. The complex has a seating capacity of 15,000.

SALT LAKE CITY

SALT LAKE CITY

Triad Center (1984–1990)

ARCHITECTS: Carpenter & Stringham, Gensler & Associates and Edwards and Daniels Associates
LOCATION: North Temple and Third West
OPEN: During business and shopping hours

Triad Center, developed by Triad America Corporation, founded by Saudi Arabian businessman Adnan Khashoggi, is an extraordinary and ambitious urban development program consisting of 30 acres. Reflective tinted glass cubes rising from a base of brick and granite are striking. Arched brick gateways welcome visitors to gardens, plazas, footpaths, shops, restaurants, a market, an ice rink that functions as an outdoor theater in the summer, and other businesses. The cornerstone of Triad Center is the renovated Mansardic Victorian pioneer mansion, Devereaux House, now functioning as a restaurant and reception center. Continuing building phases will include hotels, office buildings, condominiums, and other facilities.

Trolley Square Renovation (1904/1978/)

ARCHITECTS: Original: Albert L. Christensen. Renovation: Fred Babcock/Architects/Planners
LOCATION: 5th South and 7th East
OPEN: During business and shopping hours

Originally functioning as a trolley car terminal, this large complex of buildings, with exteriors recalling Flemish parapets, has been delightfully restored and renovated. Trolley Square, simply constructed of frankly exposed brick, iron, and glass, is a unique early example of structural design in the state. A network of interior spaces is particularly exhilarating with a collection of shops, restaurants, markets, and movie houses.

SALT LAKE CITY

ZCMI Center Renovation and Addition (1976)

ARCHITECTS: Gruen Associates
LOCATION: 15 South Main Street
OPEN: During business and shopping hours

ZCMI (Zion's Co-operative Mercantile Institution) was the nation's first department store and has been a landmark in Utah since 1876. (The original architects were William H. Folsom and Obed Taylor). Gruen and Associates have sensitively renovated the exquisite cast-iron work and incorporated bold modern additions that complement the decorative facade. The entire complex is one of the country's largest downtown shopping centers.

SNOWBIRD

Snowbird Village (1972–)

ARCHITECTS: Brixen & Christopher
LOCATION: Little Cottonwood Canyon, UT 210, just S of Alta

Capitalizing on its beautiful mountain setting, Snowbird Village is part of a thoughtfully planned recreational development including a 160-unit condominium concrete structure. Supportive facilities for the popular ski and summer resort include shops, restaurants, recreation, and convention spaces. Blending boldly expressed concrete, stone, cedar, and glass materials, Snowbird Village complements its surroundings. Note the sod and grass roof covering the lodge. This was purposely planned so as not to be an intrusion on the landscape.

ADDITIONAL MODERN STRUCTURES OF INTEREST

PROVO

Harris Fine Arts Center at Brigham Young University (1962–64)
ARCHITECTS: William L. Periera & Associates
LOCATION: Brigham Young University, NW area of campus

Constructed of golden-buff brick and off-white cast stone, this functional center for the arts features exterior vertical fin shields and a spacious interior atrium exhibit space.

Tanner Building at Brigham Young University (1982)
ARCHITECTS: Fowler Ferguson Kingston Ruben Associates
LOCATION: Brigham Young University, W side of campus

This strongly expressed building is faced with granite and features the only major large atrium space in the state.

Utah Technical College (1975–84)
ARCHITECTS: Fowler Ferguson Kingston Ruben, Neil Astle and others
LOCATION: 1395 N. 150 E., just off I 15

This sprawling complex is based on a consistent 30-foot by 30-foot module design.

SALT LAKE CITY

General Church Office Building, Headquarters for The Church of Jesus Christ of Latter-Day Saints (1975)
ARCHITECT: George Cannon Young
LOCATION: Between Main & State Streets on North Temple

This streamlined 450-foot structure is one of Utah's tallest buildings. The clean structural lines of the tower contrast significantly with its historical surroundings.

Natorium (1970)
ARCHITECTS: Robert A. Fowler Associated Architects
LOCATION: University of Utah campus

Massing of strong forms and sensitive handling of materials provides visual interest for this complex.

Northwest Energy Building (1981)
ARCHITECTS: Fowler Ferguson Kingston Ruben
LOCATION: 295 Chipeta Way at University of Utah Research Park

This major office building complex was designed for open office planning featuring unusual color schemes. The horizontally expressed aluminum, steel, and glass structure nestles into its hillside setting, taking advantage of a panoramic view of the valley and mountains.

Prudential Building (1962–64)
ARCHITECTS: William L. Periera & Associates of Los Angeles
LOCATION: 115 South Main Street

The Prudential Building features a five-story atrium with floors suspended from two beams at rooftop level. The construction design was one of the first of its type in Utah.

SNOWBIRD

Mid Gad Valley Restaurant (1974)
ARCHITECTS: Enteleki Architecture
LOCATION: Little Cottonwood Canyon Road, UT 210, 1 mi. S of Alta

This bridge-like structure beautifully relates to the surrounding ski slopes. Constructed primarily of wood, the restaurant is accessible only by ski lift.

SOUTH JORDAN

Jordan River Temple (1981)
ARCHITECT: Emil B. Fetzer
LOCATION: 10200 South 1300 West

Faced with cast stone concrete and marble chips, the central tower of this stately Temple soars 200 feet and is topped with a golden angel rising another 20 feet.

VERNAL

Dinosaur National Monument (1958)
ARCHITECTS: Anshen & Allen
LOCATION: c. 20 miles ESE of Vernal on
US 40 E., 13 miles, then Hwy. 147 N. for 7
miles (Follow the signs)

This spacious Visitor's Center is uniquely built
around prehistoric dinosaur diggings atop a
rugged hillside.

• Lyndonville

• Burlington

Barnet •

Brattleboro •

Vermont

BURLINGTON

Billings Student Center

(1883–85)

ARCHITECT: Henry Hobson Richardson
LOCATION: University of Vermont, Main
Campus via Colchester Avenue on
University Place
OPEN: Lobby open weekdays 7:30–11 PM,
weekends, 9 AM–10 PM when school is in
session

Constructed of heavy rusticated stone, the
Billings Student Center bears all the architectural trappings employed by the "Great
Romanesque Revivalist," Henry Hobson
Richardson. The enormous massive entry arch
beckons the visitor into the impressive multi-
use interior spaces. Many Richardson fans
come to see this interesting work by the
"father of modern architecture in America."
The octagonal end bay and towering turret
admirably dominate the building's plan.

BURLINGTON

Cathedral of The Immaculate Conception (1978)

ARCHITECTS: Edward Larrabee Barnes
Associates
LOCATION: 20 Pine Street, downtown
Burlington
OPEN: Mon.–Fri., 9–5:30, Sat., 9–6:30, Sun.
7–1:30

Although this well executed religious structure recalls themes from the past, it is
nevertheless considered an original and creative endeavor. Inspired by Henry Hobson
Richardson's beautiful landmark, Billings Library close by, Barnes' Cathedral of the
Immaculate Conception employs the neo-
Romanesque style with its series of arches
and masonry construction. A modern interpretation is achieved through the unique
sloping roofline topped with a simple cross.

BURLINGTON (Essex Junction)

IBM Facility (1970–72)

ARCHITECTS: Curtis & Davis
LOCATION: Robinson Parkway (E off VT 2A, about .5 miles S of junction with VT 15)
OPEN: Grounds and reception area during business hours

The IBM Facility is a commendable aesthetic achievement for a manufacturing plant. The 3-story complex is efficiently connected to some existing buildings owned by IBM, creating a pleasant and unified working space. Importance was placed on location for the complex—a lovely country setting on a river's edge, rather than in a crowded industrial area. The IBM's Facility is a superb example of concern for the employee's working environment.

LYNDONVILLE

Lyndon State College Library (1975)

ARCHITECTS: The Perkins & Will Partnership
LOCATION: Lyndon State College campus
OPEN: During school hours

The quiet design statement projected by the Lyndon State College Library is a perfect solution for the building's beautiful wooded setting. Straddling the edge of a pond, the low rambling structure complements the gently rolling hill. The award-winning library is constructed of concrete forms generously incorporating glass window arrangements to take full advantage of the view. Interiors are successfully planned for function and a pleasant environment for study.

ADDITIONAL MODERN STRUCTURES OF INTEREST

BARNET

Karme Choling, Buddhist Meditation and Study Center
ARCHITECT: Harold Rolls
LOCATION: On Star Route or West Barnet Road (Exit 18 on I-91)

Karme-Choling, in the Buddhist sense, is an absence of confusion. Four wood-framed buildings house the center, planned to harmoniously relate to New England's rural architecture.

BRATTLEBORO

Famolare Headquarters (Now Vermont Yankee Nuclear Power) (1977)
ARCHITECTS: Banwell, White & Arnold
LOCATION: On Ferry Road, 1 mile N of I-91, Exit 3

Located in a mountainous and farm setting, this new office complex for a shoe manufacturer features innovative energy conservation design.

BURLINGTON

The Vermont Regional State Office Building (1969)
ARCHITECTS: Linde-Hubbard Associates
LOCATION: 39 Pearl Street

Exposed sand-blasted concrete, brick, and glass are the construction materials for this bold new government complex.

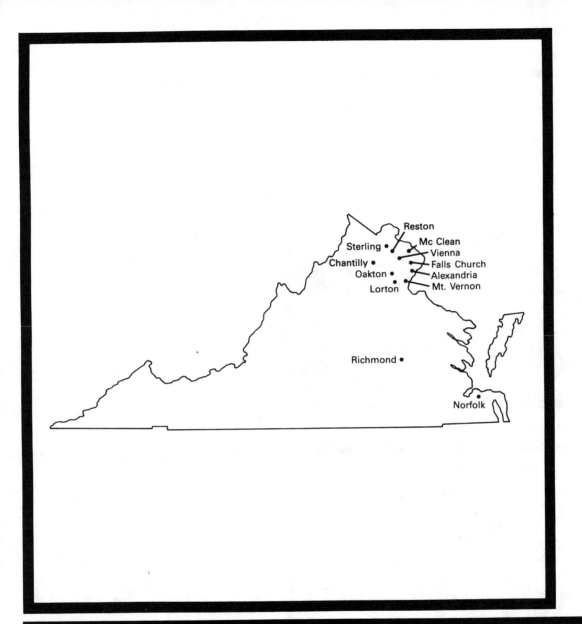

Reston
Mc Clean
Sterling
Vienna
Chantilly
Falls Church
Oakton
Alexandria
Lorton
Mt. Vernon

Richmond

Norfolk

Virginia

CHANTILLY

Dulles Airport (1958–62/1979–82)

ARCHITECTS: Eero Saarinen & Associates
LOCATION: Exit 12 from Beltway (IS 495),
Dulles Access Road
OPEN: Always open

The late Eero Saarinen felt Dulles Airport was his finest architectural achievement—and most experts agree. Desiring to express the dynamics and tension of takeoff, the upswept structure of glass and concrete dynamically accomplishes the sensation. Saarinen ingeniously designed mobile units to facilitate transportation from check-in point to the airplane. Other facilities and detailing were also planned by the master architect before his untimely death. The bold structure makes an exciting silhouette against the lush countryside setting.

MOUNT VERNON

Pope-Leighey House (1940–41)

ARCHITECT: Frank Lloyd Wright
LOCATION: At Woodlawn Plantation, NW
off US 1, C. 14 miles S of Washington D.C.
OPEN: Mar.–Oct., Sat.–Sun. 9:30–4:30

Although not as commonly known or as admirably designed as Wright's other residential works, this house is one of the few open to the public. On a small scale, it exemplifies many of the master's advanced building ideas for the small, inexpensive home. The structure was moved to its present site in 1965—saved from demolition. Further up the path is stately Woodlawn Plantation.

NORFOLK

Scope-Cultural and Convention Center

(1971 and 1972)

ARCHITECTS: William & Tazewell Partnership with Pier Luigi Nervi
LOCATION: Charlotte St., Monticello Ave., Brambletown Ave., and Paul's Boulevard
OPEN: During special events

Consisting of a stately vertical multi-storied building and a marvelous circular domed structure, this facility provides a myriad of public acitivies. The large innovative complex is located on the eastern edge of downtown Norfolk. The Convention and Sports Hall commands the most attention with its astounding V-shaped supports and exposed concrete triangles. The spectacular dome design was engineered by Italy's famed late architect, Pier Luigi Nervi, who is well-known for his Palettzo del Sporto for the Rome Olympics of 1960.

OAKTON

AT&T Long Lines (1980)

ARCHITECTS: Kohn Pedersen Fox
LOCATION: 3033 Chain Bridge Road (from Route 123)
OPEN: Mon.–Fri., 7 AM–3:30 PM (Tours available)

A magnificent glass-arched employees' entrance introduces the suburban Eastern Regional Headquarters for AT&T Long Lines. Curved, diagonal, and straight forms combine effectively in a rhythmic complex of offices that are arranged around a sunlit galleria. Sixteen hundred workers are accommodated in the large facility that is sensitively sited on thirty-four acres of Virginia countryside. The attractive and dignified building also functions admirably to meet the needs of the workers.

RESTON

Reston New Town and Lake Anne Village (1965 to present)

ARCHITECTS: Conklin & Rossant with others
LOCATION: NW on VA 7, then W on VA 606 from Washington D.C.
OPEN: Public facilities in village during business hours

Reston is an admirable solution to twentieth century suburban living and one of America's first "New Towns." With all the advantages of a natural country setting, complete with a manmade lake, Reston is conveniently close to Washington D.C. Although not without serious problems, Reston, with its attractive landscaping and variety of living quarters, still remains a trendsetter for similar developments.

RICHMOND

Best Products Co. (1981)

ARCHITECTS: Hardy, Holzman & Pfeiffer Assoc.
LOCATION: Off I-95, exit East Parham
OPEN: 8:15–5:00, Tours by appointment (Mon.–Fri.)

A marvelous Art Deco update, Best Products Co. has a stunning entrance flanked by two huge eagle sculptures that support cylindrical light fixtures. These eagles were originally designed in the Art Deco Style in 1939 for an airlines building in New York (the eagle was a typical motif of the period). The new corporate headquarters features a curved front facade of glass block—a favorite building material during the Art Deco period. The glass wall is capped with a terracotta cornice that stabilizes the design.

RICHMOND

Philip Morris Factory (1972–74)

ARCHITECTS: Skidmore, Owings and Merrill
LOCATION: 3601–4201 Commerce Road
OPEN: Tours Mon.–Fri. 9–4

A series of bold mechanical towers are uniformly centered around beautiful gardens in the open pockets of this dramatic facility. Pleasantly arranged for the factory's employees, the white concrete complex was designed to facilitate the process of making 4,000 cigarettes a minute. (The procedure was the same 100 years ago, but now machines accomplish the task at a much faster rate). Situated close to the freeway, the building generates excitement through the use of form, space, and landscaping.

VIENNA

The Filene Center and Wolf Trap Farm Park (1968–71)

ARCHITECTS: MacFadyen & Knowles with Alfredo de Vido
LOCATION: Washington Memorial Parkway from Washington D.C. to Beltway, the Dulles Access Road or VA 7 to Trap Road
OPEN: June–mid-Sept. for performances

"The country's first park for the performing arts" was bequeathed by Mrs. Catherine Filene Shouse in 1966 as a memorial to her parents. Playing up the natural sloping terrain, the architects have created an engaging theater and concert hall seating 3,500 patrons, with hillside seating for an additional 3,000. The massing of forms and lines for the structure is intriguing and functional, with sides that open to the outside. A wide variety of performing arts are held here during summer months.

ADDITIONAL MODERN STRUCTURES OF INTEREST

FALLS CHURCH

Fountain of Faith, National Memorial Park (1952)
DESIGNER: Carl Milles
LOCATION: US 29 and 211, 2 miles W of town on Lee Highway

This fascinating modern sculptural oasis in the middle of a cemetery was created by the prominent Swedish sculptor, Carl Milles. Wonderful life-size figures are stylized and captured amidst cascades of spraying water.

GREENWAY

Science Building (1975)
ARCHITECTS: Arthur Cotton Moore Associates
LOCATION: The Madeira School campus

This Science facility for a private girls' school is constructed of steel, wood, and concrete and utilizes efficient solar collectors.

LORTON

Ann Mason Building (1977)
ARCHITECTS: Philip Ives Associates
LOCATION: Gunston Hall Plantation

A large, modern Visitors Center for the historic Georgian mansion, the Ann Mason Building is arranged in an interesting series of forms.

MC CLEAN

Immanuel Presbyterian Church (1982)
ARCHITECTS: Hartman-Cox
LOCATION: 888 Dolley Madison Blvd.

The overall aesthetic effect of this spartan white church is reminiscent of the traditional farmhouse.

RICHMOND

First Unitarian Church of Richmond (1970)
ARCHITECTS: Ulrich Franzen and Associates
LOCATION: 1000 Blanton Avenue

Designed to reflect the changing nature of religious instruction and worship, this church is uniquely planned yet fits nicely into its neighborhood setting.

Philip Morris Operations Center (1982)
ARCHITECTS: Davis, Brody & Associates
LOCATION: 2001 Walmsley

The newest addition to the huge Philip Morris enterprises, this brilliant white complex is given emphasis through the placement of bright red sculpture by Ivan Chermayeff.

Reynolds Metals Building (1955–58)
ARCHITECTS: Skidmore, Owings and Merrill
LOCATION: 6601 West Broad Street (US 250) at Dickens Road

The Reynolds Building is a highly successful administrative building located in a pleasant country setting. Courtyards, terraces, fountains, and lush plantings further humanize the facility.

STERLING

Christ The Redeemer Parish Center (1981)
ARCHITECTS: Lawrence Cook & Associates
LOCATION: 306 East Leesburg Pike

Strong geometric forms supported by earth beams are featured in this energy-efficient religious structure.

VIENNA

Tycon Towers (1985)
ARCHITECTS: Philip Johnson/John Burgee
LOCATION: 8000 Mimosa

Comprising three towers, these brick, aluminum, and glass buildings feature a series of projecting bow-type cylinders rising the full height of the structure.

Seattle

● Mercer Island

● Tacoma

● Olympia

Spokane ●

Richland ● ● Pasco

Washington

OLYMPIA

The Evergreen State College
(1968–72)

ARCHITECTS: Durham Anderson Freed Company with various architects
LOCATION: Cooper Point Peninsula, W on Harrison Ave. and Mud Bay Rd., N on Overhulse Rd., just NW of town
OPEN: Continuously open

Designed to take full advantage of the beautiful sweeping landscape, the Evergreen State College is neatly incorporated on 990 acres of wooded area. The new four-year College is an engaging and well-planned facility geared to enhance the student's learning and aesthetic experience. Noteworthy buildings include the *ACTIVITIES BUILDING* by Kirk, Wallace & McKinley; the *LIBRARY* by Durham, Anderson, Freed; the *GROUP INSTRUCTION BUILDING* by Harris, Reed & Litzenberger; and the *LABORATORY BUILDING* by Naramore, Bain, Brady & Johanson.

PASCO

Art-Drama Music Complex
(1970–71)

ARCHITECTS: Brooks Hensley Creager
LOCATION: Columbia Basin Community Center
OPEN: During school hours

Bold concrete masses of the Art-Drama-Museum are uniquely sliced with pedestrian walks channelling traffic to various functional spaces including faculty offices, workshops, exhibit areas, and a stage theater. Surrounded by a rather barren landscape, the boxy structure's design is focused inward with limited fenestration on the thick exterior perimeter walls—creating an actual barrier from the hot sun. The award-winning complex has been admired for its "sense of integrity however different its appearance from the norm."

SEATTLE

Pacific Science Center (1962)

ARCHITECT: Minoru Yamasaki and
Naramore, Bain, Brady & Johnson
LOCATION: 200 2nd Avenue North
OPEN: Daily, from 10:00 AM

Built for the 1962 Seattle World's Fair, the
gleaming white United States Science pavilion
was the most popular building at the
exposition. The buildings, centered around a
refreshing central courtyard with pools, fountains, and seating, feature a network of
delicate contemporary gothic arches and
tracery. This design theme is carried out and
magnified with soaring lacy pointed arched
structures that hover over the courtyard. Of
additional interest in the area is the *SEATTLE
SPACE NEEDLE* with its revolving restaurant.

SEATTLE

Seattle Aquarium (1977)

ARCHITECTS: Fred Bassetti & Company
LOCATION: Pier 59 on Waterfront Park
OPEN: May–Sept., daily 10–9, Oct.–Apr.,
daily 10–5

The Seattle Aquarium occupies an old pier on
the waterfront, creating an impressive addition to the area. The wood, metal, and
concrete structure brilliantly encloses space
housing fascinating exhibits of marine life
arranged in a manner that entices the visitor
from one display to another. Part of an
existing building on the site functions as a
bookshop and introductory lobby for the
aquarium.

SEATTLE

Seattle–First National Bank

(1968–69)

ARCHITECTS: Naramore, Bain, Brady & Johanson
LOCATION: 4th Ave. between Madison and Spring Streets
OPEN: During business hours

A pleasant and welcoming street level plaza with trees, seating, and an intriguing Henry Moore sculpture introduces this impressive banking complex. The boxy structure rises 50-stories supported by gigantic aluminum-covered steel corner columns. Ceiling to floor windows are set back, enclosing a lobby space and providing a stunning background for a display of colorful contemporary art. Interiors are professionally and harmoniously executed throughout.

SPOKANE

Riverpark Center Opera House (1972–74)

ARCHITECTS: Walker, McGough, Foltz & Lyerla
LOCATION: Spokane Falls Boulevard at Washington Street
OPEN: For performances and events

Built as part of the 1974 Exposition held in Spokane, Riverpark Center Opera House and exhibition hall makes a dynamic silhouette in its urban setting on the riverbank. The strongly angled structure of concrete and dark tinted glass is appealing from all vantage points. Interiors are simple and dignified. Functional facilities in the auditorium are particularly admirable.

TACOMA

Christ Episcopal Church

(1968–69)

ARCHITECTS: Paul Thiry
LOCATION: 310 North K Street
OPEN: Inquire at church office, Mon.–Fri.
9–5

A composition of square, rounded, and diagonal forms entice the visitor to explore this unique church. The interior space is especially interesting. A large ring, supporting lighting fixtures, hovers over the seating area. Natural and artificial lighting add to the drama of the area, emphasizing texture, form, and stained glass. Items saved from an old destroyed church on the site are featured in the contemporary building, bringing an added dimension of contrast with the old and new.

TACOMA

Weyerhaeuser Headquarters

(1969–71)

ARCHITECTS: Skidmore, Owings and Merrill
LOCATION: About 8 miles from Tacoma, N on IS 5, exit 142 B, E on WA 18, first road N
OPEN: During business hours by appointment only

The Weyerhaeuser Headquarters is a superb creation—and one of the finest buildings of its type in the nation. The strong horizontal levels of the complex, with its deeply recessed windows, stretch across the wooded terrain. The levels are strikingly staggered to conform to the changing contours of the land. The architects met the challenge of providing an openness with nature and a pleasant environment for employees. Additionally, the building was designed for energy efficiency. Open office planning and interior furnishings are excellent.

ADDITIONAL MODERN STRUCTURES OF INTEREST

MERCER ISLAND

The Mercer Island, Washington, Presbyterian Church (1963)
ARCHITECT: Paul Thiry
LOCATION: 3605 84th Avenue S.E.

Thiry said of this design: "I set out to create a "tent" to offer shelter for worship—to keep the congregation close to nature."

RENTON

Gene Coulon Memorial Beach Park (1982)
ARCHITECTS: Jones & Jones
LOCATION: On banks of Lake Washington (12 mi. SSE of Seattle)

Beautifully located along Lake Washington, this 53-acre park features award winning pavilions housing a picnic shelter, boat house, restaurant/snack bar, and other public facilities. A mile pedestrian trail, boat rentals, swimming, tennis and other activities are available.

RICHLAND

Batelle Memorial Institute's Pacific Northwest Laboratories (1968)
ARCHITECTS: Naramore, Bain, Brady & Johanson
LOCATION: George Washington Way at Batelle Blvd. about 5 miles NW of Richland

This large complex, designed for the "use of science for the benefit of all mankind," has a reception area and grounds open to the public during business hours.

Central United Protestant Church (1963–65)
ARCHITECTS: Durham Anderson Freed Company
LOCATION: 1124 Stevens Drive (north of hospital)

Simplicity of materials and effective lighting are beautifully combined in this religious structure.

SEATTLE

Bagley Wright Theatre (1983)
ARCHITECTS: The NBBJ Group
LOCATION: 155 Mercer Street

Narrow red stripes define the bands of bright green stucco providing a dynamic visual image. One of Seattle's most "nortorious" structures.

Calvary Lutheran Church (1960s)
ARCHITECT: Robert D. Theriault
LOCATION: 7002 23rd N.W.

This church, constructed of red cedar and stained glass, is boldly formed, creating a striking impression in its wooded setting. The interior soaring nave is particularly interesting.

Condon Hall, School of Law/Law Library (1976)
ARCHITECTS: Mitchell/Giurgola
LOCATION: The University of Washington, just off main campus

This strongly designed library of concrete forms clearly states its function and purpose.

Fourth & Blanchard Building (1978)
ARCHITECTS: Chester L. Lindsey
LOCATION: Fourth & Blanchard in Denny Regrade district

A connected, twin-tower, steel structure sheathed with reflective glass and 45-degree angled roofs.

Freeway Park (1974–76)
LANDSCAPE ARCHITECTS: Lawrence Halprin & Associates
LOCATION: Seneca Street between 6th and 8th

Ingeneously created, Freeway Park is located by a noisy freeway, but instead of succumbing to this environment, the park has been designed to function as an inviting area, alive with waterfalls, trees, and plants.

Gas Works Park (1978)
ARCHITECTS: Richard Haag Associates
LOCATION: Point jutting into Lake Union near entrance to Lake Washington Ship Canal

This "funky," "gigantic walk-through Tinker Toy" is a delightful renovation of a 72-year-old industrial park.

Hillclimb Court Condominiums (1983)
ARCHITECTS: Olson/Walker
LOCATION: Just E of Alaska Way freeway at 1421 Western Avenue

A successful new housing development on a difficult site. The Art Deco styled complex is centered around nicely landscaped courtyards.

I.B.M. Office Building (1963)
ARCHITECT: Minoru Yamasaki
LOCATION: 1200 Fifth Avenue

The outer wall of this stately complex is constructed of steel pipes enclosed in concrete spaced at 28 inches. Bold marble arches at the base of the structure provide variety and contrast. Notice the delicate handling of the corners. A sunken plaza below the arches provides further emphasis.

Juanita High School (1970–72)
ARCHITECTS: Kirk, Wallace & McKinley
LOCATION: N on IS 405, take Exit 20 B (NE 12th Street), W on 124th to 100th Ave., NE, N to 132nd St., E to school in Kirkland, Seattle

One of the finest and most inventive educational facilities in the nation.

L.C. Smith Building (1914)
ARCHITECTS: Gaggin & Gaggin
LOCATION: Yesler Way at 2nd Avenue

Although not as well known, this 35-story skyscraper, built on an irregular site, was for years the tallest structure north of San Francisco and west of the Mississippi.

North Seattle Community College (1968–70)
ARCHITECTS: Edward and John Mahlum

LOCATION: Exit 172 from IS 5, W on North 8th Street, N on Meridian Avenue

This well-planned campus for 6,000 students features a unique instructional core.

The Norton Building (1960)
ARCHITECTS: Skidmore, Owings & Merrill with others
LOCATION: Entrance on Second Street and First Street

This 21-story glass curtain wall tower is Seattle's first tall building built since the 1920s.

Pioneer Square Historic District (1890s/1970s)
ARCHITECTS: Various architects
LOCATION: Yesler Way at 1st Avenue South

A pleasant and commendable downtown revitalization program Pioneer Square includes an exquisite restored glass and iron pavilion and many updated buildings of interest.

Seattle Central Community College (1973–76)
ARCHITECTS: Kirk, Wallace & McKinley
LOCATION: Broadway at East Pine Street

Located on the edge of the downtown district, this campus is planned for convenience and maximum efficiency.

Weston Hotel (Formerly the Washington Plaza Hotel) (1969)
ARCHITECTS: John Graham & Company
LOCATION: 1900 5th

The unusual metal and glass circular hotel is crowned with an aluminum parapet that encircles the structure.

TACOMA

St. Joseph's Hospital (1975)
ARCHITECTS: Bertrand Goldberg & Associates
LOCATION: 1718 South I Street

This extraordinarily-formed 13-story hospital has a wavy shell exterior punctuated with oval fenestration.

**Tacoma Art Museum (Renovation of
Pacific National Bank)** (1971)
ARCHITECTS: Alan Liddle
LOCATION: 12th and Pacific Avenue

No changes were made to the exterior of this
1920s building, but the interior was interestingly converted into a spacious modern
museum. (The old bank vault in the basement was converted into a children's theater.)

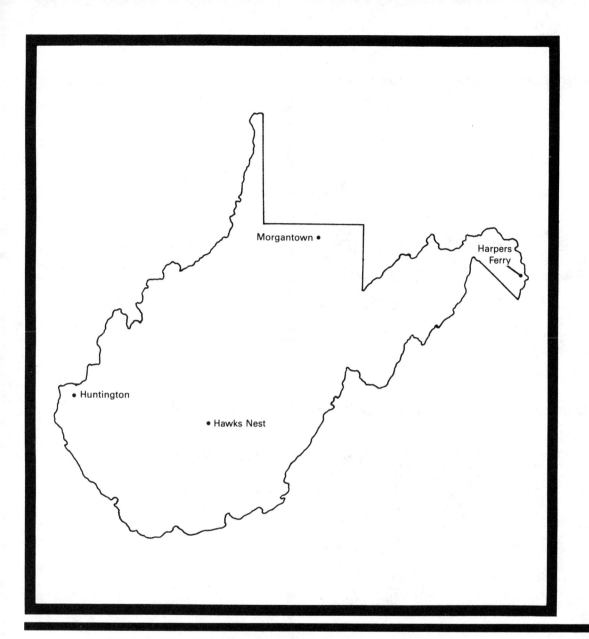

Morgantown •

Harpers
Ferry
•

• Huntington

• Hawks Nest

West Virginia

HARPERS FERRY

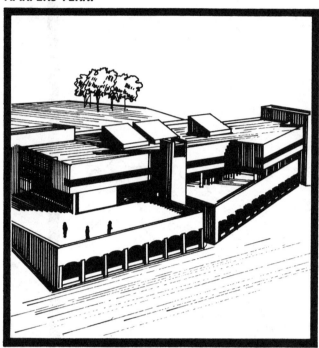

The Interpretive Facilities Building (1970)

ARCHITECTS: Ulrich Franzen and Associates
LOCATION: At confluence of Shenandoah & Potomac Rivers
OPEN: Grounds always open, Visitor's lobby 8–5

Located on one of America's most interesting historical spots, this new building for the National Park Service was designed to enhance and respect its important setting. The low, rambling office building complex, inspired by ancient Roman aquaducts, was built on a high crest above the old town serving the entire National Park system. A panoramic view from the balcony of the facility is breathtaking.

HAWKS NEST

Hawks Nest Lodge 1967

Hawks Nest State Park

ARCHITECTS: TAC (The Architects' Collaborative)
LOCATION: On US 60, W of Ansted, c. 45 miles SE of Charleston
OPEN: Daily

Allowing nature with its magnificent beauty to be emphasized instead of the building, the architects have incorporated a keenly sensitive structure relating to the setting. The complex is located amidst the tall trees on a mountainside, with levels cascading down from the street floor. Wood, brick, rough concrete, and glass are simply employed but tremendously effective throughout for the visitor's enjoyment. TAC was founded by the late master architect and founder of the Bauhaus, Walter Gropius.

HUNTINGTON

Huntington Gallery Addition
(1970)

ARCHITECTS: Walter Gropius and The
Architects' Collaborative
LOCATION: Park Hills
OPEN: Tues.–Sat., 10–5, Sun., 12 noon to
5:00

The new addition of the Huntington Gallery
features a series of interrelated boxes arranged in a U-shape housing, a new gallery
space, a 300-seat auditorium, and a research
library. Concrete, brick, and glass are combined to create a building of tranquility and
simplicity—a perfect background for enjoying
art. The gallery, with its courtyards, is
pleasantly located in a meadow setting,
adding to the expressive architectural approach. Both artificial and natural lighting is
planned to enhance the art exhibits within.
Half vaults projecting from the roof provide
the natural lighting.

MORGANTOWN

West Virginia University
Coliseum (1970)

ARCHITECTS: C.E. Silling & Associates
LOCATION: US 19 (Monongahela Blvd.) at
Patterson Dr. (2 mi. W. of town)

The large concrete Coliseum is a dramatic
focal point on West Virginia University campus, especially at night when lighting
accentuates the structure's design elements.
Forty peripheral slender arches support the
building's dome. The dome itself is spec-
tacularly engineered, based on precise
mathematical calculations. The Coliseum seats
more than 13,000 spectators for a variety of
events.

Rhinelander •

Appleton
•

Richland
Center •
Columbus •

Spring Green •
Brookfield
•
Madison •
Milwaukee •

Racine •
Lake Benet •

Wisconsin

BENET LAKE

St. Benedict's Abbey (1978)

ARCHITECT: Stanley Tigerman
LOCATION: c. 1/2 mi. NE of Antioch, Ill., on Illinois-Wisconsin border on Nelson Rd.
OPEN: 9:00 AM to 5:00 PM daily

This "buried" church reflects the desire of the monks of St. Benedict's to create a new modern church that would "present an unpretentious image, to seem accessible to all." The 68-foot-long underground building is concealed by a 9-foot-wide sloping roof that is meant to express a crown of thorns. The interior was also designed to convey the "increased liberalism of the Catholic Church today."

MADISON

First Unitarian Meeting House (1949–51)

ARCHITECT: Frank Lloyd Wright
LOCATION: 900 University Bay Drive, 1 block N of University Ave at W edge of University of Wisconsin campus
OPEN: Tues.–Fri., 9–4, Sat., 9–12

Composition of lines and massing for this Meeting House shows the master architect's creative talents. The triangular copper roof design was inspired by hands in the position of prayer. Wright, always keenly aware of the relationship of the structure to the land, designed this triangular complex nestled closely to the terrain. The principle source of lighting within the building floods the pulpit area.

MILWAUKEE

Annunciation Greek Orthodox Church (1959–61)

ARCHITECT: Frank Lloyd Wright
LOCATION: N 92nd and W Congress
Streets, W from downtown
OPEN: Mon.–Sat. 10–3

The visual aspects of the stunning Greek Orthodox Church are immediately apparent with the first glimpse of the sky-blue painted copper domed roof. The circular form is found everywhere—a shape that the great architect was preoccupied with toward the end of his life. Inspiration for the building's design and plan was based on eastern Europe prototypes, in particular, Santa Sophia (537), the Mother Church in Instanbul. Greek Orthodox symbolism is incorporated into the total design outlook—a goal Wright was determined to convey.

MILWAUKEE (Waywatosa)

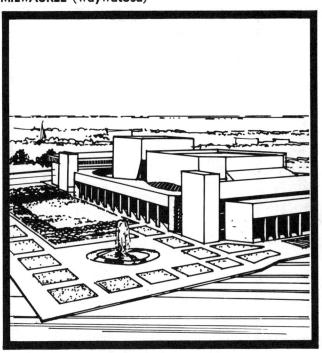

Center for The Performing Arts (1968–69)

ARCHITECTS: Harry Weese & Associates
LOCATION: North Water Street between
East Kilbourn Avenue and East State Street
OPEN: During performances

Sheathed with travertine, the massing of strong forms employed for this center make a dignified and prominent addition to Milwaukee's downtown area. Landscaping and terracing down to the riverside close by is aesthetically pleasing and inviting. A large concert hall dominates the interior space flanked by a small recital hall, repertory theater, and a banquet pavilion.

MILWAUKEE

First Wisconsin Center

(1973–74)

ARCHITECTS: Skidmore, Owings & Merrill
LOCATION: East Wisconsin Ave. between
North Cass, North Van Buren, and East
Michigan
OPEN: During business hours

Strikingly impressive on Milwaukee's water-front, the Wisconsin Center is an innovative commercial complex. Gleaming white mullions and zigzagging supports contrast beautifully with the tinted glass fenestration. A series of trusses adds to the building's impact. Landscaping is brilliantly handled enhancing the surrounding areas. Interior treatments include enormous trees suitable in scale to the vast spaces.

MILWAUKEE

Milwaukee County War Memorial (1953–57)

Art Center (1976)

ARCHITECTS: Eero Saarinen/Kahler, Slater & Fitzhugh Scott, Inc.
LOCATION: 750 North Lincoln Memorial Drive
OPEN: Tues, Wed, Fri., 10–5, Thurs., noon–9:00 PM Sun. 1–6 PM, Sat., 10–5. Tours available: call (414) 271-9508

On a hilltop overlooking Lake Michigan, these two bold concrete structures make a strong silhouette on the shoreline. Saarinen's original cantilevered Memorial is sensitively comple-mented by the new Art Center addition. The roof of the new flexible art space provides a walking surface and sculpture setting for the soaring War Memorial. The entire complex is one of unity, variety, and drama—an ideal background setting for interesting exhibits.

RACINE

S.C. Johnson Offices (1936–39)
Laboratory (1947–50)

ARCHITECT: Frank Lloyd Wright
LOCATION: 1525 Howe St., Franklin St.
between 15th and 16th
OPEN: Tours daily, Mon.–Fri.

Considered one of the first important factory
complexes in the United States, the large
manufacturer of wax products stresses the
importance of humanism in a working environment. An 8-story brick and glass tower
balances the 1-and-2-story red brick main
building featuring bands of glass tubing at the
cornice line. The vast administrative space is
supported by a forest of slender mushroom-
shaped columns carried throughout the complex, providing a unifying design element. A
rich red color theme, used for furnishings
and backgrounds, accents the brick and glass
construction.

SPRING GREEN

Taliesin Spring Green Vicinity
(1902–3/1952–)

ARCHITECTS: Frank Lloyd Wright and The
Taliesin Fellowship
LOCATION: Off State Highway 23, 2 1/2
miles W of entrance to Tower Hill State Park
OPEN: "Hillside" School: Tours daily
Jul–Labor Day: Mon.–Sat., 10–4, Sun., 12–4.
Spring Green Restaurant daily

Many admirers of the great master modern
architect make a pilgrimage to view numerous
structures by Wright built in his home town.
Wright's own home, Taliesin III, is not open to
the public at this time. Information and maps
are available directing tourists to a number of
structures either by Wright or Taliesin Fellowship. Most of the buildings are constructed
of local sandstone, stucco, and natural wood.

ADDITIONAL MODERN STRUCTURES OF INTEREST

APPLETON

AID Association For Lutherans (1977)
ARCHITECTS: John Carl Warnecke & Associates
LOCATION: 4321 N. Ballard Road

The illumination plan for this long, low white complex is outstanding. The building with its visitor's center is functionally efficient.

BROOKFIELD

Sales Office for L.M. Berry & Co. (1979)
ARCHITECTS: Charles Davis and Michael Gelick
LOCATION: 13600 Bishops Court

A building constructed of a metal panel skin arranged in horizontal bands rounded at the corner, this structure recalls the Art Deco period.

COLUMBUS

Farmers and Merchants Union Bank (1919)
ARCHITECT: Louis H. Sullivan
LOCATION: Corner of James St. and Broadway

One of the last commissions of the great early modern architect.

MADISON

New Madison Civic Center (1980)
ARCHITECTS: Hardy Hotzman Pfeiffer Associates
LOCATION: On State and Henry Streets

An intriguing refurbished cinema facade is incorporated into the new post-modern design of this center. The complex interestingly angles through the block, providing dramatic space.

U.S. Forest Products Laboratory (1932)
ARCHITECTS: Holabird & Root
LOCATION: 501 Walnut Street

An early important structure of the Art Deco style.

MILWAUKEE

Marine Plaza (Marine Bank, N.A.) (1962)
ARCHITECTS: Harrison and Abramovitz
LOCATION: Riverfront, 111 East Wisconsin Avenue

A sleek high-rise with an entrance pavilion by the architects of the United Nations Building in New York City.

MGIC Investment Corporation (1973)
ARCHITECTS: Skidmore, Owings & Merrill with Warren Platner
LOCATION: MGIC Plaza

The interior detailing of this small corporate headquarters is exquisite. The striking white structure interestingly contrasts with the stately traditional City Hall close by.

St. Margaret Mary Parish (1977)
ARCHITECTS: Rugg, Knopp & Lambert, Inc.
LOCATION: 3930 No. 92nd St. (Capitol Dr., NW Milwaukee)

Natural stone is excitingly employed both inside and out for the construction of this religious structure.

RACINE

"Wingspread" Conference Center, Johnson House (1937)
ARCHITECT: Frank Lloyd Wright
LOCATION: Off East Four Mile Road, 1/2 mile past Hunt Club Road at Wind Point. NE of Racine

Only a few of Wright's famous "Prairie Houses" are open to the public. ("Wingspread" is open by appointment: telephone (414) 639-3211.) The Johnson House is one of Wright's most innovative residential projects. The plan wraps around the fireplace with four wing extensions. This feature is highlighted by triple bands of skylights.

RHINELANDER

First National Bank (1910–1911)
ARCHITECTS: Purcell, Feick, and Elmslie
LOCATION: West Davenport and Stevens
Street

An excellent example of Prairie architecture, this commercial building was inspired by Sullivan and Wright.

RICHLAND CENTER

A.D. German Warehouse (1915)
ARCHITECT: Frank Lloyd Wright
LOCATION: 300 South Church St. (US 14)

The building, recently converted into a museum, features a solid red brick mass on the lower three stories topped with a fascinating patterned concrete upper tower.

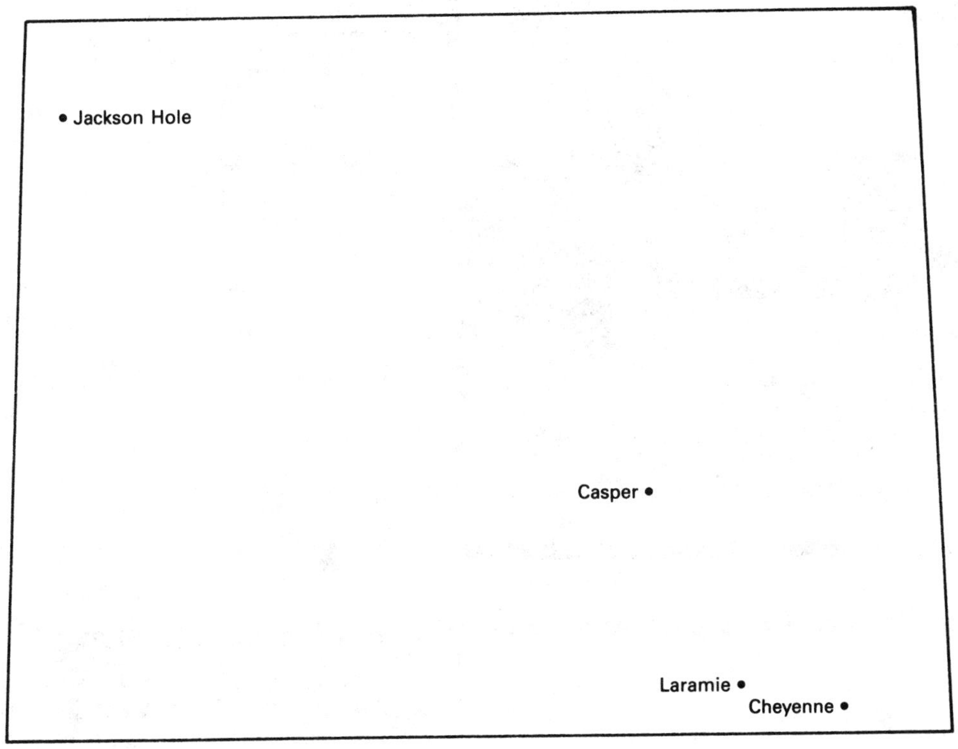

- Jackson Hole

Casper ●

Laramie ●
Cheyenne ●

Wyoming

CHEYENNE

First United Church Education Building Addition

(1967)

ARCHITECTS: J.P. Julien/Muchow Associates
LOCATION: 18th Street between Central and Warren Avenues
OPEN: Mon.–Fri., 8–4, Sunday services

Projecting a low-profile image in its neighborhood and urban setting, the First United Methodist Church Education Building is a fine addition to this western city. The complex was sensitively planned to respect and complement the existing First United Church, built in 1890, close by. The use of simple materials and forms are functionally arranged, surrounded by well-landscaped grounds.

LARAMIE

Ames Monument (1881–82)

ARCHITECT: Henry Hobson Richardson
LOCATION: Off IS 80 at Veedauwoo exit, SW c. 2 miles on Blair Road (c. 18 miles SE of Laramie)
OPEN: Always

Creating a strong outline on the Wyoming desert terrain, the Ames monument is dedicated to Oliver and Oakes Ames, two brothers who pioneered the area for the Union Pacific Railroad a short distance away. The irregular form, constructed of ashlar, rises sixty feet high with plaques near the pinnacle dedicated to the Ames brothers. Describing the intriguing monument, one author wrote, "I never saw a monument so well befitting its situation or a situation so well befitting the special character of a particular monument." (Mr. Olmsted, *Henry Hobson Richardson.)*

LARAMIE

First United Methodist Church (1968)

ARCHITECTS: Muchow Associates, George Hoover, principle designer
LOCATION: 1215 Gibbon Street (3 blocks N of Univ. of Wyoming campus)
OPEN: Mon.–Fri., 8:30–4:30, all day on Sunday

Stark and simple in its physical appearance, the striking First Methodist Church gains interest through its unique soaring monolithic form. Two slender crosses adorn each end of the roof peaks. A low wall of masonry construction surrounds the structure contrasting with the church itself yet providing a courtyard of privacy. The interior sanctuary is unique with strong upward forms culminating in a triangular point. Although the design has been applauded, there have been some concerns for adequate insulation and effective use of materials.

JACKSON HOLE

Americana Snow King Inn (1975)

ARCHITECTS: MacFadyen/De Vido and Corbett/Dehnert/Associates
LOCATION: Turn off Main St. to the end of Snow King Avenue
OPEN: Continuously

Situated amidst spectacular mountain scenery, the 200-room Ramada Snow King Inn rambles across the rolling terrain. The complex, constructed of wood, beautifully relates to its environment. With ski facilities close by and numerous summer activities available, this resort hotel attracts many visitors. The rustic design approach captures the spirit of the wilderness and this theme is carried throughout the interior spaces. Wood, stone, stucco, concrete, and glass are attractively massed for maximum efficiency. The exposed truss beam ceiling in the lobby areas is particularly attractive and impressive.

ADDITIONAL MODERN STRUCTURES OF INTEREST

CASPER

Durbin Center (1981)
ARCHITECTS: Gerald Deines & Associates
LOCATION: 145 South Durbin

The Durbin center is constructed of precast/prestressed concrete components with a striated texture and functions as an office building complex.

Wyoming National Bank (1964)
ARCHITECT: Charles Deaton
LOCATION: 234 East First Street

A bold 94-foot dome supported by 17 leaf-shaped concrete blades uniquely shape the plan of this unusual bank. The sculptural effect is also carried throughout the interior spaces.

Bibliography

Ball, Victoria Kloss. *Architecture and Interior Design*. New York: John Wiley and Sons, Inc., 1980.

Bardeschi, Marco Dezzi. *Frank Lloyd Wright*. New York: Hamlyn, 1970.

Bastland, Knud. *Jose Luis Sert*. New York: Frederick Praeger, Publications, 1980.

Boesiger, Willy. *Le Corbusier* (1957–1965), Vol. 7. London: Thames and Hudson, 1965.

Breuer, Marcel. *New Buildings and Projects*. New York: Praeger Publishers, Inc., 1970.

Diamonstein, Barbaralee. *American Architecture Now*. New York: Rizzoli, 1980.

Fleming, John and Hugh Honour. *Dictionary of the Decorative Arts*. New York: Harper & Row, 1977.

Frampton, Kenneth. *Modern Architecture: A Critical History*. New York: Oxford University Press, 1980.

Frampton, Kenneth and Yukio Futagawa. *Modern Architecture 1851–1945*. New York: Rizzoli, 1983.

Gleve, Paul. *The Architecture of Los Angeles*. Los Angeles: Rosebud Books, 1981.

Harling, Robert. *Dictionary of Design and Decoration*. New York: Viking Press, 1973.

Heinz, Thomas A. *Frank Lloyd Wright*. New York: St. Martin's Press, 1982.

Heyer, Paul. *Architects on Architecture*. New York: Walker and Company, 1978.

Hitchcock, Henry Russell. *Philip Johnson Architecture: 1949–1965*. New York: Holt, Rinehart & Winston, 1966.

Hofmann, Werner and Udo Kultermann. *Modern Architecture in Color.* New York: Viking Press, 1970.

Janson, H.W. *History of Art.* New York: Prentice-Hall, Inc. and Harry Abrams, Inc., 1969.

Jencks, Charles. *The Language of Post-Modern Architecture.* New York: Rizzoli International Inc., Publishers, 1981.

Jencks, Charles. *Late Modern Architecture.* New York: Rizzoli International Publications, Inc., 1981.

Jencks, Charles and William Chaitkin. *Architecture Today.* New York: Harry N. Abrams, Inc., Publishers, 1982.

Klein, Dan. *Art Deco.* New York: Crown Publishers, 1974.

Mang, Karl. *History of Modern Furniture.* New York: Harry N. Abrams, Inc., Publishers, 1979.

Miller, Nory. *Johnson/Burgee: Architecture.* New York: Random House, 1979.

Papachristou, Tician. *Marcel Breuer New Buildings and Projects.* New York: Praeger Publishers, 1970.

Pastier, John. *Cesar Pelli, Monographs in Contemporary Architecture.* New York: Whitney Library of Design, an imprint of Watson-Guptill Publications, 1980.

Peter, John. *Masters of Modern Architecture.* New York: Bonanza Books, 1958.

Pevsner, Nikolaus, Fleming, John, and Hugh Honour. *A Dictionary of Architecture.* Woodstock, New York: The Overlook Press, 1976.

Pevsner, Nikolaus. *Pioneers of Modern Design: From William Morris to Walter Gropius.* Rev. and partly rewritten ed. England: Penquin Books. New York and Harmondsworth, 1975.

Philip Johnson. *Architect: The First Forty Years.* New York: The Municipal Art Society of New York, 1983.

Reader's Digest editors. *Illustrated Guide to the Treasures of America.* Pleasantville, New York: The Reader's Digest Association, Inc., 1974.

Reid, Richard. *The Book of Buildings.* Chicago: Rand McNally, 1980.

Richards, J.M., ed. *Who's Who in Architecture from 1400 to the Present.* New York: Holt, Rinehart and Winston, 1977.

Scully, Vincent Jr. *Modern Architecture: The Architecture of Democracy.* New York: George Braziller, 1974.

Smith, G.E. Kidder. *A Pictorial History of Architecture in America.* New York: American Heritage Publishing Co. Inc., Vol. I and II, 1976.

Smith, G.E. Kidder, with the Museum of Modern Art. *The Architecture of the United States—New England and the Mid-Atlantic States.* Garden City, New York: Anchor Press/ Doubleday, 1981.

Smith, G.E. Kidder, with the Museum of Modern Art. *The Architecture of the United States—The Plains States and Far West.* Garden City, New York: Anchor Press/Double-day, 1981.

Smith, G.E. Kidder, with the Museum of Modern Art. *The Architecture of the United States—The South and Midwest. Garden City, New York: Anchor Press/Double-day, 1981.*

Smithson, Alison and Peter Smithson. *The Heroic Period of Modern Architecture.* New York: Rizzoli International Publications, Inc., 1974.

Spade, Rupert. *Eero Saarinen.* New York: Simon and Schuster, 1971.

Spade, Rupert. *Paul Rudolph.* New York: Simon and Schuster, 1971.

Van Rensselaer, Marina Griswold. *Henry Hobson Richardson and His Works.* New York: Dover Publications, Inc., 1969.

Whiton, Sherrill. *Elements of Interior Design.* New York: J.B. Lippincott Company, 1974.

PERIODICALS

Progressive Architecture. Volumes 46-65.

A.I.A. Journal. Volumes 43-72.

Architectural Record. Volumes 127-172

Architectural Review

Architecture Minnesota, ASAIA Guidebook Committee. James P. Cramer, Publisher.

Process: Architecture, A. Quincy Jones: The Oneness of Architecture. No. 41. Tokyo Bunji Murotani, publisher. Van Nostrand Reinhold Company, Inc., New York, Exclusive Distributor.

Index

ARCHITECTS LISTING

BUILDINGS LISTING